Statements of the LDS First Presidency

STATEMENTS OF THE LDS FIRST PRESIDENCY

A TOPICAL COMPENDIUM

COMPILED BY GARY JAMES BERGERA

FOREWORD BY DALE C. LECHEMINANT

Signature Books • Salt Lake City • 2007

Printed on acid-free paper; composed, printed, and bound in the United States of America.

www.signaturebooks.com

Cover design by Ron Stucki.

12 11 10 09 08 07 6 5 4 3 2 1

LIBRARY OF CONGRESS CATALOGING-IN-PUBLICATION DATA

Church of Jesus Christ of Latter-day Saints. First Presidency.

Statements of the LDS First Presidency : a topical compendium / compiled by Gary James Bergera ; foreword by Dale C. LeCheminant.

p. cm.

Includes bibliographical references.

ISBN-13: 978-1-56085-195-0 (pbk. : alk. paper)

ISBN-10: 1-56085-195-3 (pbk. : alk. paper)

1. Church of Jesus Christ of Latter-day Saints—Doctrines—Handbooks, manuals, etc. I. Bergera, Gary James. II. Title.

BX8635.3.C38 2007

289.3'32—dc22

2006048908

Contents

Foreword

Dale C. LeCheminant
Instructor-Retired, LDS Institute of Religion,
University of Utah, Salt Lake City

For anyone interested in the doctrinal and theological teachings of The Church of Jesus Christ of Latter-day Saints, it is essential to have a reliable source of authoritative statements. Members and non-members alike frequently express individual views on LDS teachings in articles and books, in addresses and sermons. Many so write and speak. The results are legion. But what are the documents that define the Church's official teachings? Where does one easily find these?

Scriptures, Latter-day Saints believe, lead the list of official sources and are the subject of sundry guides to help readers locate various topics. Members carry the Holy Bible, Book of Mormon, Doctrine and Covenants, and Pearl of Great Price into meetings where lessons and discussions are given on Church doctrine, and they follow the teachers' or speakers' quotations from authorized texts.

The scriptures and their helps are found in the homes of members and others interested in the Church. However, there has not been an easily accessible one-volume compilation of the official statements from the highest Church leadership quorum, the First Presidency, which is perhaps the most significant source of doctrine and theology. These extra-scriptural statements are important because they authoritatively clarify Church teachings—explaining and interpreting the scriptures for the contemporary Church. To be most useful, a collection of these statements should provide readers with easy access to specific topics, be as complete as possible, be arranged alphabetically, and cover all written sources in which declarations of the First Presidency have appeared, whether the sources are in public or private repositories.

The compiler of the present one-volume collection has endeavored to meet these requirements in locating official doctrinal and theological statements, both in Church and university libraries and archives and in private possession. The collection features both statements of the First Presidency and authoritative statements issued under their aegis. Together, these constitute the position of the LDS Church on a wide variety of issues.

Statements by the First Presidency and by those acting at their request and with their approval define doctrine. Their words take precedence over other statements. This is true because the Church teaches that God's current prophets reveal His will to His Church today. The present compilation is a welcome addition to the library of any and all who seek the declarations of authorized views of The Church of Jesus Christ of Latter-day Saints for our day.

Introduction

Since its formation in 1832, the First Presidency of The Church of Jesus Christ of Latter-day Saints has regularly issued official declarations on matters of interest to Church members. Most often, the Presidency addresses practical matters of administration, governance, and policy. Periodically, but no less importantly, the Church's governing priesthood quorum offers pronouncements of belief, doctrine, theology, and morals. The present compilation gathers together these latter statements into one volume.

Among the guidelines used to determine the kinds of statements to be included are the following. The statement should be:

- Primarily doctrinal or theological, broadly defined; and
- Signed by at least two members of the First Presidency, or by a member of the Presidency on behalf of the others; or in the absence of a First Presidency by the President of the Quorum of the Twelve Apostles on behalf of the quorum or by the entire quorum; or
- Explicitly authorized by, if not composed by or carrying the signatures of, the First Presidency and/or Quorum of the Twelve Apostles.

While other compilers might have selected differently, these criteria help to ensure that the declarations appearing here represent, at the time they were announced, the position of the LDS Church.

The statements are arranged topically in reverse chronological order. For each statement, the source appears in small capital letters, usually in abbreviated form, at the end of the excerpt. A key to the abbreviations follows this introduction. "IBID.," short for the Latin *ibidem,* "in the same place," refers to the citation appearing at the end of the previous excerpt.

I selected what seemed to be the most relevant portion(s) of each, sometimes lengthier, statement. Those interested in the complete texts should consult James R. Clark's six-volume *Messages of the First Presidency of The Church of Jesus Christ of Latter-day Saints.* In addition, complete sets and/or microfilm or digital copies of most major LDS newspapers and magazines, as well as other documents, are available in the LDS Church Family History Library and in the LDS Church History Library in Salt Lake City. Of particular interest is the "Journal History of The Church of Jesus Christ of Latter-day Saints," a multi-volume scrapbook of primary and secondary sources, including many First Presidency statements. The "Journal History" is available in both of the above libraries, and a significant portion is also available in DVD format on *Selected Collections from the Archives of The Church of Jesus Christ of Latter-day Saints,* vol. 2 (Provo, Utah: Brigham Young University Press, 2002).

In some instances, personal correspondence is quoted, copies of which (in addition to those excerpted in the "Journal History") may be found in the following collections: the James R. Clark Papers and J. Reuben Clark Jr. Papers, Special Collections, Harold B. Lee Library, Brigham Young University; and the David J. Buerger Papers, Scott G. Kenney Papers, H. Michael Marquardt Papers, David O. McKay Papers, and Max H. Parkin Papers, Special Collections, J. Willard Marriott Library, University of Utah. Also helpful were separate unpublished compilations prepared by Dennis "C" Davis and Gregory A. Prince, in private possession.

Readers should know that I silently modernized some non-traditional or archaic forms of punctuation, although only if the original intent was clear and the change did not affect meaning. I also silently standardized capitalization in some instances in conformity with the *Style Guide for Publications of The Church of Jesus Christ of Latter-day Saints* (3rd ed., 1998). A few statements feature emphasis in *italicized* or FULLY CAPITALIZED words, which in every case follows the original usage.

My intent for this volume is strictly educational; my goal to provide an accessible collection of instructive, informative excerpts. *Statements of the LDS First Presidency* is not a history of the development of LDS doctrine, nor does it track changes in wording or shifts in emphasis over time. It should also be stressed that this work is neither endorsed nor sanctioned in any way by the LDS Church. The arrangement, editing, presentation, and selection are entirely my own, and I alone am responsible for all errors.

Abbreviations

"Attitudes"	"Attitudes of The Church of Jesus Christ of Latter-day Saints toward Certain Medical Problems," prepared for the First Presidency, June 3, 1974.
"Basic Doctrines"	"The Basic Doctrines of the Gospel of Jesus Christ Essential to Developing a Religious Education Curriculum as Revealed to Ancient and Modern Prophets," approved by the LDS Church Board of Education, Mar. 5, 1971.
Brief Statement	*A Brief Statement of Principles of the Gospel Based Largely upon the Compendium (Richards-Little) with Excerpts from Other Writings* (Church of Jesus Christ of Latter-day Saints, 1943).
Bulletin	*The Bulletin,* successor to the *Priesthood Bulletin,* published from Aug. 1980 through early 1997. The Sept. 1982 issue explained: "[it] contains current information and instruction from Church headquarters to local priesthood and auxiliary leaders."
BYU Years	*Brigham Young University: The First One Hundred Years,* ed. Ernest L. Wilkinson, 4

	vols. (Brigham Young University Press, 1976).
Church Handbook	*Church Handbook of Instructions, Book 1: Stake Presidencies and Bishoprics* (Church of Jesus Christ of Latter-day Saints, 1998) is the most current edition of the "authoritative guide for local Church leaders" (*Encyclopedia of Mormonism* [Macmillan Publishing Company, 1992], 2:541). It has appeared under various titles and undergone twenty-five revisions since first published in 1899. For the first ten years it was known as *Annual Instructions*, then in 1913 as *Circular of Instructions,* in 1921 as *Instructions to Bishops and Counselors, Stake and Ward Clerks,* from 1928 through 1944 as *Handbook of Instructions,* and from 1960 through 1989 as *General Handbook of Instructions*. All versions are referred to in the present work as *Church Handbook*.
Church Handbook 2	*Church Handbook of Instructions, Book 2: Priesthood and Auxiliary Leaders* (Church of Jesus Christ of Latter-day Saints, 1998).
Church News	*Church News*, a weekend insert to the *Deseret News,* periodically containing pronouncements from the First Presidency.
"Dear Brethren"	Letters from the First Presidency to general, regional, and/or local Church officials.
Deseret News	*Deseret News* is the Church's daily newspa-

	per, *Deseret Morning News* after June 8, 2003; its predecessors include the *Deseret News Weekly*.
"Desirable Objectives"	"Some Desirable Objectives to Be Sought in International Cooperation: A Statement by the First Presidency of The Church of Jesus Christ of Latter-day Saints," May 14, 1965.
Elder's Journal	Official publication of North American missions of the LDS Church, 1903-1907; predecessor to the *Liahona.*
Ensign	The *Ensign* magazine, 1971 to the present, the official monthly publication of the LDS Church, with "First Presidency Message" as a regular feature.
"Evolution and Origin"	"Evolution and the Origin of Man," approved by the BYU Board of Trustees (composed of The First Presidency and others), June 1992.
Faith in God	*Faith in God for Boys* (Church of Jesus Christ of Latter-day Saints, 2003).
Family Home Evening	The Church's annual publication for families, sometimes carrying a message from the First Presidency. The title varies (*Family Home Evenings,* 1970, 1971) or adds a subtitle (*The Law*, 1973; *Love Makes Our House a Home,* 1974; *Heaven in Our Home* 1980).
Friend	*The Friend,* the LDS Church's monthly

	magazine for children, 1971 to the present.
Helps and Suggestions	*Helps and Suggestions for Ward Bishoprics* (Presiding Bishopric of the Church of Jesus Christ of Latter-day Saints, Jan. 1956), "approved by the First Presidency."
Hymns	*Hymns of the Church of Jesus Christ of Latter-day Saints* (Church of Jesus Christ of Latter-day Saints, 1985).
Improvement Era	Official LDS Church publication, 1897-1970, predecessor to the *Ensign.*
"Issues Resources"	Statements posted on the official LDS Church website, *Church of Jesus Christ of Latter-day Saints*, at www.lds.org/newsroom, accessed 2006. "The Church of Jesus Christ of Latter-day Saints has issued official statements regarding many of the social issues of today [i.e., Abortion, Child Abuse, Civic Involvement, Embryonic Stem-cell Research, Euthanasia and Prolonging Life, Political Neutrality, and Same-Gender Attraction]. Several of these statements are collected here."
"Journal History"	"Journal History of The Church of Jesus Christ of Latter-day Saints," a multi-volume daily scrapbook, including news releases issued by the Church, arranged by date, for use by the public.
Liahona	Official periodical of North American

missions of the LDS Church, 1907-45, successor to the *Elder's Journal.* (This does not refer to the foreign-language editions of the *Ensign* published under the name *Liahona.*)

Messages — *Messages of the First Presidency of the Church of Jesus Christ of Latter-day Saints*, comp. James R. Clark, 6 vols. (Bookcraft, 1965-75), covering the years 1833-1951.

Millennial Star — *Latter-day Saints' Millennial Star*, official British organ of the LDS Church, 1840-1970.

Patriarchs — *Information and Suggestions for Patriarchs* (Church of Jesus Christ of Latter-day Saints, 1981).

Planning Calendar — *1987 Planning Calendar* (Church of Jesus Christ of Latter-day Saints, 1986).

Preach My Gospel — *Preach My Gospel: A Guide to Missionary Service* (Church of Jesus Christ of Latter-day Saints, 2004; approval of English text Jan. 2005). A First Presidency message reads: "*Preach My Gospel* is intended to help you be a better-prepared, more spiritually mature missionary and a more persuasive teacher. We urge you to use it daily in your personal and companion preparation."

Priesthood Bulletin — The *Priesthood Bulletin,* published by the LDS Church from 1964 to mid-1974, succeeded by the *Bulletin.*

Priesthood Handbook	*Melchizedek Priesthood Handbook* (Council of the Twelve Apostles, 1948). An introductory statement from the First Presidency reads: "This Handbook is issued for the help and guidance of priesthood supervisors and officers in the performance of their duties in carrying forward the approved procedure of the Church."
Priesthood Study Guide	The adult male priesthood course manual, variously titled but with "Personal Study Guide" and/or "Melchizedek Priesthood Lessons" in the title or subtitle. The 1985 edition was *Search These Commandments: Melchizedek Priesthood Personal Study Guide.* Other variations: *Magnifying the Priesthood in the Home* (1965), *A Light unto the World* (1967), *When Thou Art Converted, Strengthen Thy Brethren* (1974), *A Royal Priesthood* (1975), *My Errand from the Lord* (1976), *Prepare Ye the Way of the Lord* (1978), and *Put On Thy Strength, O Zion* (1980).
Principles	*Principles of the Gospel* (Church of Jesus Christ of Latter-day Saints, 1976), intended for LDS servicemen, endorsed by the First Presidency on p. 9.
Progress	*Progress of the Church* (LDS Presiding Bishopric, Jan. 1941).
Quick Facts	*Quick Facts: Overview of the Essential History, Doctrine and Organization of The Church of Jesus Christ of Latter-day Saints*

(Church of Jesus Christ of Latter-day Saints, 2005), available at www.lds.org/newsroom (accessed 2006-2007).

Servicemen's Program — *Handbook of the LDS Servicemen's Program* (Church of Jesus Christ of Latter-day Saints, June 1961), for LDS Church leaders caring for servicemen, introduced on p. 3 by the First Presidency: "We are issuing" this publication "for your information and guidance."

Stake Missions — *Handbook for Stake Missions of the Church of Jesus Christ of Latter-day Saints* (Church of Jesus Christ of Latter-day Saints, June 1960), "issued by the First Presidency."

Strength of Youth — *For the Strength of Youth: Fulfilling Our Duty to God* (Church of Jesus Christ of Latter-day Saints, 2000). The LDS Church's *Guidebook for Parents and Leaders of Youth* (2001) reads: "*For the Strength of Youth* is a guide given by the First Presidency of the Church to young men and young women." Similar sentiments were expressed by the First Presidency in previous editions of *For the Strength of Youth*: "We [First Presidency] wish to endorse what has been here written" (1968); "The First Presidency and Quorum of the Twelve have reviewed, accepted, and endorsed this pamphlet, which is printed at their request and with their approval for the information, guidance, and blessings of the youth of the Church" (1990).

True to Faith	*True to the Faith: A Gospel Reference* (Church of Jesus Christ of Latter-day Saints, July 2004). The First Presidency's introduction reads: "This book is designed as a companion to your study of the scriptures and the teachings of the latter-day prophets. We encourage you to refer to it as you study and apply gospel principles. Use it as a resource when you prepare talks, teach classes, and answer questions about the Church."
Welfare Plan	*Welfare Plan of The Church of Jesus Christ of Latter-day Saints: Handbook of Instructions* (General Church Welfare Committee, 1952), "prepared under the direction of, and approved by, the First Presidency of the Church of Jesus Christ of Latter-day Saints."
Woman's Exponent	*The Woman's Exponent* (1872-1914), a monthly newspaper published by the leadership of the LDS Church's female Relief Society, including periodic statements from the First Presidency.

A

Aaronic Priesthood, *see* priesthood

abortion. *See also* life, sanctity of

The Church of Jesus Christ of Latter-say Saints believes in the sanctity of human life. Therefore, the Church opposes elective abortion for personal or social convenience, and counsels its members not to submit to, perform, encourage, pay for, or arrange for such abortions.

The Church allows for possible exceptions for its members when:

• Pregnancy results from rape or incest, or

• A competent physician determines that the life or health of the mother is in serious jeopardy, or

• A competent physician determines that the fetus has severe defects that will not allow the baby to survive beyond birth.

The Church teaches its members that even these rare exceptions do not justify abortion automatically. Abortion is a most serious matter and should be considered only after the persons involved have consulted with their local Church leaders and feel through personal prayer that their decision is correct.

The Church has not favored or opposed legislative proposals or public demonstrations concerning abortion. "ISSUES RESOURCES" 2006

Members of The Church of Jesus Christ of Latter-day Saints

must not submit to, perform, encourage, pay for, or arrange for an abortion. If you encourage an abortion in any way, you may be subject to Church discipline. *TRUE TO FAITH*, 2004

Church leaders have said that some exceptional circumstances may justify an abortion, such as when pregnancy is the result of incest or rape, when the life or health of the mother is judged by competent medical authority to be in serious jeopardy, or when the fetus is known by competent medical authority to have severe defects that will not allow the baby to survive beyond birth. But even these circumstances do not automatically justify an abortion. Those who face such circumstances should consider abortion only after consulting with their local Church leaders and receiving a confirmation through earnest prayer. IBID.

The Church opposes elective abortion for personal or social convenience. Members must not submit to, perform, encourage, pay for, or arrange for an abortion. The only possible exceptions are when:

1. Pregnancy resulted from rape or incest.
2. A competent physician determines that the life or health of the mother is in serious jeopardy.
3. A competent physician determines that the fetus has severe defects that will not allow the baby to survive beyond birth.

Even these exceptions do not justify abortion automatically. Abortion is a most serious matter and should be considered only after the persons responsible have consulted with their bishops and received divine confirmation through prayer. *CHURCH HANDBOOK*, 1998

The practice of elective abortion is fundamentally contrary to the Lord's injunction: "Thou shall not steal, neither commit adultery, nor kill, nor do anything like unto it" (D&C 59:6). We urge all to preserve the sanctity of human life and thereby realize the happiness promised to those who keep the commandments of the Lord. *DESERET NEWS*, JAN. 12, 1991

The Church of Jesus Christ of Latter-day Saints as an institution has not favored or opposed specific legislative proposals or public demonstrations concerning abortion.

Inasmuch as this issue is likely to arise in all states in the United States of America and in many other nations of the world in which the Church is established, it is impractical for the Church to take a position on specific legislative proposals on this important subject.

However, we continue to encourage our members as citizens to let their voices be heard in appropriate and legal ways that will evidence their belief in the sacredness of life. IBID.

As far as has been revealed, the sin of abortion is one for which a person may repent and gain forgiveness. *CHURCH NEWS*, JUNE 5, 1976

The Church opposes abortion and counsels its members not to submit to or perform an abortion except in the rare cases where, in the opinion of competent medical counsel, the life or good health of the mother is seriously endangered or where the pregnancy was caused by rape and produces serious emotional trauma in the mother. Even then it should be done only after counseling with the local presiding priesthood authority and after receiving divine confirmation through prayer.

Abortion must be considered one of the most revolting and sinful practices in this day, when we are witnessing the frightening evidence of permissiveness leading to sexual immorality.

Members of the Church guilty of being parties in the sin of

abortion must be subjected to the disciplinary action of the councils of the Church as circumstances warrant. In dealing with this serious matter, it would be well to keep in mind the word of the Lord stated in the fifty-ninth section of the Doctrine and Covenants, verse 6, "Thou shalt not steal; neither commit adultery, nor kill, nor do anything like unto it."

As to the amenability of the sin of abortion to the laws of repentance and forgiveness, we quote the following statement made by President David O. McKay and his counselors, Stephen L Richards and J. Reuben Clark, Jr., which continues to represent the attitude and position of the Church:

"As the matter stands today, no definite statement has been made by the Lord one way or another regarding the crime of abortion. So far as is known, He has not listed it alongside the crime of the unpardonable sin and shedding of innocent human blood. That He has not done so would suggest that it is not in that class of crime and therefore that it will be amenable to the laws of repentance and forgiveness."

This quoted statement, however, should not, in any sense, be construed to minimize the seriousness of this revolting sin.
CHURCH NEWS, JAN. 27, 1973

The Church takes the view that any tampering with the fountains of life is serious, both morally and physiologically. The Lord's command imposed upon all Latter-day Saints is to "multiply and replenish the earth" [Gen. 1:28]. Nevertheless, there may be conditions where abortion could be justified, but such conditions must be determined acting upon the advice of competent, reliable physicians, preferably members of the Church, and in accordance with the laws pertaining thereto.

No definite statement has been made by the Lord one way or another regarding the crime of abortion. So far as known,

He has not listed it alongside the crime of the unpardonable sin and shedding of innocent human blood. That He has not done so would suggest that it is not in that class of crime and therefore it will be amenable to the laws of repentance and forgiveness. FIRST PRESIDENCY, LETTER DATED NOV. 2, 1970

To take means to prevent the due process of nature following conception is a crime. DAVID O. MCKAY TO "DEAR BROTHER," MAR. 6, 1942

[N]o one who has deliberately committed murder can be permitted to be baptized into the Church of Christ, and we regard those who intentionally destroy their children before birth as included in this prohibition. WILFORD WOODRUFF AND JOSEPH F. SMITH TO JOB PINGREE, JAN. 23, 1894

You ask me if you shall baptize a person whom you know to be guilty of foeticide. I presented the question to the Apostles, in council, and it was decided that you ought not; that the commission of this sin, common and frequent though it be, is next akin to murder, and no murderer hath eternal life abiding in him. FRANKLIN D. RICHARDS TO ROBERT G. BERRETT, NOV. 14, 1879

abuse. *See also* child abuse

Abuse is the treatment of others or self in a way that causes injury or offense. It harms the mind and the spirit and often injures the body as well. It can cause confusion, doubt, mistrust, and fear. It is a violation of the laws of society and is in total opposition to the teachings of the Savior. The Lord condemns abusive behavior in any form—physical, sexual, verbal, or emotional. Abusive behavior may lead to Church discipline. *TRUE TO FAITH*, 2004

The Church's position is that abuse cannot be tolerated in any form. Those who abuse or are cruel to their spouses, children, other family members, or anyone else violate the laws of God and man. *CHURCH HANDBOOK*, 1998

No man is worthy of the priesthood who abuses his wife, the mother of his children. GORDON B. HINCKLEY, "FIRST PRESIDENCY MESSAGE," *ENSIGN*, AUG. 1997

accountability

The principle of accountability is fundamental in God's eternal plan. We will all stand before the Lord at the last judgment and give an accounting for what we have done with the opportunities He has given us (see Alma 5:15-19; D&C 137:9). *PREACH MY GOSPEL*, 2005

Although we are redeemed unconditionally from the universal effects of the Fall, we are accountable for our own sins. *TRUE TO FAITH*, 2004

Members who have mental disabilities and cannot knowingly repent may be considered by the bishop as not accountable. These persons need not be baptized, regardless of their age. They are "saved in the celestial kingdom of heaven" (D&C 137:10; see also Moro. 8:9-12). *CHURCH HANDBOOK*, 1998

Those who are mentally deficient do not need to be baptized, no matter what their age may be. They are not in a position to understand or be capable of repentance and, therefore, cannot be held accountable. Should they ever become mentally responsible, the ordinances of the gospel may then be administered. *CHURCH HANDBOOK,* 1940

Adam and Eve

Latter-day revelation makes clear that the Fall is a blessing and that Adam and Eve should be honored as the first parents of all mankind. *PREACH MY GOSPEL,* 2005

The consequences of the missions performed by Adam and Eve made necessary the Atonement wrought by Jesus. MARION G. ROMNEY, "FIRST PRESIDENCY MESSAGE," *ENSIGN,* SEPT. 1980

When the woman was given to Adam, he called her name Eve "because she was the mother of all living" (Moses 4:26). She was the first. Adam and Eve were the progenitors of the race. They were the first father and mother, and all the children of mortality are the offspring of this couple.

Now, this man and this woman were sealed for eternity, God being the sealer. He gave to Adam his wife, Eve. He intended that all men should live worthy to have performed this ordinance of marriage for time and all eternity. SPENCER W. KIMBALL, "FIRST PRESIDENCY MESSAGE," *ENSIGN,* OCT. 1975

Adam was the first man and Eve the first woman on this earth. They were created in the image of God, with bodies of flesh, bones, and spirit, capable of falling and being redeemed.

Adam and Eve were placed on earth in a state of innocence. They, the earth, and all things in it were pronounced very good, and without transgression would have remained in that state forever.

When Adam and Eve partook of the forbidden fruit, transgressing the law given to them by God, their nature was changed and they became subject to both spiritual and temporal deaths.

Only after Adam and Eve became mortal did they begin to multiply and replenish the earth. Because of their transgression, they, their posterity, and all other things on earth became subject to the conditions of mortality.

An infinite Atonement had to be made to overcome the power of death and sin, thereby making possible the redemption and resurrection of Adam and Eve and their posterity. "BASIC DOCTRINES," 1971

Adam and Eve were the first couple on this earth who were married for time and eternity, and this ceremony was performed by the Lord before the Fall, at which time there was no death and therefore it could not have been a time marriage.
FIRST PRESIDENCY TO RAY HILL MOORE, SEPT. 6, 1967

We have before us your letter of February 18 [1931], in which you say that in your priesthood class one brother claims that Adam "had been through the experience of mortality on another sphere before he came here; that he was a celestialized being when placed in the Garden of Eden."

What this brother means by "celestialized being" is not clear. We are informed that we all lived in the presence of God in the spirit world before we came here. In one sense we might say that this was a celestialized existence. If what is meant is that Adam had passed on to celestial glory through a resurrection before he came here, and that afterwards he was appointed to this earth to die again, the second time becoming mortal, then it is not scriptural or according to the truth. See Moses 3:7; 4:29; Abr. 5:7; Alma 42:2; also Gen. 2:7; 3:23; John 11:25-29, and many other passages of scripture–D&C 107; John 11:25-56; Rev. 21:4; Alma 11:45; 12:18; D&C 63:49; 88:14-16; 93:33-34; 2 Ne. 2:22; D&C 29:41-43.

Adam could have remained in the Garden of Eden indefinitely if he had not transgressed the law which brought to pass mortality. Since Adam had not passed through the resurrection, his spirit and body *were not* inseparably connected, hence it was possible for him to become mortal by partaking of the fruit of the tree of knowledge of good and evil. By so doing he received the seeds of death and brought to pass mortality in himself and caused all of his posterity to partake of like conditions and be subject to death.

Christ came, as we know, not subject to death, but always

having the mastery over death, to atone for Adam's transgression. The Savior said that He had life in Himself as the Father had life in Himself (John 5:26) and that He had power to lay down His life of Himself and take it again, which commandment He had received from His Father (10:15).

Adam, like all of his posterity, became a benefactor through the mission of Jesus Christ. Through the Atonement made by our Lord, Adam was redeemed from his transgression and received the resurrection. FIRST PRESIDENCY TO JOSEPH H. ELDREDGE, FEB. 26, 1931, IN *MESSAGES,* 5:289-90

Adam, our great progenitor, "the first man," was, like Christ, a pre-existent spirit, and like Christ, he took upon him an appropriate body, the body of a man, and so became a "living soul." *DESERET NEWS,* JULY 18, 1925, QUOTING *IMPROVEMENT ERA,* NOV. 1909

When President [Brigham] Young asked, "who is the Father?" he was speaking of Adam as the father of our earthly bodies, who is at our head, as revealed in Doctrine and Covenants, section 107, verses 53-56. In that sense he is one of the gods referred to in numerous scriptures, and particularly by Christ (John 10:34-36). He is the great patriarch, the Ancient of Days, who will stand in his place as "a prince over us forever," and with whom we shall "have to do," as each family will have to do with its head, according to the holy patriarchal order. Our father, Adam, perfected and glorified as a God, will be the being who will carry out the behests of the great Elohim in relation to his posterity (see Dan. 7:9-14). FIRST PRESIDENCY TO SAMUEL O. BENNION, FEB. 20, 1912, IN *MESSAGES,* 4:266-67

Speculations as to the career of Adam before he came to the earth are of no real value. We learn by revelation that he was Michael, the archangel, and that he stands as the head of his posterity on earth (D&C 107:53-56). *IMPROVEMENT ERA,* MAR. 1912, IN *MESSAGES,* 4:264-65

[I]f God made man—the first man—in His own image and likeness, he must have made him like unto Christ, and consequently like unto men of Christ's time and of the present day. That man was made in the image of Christ is positively stated in the Book of Moses: "And I, God, said unto mine Only Begotten, which was with me from the beginning, Let us make man in our image, after our likeness; and it was so. ... And I, God, created man in mine own image, in the image of mine Only Begotten created I him, male and female created I them" (2:26, 27). *IMPROVEMENT ERA,* NOV. 1909, IN *MESSAGES,* 4:200-06

It is held by some that Adam was not the first man upon this earth, and that the original human being was a development from lower orders of the animal creation. These, however, are the theories of men. The word of the Lord declares that Adam was "the first man of all men" (Moses 1:34), and we are therefore in duty bound to regard him as the primal parent of our race. It was shown to the brother of Jared that all men were created in the beginning after the image of God; and whether we take this to mean the spirit or the body, or both, it commits us to the same conclusion: Man began life as a human being, in the likeness of our Heavenly Father.

True it is that the body of man enters upon its career as a tiny germ embryo, which becomes an infant, quickened at a certain stage by the spirit whose tabernacle it is, and the child, after being born, develops into a man. There is nothing in this, however, to indicate that the original man, the first of our race, began life as anything less than a man, or less than the human germ or embryo that becomes a man. IBID.

The [Adam-God] doctrine was never submitted to the councils of the priesthood nor to the Church for approval or ratification, and was never formally or otherwise accepted by the Church. It is therefore in no sense binding upon the Church nor upon the consciences of any of the members thereof, except perhaps only so far as some may have confidence in President [Brigham] Young, believing that he had light on the subject which was not given in connection with his public mention thereof. It is thought, even if there is truth in it, that the bare mention made by Pres[ident]. Young, without indubitable evidence and authority being given of its truth, was unfortunate to say the least. JOSEPH F. SMITH TO A. SAXEY, JAN. 7, 1897

adoption

When a man and a woman conceive a child out of wedlock, their first consideration should be to marry and work toward establishing an eternal family relationship. When the probability of a successful marriage is unlikely because of age or other circumstances, unwed parents are encouraged to place their child for adoption through LDS Family Services to ensure that the baby will be sealed to temple worthy parents. *CHURCH NEWS,* NOV. 8, 2003

Adoption is an unselfish, loving decision that blesses the birth parents, the child, and the adoptive family. *CHURCH NEWS,* NOV. 23, 2002

When a child is conceived out of wedlock, the best interests of the child should be the paramount consideration. When a successful marriage is unlikely, many choose to place their children for adoption in order to provide the blessings of having a father and a mother. Adoptive placement by unwed parents is truly an act of love. *CHURCH NEWS,* NOV. 18, 2000

Unwed parents who do not marry should not be counseled

to keep the infant as a condition of repentance or out of a sense of obligation to care for one's own. Generally, unwed parents are not able to provide a stable, nurturing environment so essential for the baby's well-being. *CHURCH NEWS,* NOV. 11, 2000

An unwed parent who determines to keep the child should be treated with compassion and concern, and is encouraged to have the child given a name and a blessing. "DEAR BRETHREN," MAY 25, 1989

adultery, ***see*** **Church discipline; sexual relations**

adversity, ***see*** **suffering**

afterlife, ***see*** **resurrection**

agency

Every moment demands that we choose, over and over again, between that which comes from the Lord and that which comes from the devil. As tiny drops of water shape a landscape, so our minute-by-minute choices shape our character. JAMES E. FAUST, "FIRST PRESIDENCY MESSAGE," *ENSIGN,* JUNE 2006

All people have the gift of agency, which includes the freedom to accept or reject the gospel as taught by the prophets and apostles. Those who choose to obey are blessed, but those who ignore, reject, or distort the gospel do not receive God's promised blessings. *PREACH MY GOSPEL,* 2005

Your Heavenly Father has given you agency, the ability to choose and to act for yourself. Agency is essential in the plan of salvation. Without it, you would not be able to learn or progress or follow the Savior. With it, you are "free to choose liberty and eternal life, through the great Mediator of all men, or to choose captivity and death, according to the captivity and power of the devil" (2 Ne. 2:27). *TRUE TO FAITH*, 2004

Learn to follow your conscience. This is an important part of exercising your agency. The more you follow your conscience, the stronger it will become. A sensitive conscience is a sign of a healthy spirit. IBID.

While you are free to choose for yourself, you are not free to choose the consequences of your actions. When you make a choice, you will receive the consequences of that choice. The consequences may not be immediate, but they will always follow, for good or bad. *STRENGTH OF YOUTH,* 2001

Moral agency is a cardinal principle of obedience, and obedience comes from *love of God* and *commitment to His work.* JAMES E. FAUST, "FIRST PRESIDENCY MESSAGE," *ENSIGN,* JULY 2000

Since each one of us has his free agency, the ultimate determination of what is inspired of the Lord, what is right and wrong, true or false, can be made by each of us. JAMES E. FAUST, "FIRST PRESIDENCY MESSAGE," *ENSIGN,* SEPT. 1998

Freedom of choice is a God-given, eternal principle that carries with it moral responsibilities for the choices made. *STRENGTH OF YOUTH*, 1990

All men who dwell on the earth are subject to the influences of righteousness, and also to the influences of wickedness. They are endowed, too, with the divine gift of moral agency, in the exercise of which no person who has lived upon the earth to the age of accountability, except Jesus, has been able in all things to avoid yielding to the influence of evil. All have sinned. Each person is therefore unclean to the extent to which he has sinned, and because of that uncleanness is banished from the presence of the Lord so long as the effect of his own wrongdoing is upon him. MARION G. ROMNEY, "FIRST PRESIDENCY MESSAGE," *ENSIGN,* APR. 1985

Earth life is a period of trial for every person of two mighty forces pulling in opposite directions. On the one hand is the power of Christ and His righteousness. On the other hand is Satan and his fellow travelers. Mankind, in the exercise of their God-given moral agency, must determine to travel in company with the one or the other. The reward for following the one is the fruit of the spirit—peace. The reward for following the other is the works of the flesh—the antithesis of peace. MARION G. ROMNEY, "FIRST PRESIDENCY MESSAGE," *ENSIGN,* OCT. 1983

[T]he spiritual guidance received by each individual is strictly up to the individual. Each is enlightened by the Spirit when he comes into the world, given his free agency, and held responsible for his exercise thereof. MARION G. ROMNEY, "FIRST PRESIDENCY MESSAGE," *ENSIGN,* JANUARY 1980

We are endowed by our creator with agency. While in mortality, we live between powerful forces—the force of good and the force of evil. Between the two we must choose. There is no escape. MARION G. ROMNEY, "FIRST PRESIDENCY MESSAGE," *ENSIGN,* FEB. 1977

Free agency is the ability to choose good or evil. It is an eternal principle and an essential part of the plan of salvation. *PRINCIPLES,* 1976

If there were no opposition to good, would there be any chance to exercise your agency or right to choose? To deny you that privilege would be to deny you the opportunity to grow in knowledge, experience, and power. God has given laws with penalties affixed so that man might be made afraid of sin and be guided into paths of truth and duty (see Alma

42:20). HAROLD B. LEE, "FIRST PRESIDENCY MESSAGE," *ENSIGN,* JULY 1971

All beings are subject to divine law, obedience to which brings blessings. Disobedience results in suffering and damnation.

Man has the divine gift of agency to choose good or evil. He may worship how, where, or what he may, but only by learning and obeying celestial laws can man be exalted.

Man can choose and act for himself only as he gains knowledge of good and evil and is influenced by one or the other. "BASIC DOCTRINES," 1971

Let us never lose sight of the eternal principle enunciated by the Master that while free agency will not be trammeled by our Heavenly Father, conformity to established rules of conduct is a necessary prerequisite to the blessings promised to those who obey and keep His commandments. *STRENGTH OF YOUTH,* 1968

At the very basis of all our doctrine stands the right to the free agency of man. We are in favor of maintaining this free agency to the greatest extent possible. We look adversely upon any infringement thereof not essential to the proper exercise of police power of the state. *DESERET NEWS,* JUNE 25, 1965

We believe that the essential basis for human cooperation in any form is mutual recognition of the worth of the individual. Inherent and implied in each undertaking of the United States should stand the purpose of maintaining, promoting, and extending the free exercise of individual conscience and the protection of life. We also believe that the individual's right to the ownership and control of property is an important adjunct of such purpose. This is in line with the common law maxim that a man's home is his castle and subject only to due process of law respecting the rights of life, liberty, and conscience. "DESIRABLE OBJECTIVES," MAY 14, 1965

Let us never lose sight of the eternal principle enunciated by the Master that while free agency will not be trammeled by our Heavenly Father, conformity to established rules of conduct is a necessary prerequisite to the blessings promised to those who obey and keep His commandments. *STRENGTH OF YOUTH,* 1965

This love of our Father has been manifested ever since He gave free agency to man, and was particularly made known during the earthly life of Jesus by His teachings, death, and resurrection in the first century following His birth in mortality. *DESERET NEWS,* DEC. 15, 1954

All men have the right to believe as they wish and practice what they wish within the law. Our eleventh Article of Faith declares the principle: "We claim the privilege of worshiping Almighty God according to the dictates of our own conscience, and allow all men the same privilege, let them worship how, where, or what they may."

All this is in accordance with the great and eternal principle of free agency. "DEAR BRETHREN," JUNE 30, 1952

Even to imply that members of the Church are not to do their own thinking is grossly to misrepresent the true ideal of the Church, which is that *every individual must obtain for himself a testimony of the truth of the gospel,* must through the redemption of Jesus Christ *work out his own salvation,* and is *personally responsible to His Maker for his individual acts.* The Lord Himself does not attempt coercion in His desire and effort to give peace and salvation to His children. He gives the principles of life and true progress, but leaves every person free to choose or to reject His teachings. This plan the Authorities of the

Church try to follow. GEORGE ALBERT SMITH TO J. RAYMOND COPE, DEC. 7, 1945

[T]he Church gives to every man his free agency, and admonishes him always to use the reason and good judgment with which God has blessed him. IBID.

While we do not charge the Almighty with causing the evils of any kind that afflict humanity, and which we regard as the fruits of disobedience to His holy laws, we recognize the fact that He is over all and that He will eventually control everything to bring about His own almighty plans. The agency of man is not interfered with by divine providence. If men were not left free to choose the good and refuse the evil, or vice versa, there would be no righteousness or even reason in bringing them to judgment. In consequence of the power of volition, they become responsible beings, and therefore will receive the results of their own doings. They will be rewarded or punished according to their works, when the books are opened and they are judged out of the things written therein.

God, doubtless, could avert war, prevent crime, destroy poverty, chase away darkness, overcome error, and make all things bright, beautiful, and joyful. But this would involve the destruction of a vital and fundamental attribute in man, the right of agency. It is for the benefit of His sons and daughters that they become acquainted with evil as well as good, with darkness as well as light, with error as well as truth, and with the results of the infraction of eternal laws. Therefore He has permitted the evils which have been brought about by the acts of His creatures, but will control their ultimate results for His own glory and the progress and exaltation of His sons and daughters, when they have learned obedience by the things they suffer. The contrasts experienced in this world of mingled sorrow and joy are educational in their nature, and will be the means of raising humanity to a full appreciation of all that is right and true and good. The foreknowledge of God does not imply His action in bringing about that which He foresees, nor make Him responsible in any degree for that which man does or refuses to do. The comprehension of this principle makes clear many questions that puzzle the uninformed as to the power and works of Deity. *DESERET NEWS,* DEC. 19, 1914, IN *MESSAGES,* 4:318-26

We claim for Church officers as well as Church members all the rights and privileges of American citizens, no less and no more; and do not claim, or exercise, power to compel, or coerce, or infringe upon the liberties of any person, and all assertions to the contrary are infamously untrue. *IMPROVEMENT ERA,* JUNE 1911, IN *MESSAGES,* 4:224-29

Diversity of opinion does not necessitate intolerance of spirit, nor should it embitter or set rational beings against each other. The Christ taught kindness, patience, and charity. In His doctrine of the fatherhood of God, He implied the brotherhood of man. The message we have to bear is universal—for every nation, kindred, tongue, and people. While it is to be declared to all, it is to be enforced upon none. The free agency of man is a fundamental in the creed of the Latter-day Saints as received from the Prophet Joseph Smith as he obtained it from Jesus the Christ. Free will, free thought, free speech, free action to the line of the liberty of others form an essential part of our faith and practice. *DESERET EVENING NEWS,* DEC. 17, 1910

We believe in the free agency of man, and therefore in his individual responsibility. *IMPROVEMENT ERA,* MAY 1907, IN *MESSAGES,* 4:143-55

The religion of the Latter-day Saints relates to present conduct as well as future happiness. It influences its votaries in everything that affects human character. It is for the body as well as for the spirit. It teaches people how to live and act in this world that they may be prepared for the realities of the world to come. The Church, therefore, instructs in things temporal as well as things spiritual, so far as they relate to the Church, its properties and institutions, and the association of its adherents. But it does not infringe upon the liberty of the individual or encroach upon the domain of the state. The free agency of man is a fundamental principle which, according to the tenets of the Church, even God Himself does not suppress. Therefore, the Church does not dictate a member's business, his politics, or his personal affairs. It never tells a citizen what occupation he shall follow, whom he shall vote for, or with which party he shall affiliate. *ELDER'S JOURNAL,* JAN. 1904, IN *MESSAGES,* 4:78-83

As to the agency of man, it is by the light of Christ and the power of God that man by his agency can become exalted through obedience to the laws of God. It is by his agency that he becomes a son of perdition after having received the truth, by yielding against himself to the power of Satan. A man who by his agency conquers Satan, subdues the evil that is in him, and rises above the power of temptation and of all evil is still as much a free agent as he was when he was subject to temptation, but then he is like God or Christ—beyond the power of evil. JOSEPH F. SMITH TO JOSEPH FIELDING SMITH, APR. 3, 1900

No man's business or other secular affairs are invaded by the Church or any of its officers. Free agency and direct individual accountability to God are among the essentials of our Church doctrine. *DESERET NEWS WEEKLY,* DEC. 12, 1889, IN *MESSAGES,* 3:184-87

The nearer you can come to union in all of your agricultural, mechanical, manufacturing, commercial, political, social, and religious pursuits, the nearer you will approach to that harmony that is contemplated by the Almighty in the organization of this people. Thus giving the fullest and most complete free agency to men on the one hand, and the most perfect union of action on the other. "DEAR BRETHREN," BANNOCK STAKE, AUG. 16-17, 1884, IN *MESSAGES,* 2:357-59

This brings us again to observe that salvation is an individual work, and that so long as any person operates in a course which does not infringe upon the proper rights of others, his belief and conduct should not incur their violence, anger, or improper interference, for he is walking in his own sphere, enjoying the agency given him, and will reap the reward thereof, and all undue interference will be charged to the account of whoever thus interferes. *DESERET NEWS,* SEPT. 14, 1854, IN *MESSAGES,* 2:149-53

alcohol (consumption and sales). ***See also*** **Word of Wisdom**

Any form of alcohol, including beer, is harmful to your spirit and your body. Drinking will dull your conscience, is expensive, and could lead to alcoholism, which is self-destructive, dangerous, and deadly. *STRENGTH OF YOUTH,* 1990

Involvement by members of the Church in handling, selling, or serving of alcoholic beverages should be discouraged. Cautious consideration should be exercised before persons so involved are called to Church positions. *CHURCH HANDBOOK,* 1976

We deplore the efforts of those who attempt to broaden the sale and use of spirituous beverages, particularly among young people.

We are fully aware of the many problems that result in legally making liquor available to young men and women who generally are more prone to form new habits, good and bad, than older adults.

To lower the age for liquor consumption will only add to the mounting problems of health, crime, accidents, and broken homes which already beset our society. *CHURCH NEWS,* OCT. 27, 1973

We deplore the efforts of those who attempt to facilitate the ease with which spirituous beverages can be purchased. The inevitable effect of this is to increase the likelihood that these beverages will get into the hands of minors. Their sale over the counter in grocery stores also has the subtle effect of somehow making their purchase and consumption more commonplace and acceptable; and doing so will doubtless increase the per capita consumption of these beverages, thereby further impairing the general health and safety of the community. "DEAR BRETHREN," IDAHO STAKES, JULY 20, 1972

Drink brings cruelty into the home; it walks arm in arm with poverty; its companions are disease and plague; it puts chastity to flight; it knows neither honesty nor fair dealing; it is a total stranger to truth; it drowns conscience; it is the bodyguard of evil; it curses all who touch it.

Drink has brought more woe and misery, broken more hearts, wrecked more homes, committed more crimes, filled more coffins than all the wars the world has suffered. *IMPROVEMENT ERA,* NOV. 1942, IN *MESSAGES,* 6:170-85

American Indians

This process of redeeming the Lamanite people has been far from easy, especially for the Lamanites themselves. For a thousand years after the closing of the Book of Mormon record, these people wandered in spiritual darkness and were scattered upon the American continents and the isles of the sea. They lost their written language, their high culture, and, worst of all, their knowledge of the living God and His work. Faith was replaced by fear, rich language by crippled dialects, and an understanding of God and His ways by idolatry, even human sacrifice. Since the coming of the white man to the Americas, they have been driven mercilessly, killed, and degraded. When Columbus came, these descendants of the Book of Mormon peoples and those with whom they had mixed numbered in the millions and covered the islands of the Pacific and the Americas from Point Barrow to Tierra del Fuego. But the conquerors found a prey, and in the land southward they robbed and despoiled and slaughtered in the name of gold and silver. In the land northward the 400-year "Battle of America" drove the tribal nations, much reduced in numbers, into the far corners of desolate lands. The peoples of the isles of the sea were corrupted by European and American seamen-adventurers and were reduced nearly to extinction by disease. Someone said, "If my pen might have the gift of tears, I would write a book and call it 'The Indian,' and I would make the whole world weep." Only the most brazen soul could fail to weep when contemplating the fall of this people, and yet it was the decree of the Lord that the Lamanites should be preserved in the land, that this remnant of Joseph should again come into their promised inheritance. SPENCER W. KIMBALL, "FIRST PRESIDENCY MESSAGE," *ENSIGN,* DEC. 1975

[W]e should bear with them [i.e., native American Indians] in their ignorance, and do all that we can to reclaim them from the[ir] low and fallen condition, and to point unto them the course which they should take to enjoy the blessings of this life and to perpetuate their race upon the earth. A remnant of them will be saved; and they will become a white and delightsome people, as the prophets have foretold. This will be accomplished in the Lord's own time and in His own way. But before this will be fulfilled, the Lamanites have a terrible work to perform. They are yet to be "as a lion among the beasts of the forest, as a young lion among the flocks of sheep, who, if he goeth through, both treadeth down and teareth to pieces and none can deliver." We need not be surprised, therefore, that they are bloodthirsty and pitiless. It is their nature, as it has been developed by generations of training, and none but a race such as they are could be capable of the deeds that, we are told, they will commit. Knowing that this is their nature, we should take every precaution to guard against its manifestation in acts of violence towards us, and never place ourselves in a position to be attacked with impunity. In so doing, and always treating them with proper kindness and consideration, they will both fear and respect us. FIRST PRESIDENCY TO ORSON HYDE AND BISHOPS AND SAINTS IN SANPETE, SEVIER, PIUTE, AND SUMMIT COUNTIES, AND ERASTUS SNOW AND SAINTS IN IRON, KANE, AND WASHINGTON COUNTIES, APR. 28, 1866

[T]he *"Indians"* (so called) of North and South America are a remnant of the tribes of Israel, as is now made manifest by the discovery and revelations of their ancient oracles and records. STATEMENT, APR. 6, 1845, IN *MESSAGES,* 1:252-66

Ancient of Days, *see* Adam and Eve

angels

Angels are spirit children of our Heavenly Father (as we are) who either have not yet entered this mortal life or have already died. *PRINCIPLES,* 1976

Angels are all around you all the time, watching over and caring for you. They can help and guard you best; they can keep harm away from you most when you do what your father and mother ask you to do. FIRST PRESIDENCY TO "DEAR PRIMARY CHILDREN," NOV. 1941, IN *MESSAGES,* 6:134-35

apostasy

We now live in a time when the gospel of Jesus Christ has been restored. But unlike the Church in times past, The Church of Jesus Christ of Latter-day Saints will not be overcome by general apostasy. The scriptures teach that the Church will never again be destroyed (see D&C 138:44; see also Dan. 2:44). *TRUE TO FAITH,* 2004

Those who express private doubts or unbelief as a public chastisement of the leadership or the doctrine of the Church or as a confrontation with those also seeking eternal light have entered upon sacred ground. Those who complain about the doctrines or leadership of the Church but who lack the faith or desire to keep God's commandments risk separating themselves from the divine source of learning. They do not enjoy the same richness of the Spirit that they might enjoy if they proved their sincere love of God by walking humbly before Him, by keeping His commandments, and by sustaining those whom He has appointed to lead the Church. JAMES E. FAUST, "FIRST PRESIDENCY MESSAGE," *ENSIGN,* JULY 2000

[A]postasy refers to members who:

1. Repeatedly act in clear, open, and deliberate public opposition to the Church or its leaders.
2. Persist in teaching as Church doctrine information that is not Church doctrine after they have been corrected by their bishops or higher authority.
3. Continue to follow the teachings of apostate sects (such as those that advocate plural marriage) after being corrected by their bishop or higher authority. *CHURCH HANDBOOK,* 1998

Total inactivity in the Church or attending or holding membership in another church does not constitute apostasy. IBID.

An adult member who wishes to have his or her name removed from the membership records of the Church must send the bishop a written, signed request (not a form letter). IBID.

If a member requests name removal and a bishop or stake president has evidence of transgression that warrants convening a disciplinary council, he should not act on the request until Church discipline has been imposed or he has concluded that no disciplinary council will be held. Name removal should not be used as a substitute for or alternative to Church discipline.

If a member requests name removal and a bishop or stake president suspects transgression but lacks sufficient evidence to convene a disciplinary council, the request for name removal may be approved. IBID.

A member who has been excommunicated or disfellowshipped for advocating or teaching apostate or anti-Church doctrines must not have his disfellowshipment lifted or be readmitted to the Church without the approval of the First Presidency. *BULLETIN,* 1992-2

[I]t is unwise to contend with the critics or to be drawn to imitate their unchristianlike conduct. "DEAR BRETHREN," DEC. 1, 1983

The Lord gave Adam the principles of the gospel so that we could conduct our lives in harmony with the order of heaven and thus be able to return to Him. These same principles have been taught throughout the world's history by prophets of the Lord. Apostasy occurs when men–as groups or as individuals—reject, abandon, or disregard these principles given by the Lord. *PRINCIPLES,* 1976

When we speak of the Apostasy in a specific sense, we are usually referring to the falling away from the Church and gospel established by the Savior during his earthly ministry. IBID.

As time passed, dissensions occurred in the primitive Church. The laws governing the Church established by the Redeemer were transgressed, the ordinances were changed, the everlasting covenant was broken. Men began to teach for doctrine their own commandments; a form of worship had been established which was called Christianity, but was without the power of God which characterized the primitive Church. Spiritual darkness covered the earth, and gross darkness the minds of the people. *DESERET NEWS,* DEC. 19, 1925, IN *MESSAGES,* 5:245-48

Piety is often the cloak of error. *DESERET NEWS,* AUG. 2, 1913, IN *MESSAGES,* 4:285-86

The religion of the Latter-day Saints which the world calls "Mormonism" affirms, as the reason for its existence, the departure of the present-day Christian churches from the principles of the original Christian faith, thus necessitating a restoration of the true gospel, with its spiritual gifts, and the powers of the priesthood, as enjoyed anciently. *DESERET NEWS,* NOV. 4, 1911, IN *MESSAGES,* 4:231-51

The Latter-day Saints have a very important message to bear to the world. They declare that God has revealed Himself to the Prophet Joseph Smith, and that He has again bestowed authority upon men to administer in the ordinances of the gospel. This authority has not been upon the earth since the early era of Christianity. The "falling away" predicted by Paul in his letter to the Thessalonians has taken place, and "the man of sin" has been revealed, and hence the great need of the ushering in of another dispensation of the gospel. That God in His mercy has done this is the glad tidings which the Latter-day Saints in all sincerity proclaim to their fellowmen. *LIAHONA,* APR. 6, 1907, IN *MESSAGES,* 4:155-57

Bishops' Courts cannot consistently entertain a complaint charging a man with erroneous belief or opinion on points of doctrine, provided his belief or opinion is not expressed to the injury of others. If, however, he persists in holding them out and thereby misleads or tries to mislead others, a complaint might consistently be entertained and he tried on his fellowship. FIRST PRESIDENCY TO S. C. STEPHENS, OCT. 22, 1901

As it has been in all ages of the Church, so it is now (and so it will continue while the net gathers all sorts of fish) there are unfaithful members, they have a name to live, but are dead; and being destitute of faith are destitute of good works, are faultfinders, backbiters, evil surmisers, false prophets, apostates. *MILLENNIAL STAR,* JULY 9, 1853, IN *MESSAGES,* 2:110-19

Strange as it may appear at first thought, yet it is no less strange than true, that notwithstanding all the professed determination to live godly, apostates after turning from the faith of Christ, unless they have speedily repented, have sooner or later fallen into the snares of the wicked one, and have been left destitute of the Spirit of God, to manifest their wickedness in the eyes of multitudes. From apostates the faithful have received the severest persecutions. STATEMENT, JAN. 22, 1834, IN *MESSAGES,* 1:23-44

artificial insemination

Children conceived by artificial insemination or *in vitro* fertilization are born in the covenant if their parents are already sealed. If the children are born before their parents are sealed, they may be sealed to their parents after their parents are sealed to each other. *CHURCH HANDBOOK,* 1998

Artificial insemination with semen from anyone but the husband is strongly discouraged. However, this is a personal matter that ultimately must be left to the judgment of the husband and wife. Responsibility for the decision rests solely upon them.

Artificial insemination of single sisters is not approved. IBID.

The donation of sperm is strongly discouraged. IBID.

Surrogate motherhood is strongly discouraged. IBID.

The Church discourages artificial insemination with other than the semen of the husband. Artificial insemination with semen other than from the husband may produce problems related to family harmony. The Church recognizes that this is a personal matter which must ultimately be left to the determination of the husband and wife with the responsibility for their decision resting solely upon them. "DEAR BRETHREN," APR. 19, 1977

We feel that the Church cannot approve of artificial insemination with other than the semen of the husband. The legitimacy of offspring of artificial insemination from semen other than that of the husband is open to question. FIRST PRESIDENCY TO FRED A. SCHWENDIMAN, DEC. 3, 1971

[T]he Brethren feel that the practice of artificial insemination with other than the semen of the husband is a personal matter which must be left to the determination of the husband and wife, with the responsibility of their decision resting upon them. The Brethren perceive some serious problems arising from artificial insemination that restrain them from extending their sanction thereto. JOSEPH ANDERSON, SECRETARY TO THE FIRST PRESIDENCY, TO W. M. HESS, OCT. 8, 1968

astrology, *see* occult

Atonement. *See also* Jesus Christ

Of all the events of human history, none other approaches the Atonement of the Savior in its meaning and in its results. GORDON B. HINCKLEY, "FIRST PRESIDENCY MESSAGE," *ENSIGN*, FEB. 2007.

Our Mediator, our Redeemer, our Brother, our Advocate with the Father died for our sins and the sins of all mankind. The Atonement of Jesus Christ is the foreordained but voluntary act of the Only Begotten Son of God. He offered His life as a redeeming ransom for us all. THOMAS S. MONSON, "FIRST PRESIDENCY MESSAGE," *ENSIGN,* AUG. 2006

As a result of our Savior's great atoning sacrifice, death, and resurrection, we become the beneficiaries of His mercy and grace. In a world of trouble and uncertainty, His peace will fill our heats and ease our minds. *CHURCH NEWS,* MAR. 26, 2005

To fulfill the plan of salvation, Christ paid the penalty for our sins. He alone was able to do that. He was called and prepared in pre-earth life. He was the literal Son of God in the flesh. He was sinless and completely obedient to His Father. Though tempted, He never gave in to temptation. When the Father asked His Beloved Son to pay the price of the world's sins, Jesus was prepared and willing. The Atonement included His suffering in the Garden of Gethsemane and His suffering and death on the cross, and it ended with His Resurrection.

Though He suffered beyond comprehension—so much so that He bled from every pore and asked whether it were possible that this burden be lifted from Him—He submitted to the Father's will in a supreme expression of love for His Father and for us. This triumph of Jesus Christ over spiritual death by His suffering and over physical death by His Resurrection is called the Atonement. *PREACH MY GOSPEL,* 2005

The greatest of all acts in all history was the atoning sacrifice of our Savior and Redeemer. JAMES E. FAUST, "FIRST PRESIDENCY MESSAGE," *ENSIGN,* DEC. 2004

Jesus' atoning sacrifice took place in the Garden of Gethsemane and on the cross at Calvary. *TRUE TO FAITH,* 2004

Repentance and forgiveness are among the greatest fruits of the Atonement. JAMES E. FAUST, "FIRST PRESIDENCY MESSAGE," *ENSIGN,* APR. 2004

Christ's supreme sacrifice can find full fruition in our lives only as we accept the invitation to follow Him. This call is not irrelevant, unrealistic, or impossible. To follow an individual means to watch him or listen to him closely; to accept his authority, to take him as a leader, and to obey him; to support and advocate his ideas; and to take him as a model. Each of us can accept this challenge. HOWARD W. HUNTER, "FIRST PRESIDENCY MESSAGE," *ENSIGN,* SEPT. 1994

We worship Jesus Christ as Lord and Savior.

He lives; He is the Son of God.

He came to earth as the Only Begotten of the Father, fulfilling through His suffering in Gethsemane and upon the cross the atoning sacrifice by which all mankind may be saved. *CHURCH NEWS,* MAR. 18, 1989

In Gethsemane, the scene of His great agony, and on the

cross where He gave his life, the sinless Jesus suffered for the sins of all mankind. Through acts of infinite love and mercy He not only satisfied the demands of justice, but made effective mercy, by which men and women may be redeemed from spiritual and physical death. NEWS RELEASE, APR. 3, 1987

Jesus alone could make the required, infinite Atonement because, being the only sinless person who has ever lived upon the earth, He had a sinless life to offer and because He, being the Son of God, had power over life and death. No one could have taken His life had He not been willing to give it. "No man taketh it from me," He said, "but I lay it down of myself. I have power to lay it down, and I have power to take it again" (John 10:18). It was, therefore, through acts of infinite love and mercy that He vicariously paid the debt of the broken law and satisfied the demands of justice.

We are still further indebted to Jesus, for by His Atonement He not only satisfied the demands of the law of justice, but He made effective the law of mercy, by which men may be redeemed from spiritual death. For while they are not responsible for mortal death, they are responsible for spiritual death, which shuts them out from the presence of God. MARION G. ROMNEY, "FIRST PRESIDENCY MESSAGE," *ENSIGN,* APR. 1985

We believe that the blood of Christ, shed in the Garden of Gethsemane and on the cross of Calvary, cleanses all men from sin on condition of repentance. BRUCE R. MCCONKIE, AT REQUEST OF THE FIRST PRESIDENCY, TO THOMAS B. MCAFFEE, OCT. 18, 1978

The Atonement, therefore, is a ransom, a payment, a reconciliation made by Christ for the demands of justice. *PRINCIPLES,* 1976

Christ, being free of sin, was able to atone or pay for our sins as well as for Adam's transgression. IBID.

What then does the Atonement mean for each of us? The temporal death, the separation of body and spirit, is replaced by immortality. All men, regardless of their beliefs or righteousness, are resurrected to immortality, a rejoining of body and spirit; each of us will live forever. This comes as a gift through the grace of God (see Morm. 9:12-14).

The spiritual death is overcome according to our righteousness. Through Christ's Atonement, if we are obedient to the laws and ordinances of the gospel, have faith in the Savior, and repent of our disobedience, He forgives us of our sins, He having already paid for them. Then we can return into the presence of God. IBID.

Essential to an understanding of the aspect of the Atonement of Christ, which enables men to attain unto eternal life, is a realization that mortal man, while he lives on Earth, is enlightened by the spirit of God and that he is also tempted by Satan; that every human being who lives beyond the age of accountability yields to some degree to the temptations of Satan. Jesus, who was the Son of God in the flesh, as well as in the spirit, was the only exception.

By yielding to the temptation of Satan, we become unclean. To the extent to which we yield, we become carnal, sensual, and devilish. As a consequence, we are banished from the presence of God. Without being cleansed from the stain of our transgressions, we cannot be readmitted into the presence of God because "no unclean thing can enter into his kingdom" (3 Ne. 27:19). Men, in the exercise of their own free agency, having disqualified themselves for a place in the kingdom of God, are banished therefrom and cannot by their own unaided efforts return. If they are ever to return, atonement for their sins must be made by someone not himself banished: Jesus was that one. MARION G. ROMNEY, "FIRST PRESIDENCY MESSAGE," *ENSIGN,* DEC. 1973

Jesus Christ was chosen in the grand council in heaven and foreordained to come to earth to perform the atoning sacrifice. As the Only Begotten Son of God in the flesh, our Savior received from His Eternal Father power over death; from His mortal mother He received the capacity to die.

The Atonement by the Son of God saves all creatures from the permanent effects of temporal death and redeems every individual from spiritual death (the lasting penalties of his own transgression) if he accepts and lives the gospel of Jesus Christ. "BASIC DOCTRINES," 1971

B

baptism

Baptism by immersion is a symbol of the death, burial, and resurrection of the Savior. In a similar way, it represents the end of our old life of sin and a commitment to live a new life as a disciple of Christ. The Savior taught that baptism is a rebirth. When we are baptized, we begin the process of being born again and become spiritual sons and daughters of Christ (see Mosiah 5:7-8; Rom. 8:14-17).

We must be baptized to become members of the restored Church, The Church of Jesus Christ of Latter-day Saints, and to eventually enter the kingdom of heaven. This ordinance is a law of God and must be performed by His authority. *PREACH MY GOSPEL,* 2005

Men and women who are living together but are not married may not be baptized without first getting married or separated. Those who are married to more than one person at a time may be not baptized. IBID.

[B]aptism is by complete immersion and symbolizes the cleansing of a person from sin. Since young children are incapable of sin, they are not baptized until the age of eight, when they become accountable for their actions. *QUICK FACTS,* 2005

When we are baptized of water and of the Spirit we take upon ourselves the name of Christ and are adopted into His family. *PATRIARCHS,* 1981

[A]s part of the preparation for baptism, investigators should–

1. Be taught all of the standard missionary discussions before baptism and have come to a knowledge of the Savior.

2. Have attended regular Sunday Church meetings (such as sacrament meeting) and should feel a unity and oneness with Church members; and have been introduced to the bishop or branch president.

3. Repent, and thereafter love and serve God with all their hearts, and commit to keeping His commandments. "DEAR BRETHREN," AUG. 31, 1979

Baptism is a requirement for entrance into the celestial kingdom. *PRINCIPLES,* 1976

Baptism is for the remission of sins. In other words, through baptism we are cleansed and released from the penalty of our sins. But sins are not remitted if there is no faith and sincere repentance. IBID.

Baptism should mark the end of an old way of life and the beginning of a new, spiritual way of life. IBID.

In regard to the matter of becoming members of the House of Israel by adoption when we are baptized, this is not the doctrine of the Church. FIRST PRESIDENCY TO J. DUANE DUDLEY, MAY 17, 1974

Now, baptism into the Church is not enough to save us. It is for the remission of sins, that is true; but there is another baptism that is even more essential, and that is the baptism of the Spirit, or the bestowal of the gift of the Holy Ghost.

After we are baptized, we are confirmed. What is that confirmation for? To make us companions with the Holy Ghost; to give us the privilege of the guidance of the third member of the Godhead–companionship, that our minds might be enlightened, that we might be quickened by the Holy Spirit to seek for knowledge and understanding concerning all that pertains to our exaltation. JOSEPH FIELDING SMITH, "FIRST PRESIDENCY MESSAGE," *ENSIGN,* JUNE 1972

Baptism is a holy ordinance of great importance and should be conducted by the priesthood under the inspiration of the Lord. "DEAR BRETHREN," SEPT. 6, 1966

[O]nly those who indicate a desire to be baptized, witness that they have truly repented of all their sins, and manifest by their works that they have received of the Spirit of Christ unto the remission of their sins, shall be admitted to the Church by baptism. FIRST PRESIDENCY TO PRESIDENTS OF MISSIONS, OCT. 12, 1964

A child should be baptized on his eighth birthday or as soon thereafter as possible. Baptismal fonts should be made available the year round for this purpose. Any body of water large enough to immerse the candidate may be used, except that persons should not be baptized in bathtubs or any other such receptacles.

The person officiating must stand in the water with the candidate being baptized. He as well as the individual being baptized should be appropriately dressed. They may wear white clothing. Special care should be taken to see that the rules of modesty are not violated. Waders, hip boots, and bathing caps should not be worn by any of those concerned. *CHURCH HANDBOOK,* 1960

Baptism alone does not remit sins; it takes faith in Jesus Christ, true repentance, and then baptism performed by one having authority to bring about remission. It is the blood of Jesus Christ which cleanses from sin, but that blessing comes to the repentant believer by means of authorized baptism. JOSEPH F. SMITH TO ANDERSON LEE, NOV. 2, 1915

Bible

The New Testament is "a better testament" [Heb. 7:19, 22] because so much is left to the intent of the heart and of the mind and the promptings of the Holy Spirit. This refinement of the soul is part of the reinforcing steel of a personal testimony of Jesus Christ. If there is no witness in the heart and in the mind by the power of the Holy Ghost, there can be no testimony. JAMES E. FAUST, "FIRST PRESIDENCY MESSAGE," *ENSIGN,* SEPT. 2003

The Bible, as it has been transmitted over the centuries, has suffered the loss of many plain and precious parts. *CHURCH NEWS,* JUNE 20, 1992

Many versions of the Bible are available today. Unfortunately, no original manuscripts of any portion of the Bible are available for comparison to determine the most accurate version. However, the Lord has revealed clearly the doctrines of the gospel in these latter days. The most reliable way to measure the accuracy of any biblical passage is not by comparing different texts, but by comparison with the Book of Mormon and modern-day revelations. IBID.

While other Bible versions may be easier to read than the King James Version, in doctrinal matters latter-day revelation supports the King James Version in preference to other English translations. All of the Presidents of the Church, beginning with the Prophet Joseph Smith, have supported the King James Version by encouraging its continued use in the Church. In light of all the above, it is the English language Bible used by The Church of Jesus Christ of Latter-day Saints. IBID.

The Holy Bible is a divine library containing the works of many prophets and inspired writers. It is a revered volume in The Church of Jesus Christ of Latter-day Saints and stands as a witness to the divinity of the Savior, Jesus Christ. It is especially valuable inasmuch as it contains His teachings which, when adhered to, enhance the quality of life of the individual and of society in general. *CHURCH NEWS,* NOV. 5, 1988

The Bible is a sacred library that bears witness to the divinity of Jesus Christ, tells of His life and teachings, and of prophets and people who followed Him. The Bible has enlightened and influenced the Christian world generally as no other book has ever done. When it is read under the guidance of the Spirit, it becomes one of the most priceless volumes known to man. NEWS RELEASE, NOV. 13, 1987

When it is read reverently and prayerfully, the Holy Bible becomes a priceless volume, converting the soul to righteousness. Principal among its virtues is the declaration that Jesus is the Christ, the Son of God, through whom eternal salvation may come to all. *CHURCH NEWS,* MARCH 20, 1983

birth. ***See also*** **abortion; adoption**

The Church of Jesus Christ of Latter-day Saints has no official position on the moment that human life begins. NEWS RELEASE, MAY 26, 2005

It is a fact that a child has life before birth. However, there is no direct revelation on when the spirit enters the body. *CHURCH HANDBOOK,* 1998

[T]here is no direct revelation upon the subject of when the spirit enters the body; it has always been a moot question. That there is life in the child before birth is an undoubted fact, but whether that life is the result of the affinity of the child in embryo with the life of its mother, or because the spirit has entered it, remains an unsolved mystery. FIRST PRESIDENCY TO W. DEAN BELNAP, FEB. 12, 1970

"When does the spirit enter the body–at conception or at the first breath of life?"

Undoubtedly the nearest approach we have to definite knowledge on this subject is the statement made by the Savior, 3 Nephi 1:13, wherein He said, "Tomorrow come I into the world." This indicates that the spirit takes possession of the body at birth. Life manifest in the body before that time would seem to be dependent upon the mother. DAVID O. MCKAY TO TIENA NATE, OCT. 31, 1934

[L]ife, or the vital force, may be infused into organized matter, though the details of the process have not been revealed unto man. *IMPROVEMENT ERA,* AUG. 1916, IN *MESSAGES,* 5:26-34

birth control

It is the privilege of married couples who are able to bear children to provide mortal bodies for the spirit children of God, whom they are then responsible to nurture and rear. The decision as to how many children to have and when to have them is extremely intimate and private and should be left between the couple and the Lord. Church members should not judge one another in this matter. *CHURCH HANDBOOK,* 1998

The Lord has commanded husbands and wives to multiply and replenish the earth that they might have joy in their posterity [Gen. 1:28].

Husbands must be considerate of their wives, who have the greater responsibility not only of bearing children but of caring for them through childhood, and should help them conserve their health and strength. Married couples should exercise self-control in all of their relationships. They should seek inspiration from the Lord in meeting their marital challenges and rearing their children according to the teachings of the gospel. *CHURCH HANDBOOK*, 1983

Where husband and wife enjoy health and vigor and are free from impurities that would be entailed upon their posterity, it is contrary to the teachings of the Church artificially to curtail or prevent the birth of children. We believe that those who practice birth control will reap disappointment by and by.

However, we feel that men must be considerate of their wives who bear the greater responsibility not only of bearing children, but of caring for them through childhood. To this end the mother's health and strength should be conserved and the husband's consideration for his wife is his first duty, and self-control a dominant factor in all their relationships. "DEAR BRETHREN," APR. 14, 1969

[T]he Church has never authorized the use of methods to curtail the birth of children where the parties concerned are in possession of health and vigor and are free from impurities that would be entailed upon their posterity.

The brethren feel, however, that men must be considerate of their wives, who bear the greater responsibility not only of bearing children but of caring for them through childhood. To this end the mother's strength should be conserved and the husband's consideration for his wife is his first duty and self-control a dominant factor in all their relationships. After all, however, the Brethren recognize that this is a personal matter involving the individuals concerned, and concerning which they must make their own decision. JOSEPH ANDERSON, SECRETARY TO THE FIRST PRESIDENCY, TO W. M. HESS, JAN. 7, 1969

It is the policy of the Church to discourage the prevention of conception by any means unless the health of the mother demands it. It is also the policy of the Church to regard marital relations of husband and wife as their personal problem and responsibility to be solved and to be established between themselves as a sacred relationship. DAVID O. MCKAY, LETTER DATED SEPT. 11, 1963

[W]e advise mothers, and fathers, to be wise in their intimate relations and, if the health of the mother is involved and the welfare of the rest of the family is at stake, parents are justified in following the advice of good physicians, preferably members of the Church, who have high moral standards and will advise such measures only for the protection of the health and life of the mother and other children. HUGH B. BROWN, LETTER DATED OCT. 6, 1961

[T]he Lord has made it abundantly clear in holy writ, ancient and modern, that it is wholly wrong to interfere with the normal processes of the reproduction of life. One of the commands imposed upon all Latter-day Saints is to "multiply and replenish the earth" [Gen. 1:28]. This was the original plan given to Adam. We understand there are righteous spirits waiting on the other side to be tabernacled in mortal bodies, and that it is the duty of the Latter-day Saints to provide bodies for these spirits.

However, where the question of the life of the mother really may be at stake, the situation becomes different. No physician has sufficient wisdom to declare with absolute certainty the result of a full pregnancy upon either the life of the mother or the life of the child. Physicians of wide experiences are able more or less accurately to foretell out of their experiences what the eventuality may be of a full pregnancy. But everyone knows that while the best physicians have accurately foretold what would happen in such cases, there have been perhaps an equal number of cases in which they have made mistakes, and in which mothers have borne babies and lived thereafter as healthy as they were before, contrary to the predictions of the physicians. The Brethren wish me to say in this connection that they have heard of cases in which the administration of the Elders has brought promises and blessings which were in truth miracles from the point of view of the physician.

Under these circumstances and with their lack of knowledge of the exact situation, the Brethren suggest that you and your husband make the matter a subject of earnest prayer, and that you call in the Elders, good and righteous men, and see what the Lord has to say to you through them; that you and your husband examine your own faith, to learn where that leads you, remembering the power of faith and that the Lord Himself in creating this world acted through the power of faith and that then you reach your own conclusions as to what should be done. After all, you are the one whose life is to be hazarded, and you are the one who should determine whether the hazard should or should not be taken.

In reaching your decision, you will moreover have in mind the obligations which you have assumed toward the children you have already brought into the world and the situation that would arise if you were to be taken away and leave the children without a mother. This is a very serious consideration and should be the subject of sincere and earnest prayer to our Heavenly Father both on your own part and the part of your husband. JOSEPH ANDERSON, SECRETARY TO THE FIRST PRESIDENCY, "FEMALE OPERATION DESTROYING CHANCES FOR MOTHERHOOD," MAR. 2, 1946

We have never presumed to tell Church members how large their families should be. That is a matter that people must decide for themselves and accept the responsibility for their decision. We have always advocated large families under normal conditions. Of course, ill health, disease, and perhaps other conditions may be justifiable reasons for restraint in such matters. The first great commandment given to Adam and Eve was to multiply and replenish the earth [Gen. 1:28]. The teachings of the Church are reasonably clear upon the subject, but it is worth considering whether or not we should not avoid extremes in pressing our doctrines. HEBER J. GRANT TO SAMUEL F. SMITH, FEB. 19, 1935

[T]he health of a mother demands that there be a reasonable space between the birth of babies, and this should be accomplished in a proper manner with mutual understanding between the husband and wife. Due consideration and regard for the health of the wife should prompt the husband to refrain from intimate relations with her for at least three months after the birth of a child. DAVID O. MCKAY TO MRS. J----- G---, JAN. 21, 1935

As to the lesser sin of preventing conception, no general rule can be laid down, there are so many different circumstances distinguishing one case from another and such a difference in motives that each particular case has to be judged by itself and decided by the light of the Spirit. But we believe where persons sincerely repent and cease the practice, they should be permitted to enter the Church. This is not the unpardonable sin, and like other misdeeds, can be forgiven when penitence and reformation are shown. WILFORD WOODRUFF AND JOSEPH F. SMITH TO JOB PINGREE, JAN. 23, 1894

bishops

The bishop, assisted by two counselors, presides over the ward as presiding high priest and as president of the Aaronic

Priesthood. He is responsible for correlating all of the activities within the ward boundaries, including those of the Melchizedek Priesthood quorums and groups. He administers all ward programs (except those directed by the Melchizedek Priesthood leaders). He administers the welfare program and is the common judge in Israel, counseling and teaching members in an effort to improve their lives. His first responsibility is for directing the programs designed to teach and activate members of the Aaronic Priesthood and of the Young Women. *PRINCIPLES,* 1976

The bishop, as father of the ward, should set the example of right living and faithful observance of all gospel principles. As a husband and father, he should be kind and affectionate, and have unity and faithfulness in his family. His financial integrity should be unquestioned. He should practice economy and thrift. He should learn to distribute responsibility and get results. *CHURCH HANDBOOK,* 1940

The work of the bishop is both temporal and spiritual. He exercises general direction over all ward affairs. He should supervise but should not try to do personally all the work of his ward. It is important that each counselor, under the bishop's direction, should have charge of certain phases of the work according to his qualifications. In addition, all those who bear the priesthood, and the auxiliary association officers, in their respective spheres, should be given a measure of responsibility. *CHURCH HANDBOOK,* 1928

A very pleasing custom has been adopted in many of the large wards–that of the bishopric personally greeting the Saints as they enter the meeting-house on the Sabbath day. This practice creates a good impression and enables the bishopric to become better acquainted with those who reside in the ward. *CHURCH HANDBOOK,* 1921

The bishop of each ward should be personally acquainted with the conditions of the poor in his ward and the Relief Society should cooperate with the bishop and act under his direction in caring for them.

The bishop should use his influence to secure opportunities for persons to obtain a livelihood in his ward; to provide homes for newcomers; in fact, to help members to become self-supporting. The care and relief of the poor is not so much a question of giving charities to assist them as it is to help them to become self-supporting. This labor should be done on a well-defined plan, outlined by the bishopric of the ward and in consultation with the Relief Society officers. Each individual case should be treated according to its necessities. IBID.

The bishop is the steward of the Lord's Storehouse of the ward over which he presides, and he is personally responsible for receiving, handling, disbursing, and accounting for the tithes of the ward. *CHURCH HANDBOOK,* 1909

blood atonement. ***See also*** **capital punishment**

We do *not* believe that it is necessary for men in this day to shed their own blood to receive a remission of sins. BRUCE R. MCCONKIE, AT REQUEST OF THE FIRST PRESIDENCY, TO THOMAS B. MCAFFEE, OCT. 18, 1978

There is no such a doctrine as blood atonement in the Church today nor has there been at any time. Any statements to the contrary are either idle speculation or pure fantasy. IBID.

Except for the Atonement of Christ, which is or should be a part of the creeds of all Christian churches; and except for the use of the term "blood atonement" as a synonym–nothing more–of "capital punishment" where "enlightened" members of the Church are concerned, there is not such a doctrine in this dispensation as blood atonement. IBID.

[T]he theoretical principle of blood atonement has no application in *any* dispensation when there is a separation of church and state. IBID.

The charge so often made by apostates and other enemies of the Church, that in pursuance of an alleged doctrine of blood atonement, the Latter-day Saints put to death those unfriendly to their interests, is a cruel slander, best refuted by the fact that those who utter it walk the streets in the very midst of the community they malign, uninjured, unmolested, and treated with a tolerance and a charity that would not be shown them anywhere else on earth. JOSEPH F. SMITH TO MRS. E. E. CURRY, NOV. 11, 1912

body piercing

Latter-day prophets strongly discourage the piercing of the body except for medical purposes. *TRUE TO FAITH,* 2004

Book of Mormon. *See also* American Indians

Its [Book of Mormon's] appeal is as timeless as truth, as universal as mankind. It is the only book that contains within its covers a promise that by divine power the reader may know with certainty of its truth. GORDON B. HINCKLEY, "FIRST PRESIDENCY MESSAGE," *ENSIGN,* AUG. 2005

It [Book of Mormon] is a scripture of the New World, as certainly as the Bible is the scripture of the Old. Each of these volumes of scripture speaks of the other. Each carries with it the spirit of inspiration, the power to convince and to convert. Together they become two witnesses, hand in hand, that Jesus is the Christ, the resurrected and living Son of the living God. IBID.

The Book of Mormon narrative is a chronicle of nations long since gone. But in its descriptions of the problems of today's society, it is as current as the morning newspaper and much more definitive, inspired, and inspiring concerning the solutions of those problems. IBID.

[T]he great and stirring burden of its [Book of Mormon's] message is a testimony, vibrant and true, that Jesus is the Christ, the promised Messiah, He who walked the dusty roads of Palestine healing the sick and teaching the doctrines of salvation; who died upon the cross of Calvary; who on the third day came forth from the tomb, appearing to many. IBID.

Those who read the Book of Mormon will be blessed with an added measure of the Spirit of the Lord, a greater resolve to obey His commandments, and a stronger testimony of the living reality of the Son of God. *CHURCH NEWS,* JULY 30, 2005

The Book of Mormon, which we regard as the testament of the New World, setting forth the teachings of prophets who lived anciently in the Western Hemisphere, testifies of Him who was born in Bethlehem of Judea and who died on the hill of Calvary. To a world wavering in its faith, the Book of Mormon is another and powerful witness of the divinity of the Lord. Its very preface, written by a prophet who walked the Americas a millennium and a half ago, categorically states that it was written "to the convincing of the Jew and Gentile that Jesus is the Christ, the Eternal God, manifesting himself unto all nations." GORDON B. HINCKLEY, "FIRST PRESIDENCY MESSAGE," *ENSIGN,* APR. 2005

Joseph Smith was directed by a heavenly messenger named Moroni to a hill where gold plates had lain hidden for centuries. These gold plates contained the writings of prophets giving an account of God's dealings with some of the ancient inhabitants of the Americas. Joseph Smith translated the contents of these plates by the power of God. *PREACH MY GOSPEL,* 2005

The Book of Mormon: Another Testament of Jesus Christ is convincing evidence that Joseph Smith was a prophet and that the gospel of Jesus Christ has been restored. It is the keystone of our religion, the most powerful resource for teaching this message. Some important truths restored through Joseph Smith include the knowledge that God is our Father and that we are His spirit children, that we lived with Him before birth, and that families can live together forever in God's presence through Christ's Atonement by obeying the laws and ordinances of the gospel. IBID.

The Book of Mormon is powerful evidence of the divinity of Christ. It is also proof of the Restoration through the Prophet Joseph Smith. An essential part of conversion is receiving a witness from the Holy Ghost that the Book of Mormon is true. IBID.

The Book of Mormon came forth in this dispensation by the will of the Lord. It is a record of God's dealings with the people who lived in the ancient Americas. *TRUE TO FAITH,* 2004

The evidence for its [Book of Mormon's] truth, for its validity in a world that is prone to demand evidence, lies not in archaeology or anthropology, though these may be helpful to some. It lies not in word research or historical analysis, though these may be confirmatory. The evidence for its truth and validity lies within the covers of the book itself. The test of its truth lies in reading it. It is a book of God. Reasonable people may sincerely question its origin; but those who have read it prayerfully have come to know by a power beyond their natural senses that it is true, that it contains the word of God, that it outlines saving truths of the everlasting gospel, that it "came forth by the gift and power of God ... to a convincing of the Jew and Gentile that Jesus is the Christ" (Book of Mormon title page). GORDON B. HINCKLEY, "FIRST PRESIDENCY MESSAGE," *ENSIGN,* FEB. 2004

The Book of Mormon is a keystone [of our religion] because it establishes and ties together eternal principles and precepts, rounding out basic doctrines of salvation. It is the crowing gem in the diadem of our holy scriptures. JAMES E. FAUST, "FIRST PRESIDENCY MESSAGE," *ENSIGN,* JAN. 2004

The Book of Mormon was central to Joseph Smith's understanding of the doctrines of the gospel and of his role in the Restoration. Surely the First Vision alerted young Joseph to his special responsibilities, but he was given a fuller understanding only through translating the Book of Mormon. The nature of his prophetic responsibilities became clear during the four years before he was allowed even to obtain the plates; the confirmation of his responsibility to translate the record perhaps came only after he had the plates in his possession and was commanded to make the record available to this generation. JAMES E. FAUST, "FIRST PRESIDENCY MESSAGE," *ENSIGN,* JAN. 1996

The Book of Mormon was designed by Deity to bring men to Christ and to His Church. EZRA TAFT BENSON, "FIRST PRESIDENCY MESSAGE," *ENSIGN,* DEC. 1993

[T]he First Presidency and Council of the Twelve give close personal supervision to the translation of scriptures from English into other languages and have not authorized efforts to express the doctrinal content of the Book of Mormon in familiar or modern English. *CHURCH NEWS,* FEB. 20, 1993

[T]he Book of Mormon is the keystone of our religion–the keystone of our testimony, the keystone of our doctrine, and the keystone in the witness of our Lord and Savior. EZRA TAFT BENSON, "FIRST PRESIDENCY MESSAGE," *ENSIGN,* JAN. 1992

The Book of Mormon was written for us today. God is the author of the book. It is a record of a fallen people, compiled by inspired men for our blessing. EZRA TAFT BENSON, "FIRST PRESIDENCY MESSAGE," *ENSIGN,* JAN. 1988

The Book of Mormon brings men to Christ through two basic means. First, it tells in a plain manner of Christ and His gospel. It testifies of His divinity and of the necessity for a Redeemer and the need of our putting trust in Him. It bears witness of the Fall and the Atonement and the first principles of the gospel, including our need of a broken heart and a contrite spirit and a spiritual rebirth. It proclaims we must endure to the end in righteousness and live the moral life of a Saint.

Second, the Book of Mormon exposes the enemies of Christ. It confounds false doctrines and lays down contention (see 2 Ne. 3:12). It fortifies the humble followers of Christ against the evil designs, strategies, and doctrines of the devil in our day. The type of apostates in the Book of Mormon are similar to the type we have today. God, with His infinite foreknowledge, so molded the Book of Mormon that we might see the error and know how to combat false education, political, religious, and philosophical concepts of our time. IBID.

[W]e have not been using the Book of Mormon as we should. Our homes are not as strong unless we are using it to bring our children to Christ. Our families may be corrupted by worldly trends and teachings unless we know how to use the book to expose and combat falsehoods in socialism, rationalism, etc. Our missionaries are not as effective unless they are "hissing forth" with it. Social, ethical, cultural, or education converts will not survive under the heat of the day unless their taproots go down to the fullness of the gospel which the Book of Mormon contains. Our Church classes are not as spirit-filled unless we hold it up as a standard. The situation in the world will continue to degenerate unless we read and heed the words of God and quit building up and upholding secret combinations, which the Book of Mormon tells us proved the downfall of ancient civilizations. IBID.

The Book of Mormon is here to be handled and to be read with prayer and earnest inquiry. All the work of its critics throughout the hundred and fifty-three years of the book's presence has lacked credibility and has been without effect on those who have prayerfully read the book and received by the power of the Holy Ghost a witness of its truth. If there were no other evidence for the divine mission of Joseph Smith, the Book of Mormon would stand as an irrefutable witness of that fact. To think that anyone less than one inspired could bring forth a volume which should have so profound an effect for good upon so many others is to imagine that which simply cannot be. The evidence for the truth of the Book of Mormon is found in the lives of the millions, living and gone, who have read it, prayed about it, and received a witness of its truth. GORDON B. HINCKLEY, "FIRST PRESIDENCY MESSAGE," *ENSIGN,* AUG. 1983

The Book of Mormon, which we regard as the testament of the New World, sets forth the teachings of prophets who lived anciently in this Western Hemisphere and testifies of Him who was born in Bethlehem of Judea and who died on the hill of Calvary. To a world wavering in its faith, the Book of Mormon is another testament and powerful witness of the divinity of the Lord. Its very preface, written by a prophet who walked the Americas a millennium and a half ago, categorically states that it was written "to the convincing of the Jew and Gentile that JESUS is the CHRIST the ETERNAL GOD, manifesting himself unto all nations." IBID.

We declare that the Book of Mormon was brought forth by the gift and power of God, and that it stands beside the Bible as another witness of Jesus Christ, the Savior and Redeemer of mankind. Together they testify of His divine Sonship. *CHURCH NEWS,* APR. 12, 1980

The Book of Mormon does not in any degree conflict with or take the place of the Holy Bible, but is the strongest corroborative evidence in existence of the divine origin of that sacred record. *IMPROVEMENT ERA,* MAY 1930, IN *MESSAGES,* 5:274-86

The Book of Mormon may be termed the Bible of the western hemisphere. It is not regarded by the Latter-day Saints as a substitute for the Hebrew scriptures, but as a companion volume to that sacred book. *DESERET NEWS,* NOV. 4, 1911, IN *MESSAGES,* 4:231-51

The Book of Mormon is a witness of the dealings of God with the ancient inhabitants of this land, which is the land of Zion. *DESERET NEWS,* DEC. 19, 1908, IN *MESSAGES,* 4:188-94

The differences are so great on geographical questions amongst students of the Book of Mormon that the authorities have discountenanced the preparation of any suggestive map of America in Nephite times; consequently none have been published with the approval of the priesthood. GEORGE REYNOLDS TO E. T. LLOYD, AUG. 8, 1901

born again. ***See also*** **conversion**

Rebirth is a beautiful symbol for baptism. Just as a new infant enters a new existence in innocence and receives life, the newly baptized person begins a new life, free from sin and made more meaningful through the giving of the Spirit. Just as the infant grows and increases in intelligence and other abilities, so the baptized person may grow in spirituality. *PRINCIPLES,* 1976

A person is spiritually reborn when he receives the baptism of fire and the Holy Ghost. He receives forgiveness of his past sins and the companionship of the Holy Ghost. Those who gain exaltation in the celestial kingdom will have been born of God and have become the sons and daughters of God (see Mosiah 27:24-26). IBID.

Even though a man has been born of God, he is not guaranteed a place in the celestial kingdom. He must continue in righteousness until the end of his life (see Mosiah 2:36-37). IBID.

born in the covenant, ***see*** **sealings, children to parents**

branches

A branch is a developing Church unit with a limited number of priesthood holders. A worthy Melchizedek Priesthood holder or a worthy priest may preside over it. *CHURCH HANDBOOK,* 1985

C

caffeine drinks, *see* Word of Wisdom

capital punishment

The Church of Jesus Christ of Latter-day Saints regards the question of whether and in what circumstances the state should impose capital punishment as a matter to be decided solely by the prescribed processes of civil law. *We neither promote nor oppose capital punishment.* NEWS RELEASE, MAY 27, 2003

[T]here is no difference between a firing squad, an electric chair, a gas chamber, or hanging. Death is death and I would interpret the shedding of man's blood in legal executions as a figurative expression which means the taking of life. There seems to me to be no present significance as to whether an execution is by a firing squad or in some other way. BRUCE R. MCCONKIE, AT REQUEST OF THE FIRST PRESIDENCY, TO THOMAS B. MCAFFEE, OCT. 18, 1978

Believing in capital punishment for certain crimes, we hold that when a criminal deserves death and is legally sentenced to die, his blood should be spilt, as an atonement; but we maintain that the execution should be done legally, through the operations of courts of justice, after fair trial and conviction, and that the death penalty should be inflicted by duly qualified officers of the law, not by private individuals. JOSEPH F. SMITH TO MRS. E. E. CURRY, NOV. 11, 1912

[W]e regard the killing of a human being, except in conformity with the civil law, as a capital crime which should be punished by shedding the blood of the criminal, after a public trial before a legally constituted court of the land. *DESERET NEWS WEEKLY*, DEC. 21, 1889, IN *MESSAGES*, 3:184-87

The revelations of God to this Church make death the penalty for capital crime, and require that offenders against life and property shall be delivered up to and tried by the laws of the land. IBID.

celestial kingdom. ***See also*** **exaltation**

The celestial kingdom is the highest of the three kingdoms of glory. Those in this kingdom will dwell forever in the presence of God the Father and His Son Jesus Christ. *TRUE TO FAITH*, 2004

To gain eternal life is to be made worthy to dwell in God's presence, inheriting a place in the highest degree of the celestial kingdom. This gift is available only through the Atonement of Jesus Christ. IBID.

Although all people will be resurrected, only those who have come unto Christ and partaken of the fullness of His gospel will inherit exaltation in the celestial kingdom. IBID.

The celestial kingdom is the dwelling place of God. The highest of its three degrees will be inherited only by those who have received exaltation. In addition to faith in Christ, repentance, baptism, the laying on of hands for the gift of the Holy Ghost, and obedience to all of the Lord's commandments, they must have been sealed in the everlasting covenant of celestial marriage and must have kept the conditions of that covenant (see D&C 131:1-4). PRINCIPLES, 1976

[B]eing married in the temple is no guarantee of a place in

the celestial kingdom. The couple must be faithful to the covenants they have made, living righteously throughout the rest of their lives. IBID.

[T]here is no truth in the statement that those who may reach the celestial kingdom who do not want to live the law of polygamy will be cast into outer darkness. FIRST PRESIDENCY TO JOE J. CHRISTENSEN, JUNE 14, 1971

The Lord has been very kind and merciful in preparing a salvation so that all men may receive according to their works. Baptism is the door into the celestial kingdom, but exaltation therein is based upon obedience to other commandments and covenants. It is reasonable to believe, and the scriptures teach us, that provision has been made so that even in the celestial kingdom many may enter who have not received the fullness of exaltation, yet are worthy of a better reward than will be given to those of the terrestrial kingdom. It may be that many of these will have to spend their eternity in the celestial kingdom as servants, deprived of the fullness, and this the revelations teach us, for they receive according to that which they merit. Surely there will be servants as well as gods in the celestial kingdom. DAVID O. MCKAY TO H. C. GREGERSEN, JUNE 18, 1935

celestial marriage, *see* marriage

charity. *See also* service; welfare

[C]harity is a more perfect, more eternal form of love, which is concerned completely with righteousness and the eternal welfare of our Father's children. As such, charity is the highest attribute of godliness and perfection and is one of the most important things we must acquire: "And above all things, clothe yourselves with the bond of charity, as with a mantle, which is the bond of perfectness and peace" (D&C 88:125). *PRINCIPLES*, 1976

Children, wives, friends, and associates tend to live up to (or down to) the statements expressed about them. An honest, sincerely stated compliment helps to build character; criticism destroys it. Tearing down another's reputation or character never builds or betters our own. Expressing admiration for the accomplishments or character traits of another builds us as well as those about whom we speak. N. ELDON TANNER, "FIRST PRESIDENCY MESSAGE," *ENSIGN*, MAR. 1973

chastity, *see* sexual relations

child abuse

The abuse of a child awakens in us an intensity and breadth of emotion that is beyond adequate expression. Perhaps this crime moves us so personally because we remember what it was like to hold our own children for the first time—the overwhelming feeling of love and the deepest parental instinct to nourish, teach, and protect. It is shocking, almost inconceivable, that someone would hurt a child. It is the ultimate form of betrayal. "ISSUES RESOURCES," 2006

Simply put, The Church of Jesus Christ of Latter-day Saints has a zero-tolerance policy when it comes to child abusers. When abuse is suspected, the Church directs its members to first contact the legal authorities and then their local bishop for counseling and support. The Church cooperates fully with law enforcement in investigating incidents of child abuse and bringing perpetrators to justice. IBID.

Can child abusers who have paid the legal price for their crimes and gone through a rigorous repentance process [excommunication] with local Church leaders become members of the Church again? Yes. As Christians, we believe in forgiveness. But can they ever again, in their lifetime, serve in any capacity that would put them in direct contact with children? Absolutely not. Forgiveness does not remove the consequences of sin. Protection of the family is a first principle of the Church.

Since 1995, the Church has placed a confidential annotation on the membership record of members who previously abused children. These records follow them to any congregation where they move, thereby alerting bishops not to place them in situations with children. As far as we know, The Church of Jesus Christ of Latter-day Saints was the first religious institution to create such a tracking mechanism. We hold the family sacred and protect its children. This explains why the Church is one of the few denominations that imposes formal ecclesiastical discipline on mere members (as opposed to official clergy) for sexually abusive conduct. IBID.

If only all children had loving parents, safe homes, and caring friends, what a wonderful world would be theirs. Unfortunately, all children are not so bounteously blessed. Some children witness their fathers savagely beating their mothers, while others are on the receiving end of such abuse. What cowardice, what depravity, what shame! THOMAS S. MONSON, "FIRST PRESIDENCY MESSAGE," *ENSIGN*, JUNE 2000

A member who has been excommunicated or disfellowshipped for a sexual offense against a child or for other abuse of a child must not have his membership status changed without the approval of the First Presidency. *BULLETIN*, 1992-1

Persons cannot abuse children without offending God. A man who commits incest is unworthy to hold the priesthood or to be a member of the Church. Parents or guardians who abuse or neglect children will be held accountable before God. "DEAR BRETHREN," UTAH STAKES, MAR. 25, 1986

[N]o man who is a professed follower of Christ, and no man who is a professed member of this Church, can engage in the abuse of children without offending God, who is their Father, and repudiating the teachings of the Savior and His prophets. GORDON B. HINCKLEY, "FIRST PRESIDENCY MESSAGE," *ENSIGN*, JUNE 1985

Young victims of sexual abuse are likewise guilty of no sin where they are too young to be accountable for evaluating the significance of the sexual behavior. Even where acts are committed with the apparent consent of a young person, that consent may be ignored or qualified for purposes of moral responsibility where the aggressor occupied a position of authority or power over the young victim. "DEAR BRETHREN," FEB. 7, 1985

children

Children are entitled to the blessing of being reared in a stable family environment where father and mother honor marital vows. Having a secure, nurturing, and consistent relationship with both a father and a mother is essential to a child's well-being. *CHURCH NEWS*, NOV. 18, 2006

[N]one of us is perfect and none of us has children whose behavior is entirely in accord with exactly what we would have them do in all circumstances. "ISSUES RESOURCES," 2006

Among the other values children should be taught are respect for others, beginning with the child's own parents and family; respect for the symbols of faith and the patriotic beliefs of others; respect for law and order; respect for the property of others; respect for authority. JAMES E. FAUST, "FIRST PRESIDENCY MESSAGE," *ENSIGN*, OCT. 2005

Let parents who have been conscientious, loving, and concerned, and who have lived the principles of righteousness as best they could, be comforted in knowing that they are good parents despite the actions of some of their children. The children themselves have a responsibility to listen, to obey, and, having been taught, to learn. Parents cannot always answer for all their children's misconduct because they cannot ensure the children's good behavior. Some few children would tax even Solomon's wisdom and Job's patience. IBID.

Generally, those children who make the decision and have the resolve to abstain from drugs, alcohol, and illicit sex are those who have adopted and internalized the strong values of their homes as lived by their parents. In times of difficult decisions, they are most likely to follow the teachings of their parents rather than the example of their peers or the sophistries of the media, which glamorize alcohol consumption, illicit sex, infidelity, dishonesty, and other vices. IBID.

How much more beautiful would be the world and the societies in which we live if every father and mother looked upon their children as the most precious of their assets, if they led them by the power of their example in kindness and love, and if in times of stress blessed by the authority of the holy priesthood, and if they regarded their children as the jewels of their lives, as gifts from the God of heaven who is their Eternal Father, and brought them up with true affection in the wisdom and admonition of the Lord. GORDON B. HINCKLEY, "FIRST PRESIDENCY MESSAGE," *ENSIGN*, JUNE 2001

The best place for a child to learn the gospel is in the home. Mothers and fathers have the responsibility to teach and care for their children (D&C 68:25-28). It is also important for extended families, priesthood leaders, auxiliary leaders, and teachers to help strengthen children. The principles children learn at home and at Church will help them gain a strong foundation of testimony that they can use to make righteous choices and faithfully live the gospel of Jesus Christ. *CHURCH NEWS*, NOV. 27, 1993

A great privilege and responsibility of mortal life is bringing children into the world and then nurturing them with love and kindness as they grow to adulthood. NEWS RELEASE, MAR. 11, 1988

Begin early in exposing children to books. The mother who fails to read to her small children does a disservice to them and a disservice to herself. It takes time, yes, much of it. It takes self-discipline. It takes organizing and budgeting the minutes and hours of the day. But it will never be a bore as you watch young minds come to know characters, expressions, and ideas. Good reading can become a love affair, far more fruitful in long term effects than many other activities in which children use their time. GORDON B. HINCKLEY, "FIRST PRESIDENCY MESSAGE," *ENSIGN*, JUNE 1985

[T]raining our children is the best antidote to the materialism, irreverent secularism, declining morality, adult and juvenile delinquency, increasing crime, and general disregard for the laws of God and the dignity of man that so plague our present world. MARION G. ROMNEY, "FIRST PRESIDENCY MESSAGE," *ENSIGN*, JAN. 1985

The Church can and will assist parents in training their children. But it can only assist. The Church is not and cannot be a substitute for parents in their most urgent parental responsibility, which according to the Lord is to teach their children "to understand the doctrine of repentance, faith in Christ the Son of the living God, and of baptism and the gift of the Holy Ghost by the laying on of the hands, when eight years old" (D&C 68:25). IBID.

Parents must cultivate within the young an appreciation for the best books, reading to them the great stories which have become immortal because of the virtues they teach. Patronage of appropriate movies, viewing of suitable television programs, and expressions of appreciation for what is good and displeasure for what is bad should be part of the family experience. *CHURCH NEWS*, OCT. 28, 1984

Our youth need adults who care. They need successful models with whom they can identify. They need teachers and counselors who can show the way to opportunity. They need to experience the rewards of earning their own income and using and developing their talents. They need a chance to explore career opportunities to see how adults function as employers and employees. They need to understand the relationship of the world of learning and the world of work. *CHURCH NEWS*, MAY 14, 1977

Youth is the one resource that must be developed fully if a nation is to prosper. IBID.

Our children should be taught to sustain themselves by their own industry and skill, and not only to do this, but to help sustain others, and that to do this by honest toil is one of the most honorable means which God has furnished to his children here on the earth. STATEMENT, OCT. 10, 1887, IN *MESSAGES*, 3:133-55

Christmas

Christmas is more than trees and twinkling lights, more than toys and gifts and baubles of a hundred varieties. It is love. It is the love of the Son of God for all mankind. It reaches out beyond our power to comprehend. It is magnificent and beautiful. GORDON B. HINCKLEY, "FIRST PRESIDENCY MESSAGE," *ENSIGN*, DEC. 1997

Times change, years speed by; but Christmas continues sacred. It is through giving, rather than getting, that the Spirit of Christ enters our lives. God still speaks. He prompts. He guides. He blesses. He gives. THOMAS S. MONSON, "FIRST PRESIDENCY MESSAGE," *ENSIGN*, DEC. 1995

While merchandising and social activities have become part of Christmastime in many lands, it is important that we look beyond the commercialism of the season and focus on Him whose birth it commemorates–the Son of God, the Redeemer, the promised Messiah. *CHURCH NEWS*, DEC. 4, 1993

The Christmas season for many in the world is one of joy and warm feelings for family and friends and of gratitude for bounteous blessings. The reason for such warmth of emotion is the Spirit of Him whose birth we celebrate. He came to Earth as the Son of God, the Prince of Peace. To the degree that we have blended His gospel into our lives, we have partaken of the peace which He came to bring.

We recognize that there are those for whom this special season passes virtually unnoticed because of their unrelenting suffering from war, hunger, and other afflictions. Let those who are blessed remember those who suffer in our prayers, thoughts, and deeds. *CHURCH NEWS*, DEC. 5, 1992

The Christmas season offers an opportunity to renew our quest for the true Spirit of Christ and to focus our attention not only on His birth, but also the teachings of His mortal ministry, the incredible sacrifice made for us all through His suffering and death, and His glorious Resurrection and the accompanying assurance of everlasting life to all humankind. NEWS RELEASE, DEC. 18, 1986

We pray that all may seek the peace that is to be found in Christ; that all may look beyond the merchandising and socializing to the One whose birth we celebrate. Among the many lands where Christmas is observed, there is a great variety of holiday traditions. We would encourage a tradition of worshiping the Savior through loving service to fellowmen. May the kindness, forgiveness, and personal righteousness demonstrated by the Savior be manifest in the lives of countless people throughout the world. For, just as Bethlehem's bright star guided the Wise Men to the Savior, Christlike lives today can be a bright beacon to the many who do not yet know of their Redeemer. NEWS RELEASE, DEC. 9, 1984

At this sacred season, let us not lose sight of the real meaning of Christmas. Christmas means giving–giving of self; giving of substance; giving of heart and mind and strength in assisting those in need and in spreading the cause of His eternal truth.

Christmas means compassion, love, forgiveness, and peace. NEWS RELEASE, DEC. 15, 1983

Christmas means a solemn mood and a sacred feeling blending with an air of joyful celebration, to elevate the spirit and promote good will. NEWS RELEASE, DEC. 20, 1980

Reading the scriptures should be part of a meaningful Christmas observance. *CHURCH NEWS*, DEC. 20, 1975

Make Christmas a prayerful event. Before the gifts are opened, before the stockings are taken from the fireplace and before the bright lights of the home movie cameras are turned on, take a few sacred moments and kneel with your family in humble prayer. IBID.

No worry or anxiety over the choosing and giving of gifts, no enjoyment of holiday feasts, no decorations however modern or attractive, no social parties however jovial should ever overshadow the fact that Christmas is the celebration of the birth of Jesus Christ who came to give *Life, Light,* and *Peace* to all mankind, and who marked the *Way* by which these eternal blessings may be obtained. *DESERET NEWS*, DEC. 15, 1954

Let [Christmas] be a time for family reunions, for the settlement of all grievances, and for the exercise of true charity and benevolence toward all. *DESERET NEWS*, DEC. 14, 1949

Let us cherish the hope that some day the friendly, unselfish, generous, mutually helpful spirit that characterizes the Christmastide will dominate human society. *DESERET NEWS*, DEC. 15, 1948

There is a joy in Christmas which is unsurpassed by any other season or event in the year. It is the joy that comes from losing self for the happiness of others. *DESERET NEWS*, DEC. 19, 1936

Whether it was on the night of the 25th day of December, or on some other date, that the angel of the Lord announced to the shepherds who watched over their flocks on the hills of Judea, the birth, in the city of David, of a Savior, who was Christ the Lord, The Church of Jesus Christ of Latter-day Saints joins with other Christian churches and people in commemorating this most important event in the history of the world. *DESERET NEWS*, DEC. 17, 1932, IN *MESSAGES*, 5:312-13

Our celebration of the Christmastide should be so ordered that holy angels can approve and in spirit participate with us; then shall our joys and festivities be acceptable to Him whose birth we honor. May families be united and individuals moved upon by the Christmas spirit in rich measure, that thanksgiving and praise, accompanied by benevolent ministry to those in need, may sanctify our hearts and homes! *DESERET NEWS*, DEC. 20, 1930, IN *MESSAGES*, 5:286-89

The time of the Savior's birth has become established as the "Meridian of Time" by which years, centuries, and millenniums are counted forward and computed back, so that it has come to be acknowledged by Christian, Jew, and Pagan as the pivotal event in the chronicles of mankind. IBID.

Whether or not the 25th day of December is the proper date of the birth of Christ, our Lord, matters little; we join with other Christian people in celebrating it as such, and if we observe it in the true spirit of the Master, renewing the covenant which we have made that we are willing to take upon us His name, and keep the commandments which He has given, our offering will be accepted. *DESERET NEWS*, DEC. 19, 1925, IN *MESSAGES*, 5:245-48

The chronological inaccuracy that has fixed the Nativity as of December 25 is of minor importance compared with the supreme truth of the event itself. *DESERET NEWS*, DEC. 17, 1921, IN *MESSAGES*, 5:208-11

Church

Activity is the genius of this Church. It is the process by which we grow. GORDON B. HINCKLEY, "FIRST PRESIDENCY MESSAGE," *ENSIGN*, OCT. 2006

The official name of the Church is The Church of Jesus Christ of Latter-day Saints. We worship Him [Jesus Christ] as Lord and Savior. The Bible is our scripture. We believe that the prophets of the Old Testament who foretold the coming of the Messiah spoke under divine inspiration. We glory in the accounts of Matthew, Mark, Luke, and John setting forth the events of the birth, ministry, death, and Resurrection of the Son of God, the Only Begotten of the Father in the flesh. Like Paul of old, we are "not ashamed of the gospel of [Jesus]

Christ; for it is the power of God unto salvation" (Rom. 1:16). And like Peter, we affirm that Jesus Christ is the only name "given among men, whereby we must be saved" (Acts 4:12). GORDON B. HINCKLEY, "FIRST PRESIDENCY MESSAGE," *ENSIGN*, APR. 2005

While the term "Mormon Church" has long been publicly applied to the Church as a nickname, it is not an authorized title, and the Church discourages its use. *QUICK FACTS*, 2005

The very foundation, history, and name of The Church of Jesus Christ of Latter-day Saints bear ample testimony that God the Father and His Son, Jesus Christ, who atoned for the sins of mankind and died on the cross, are the center of Church theology and worship. IBID.

The Church of Jesus Christ of Latter-day Saints is Christian but is neither Catholic nor Protestant. Rather, it is a restoration of the original Church established by Jesus Christ. IBID.

As a member of The Church of Jesus Christ of Latter-day Saints, you are a child of the covenant (see 3 Ne. 20:25-26). You have received the everlasting gospel and inherited the same promises given to Abraham, Isaac, and Jacob. You have the right to the blessings of the priesthood and to eternal life, according to your faithfulness in receiving the ordinances of salvation and keeping the associated covenants. Nations of the earth will be blessed by your efforts and by the labors of your posterity. *TRUE TO FAITH*, 2004

Membership in the Church calls forth a determination to serve. A position of responsibility may not be of recognized importance, nor may the reward be broadly known. Service, to be acceptable to the Savior, must come from willing minds, ready hands, and pledged hearts. THOMAS S. MONSON, "FIRST PRESIDENCY MESSAGE," *ENSIGN*, MAR. 2004

If there is any people in this world who believe in Jesus Christ, it is the people of this Church. The Church carries His name. He is the central figure in all of our worship. GORDON B. HINCKLEY, "FIRST PRESIDENCY MESSAGE," *ENSIGN*, JUNE 1999

We see a wonderful future for the Church, even though we live in a very uncertain world. If we will cling to our values, if we will build on our spiritual heritage, if we will walk in obedience before the Lord, if we will simply live the gospel, we will be blessed in magnificent and wonderful ways. *CHURCH NEWS*, AUG. 15, 1998

The mission of the Church is to help individuals and families come unto Christ and obtain eternal life (see Moro. 10:32; Moses 1:39). *CHURCH HANDBOOK* 2, 1998

The Church is the great reservoir of eternal truth from which we can constantly and freely drink. It is the preserver of standards, the teacher of values. Latch on to those values. Bind them to your hearts; let them become the lodestar of your lives to guide you as you move forward in the world of which you will become an important part. GORDON B. HINCKLEY, "FIRST PRESIDENCY MESSAGE," *ENSIGN*, JUNE 1996

The mission of the Church is to save souls by proclaiming the gospel, perfecting the Saints, and redeeming the dead. EZRA TAFT BENSON, "FIRST PRESIDENCY MESSAGE," *ENSIGN*, OCT. 1992

We should be willing to generously give of our time, talents, and means to the Church. No matter what happens to the world, the Church will grow in strength and will be intact when the Lord comes again. EZRA TAFT BENSON, "FIRST PRESIDENCY MESSAGE," *ENSIGN*, DEC. 1988

The purpose of the Lord's Church is to further the progress of every son and daughter of God toward the ultimate blessings of eternal life. EZRA TAFT BENSON, "FIRST PRESIDENCY MESSAGE," *ENSIGN*, SEPT. 1987

This Church is true. It will weather every storm that beats against it. It will outlast every critic who rises to mock it. It was established by God our Eternal Father for the blessing of His sons and daughters of all generations. It carries the name of Him who stands as its head, even the Lord Jesus Christ, the Savior of the world. It is governed and moves by the power of the priesthood. It sends forth to the world another witness of the divinity of the Lord. GORDON B. HINCKLEY, "FIRST PRESIDENCY MESSAGE," *ENSIGN*, SEPT. 1985

[O]ur main purpose is the same as that of our Heavenly Father–to bring to each soul the gospel, which can open the doors to eternal life for that individual. Our objective is not for power or domain; it is totally spiritual. And to every nation and people which opens its borders to the gospel will come unbelievable blessings. SPENCER W. KIMBALL, "FIRST PRESIDENCY MESSAGE," *ENSIGN*, APR. 1984

The Church is designed to enlarge and develop the powers of our spirits, to educate us for eternity and to help us live intelligently and joyfully in mortality. The gospel and its teachings lead us to Christlike living, which in turn leads us not only toward exaltation but toward knowledge. SPENCER W. KIMBALL, "FIRST PRESIDENCY MESSAGE," *ENSIGN*, SEPT. 1983

The Lord revealed that the Church should bear the name The Church of Jesus Christ of Latter-day Saints, "for thus shall my church be called in the last days" (D&C 115:4). We feel that some may be misled by the too frequent use of the term "Mormon Church." We should talk, rejoice, and preach of Christ, and we should assist others in understanding the source to which "they may look for a remission of their sins" (2 Ne.

25:26). Christian living and service should support our verbal expressions of testimony. FIRST PRESIDENCY, LETTER DATED OCT. 1, 1982

Our Heavenly Father's fundamental teachings are the same yesterday, today, and forever. Even though the world has turned to much evil, the Lord's Church cannot and will not change the Master's teachings. SPENCER W. KIMBALL, "FIRST PRESIDENCY MESSAGE," *ENSIGN*, OCT. 1982

We solemnly affirm that The Church of Jesus Christ of Latter-day Saints is in fact a restoration of the Church established by the Son of God, when in mortality He organized His work upon the earth; that it carries His sacred name, even the name of Jesus Christ; that it is built upon a foundation of apostles and prophets, He being the chief cornerstone; that its priesthood, in both the Aaronic and Melchizedek orders, was restored under the hands of those who held it anciently–John the Baptist, in the case of the Aaronic, and Peter, James, and John in the case of the Melchizedek. *CHURCH NEWS*, APR. 12, 1980

The Church, or God's kingdom on earth, is organized under the direction and authority of the priesthood to teach the gospel and administer the ordinances that lead us to exaltation. *PRINCIPLES*, 1976

[I]n its most general sense, the word *Zion* means "the pure in heart," or those who have been born again, worthy members of the Lord's Church (see D&C 97:21). IBID.

[T]he Church organization exists to assist the family and its members in reaching exaltation. *FAMILY HOME EVENING*, 1973

Only persons who are fully loyal to the Church and its officers and who are willing to live our standards and adhere to our orthodox teachings should be appointed to instructional or leadership positions or be granted other privileges of the Church. "DEAR BRETHREN," SALT LAKE METROPOLITAN AREA, NOV. 30, 1972

As the kingdom of God is extended through the earth, the ideal society, known as Zion, is developed.

The Lord has provided the following guides by which His children may be led to a Zion condition:

a. The standard works of the Church.

b. The prophet of the Church, who receives revelation from the Lord for the Church and for the world. Other prophets, seers, and revelators who assist in teaching, directing, and governing the Church.

c. Individuals receive revelation for their stewardships.

d. The priesthood and its quorums.

e. The Church organizations and priesthood programs. "BASIC DOCTRINES," MAR. 5, 1971

The mission of The Church of Jesus Christ of Latter-day Saints is to bring this knowledge to the world, to declare that Christ is the living head of the kingdom of God on the earth. *CHURCH NEWS*, DEC. 19, 1964

We give assurance to all people that The Church of Jesus Christ, our Lord, is established in the world through revelations and ministrations to the Prophet Joseph Smith and his associates, and that the Church will never more be thrown down or given to another people. We bear testimony that the Church has been set up after the pattern of the Primitive Church, with the same officers and priesthood organization that existed and functioned in the establishment created by the Savior himself and His disciples. *DESERET NEWS*, DEC. 16, 1953

The Lord is with His work. He will not forsake it. It has been put in the earth not merely for a century or a millennium. It is established for eternity. It will triumph over all opposition. *DESERET NEWS*, DEC. 12, 1951

To be true to our heritage, we must face, with fortitude and unflinching courage, the great duty that is ours—the spiritual rejuvenation of mankind. *DESERET NEWS*, JULY 24, 1947

We of this Church stand as the sole possessors of these mighty forces ["the eternal principles of the everlasting gospel of Christ and the rights and powers of the priesthood of Almighty God"] which we have for our own blessing, salvation, and exaltation, not only, but also we hold them in trust for all mankind, those who now live, those who are dead and gone, and those to be born in the future, that they, too, all of them who will receive and obey the gospel, may likewise be saved and exalted. *IMPROVEMENT ERA*, NOV. 1942, *IN MESSAGES,* 6:170-85

The Lord has established His Church in these latter days that men might be called to repentance, to the salvation and exaltation of their souls. *IMPROVEMENT ERA*, MAY 1942, IN *MESSAGES*, 6:148-63

[T]he Church was established for the purpose of preaching righteousness, and of leading men to live righteous lives obedient to the commandments of the Lord. "DEAR BRETHREN," DEC. 23, 1941, IN *MESSAGES*, 6:141-43

The Church is the organized priesthood of God; the priesthood can exist without the Church, but the Church cannot exist without the priesthood. The mission of the Church is first, to teach, encourage, assist, and protect the individual member in his striving to live the perfect life, temporally and spiritually, as laid down in the gospel—"Be ye perfect, even as your Father which is in Heaven is perfect," said the Master [Matt. 5:48]; secondly, the Church is to maintain, teach, encourage, and protect, temporally and spiritually, the membership as a group in its living of the gospel; thirdly, the Church is militantly to proclaim the truth, calling upon all men to repent, and to live in obedience to the gospel, "for every knee must bow and every tongue confess" [Philip. 2:10-11; D&C 76:110]. *CHURCH NEWS*, AUG. 13, 1938, IN *MESSAGES*, 6:44-58

[T]his is the mission that has been assigned to us, to warn the nations of impending judgments, to preach the gospel of the Redeemer, whose birth we at this season commemorate, and to invite all to come unto Christ and receive the benefits of His glorious Atonement. "Mormonism," so-called, is in the world for the world's good. Its missionary system has no other purpose than to bless and benefit. It has no quarrel with the creeds and sects of the day. It stands for peace, the peace of God "which passeth understanding." It is ever ready to do good in every possible way. It pleads for a return to the faith "once delivered to the Saints," believing that such a course will save humanity from the sins of the world and eventually exalt men in the presence of God, the Father, and Jesus Christ, the Son, "who is the Light and Life of the World." *DESERET NEWS*, DEC. 15, 1923, IN *MESSAGES*, 5:232-33

It is the mission and pleasure of the Latter-day Saints to proclaim the establishment of the Church or spiritual kingdom of Christ, anew, to be developed into His literal earthly kingdom at His personal advent. *DESERET NEWS*, DEC. 16, 1911, IN *MESSAGES*, 4:252-58

[N]o one on the face of God's footstool need fear the growth and spread of "Mormonism," for it is the truth revealed anew and from heaven, and it promotes freedom, peace, industry, temperance, faith, hope and charity, and stands for human rights, the salvation of mankind, and the glory of the most high God. *IMPROVEMENT ERA*, JUNE 1911, IN *MESSAGES*, 4:224-29

[T]he Church of Jesus Christ of Latter-day Saints must of necessity stand independent and alone, entirely free from alliances with man-made institutions; and as the Church is made up of its members, it follows as a sequence that they in like manner must themselves partake of the same spirit and also be free. "DEAR BRETHREN," DEC. 16, 1907, IN *MESSAGES*, 4:167-71

Our religion is interwoven with our lives, it has formed our character, and the truth of its principles is impressed upon our souls. *IMPROVEMENT ERA*, MAY 1907, IN *MESSAGES*, 4:143-55

The Church of Christ is with the Saints. It has committed to it the law of God for its own government and perpetuation. It possesses every means for the correction of every wrong or abuse or error which may from time to time arise, and that without anarchy, or even revolution; it can do it by processes of evolution–by development, by an increase of knowledge, wisdom, patience, and charity. *DESERET NEWS*, NOV. 13, 1905, IN *MESSAGES*, 4:108-20

If our religion does not lead us to love our God and our fellow men and to deal justly and uprightly with all men, then our profession of it is in vain. STATEMENT, OCT. 10, 1887, IN *MESSAGES*, 3:133-55

God, our God, has promised in every age, and has renewed the promise with succeeding generations, that in the latter days he would perform his great and wonderful work, and the kingdom and the greatness of the kingdom should never be given to another people. JOHN TAYLOR TO JOHN HENRY SMITH, NOV. 7, 1884

A union in all things, temporal and spiritual, is the ultimate destiny of the Latter-day Saints, and God's kingdom can never be fully established upon the earth until this is brought about. JOHN TAYLOR TO P. C. MERRILL, APR. 10, 1878

Our holy religion brings us in contact with long established error, and the traditions of centuries, which are prevalent throughout the world; hence are we necessarily a peculiar and separate people, whose best interests and preservation depend upon union and self-dependence, upon practicing virtue, industry, and sobriety, and manifesting our faith by our works in magnifying our priesthood, and in serving our God by keeping ourselves pure and unspotted in this wicked and adulterous generation. *MILLENNIAL STAR*, AUG. 11, 1855, IN *MESSAGES*, 2:159-71

The kingdom which we are establishing is not of this world, but is the kingdom of the Great God. It is the fruit of righteousness, of peace, of salvation to every soul that will receive it, from Adam down to his latest posterity. Our good will is towards all men, and we desire their salvation in time and eternity; and we will do them good so far as God will give us the power, and men will permit us the privilege; and we will harm no man; but if men will rise up against the power of the Almighty to overthrow His cause, let them know assuredly that they are running on the bosses [ornaments] of Jehovah's buckler [shield], and, as God lives, they will be overthrown. *MILLENNIAL STAR*, MAR. 14, 1848, IN *MESSAGES*, 1:323-35

As this work progresses in its onward course, and becomes more and more an object of political and religious interest and excitement, no king, ruler, or subject, no community or individual, will stand *neutral.* All will at length be influenced by one spirit or the other, and will take sides either for or against the kingdom of God, and the fulfillment of the prophets, in the great restoration and return of His long dispersed covenant people. STATEMENT, APR. 6, 1845, IN *MESSAGES*, 1:252-66

Church discipline. ***See also*** **confession; disfellowshipment; excommunication; probation**

Wise discipline reinforces the dimensions of eternal love. JAMES E. FAUST, "FIRST PRESIDENCY MESSAGE," *ENSIGN*, SEPT. 2006

Church discipline is an inspired process that takes place over a period of time. Through this process and through the Atonement of Jesus Christ, a member can receive forgiveness of sins, regain peace of mind, and gain strength to avoid transgression in the future. Church disciplinary action is not intended to be the end of the process. It is designed to help Heavenly Father's children continue in their efforts to return to full fellowship and the full blessings of the Church. The desired result is that the person make whatever changes are necessary to repent completely. *TRUE TO FAITH*, 2004

The purposes of Church discipline are (1) to save the souls of transgressors, (2) to protect the innocent, and (3) to safeguard the purity, integrity, and good name of the Church. These purposes are accomplished through private counsel and caution, informal probation, formal probation, disfellowshipment, and excommunication ... *CHURCH HANDBOOK*, 1998

Because formal Church discipline is ecclesiastical, not civil or criminal, court procedures of the state or nation do not apply. However, procedures in a Church disciplinary council must be fair and considerate of the feelings of all who participate. IBID.

Local presiding officers should not expect General Authorities to tell them how to decide difficult matters. Decisions on Church discipline are within the discretion and authority of local presiding officers as they prayerfully seek guidance from the Lord. IBID.

Normally, evidence of repentance is the most important single factor in determining how to accomplish the first purpose of Church discipline: saving the soul of the transgressor. Genuine repentance is demonstrated more reliably by righteous actions over a period of time than by intense sorrow during a single interview. Judgments about the adequacy of repentance require spiritual discernment. Factors to consider include the nature of the confession, depth of sorrow for the sin, success in forsaking the sin, strength of faith in Jesus Christ, faithfulness in obeying other commandments, truthful communications to Church officers, restitution to injured persons, obedience to legal requirements, and willingness to follow the direction of Church authorities. IBID.

Certain transgressions of Church members are serious enough that repentance can be brought about only by proper Church discipline carried out under the inspiration of the Lord through an established judicial system administered by the priesthood. Priesthood leaders should always remember that Church courts are courts of love and redemption, not of retribution. *CHURCH HANDBOOK*, 1985

The time just after an individual has been disfellowshipped or excommunicated is critical and difficult for him or her and, equally important, for members of his or her family. During this time, leaders as well as Church members should be especially patient and sensitive to the needs of those involved. Leaders as well as members should seek constant guidance from the Holy Spirit in assisting and encouraging those who have been disciplined, their companions, and their families. They may have a greater need for sustained love and considerate attention than at any other time. Such genuine concern can give them hope, a great incentive to repentance, and can assure them that they have not been abandoned.

Stake presidents and bishops are to consider the status regularly of those who have been disciplined and be sure everything possible is being done to help them regain the full blessings of the gospel. *BULLETIN*, OCT. 1983

Priesthood leaders should always remember that Church courts are courts of love and redemption, not of retribution. "DEAR BRETHREN," JUNE 1, 1979

When an interview reveals a transgression not previously resolved with the appropriate priesthood leader, the length of elapsed time, the present worthiness of the individual, the extent to which the transgression is widely known, and the quality of repentance must all be carefully considered in deciding (a) whether formal disciplinary action is to be taken; and (b) the nature of any discipline to be imposed. Where circumstances warrant, including evidence of sincere repentance, a common judge has the right to waive court action. "DEAR BRETHREN," AUG. 29, 1977

Courts of the Church are not courts of retribution and should be held in a spirit of love. They are held to try persons alleged to have transgressed the moral law or violated the principles taught by the Church, and to purge iniquity from the Church. *CHURCH HANDBOOK*, 1976

Church courts are held to try members (1) who have apostatized, (2) who have been convicted in civil and criminal courts for certain crimes, (3) who have committed sexual transgressions such as adultery, fornication, homosexuality, incest, child molesting, or other transgressions of this nature, (4) who are guilty of murder, advocating or practicing plural marriage, intemperance, cruelty to spouse or children, or unchristianlike conduct in violation of the law and order of the Church. *PRINCIPLES*, 1976

When a moral transgression occurs, and the priesthood leader involved has knowledge of it, he should not hesitate to convene a Church court and to try the transgressor for his membership, if the circumstances appear to require it.

In determining whether to convene a court, a priesthood leader should take into account the gravity of the offense, whether the confession was voluntary, whether the transgressor has confessed and made recompense to those injured by the transgression, whether and to what extent others are conscious of the transgression, whether there has been a complete forsaking of the sin, whether the transgressor occupies a position of special importance in the Church, and whether the transgressor has had his temple endowment. "CHURCH COURTS," ATTACHED TO A REVISION OF ELDER ROBERT L. SIMPSON'S GENERAL CONFERENCE ADDRESS, APR. 1972

It has come to our attention that some wives of non-members have been excommunicated because their husbands refuse to permit them to be active. Unless the person involved requests specifically that her name be removed from the records of the Church and does so in writing, and the bishop or branch president has satisfied himself that this is her firm desire, the individual concerned should not be cited to appear before a bishop's court to answer for her standing, nor should the individual's name otherwise be removed from the records of the Church.

It is most important that we recognize that the purpose of the gospel is to save souls. Bishops, branch presidents, and home teachers should labor diligently and untiringly with inactive and neglectful members in an effort to reactivate them and bring them to an understanding of the glorious truths of the gospel. "DEAR BRETHREN," AUG. 21, 1967

When young unmarried people are involved in sexual sin, every consideration should be given to helping them adjust their situation so that if possible they may live normal lives. Too severe action often defeats the ends of justice. *CHURCH HANDBOOK*, 1963

Bishops have the right to waive Church court action upon proper evidence of genuine repentance. It should be remembered, however, that forgiveness comes only from the Lord. IBID.

First: May a person who has been excommunicated from the Church on a charge of adultery, after a number of years, be granted baptism if he has repented and observed the laws in the covenant of marriage?

Yes. A person who is truly repentant and who desires to be reinstated in the Church should be admitted.

Second: Should persons guilty of adultery be dealt with for their membership or for their fellowship in the Church?

Every case should be considered on its merits. If the sin was committed in secret, and the person has confessed, the case should not be made public, but the authority to whom the confession is made should grant the forgiveness asked and the person be permitted to retain his or her membership in the Church. If, however, the case is a flagrant one and known publicly, then such necessary restitution should be made as seems fitting to the presiding authorities (see D&C 42:90-93). FIRST PRESIDENCY TO REUBEN M. WIBERG, AUG. 14, 1935

The Church does not inflict temporal punishment. But it does not shelter law-breakers from the arm of the law. *CHURCH HANDBOOK*, 1934

It is difficult to give any set rule for the handling of cases involving moral conduct. Each case must, of course, be considered on its merits and according to the seriousness of the offense. IBID.

The prevailing opinion in cases involving young unmarried couples who are obliged to marry is to be as lenient as possible, considering always their future lives and the effect which unnecessary publicity may have upon them. Too severe action often defeats the ends of justice. This would be more harmful to the individuals, to their families, and the community than any good which is hoped to accomplish by drastic measures. IBID.

The penalty of adultery is excommunication, that is, where the party in transgression has received his or her endowments. But should there be mitigating circumstances attending the case, it would be proper that they be considered when the party or parties are being dealt with, although it is difficult to conceive of mitigating circumstances in adultery cases except, perhaps, on the part of the woman in the case.

Where parties guilty of adultery have not received their endowments, they should be forgiven for the first offense on their manifesting evidences of genuine repentance, but failure on their part to bring forth the fruits of repentance, they should be cast out or excommunicated, as the revelation on this subject directs. FIRST PRESIDENCY TO GEORGE MUMFORD, MAR. 18, 1901

As to the proper method of dealing with what are called minor sins, the presidents of stakes and bishops have it in their power to decide. That there has been too much looseness upon these points in many places appears clear to us from the reports which reach us. Sabbath breaking, drunkenness, blasphemy, and sins of this character forbidden by the word of

God should not be allowed to pass unreproved by the officers of the Church. Of course, where laxity has prevailed upon these points in the past, wisdom would dictate to all in authority to proceed carefully and not rush from one extreme to the other ... Then if they continue their violations they should be dealt with. If they hold the priesthood, it might be well, as you suggest, to suspend them from that in the first place. If they will not then repent, their fellowship can be withdrawn. JOHN TAYLOR AND GEORGE Q. CANNON TO FRANKLIN SPENCER, OCT. 22, 1885

church and state

The Church rarely takes a position on pending legislation, and does so only when it involves an important moral issue, or directly affects the activities or programs of the Church. *CHURCH NEWS*, MAY 27, 2000

[T]he Church expects that all lawmakers will vote their consciences and their views of the best interest of their country. IBID.

As the ruling principle of conduct in the lives of many millions of our citizens, religion should have an honorable place in the public life of our nation, and the name of Almighty God should have a sacred use in its public expressions. *CHURCH NEWS*, OCT. 27, 1990

During the course of our history, members of our Church have been the victims of official persecution motivated by religious intolerance. We are, therefore, committed by experience as well as by precept to the wisdom of Constitutional principle that government and public officials should maintain a position of respectful neutrality in the matter of religion. *CHURCH NEWS*, MAR. 17, 1979

[T]he Constitutional principle of neutrality toward religion does not call for our nation to ignore its religious heritage, including the religious motivations of its founders and the powerful religious beliefs of generations of its people and its leaders. IBID.

As the ruling principle of conduct in the lives of many millions of our citizens, religion should have an honorable place in the public life of our nation, and the name of Almighty God should have sacred use in its public expression. We urge our members and people of good will everywhere to unite to protect and honor the spiritual and religious heritage of our nation and to resist the forces that would transform the public position of the United States from the Constitutional position of neutrality to a position of hostility toward religion. IBID.

The Church is not a political organization and proclaims the separation of church and state. Often the Church does, however, offer its members advice and council when civil governments become involved with matters affecting the religious and general moral state of the people.

The standard of the Church is that man should be free to worship according to the dictates of his conscience so that he may be held accountable for his actions; however, in countries where this is not allowed, the members of the Church should meet as the law of the country permits. They should try, through due process of the law, to obtain as much religious freedom as possible. *PRINCIPLES*, 1976

As with ... non-moral issues which may be brought before the voter by referendum, we reiterate the advice given by leaders of the Church from time to time that it is the duty of every citizen to act in accordance with his or her convictions.

We have not in the past, nor do with now, seek to bring coercion or compulsion upon the Church as to their actions. On the contrary, we have urged and do now urge that all citizens study the issue carefully and then act according to their honest convictions. *CHURCH NEWS*, MAY 13, 1972

The framers of the Constitution intended that government be free of church domination and that churches correspondingly be free of governmental regulation. By means of the First Amendment to the United States Constitution, the framers intended to create "a wall of separation between church and state." FIRST PRESIDENCY TO FRANK E. MOSS, WALLACE F. BENNETT, SHERMAN P. LLOYD, AND LAWRENCE W. BURTON, FEB. 24, 1967

We do not believe it just to mingle religious, or anti-religious, influence with civil government, whereby one religious society is fostered and another proscribed in its spiritual privileges, and the individual rights of its members, as citizens and as men, denied. "DESIRABLE OBJECTIVES," 1965

The Church of Jesus Christ of Latter-day Saints holds to the doctrine of the separation of church and state; the non-interference of church authority in political matters; and the absolute freedom and independence of the individual in the performance of his political duties. If at any time there has been conduct at variance with this doctrine, it has been in violation of the well-settled principles and policy of the Church.

We declare that from principle and policy, we favor:

The absolute separation of church and state;

No domination of the state by the church;

No church interference with the functions of the state;

No state interference with the functions of the church, or with the free exercise of religion;

The absolute freedom of the individual from the domination of ecclesiastical authority in political affairs;

The equality of all churches before the law.

The re-affirmation of this doctrine and policy, however, is predicated upon the express understanding that politics in the states where our people reside shall be conducted as in other parts of the Union; that there shall be no interference by the state with the Church, nor with the free exercise of religion. *IMPROVEMENT ERA*, MAY 1907, IN *MESSAGES*, 4:143-55

On behalf of the Church of which we are leading officers, we desire again to state to the members and also to the public generally that there has not been, or is there, the remotest desire on our part or on the part of our co-religionists to do anything looking to a union of church and state. *DESERET NEWS WEEKLY*, APR. 6, 1896, IN *MESSAGES*, 3:273-77

Church government and civil government are distinct and separate in our theory and practice, and we regard it as part of our destiny to aid in the maintenance and perpetuity of the institutions of our country. *DESERET NEWS WEEKLY*, DEC. 21, 1889, IN *MESSAGES*, 3:184-87

civil marriage, *see* marriage

class distinctions

The divine child was born amid the lowliest surroundings, in contrast to royal luxury, as a reminder to the world that the humblest and most downtrodden of mankind, as well as those in more favored circumstances, are of the lineage of God and subjects of His loving care. *DESERET NEWS*, DEC. 14, 1949

Under the present system of affairs, those who supply themselves and their families with luxuries and advantages that are denied their neighbors are in danger of becoming separated from the bulk of the people and forming a distinct class. But the day will come when a more perfect order will be introduced. Then it will be said there are no poor and no rich in Zion—that is, we shall not be divided into classes, but shall all possess everything of this character necessary to our comfort and happiness. But until then, if we wish our families and ourselves to remain Latter-day Saints, we must be especially careful to guard against the deceitfulness of riches. STATEMENT, OCT. 10, 1887, IN *MESSAGES*, 3:133-55

In union there is strength; but how can a people become united while their interests are diversified? How can they become united in spiritual matters, and see eye to eye [in that] which they can only partly understand until they become united in regard to temporal things, which they do comprehend? *MILLENNIAL STAR*, JULY 8, 1854, IN *MESSAGES*, 2:127-43

coffee, *see* Word of Wisdom

Columbus

Columbus, discovering America, moved under the Lord's inspiration. So did the Pilgrim fathers. Washington sought and obtained God's inspiration at Valley Forge, as did Lincoln before Gettysburg. The men who set up the constitutional government of the United States did so under the Lord's inspiration. He was the source of their wisdom. MARION G. ROMNEY, "FIRST PRESIDENCY MESSAGE," *ENSIGN*, SEPT. 1982

It was all part of God's plan—the coming of Columbus, the colonization, wise men raised up to frame the Constitution, Joseph Smith prepared for his part in the restoration of the gospel, even the persecution which drove the Saints to the Rocky Mountains where the Church could continue to grow. N. ELDON TANNER, "FIRST PRESIDENCY MESSAGE," *ENSIGN*, JULY 1976

The coming of Columbus to America had been foretold

centuries before he sailed from the port of Palos, in Spain. The Spirit of the Lord was upon him, was his guide and protector in his great adventure, and led him to the shores of a new world. *IMPROVEMENT ERA*, MAY 1930, IN *MESSAGES*, 5:274-86

commercialism

The Church of Jesus Christ of Latter-day Saints has long refrained from actual or implied endorsement of any commercial product, either by written or spoken word. Neither headquarters Church facilities nor local Church properties should be used for merchandising efforts, commercially oriented business meetings, display, or for supporting photography or video recordings presenting a particular product or service. FIRST PRESIDENCY TO GENERAL AUTHORITIES, MANAGING DIRECTORS, AND DEPARTMENT HEADS, AUG. 16, 1982

Religious meetings and classes are not the proper places for advocating schemes for the financial profit of individuals or special groups or organizations, or for political advantage. *CHURCH HANDBOOK*, 1976

Church meetings, classes, and facilities are to be used solely for the purpose of worship, religious training, or programmed activities of the Church.

These meetings and facilities are not to be used to promote business ventures or investment enterprises. Commercial activities for the purpose of making profit by selling products or services or by demonstrating wares in Church classes are out of harmony with the purpose of religious meetings. *BULLETIN*, JUNE 1975

From time to time individuals or groups engaged in promoting some business, political, or social welfare organization take improper advantage of the people by invoking quotations from standard Church works and from Church authorities, and by arguing in Church gatherings in support of their propositions. Any business, political, or social scheme which requires bolstering by arguments based on Church doctrine or history is one of which the people may well be careful. *CHURCH HANDBOOK*, 1963

Our buildings are dedicated to the service of the Lord. Nothing should be permitted in them that is not in harmony with that purpose, regardless of the auspices under which gatherings are held. *CHURCH HANDBOOK*, 1940

common consent. *See also* agency

Every officer in the Church should be chosen by revelation through proper authority, but in order to serve as an officer, he must be approved by the people he will serve.

By raising his hand in a sustaining vote, each Church member agrees to support the officer in his position, helping him fulfill his calling.

The law of common consent does not apply to accepting or rejecting revelations from the Lord. Members of the Church may bind themselves by covenant to obey revelations and laws, but they cannot vote on the validity of those revelations.

The law of common consent is a basic principle that allows Church members to exercise their free agency. *PRINCIPLES*, 1976

Communism

The Church of Jesus Christ of Latter-day Saints, in the totality of its principles and doctrines, takes an unalterable position against Communism and its atheistic foundations. The leaders of the Church encourage members to take seriously the responsibility and privileges that are theirs as citizens, and to participate actively in political affairs of the Country on a local, state, and national basis, as the means by which our rights as citizens can be safeguarded and advanced. CLARE MIDDLEMISS, SECRETARY TO DAVID O. MCKAY, DEC. 8, 1965

Communism is not a political party nor a political plan under the Constitution; it is a system of government that is the opposite of our constitutional government, and it would be necessary to destroy our government before Communism could be set up in the United States.

Since Communism, established, would destroy our American constitutional government, to support Communism is treasonable to our free institutions, and no patriotic American citizen may become either a Communist or supporter of Communism.

To our Church members we say—Communism is not the United Order, and bears only the most superficial resemblance thereto; Communism is based on intolerance and force, the United Order upon love and freedom of conscience and action; Communism involves forceful despoliation and confiscation, the United Order voluntary consecration and sacrifice.

Communists cannot establish the United Order, nor will Communism bring it about. The United Order will be established by the Lord in His own due time and in accordance with the regular prescribed order of the Church.

Furthermore, it is charged by universal report, which is not successfully contradicted or disproved, that Communism undertakes to control, if not indeed to prescribe, the religious life of the people living within its jurisdiction, and that it even reaches its hand into the sanctity of the family circle itself, disrupting the normal relationship of parent and child, all in a manner unknown and unsanctioned under the Constitutional guarantees under which we in America live. Such interference would be contrary to the fundamental precepts of the gospel and to the teachings and order of the Church.

Communism being thus hostile to loyal American citizenship and incompatible with true Church membership, of necessity no loyal American citizen and no faithful Church member can be a Communist.

We call upon all Church members completely to eschew Communism. The safety of our divinely inspired constitutional government and the welfare of our Church imperatively demand that Communism shall have no place in America. *DESERET NEWS*, JULY 3, 1936

confession. ***See also*** **Church discipline**

Repentance requires that all sins be confessed to the Lord. "By this ye may know if a man repenteth of his sins–behold, he will confess them and forsake them" (D&C 58:43). Members also should confess to their presiding officer if they have committed serious transgressions. Members who voluntarily and completely confess transgressions demonstrate that they have begun the process of repentance. *CHURCH HANDBOOK*, 1998

Disclosure of the identity of others who participated in a transgression may be *required* when it is necessary to restore or protect persons who have been or may be seriously injured as a result of the transgression. IBID.

Information received in a member's confession cannot be used as evidence in a disciplinary council without the member's consent. IBID.

[F]orgiveness can never come without repentance. And repentance can never come until one has bared his soul and admitted his actions without excuses or rationalizations. He must admit to himself that he has sinned, without the slightest minimization of the offense or rationalizing of its seriousness, or without soft-pedaling its gravity. He must admit that his sin is as big as it really is and not call a pound an ounce. Those persons who choose to meet the issue and transform their lives may find repentance the harder road at first, but they will find it the infinitely more desirable path as they taste of its fruits. SPENCER W. KIMBALL, "FIRST PRESIDENCY MESSAGE," *ENSIGN*, OCT. 1982

The Lord requires that major sins be confessed to a proper Church authority. These sins include adultery, fornication, other sexual sins, and other sins that are equally as serious.

Confession must be voluntary. If it is forced after an offense is discovered, a greater penalty will be exacted. Voluntary confession is far more acceptable in the sight of the Lord and truly indicates the desire in the heart of the transgressor to overcome the sin. A forced confession usually follows a path of lies and excuses which add greater weight to the sin and add other sins to it. *PRINCIPLES*, 1976

While the major sins call for confession to a Church authority, it should be understood that this is neither necessary nor desirable for all sins. Less serious sins need only be confessed to any person we may have hurt, and sins involving no one but ourselves need be confessed only to the Lord. IBID.

As to whether a bishop or branch president can use information obtained in a confidential confession as evidence in a Church court trial, it is felt that the duty of confidentiality which a common judge has toward one who confesses would preclude the use of such information as evidence. This assumes, of course, that the confession is wholly voluntary and is not made in connection with an investigation being conducted. In cases of voluntary confession where the common judge feels that formal disciplinary action is necessary, either to cleanse the Church or to bring about full repentance, he can and should persuade the transgressor to release him from his duty of confidentiality and to submit to a Church court trial. Where such a release is obtained, it is permissible to use information learned in a voluntary confession as evidence in a Church court trial. It is apparent that failure to heed these formalities would significantly compromise the role of a common judge as a confidential advisor.

As to whether a bishop or branch president can be the sole witness against an accused, testifying from that which he has learned in a voluntary confession, if the accused has released the common judge from the duty of confidentiality, the confession would then be sufficient evidence to support a charge in a Church court proceeding. FIRST PRESIDENCY TO JOHN PRESTON CREER, MAR. 9, 1973

All sins should be confessed to the Lord; those involving moral turpitude and for which the court procedures of the Church might be instituted should also be confessed to the bishop. Bishops may upon repentance waive the court procedures, thus forgiving the transgressor as far as the Church is concerned (see D&C 42:25-28). Ultimate forgiveness comes only from the Lord. *CHURCH HANDBOOK*, 1968

Church members may afford themselves of the privilege of confessing to their bishop such sins as might affect their standing in the Church or their rights to enjoy the privileges of the Church, and of receiving from them such counsel, guidance, and help as the Spirit of the Lord may indicate.

Forgiveness comes only from the Lord, but for contrite and repentance persons bishops may elect to waive any formal trial or penalty within the power of the Church to impose. The bishop will keep such totally confidential. *CHURCH HANDBOOK*, 1963

It is not necessary in all cases that those whose offenses are not generally known shall be required to confess in public. CHURCH HANDBOOK, 1913

Those who sin against many should repent before many, and where only few are wronged, they only should be asked to forgive. JOSEPH F. SMITH TO SUSA Y. GATES, APR. 30, 1891

conscientious objection

Conscientious objectors may teach in the Church (home teach, Sunday School, priesthood, etc.) provided they are worthy of these positions and with the understanding that they avoid teachings or discussions pertaining to war and their attitude toward it. The same would apply to the matter of their holding office in the Church.

There certainly could be no objection to their partaking of the sacrament if they are otherwise worthy. They could also be given recommends to the temple provided they are sincere in their beliefs and are maintaining the standards of the Church.

It would be contrary to Church policy to disfellowship men because they have conscientious objections regarding participating in military combat activities. JOSEPH ANDERSON, SECRETARY TO THE FIRST PRESIDENCY, LETTER DATED OCT. 21, 1971

[T]he Church itself has never taken the position which is taken by the Quakers and other churches; therefore mere membership in the Church does not make one a conscientious objector. As you of course are aware, there are thousands of young men of the Church in the army, assigned to the various services in the military.

As the Brethren understand, the existing law provides that men having "conscientious objections" may be excused from combat service. There would seem to be no objection to a man availing himself to the exemptions provided by law. JOSEPH AN-

DERSON, SECRETARY TO THE FIRST PRESIDENCY, LETTER DATED FEB. 1, 1968

consecration, law of

Through this law [of consecration], the Lord asks us to make available for the building of His kingdom and the care of the needy that which He has given us, both our possessions and ourselves.

At this time, the Lord does not ask us to give all our time or all our possessions to His work, but He does expect us to be willing and able to give of our time in Church service and of our money in tithing, fast offerings, and the other contributions which sustain the work and the kingdom. Thus, by faithfully accepting and fulfilling Church callings, by faithfully paying tithing and voluntarily making the other contributions asked of us, we show the Lord our willingness to obey the law of consecration.

However, the time will come when the Lord will expect His Saints to obey the law of consecration in full. *PRINCIPLES*, 1976

Constitution of the United States

Prophets beginning with Joseph Smith have loved and sustained the Constitution. The Prophet Joseph Smith said, "The Constitution of the United States is a glorious standard; and it is founded in the wisdom of God. It is a heavenly banner." President Lorenzo Snow said, "We trace the hand of the Almighty in framing the Constitution of our land and believe that the Lord raised up men purposely for the accomplishment of this object" (see D&C 101:80). We should, therefore, in the tradition of our Founding Fathers, learn the principles of the Constitution and abide by its precepts. "DEAR BRETHREN," UNITED STATES, JAN. 15, 1987

Because some Americans have not kept faith with our Founding Fathers, the Constitution faces severe challenges. Those who do not prize individual freedom are trying to erode its great principles. We believe the Constitution will stand, but it will take the efforts of patriotic and dedicated Americans to uphold it. President John Adams, our nation's second president, offered a special insight into the Constitution when he said: "Our Constitution was made only for a moral and religious people. It is wholly inadequate to the government of any other." Thus we, as Latter-day Saints, must be vigilant in doing our part to preserve the Constitution and safeguard the way of life it makes possible. IBID.

We recognize the hand of God in the shaping of our Constitution and our nation. *CHURCH NEWS*, MAY 2, 1981

Despite the troubles we face as a nation, we are reminded of the genius of the Founding Fathers who established the Republic under which we live. For nearly two centuries we have been prospered and blessed by a constitution which Gladstone declared to be "that most wonderful work ever struck off at a given time by the brain and purpose of man." "DEAR BRETHREN," UNITED STATES, JUNE 29, 1979

Under the divinely inspired Constitution of these United States, the choice of leadership in government rests with the governed. *SALT LAKE TRIBUNE*, OCT. 24, 1976

The United States of America is a nation with a spiritual foundation. The men who framed the Constitution were directed by the Spirit of the Lord in establishing the basic freedoms guaranteed the citizens of this country. But the United States of America will remain free only as long as we continue to be law-abiding, God-fearing people (see 2 Ne. 10:11-12; Ether 2:8-12). The Church and its members can play a significant role in maintaining moral standards and, thus, our freedoms. *PRINCIPLES*, 1976

[T]his land [United States of America], chosen above all others, raised up by the Lord in these latter days as a land of promise to all the world, was a land prepared in every way for the reestablishment of the Lord's Church, a land where the people have been warned to keep the commandments of the Lord or suffer their own destruction if they do not. The Constitution was established through the inspiration of God to preserve the liberty of the people and to maintain His promise. IBID.

The Church of Jesus Christ of Latter-day Saints deplores all actions which are in violation of the laws of the land, and reaffirms its basic teachings of "obeying, honoring, and sustaining the law," and of "being subject to kings, rulers, and magistrates" [AofF 1:12]. On the basis of revealed scripture, we regard the Constitution of the United States as a divinely inspired document, and express our full loyalty to those now newly sustained to uphold the laws of this land and maintain its dignity among nations of the world. *ENSIGN*, OCT. 1974

In these challenging days, when there are so many influences which would divert us, there is a need to rededicate ourselves to the lofty principles and practices of our Founding Fathers. While we must never permit an erosion of the freedoms the Constitution guarantees, we cannot let permissiveness replace responsibility. *ENSIGN*, NOV. 1973

Under the blessings of liberty secured by the Constitution, we must continue to pursue excellence and progress, but we must recognize that to move forward we must ever hold fast to those moral laws of the Lord which do not change. IBID.

We believe that the Constitution of the United States was

divinely inspired, that it was produced by "wise men" whom God raised up for this "very purpose," and that the principles embodied in the Constitution are so fundamental and important that, if possible, they should be extended "for the rights and protection" of all mankind. "DEAR BRETHREN," DEC. 15, 1969

It is a part of our "Mormon" theology that the Constitution of the United States was divinely inspired; that our Republic came into existence through wise men raised up for that very purpose. We believe it is the duty of the members of the Church to see that this Republic is not subverted either by any sudden or constant erosion of those principles which gave this nation its birth. DAVID O. MCKAY TO ERNEST L. WILKINSON, MAY 25, 1967, IN *BYU YEARS*, 4:544-45

All Latter-day Saints, whatever their nativity, are taught by their leaders and by their sacred books to revere the Constitution of the United States as a divinely inspired instrument, which they and the friends of freedom everywhere are under obligation to maintain and defend, in order to perpetuate the principles upon which the Republic was founded. *DESERET NEWS*, NOV. 4, 1911, IN *MESSAGES*, 4:231-51

We have rights under the Constitution, and however much these may be denied to us, it is still our bounden duty to contend for them, not only in behalf of ourselves, but for all our fellow citizens and for our posterity, and for humanity generally throughout the world. Were we to do less than this, we would fail in performing the mission assigned to us, and be recreant to the high trust which God has reposed in us. STATEMENT, MAY 26, 1885, IN *MESSAGES*, 3:13-17

[T]he Constitution of the United States is a glorious standard; it is founded in the wisdom of God. It is a heavenly banner; it is to all those who are privileged with the sweets of its liberty, like the cooling shades and refreshing waters of a great rock in a thirsty and weary land. It is like a great tree under whose branches men from every clime can be shielded from the burning rays of the sun. STATEMENT, MARCH 25, 1839, IN *MESSAGES*, 1:88-104

conversion

Joining the Church is a serious thing. Each convert takes upon himself or herself the name of Christ with an implied promise to keep His commandments. But coming into the Church can be a perilous experience. Unless there are warm and strong hands to greet you, unless we reach out to you with love and concern, you may begin to wonder about the step you have taken. Unless there are friendly hands and welcome hearts to greet you and lead you along the way, you may drop by the side. We have the challenge of helping you to strengthen your testimony of the truth of this work. We cannot have you walking in the front door and out the back! Every one of you is precious. Every one of you is a son or daughter of God. GORDON B. HINCKLEY, "FIRST PRESIDENCY MESSAGE," *ENSIGN*, OCT. 2006

To be able to receive the blessing of eternal life, we need to be "spiritually minded" and conquer our unrighteous desires. We need to change. More accurately, we need to be *changed,* or converted, through the power of the Savior's Atonement and through the power of the Holy Ghost. This process is called conversion.

Conversion includes a change in behavior, but it goes beyond behavior; it is a change in our very nature. It is such a significant change that the Lord and His prophets refer to it as a rebirth, a change of heart, and a baptism of fire. *TRUE TO FAITH*, 2004

By learning of Him, by believing in Him, by following Him, there is a capacity to become like Him. The countenance can change; the heart can be softened; the step can be quickened; the outlook enhanced. Life becomes what it should become. Change is at times imperceptible, but it does take place. THOMAS S. MONSON, "FIRST PRESIDENCY MESSAGE," *ENSIGN*, JAN. 2003

Make a special effort to reach out to new converts and to those who are less active. Help them feel welcome among your group of friends. You can strengthen them by sharing your testimony and by setting a good example. *STRENGTH OF YOUTH*, 2001

To be born again means that we must exercise a faith that does not waver and is not easily distracted. JAMES E. FAUST, "FIRST PRESIDENCY MESSAGE," *ENSIGN*, JUNE 1998

Conversion is a lifelong process that includes:

Having faith in Jesus Christ and exercising faith unto repentance.

Receiving the saving ordinances of the gospel, including temple ordinances and partaking of the sacrament weekly to renew baptismal covenants.

Praying daily and studying the gospel of Jesus Christ in the scriptures and the teachings of latter-day prophets.

Obeying God's commandments, such as the laws of chastity, tithing, and honesty, and following the counsel of Church leaders.

Loving God and loving and serving others with "the pure love of Christ" (Moro. 7:47).

Strengthening the family by praying together, studying the scriptures together, and loving and caring for one another.

Attending Church meetings and serving in Church callings and assignments.

Sharing the gospel with friends and relatives.

Identifying and submitting deceased ancestors' names for temple ordinances and doing temple work as often as circumstances allow. *CHURCH HANDBOOK* 2, 1998

Individuals remain converted to the gospel when they acquire a testimony of new truths in a spiritual conversion and make the social transition to new friends and new patterns of life. IBID.

Every new member needs three things–a friend, a responsibility, and spiritual nourishment through gospel study. All members are responsible to fellowship those who are new and to help them feel the strength of the gospel. Each new member should feel the influence of loving and caring friends within the Church. The personal influence of Church members is one of the most powerful factors in helping new members achieve an enduring conversion and continued activity in the Church. *ENSIGN*, AUG. 1997

A person will never be truly on the road to conversion until he has at least a beginning witness that Joseph Smith was a prophet of God and that the Book of Mormon is another testament of Christ. Further, members of this Church must accept, and its missionaries must teach, some absolutes. These absolutes are:

1. That Jesus is the Christ, the Savior and the Redeemer of all mankind through His Atonement.
2. That through Joseph Smith, a prophet of God, the gospel of Jesus Christ was restored in its fullness.
3. That the Book of Mormon is another testament of Christ.
4. That all of the Presidents of the Church since Joseph Smith have successively possessed the keys and authority which was restored through Joseph Smith.
5. That Gordon B. Hinckley is the prophet, seer, and revela-

tor to the world at this time. JAMES E. FAUST, "FIRST PRESIDENCY MESSAGE," *ENSIGN*, JAN. 1996

Converts are those who have been taught and have accepted the restored gospel of Jesus Christ. They are those into whose hearts has come a new faith and into whose minds has come a new understanding. They are those into whose lives has come a new desire to live up to higher standards of behavior. They are those who have come to know a new happiness and an enlarged circle of friends. They are those whose sights have been raised to a new understanding of the eternal purposes of God. Converts are tremendously important because they are men, women, and children who have repented of past ways and adopted new patterns of living. GORDON B. HINCKLEY, "FIRST PRESIDENCY MESSAGE," *ENSIGN*, DEC. 1986

Our responsibility as brothers and sisters in the Church is to help those who may be lost to find their way, and to help those who have lost that which is precious to find their treasure again. The scriptures clearly teach us that every member has the obligation to strengthen his fellow members. SPENCER W. KIMBALL, "FIRST PRESIDENCY MESSAGE," *ENSIGN*, JUNE 1983

[W]e should gain a knowledge of the plan of salvation and a realization that it is the only way to peace and happiness in this world and eternal life in the world to come. We should make a total commitment to, above everything else, convey by word and deed our knowledge and testimony to our fellowmen, that they may receive and rejoice in it.

Through studying the scriptures, we should know what the Lord has revealed through His prophets concerning the plan of salvation. From regular night and morning prayer and honest compliance with gospel teachings, we should enjoy the peace and spirit of the gospel. By earnestly and specifically seeking it, we should, by the power of the Holy Ghost, obtain and retain a testimony of its divine truth. We should be so converted and dedicated to it that our total lives are influenced thereby. The right and wrong of our decisions and actions should be consistently determined by its light. If they were, we would make no mistakes in our judgments and actions on the vexing questions and problems of our day. MARION G. ROMNEY, "FIRST PRESIDENCY MESSAGE," *ENSIGN*, MAR. 1983

Our role as missionaries is not primarily to *convince* people of the truthfulness of the gospel. If the Lord were primarily interested in *convincing* people of the divine nature of this work, He could, and perhaps would, demonstrate His powers in such a way that large numbers of people could know the truth in a relatively brief period of time. He could speak if He chose, and all the people on Earth could hear in their own language. Or He could emblazon His words in the sky, where all could read or see them. But if those persons thus convinced did not really change their lives for the better, repent of their sins, and turn to Him in righteousness, they would be worse off than before and would be more insensitive to the whisperings of the Holy Spirit.

No, the Lord is not primarily interested in having His children only *convinced* of His work. He would like them to be *converted* to the gospel. Truly converted persons change their old sinful ways and turn to a new life in Christ; there is truly a "converting" or a changing in their lives. SPENCER W. KIMBALL, "FIRST PRESIDENCY MESSAGE," *ENSIGN*, OCT. 1977

The Church will always be a church filled with converts. Whether the place be Salt Lake City, or Sao Paulo, Los Angeles or London, Tokyo or Turino, Italy, it is the Lord's plan that there be converts among us, brothers and sisters newly brought into the fold of Christ through the efforts of their loving friends and neighbors. Let us fellowship and love each other in the true spirit of the gospel. SPENCER W. KIMBALL, "FIRST PRESIDENCY MESSAGE," *ENSIGN*, SEPT. 1975

Experience has taught us that we lose some new members who get discouraged before their roots are set and when special attention is not given them. *STAKE MISSIONS HANDBOOK*, 1960

There are many places in the organizations where even new members could serve almost immediately, such as in the choir, as ushers, in welfare, on committees, as secretaries, and a little later as counselors, assistants, and in not too long a time even in leadership positions as their experience, judgment and ability, and worthiness justify. IBID.

[T]he welcome of new members should be instant, spontaneous, and genuine. All the converts must be made to feel that they have come into a brotherhood and sisterhood which is warm and real. When converts join the Church they often give up their former associates and turn to the Church for companionship and direction. The bishopric, the branch officers, the ward teachers, the quorum officers, all the auxiliary leaders, and neighbors particularly should at the very first opportunity extend the hand of fellowship. Few things can be more discouraging than a cold reception in the Church, which has been represented to the converts as being founded upon the exalted concept that all belong to one family in the fatherhood of God and the brotherhood of man. "DEAR BRETHREN," MARCH 15, 1956

[I]t frequently happens that when some man or woman, unusual or outstanding because of achievement or creed or color, joins the Church and brings with him a burning, eloquent testimony, with faith-promoting experiences, we joy so much in hearing of his conversion that we impose upon him by repeatedly asking him, now in one ward or organization, now in another, to relate and re-relate it to us. But experience over the years, even from the foundation of the Church, shows that too frequently we injure rather than benefit the new convert by this course. Sometimes these converts get a distorted view of their relationships to other members and their importance and value in the service of the Lord. The wiser course, as repeatedly proved, is to permit the new convert to have time to orient himself in the doctrines and activities of the Church, by a humble participation with us in the glories thereof, and when this is done we not only allow time for the convert to solidify himself in his new-found truth, but to bear thereafter a testimony that is strengthened and ripened. Give the new convert a full opportunity to grow steadily and naturally without exploitation, that he may hold fast to the end. Too much attention and commendation frequently have a tendency to dull the edge of the faith and works that carry us to the exaltation we all seek. "DEAR BRETHREN," JUNE 30, 1952

The elders should not be discouraged. They should constantly bear in mind that none cometh unto the Son except the Father draweth them; and that therefore if people cannot receive the Spirit of the Father, they cannot receive the doctrines of His Son, and as a consequence cannot be made partakers with us of the heavenly word. LORENZO SNOW TO FRANCIS M. LYMAN, AUG. 10, 1901

Inasmuch as we claim to be Saints of the Most High God, our every act must conform to our professions under all circumstances. JOHN TAYLOR TO WILLIAM BUDGE, JULY 28, 1879

In our intercourse with the world we find that we have more to do with the poor and those of low estate, and we might say of low worldly esteem, than those of any other class. This only affords another of those strong testimonies of the

Lord Jesus in behalf of this being His people, His Church, His kingdom. Truly, "the poor ye have always with you" [Matt. 26:11], and it behooveth us to learn them how to live, how to combine their elements, that they also by their own exertions may draw support from Nature's great storehouse, which is ample for all. *MILLENNIAL STAR*, APR. 18, 1857, IN *MESSAGES*, 2:192-211

The gospel of salvation now as anciently finds more ready access to the poor than the rich, forcibly illustrating and confirming the truthfulness of the remark of our Savior, "how hardly shall they that have riches enter into the kingdom of God" [Mark 10:23]. The poor, down-trodden oppressed of ages, whom the aristocratical lordlings have for centuries continually crushed with the iron heel of despotism, feel, when the light of truth and salvation penetrates their minds, a new impulse to try again, to redeem themselves and their posterity from the thraldom of ignorance, wickedness, error, superstition, and tyranny which so long enchained them and their fathers. They are inspired by an all-absorbing desire to rise above and throw off the filth and abominations, mystery, corruption, and worse than Egyptian darkness [or] wicked Babylon, and bask in the sunlight of pure principles emanating from Heaven's King; to rejoice with the Saints in Zion, and become co-workers in that cause which, having redeemed them, may enable them to contribute a share in the redemption of others who are still in the bonds of iniquity and gall of bitterness. IBID.

creation (temporal and spiritual)

You are a spirit child of God, and your body is created in His image. *TRUE TO FAITH*, 2004

As a beneficiary of all the beauties of creation, you can care for the earth and help preserve it for future generations. IBID.

We are all children of God, and there is something of His

divinity within each of us. We are more than a son or daughter of Mr. and Mrs. So-and-So who reside in such-and-such a place. We are of the family of God, with such a tremendous potential for excellence. GORDON B. HINCKLEY, "FIRST PRESIDENCY MESSAGE," *ENSIGN*, SEPT. 1999

God left the world unfinished for man to work his skill upon. He left the electricity in the cloud, the oil in the earth. He left the rivers unbridged and the forests unfelled and the cities unbuilt. God gives to man the challenge of raw materials, not the ease of finished things. He leaves the pictures unpainted and the music unsung and the problems unsolved, that man might know the joys and glories of creation. THOMAS S. MONSON, "FIRST PRESIDENCY MESSAGE," *ENSIGN*, MARCH 1988

There is a mighty strength that comes of the knowledge that you and I are sons and daughters of God. Within us is something of divinity. One who has this knowledge and permits it to influence his life will not stoop to do a mean or cheap or tawdry thing. GORDON B. HINCKLEY, "FIRST PRESIDENCY MESSAGE," *ENSIGN*, OCT. 1984

Men are eternal beings, spirit children of God. They were born to Him in the spirit world. There they dwelt with Him before the earth was. Their destiny is to continue to live on eternally after mortal death. MARION G. ROMNEY, "FIRST PRESIDENCY MESSAGE," *ENSIGN*, FEB. 1977

[M]an—YOU—is the greatest of all God's creations, and everything was created for him, over which he will have full dominion. He is blessed with the ability to think, to know good from evil, and a spirit by which he can communicate with God, and a physical body with which he is able to do the daily things he wants to do. N. ELDON TANNER, "FIRST PRESIDENCY MESSAGE," *ENSIGN*, FEB. 1976

We are all the spirit children of God; we are His supreme creation; the earth and all that pertains to it is for the growth, development, and satisfaction of all mankind. SPENCER W. KIMBALL, "FIRST PRESIDENCY'S MESSAGE," *ENSIGN,* OCT. 1975

This earth was organized so that each man could obtain a body of flesh and bones with the power of procreation. Each resurrected person will have his body forever.

Men come on earth to gain experience and to be tested.

Men are that they might have joy. Eternal happiness is the object and design of man's existence.

All things on the earth have a purpose in their creation. "BASIC DOCTRINES," 1971

[W]e know of no justification for claiming that "man was placed on the earth on the seventh day." FIRST PRESIDENCY TO WILLIAM E. BERRETT, DEC. 9, 1969

The earth was created spiritually before the temporal creation. Man himself is the spirit child of God, whose destiny is to return to the presence of the Lord whence he came. *DESERET NEWS*, DEC. 12, 1956

The Church of Jesus Christ of Latter-day Saints, basing its belief on divine revelation, ancient and modern, proclaims man to be the direct and lineal offspring of Deity. By His almighty power, God organized the earth and all that it contains, from spirit and element, which exist co-eternally with Himself. *DESERET NEWS*, JULY 18, 1925, QUOTING *IMPROVEMENT ERA*, NOV. 1909

God created the earth as an organized sphere; but He certainly did not create, in the sense of bringing into primal existence, the ultimate elements of the materials of which the earth consists, for "the elements are eternal" (D&C 93:33). *IMPROVEMENT ERA*, AUG. 1916, IN *MESSAGES*, 5:26-34

The creation was two-fold, firstly spiritual, secondly temporal. *IMPROVEMENT ERA*, NOV. 1909, IN *MESSAGES*, 4:200-06

[I]f God made man–the first man–in His own image and likeness, He must have made him like unto Christ, and consequently like unto men of Christ's time and of the present day. IBID.

cremation

Normally, cremation is not encouraged. However, in some countries the law requires it. The family of the deceased must decide whether to cremate the body, taking into account any laws governing burial or cremation. Where possible, the body of the deceased member who has been endowed should be dressed in temple clothing when the body is cremated ... A funeral service may be held. *CHURCH HANDBOOK*, 1998

The Church has never encouraged cremation as a method of disposing of the remains of the dead. It believes it is proper to consign them to mother earth, which has always been the custom. Although cremation is discouraged, the local laws must be observed and the final decision left with the family and the loved ones. "ATTITUDES," 1974

Cremation is discouraged. Wherever possible the dead should be consigned to the earth and nothing should be done that is destructive of the body; that should be left to nature. If bodies are to be cremated, funeral services are to be held in the usual way, but the disposition of the ashes usually makes unnecessary the offering of graveside or dedicatory prayers. Temple garments and robes should be removed before the body is cremated. *CHURCH HANDBOOK*, 1963

[T]he Church has never encouraged cremation as a proper method of disposing of the remains of the dead. We believe it proper to consign them to mother earth—that has always been the custom. We suppose that perhaps in the ultimate results it makes little difference what disposition is made of the bodies of those who die. The practice of the Latter-day Saints has been to adhere to the policy that the bodies of those who die be buried in the earth. JOSEPH ANDERSON, SECRETARY TO THE FIRST PRESIDENCY, TO LAWRENCE F. MOORE, OCT. 25, 1935

The Church has never expressed itself officially on the question of cremation, perhaps for the reason that the idea of deviating from the time honored custom of burying our dead in the earth has never appealed to any of its General Authorities, and we may add that we hardly think it ever will. FIRST PRESIDENCY TO HYRUM W. VALENTINE, MAR. 18, 1916

D

death. *See also* **resurrection**

It may be harder for our rising generation to be faithful, perhaps in some ways even more challenging than pulling a handcart across the plains. When someone died in the wilderness of frontier America, that person's physical remains were buried and the handcarts continued west, but the mourning survivors had hope for their loved one's eternal soul. However, when someone dies spiritually in the wilderness of sin, hope may be replaced by dread and fear for the loved one's eternal welfare. JAMES E. FAUST, "FIRST PRESIDENCY MESSAGE," *ENSIGN,* JUNE 2006

Death does not change our personality or our desires for good or evil. Those who chose to obey God in this life live in a state of happiness, peace, and rest from troubles and care. Those who chose not to obey in this life and did not repent live in a state of unhappiness. *PREACH MY GOSPEL,* 2005

Frequently, death comes as an intruder. It is an enemy that suddenly appears in the midst of life's feast, putting out its lights and its gaiety. Death lays its heavy hand upon those dear to us and, at times, leaves us baffled and wondering. In certain situations, as in great suffering and illness, death comes as an angel of mercy. But to those bereaved, the Master's promise of peace is the comforting balm which heals: "Peace I leave with you, my peace I give unto you: not as the world giveth, give I unto you. Let not your heart be troubled, neither let it be afraid" (John 14:27). "I go to prepare a place for you ... ; that where I am, there ye may be also" (14:2-3). THOMAS S. MONSON, "FIRST PRESIDENCY MESSAGE," *ENSIGN*, MAR. 2004

This life is a part of eternity. This is one stage of our eternal lives. When we die, we will go on to purposeful, active, challenging living. The life on the other side of the veil will be somewhat like the life here. If we have been clean and decent and good here, we will go on in that same spirit. If we have been rascals, we will go in that same spirit. GORDON B. HINCKLEY, "FIRST PRESIDENCY MESSAGE," *ENSIGN*, APR. 2002

All of us will die. But that will not be the end. Just as He in the spirit world taught those who were capable of being taught, even so shall each of us continue as individual personalities capable of learning and teaching and other activities.

And just as He took up His body and came forth from the tomb, even so shall all of us enjoy a reunion of body and spirit to become living souls in the day of our own resurrection. GORDON B. HINCKLEY, "FIRST PRESIDENCY MESSAGE," *ENSIGN*, APR. 1997

Even before the fall of Adam, which ushered death in this world, our Heavenly Father had prepared a place for the spirits who would eventually depart this mortal life. At the time of Jesus' death, the spirit world was occupied by hosts of our Father's children who had died–from Adam's posterity to the death of Jesus–both the righteous and the wicked.

There were two grand divisions in the world of spirits. Spirits of the righteous (the just) had gone to paradise, a state of happiness, peace, and restful work. The spirits of the wicked (the unjust) had gone to prison, a state of darkness and misery (see Alma 40:12-15). Jesus went only to the righteous– to paradise. EZRA TAFT BENSON, "FIRST PRESIDENCY MESSAGE," *ENSIGN*, APR. 1993

Death comes to all mankind. It comes to the aged as they walk on faltering feet. Its summons is heard by those who have scarcely reached midway in life's journey, and often it hushes the laughter of little children. Death is one tragic fact that no one can escape or deny. THOMAS S. MONSON, "FIRST PRESIDENCY MESSAGE," *ENSIGN,* FEB. 1993

Life is eternal. We are eternal beings. We lived as intelligent spirits before this mortal life. We are now living part of eternity. Our mortal birth was not the beginning. Death, which faces all of us, is not the end. EZRA TAFT BENSON, "FIRST PRESIDENCY MESSAGE," *ENSIGN,* AUG. 1991

The spirit world is not far away. Sometimes the veil between this life and the life beyond becomes very thin. Our loved ones who have passed on are not far from us. IBID.

In being born into this world as human souls, our spirits–which are the offspring of God–enter into our bodies, which are the offspring of our mortal parents; at death the spirit and the body are separated. That's all death is, a separation of the spirit and the body. The body returns in time to the dust or earth matter, and the spirit goes to the spirit world.

When we are resurrected, the spirit reenters the body, and each of us will become a soul again, our spirit and body never again to be separated. "And the resurrection from the dead is the redemption of the soul" (D&C 88:16). MARION G. ROMNEY, "FIRST PRESIDENCY MESSAGE," *ENSIGN,* SEPT. 1984

Death is the separation of the eternal spirit and the mortal body. Although the physical body dies, the spirit is immortal and lives on. Death is as necessary as birth in order for man to progress. *PRINCIPLES,* 1976

Although at death man leaves behind his earthly possessions and loved ones, he takes with him through the eternities his knowledge, character, priesthood, and other spiritual attainments (see D&C 131:18-19). And if he is worthy of exaltation, he will be reunited with his family as well. Death is just another necessary step toward exaltation. IBID.

Paradise is that part of the spirit world where the spirits of the righteous dwell while awaiting their resurrection. IBID.

Spiritual death means to be separated from the presence of the Lord, to die as to things of righteousness, to die as to the things of the Spirit. IBID.

Those who die without hearing the gospel in this life have the opportunity to hear the gospel in the postmortal spirit world and thus become potential heirs of salvation and exaltation. "BASIC DOCTRINES," 1971

We further testify that the Father, who lets no sparrow fall to the ground unnoticed, guards and protects those who live righteously in Him, and that we shall "Fear not them which kill the body, but are not able to kill the soul but rather fear him which is able to destroy both soul and body in hell" (Matt. 10:28). *BRIEF STATEMENT*, 1943

[W]hen the spirits of mankind leave their bodies ... they all go to the world of spirits, the good to dwell with the good, the wicked with the wicked. The part of that spirit world where the just dwell is called Paradise, the other part of that sphere is variously called Gehenna, Sheole, Hades, or Hell. The "burning in hell" of "lake of fire and brimstone" is figurative, denoting the sufferings of the willfully corrupt and intentionally rebellious, and "Abraham's bosom," the "sweet rest in heaven," or "rest from their labors" denoting the peace, deliverance from sorrow and the powers of darkness that come to the righteous. This is a degree of temporary retribution, and briefly explains the condition of the departed until the resurrection, when all are to be "judged according to their works" so as to receive that degree of glory to which they will be entitled in the future, as Paul partly explained (1 Cor. 15:41-44), and more fully in the Doctrine and Covenants 76 ... [W]hen the thief on the cross repented and departed this life, he accompanied Jesus to paradise, but Jesus bridged over the "great gulf" that divided the two divisions of the spirit world, and "went and preached to the spirits in prison, who were disobedient in the days of Noah," and afterwards "led captivity captive" (1 Pet. 3:18-22) [Eph. 4:8]. FIRST PRESIDENCY TO D. W. DILLINGHAM, JULY 29, 1918

debt

Many people do not believe that serious recession will ever come again. Feeling secure in their expectations of continuing employment and a steady flow of wages and salaries, they obligate their future income without thought of what they would do if they should lose their jobs or if their incomes were stopped for some other reason. But the best authorities have repeatedly said that we are not yet smart enough to control our economy without downward adjustments. Sooner or later these adjustments will come. EZRA TAFT BENSON, "FIRST PRESIDENCY MESSAGE," *ENSIGN,* JUNE 1987

There may never be a more favorable time than now for most people to get their financial house in order so far as debt is concerned. Yes, let us live within our income. Let us pay as we go. Let us "pay thy debt, and live! [2 Kgs. 4:1-7]." IBID.

The key to spending less than we earn is simple–it is called discipline. Whether early in life or late, we must all eventually learn to discipline ourselves, our appetites, and our economic desires. How blessed is he who learns to spend less than he earns and puts something away for a rainy day. N. ELDON TANNER, "FIRST PRESIDENCY MESSAGE," *ENSIGN*, JUNE 1982

One of the most common forms of indebtedness today is installment buying. Not only does installment buying tie up future earnings and increase the price of the item, even more important is the fact that it often causes people to become entangled in the material things of this world; they become dissatisfied with what they have and covet greater material possessions, to the exclusion of spiritual concerns. Indebtedness destroys peace of mind, endangers family relationships, and can weaken spirituality, because when we are in debt we are literally in bondage (see D&C 19:35). *PRINCIPLES,* 1976

The members of the Church would be wise to go into debt only for absolute necessities, to pay for all else at the time of purchase, and to save constantly both to escape past debt and to avoid future debt. IBID.

[I]n gathering funds for Church purposes, individual members [should] be encouraged to contribute on a voluntary basis what they feel they can afford and specify the time in which they are able to do it. Over the years the Church Authorities have advised the people to avoid debt. It would be inconsistent to encourage them to borrow money in order to pay Church assessments. "DEAR BRETHREN," DEC. 20, 1965

We know how strong is the temptation to the ordinary man, when times are good and money easy to obtain, to make unnecessary expenditures, often on borrowed capital, which, in too many instances, means the mortgaging of the home, and too frequently ends in its loss. Could our voices be heard throughout the regions where the Latter-day Saints most largely dwell, they would be raised in protest against this practice of endangering our hold on the roof that covers those who rightly look to us for care and protection—our wives and children. We can conceive of but few conditions where such would be permissible, much less commendable. In flush times like the present, our advice is: Get out of debt, and then keep out. *DESERET NEWS*, DEC. 17, 1904, IN *MESSAGES*, 4:92-98

[S]hun debt. Be content with moderate gains, and be not misled by illusory hopes of acquiring wealth. STATEMENT, OCT. 10, 1887, IN *MESSAGES,* 3:133-55

devil, *see* Satan

diaries/journals, *see* history

disfellowshipment. *See also* Church discipline

A person who is disfellowshipped is still a member of the Church but is no longer in good standing. Disfellowshipment is a severe action that may be adequate for all but the most serious transgressions.

A person who is disfellowshipped may not hold a temple recommend, serve in a Church position, or exercise the priesthood in any way. He should be encouraged to attend public Church meetings if his conduct is orderly, but he may not give a talk, offer a public prayer, partake of the sacrament, or participate in the sustaining of Church officers. *CHURCH HANDBOOK,* 1998

One is not left in disfellowshipment indefinitely. If he repents, he is brought back into full fellowship. If he does not repent, he may be excommunicated. *CHURCH HANDBOOK,* 1976

By definition disfellowshipment is a probationary state. "DEAR BRETHREN," MAY 7, 1973

divorce

The Church has always looked with disfavor upon divorce, and has discouraged it strongly. *CHURCH HANDBOOK*, 1960

To a people who believe, as we do, that true marriage was divinely instituted for the multiplication of mankind, and is not a union for time alone, but reaches into the eternities, the disruption of families by divorce is an evil of no ordinary character, not only bearing a harvest of sorrow and suffering in this life, but also having a far-reaching influence into the world beyond the grave, and possibly involving others in ruin who had no voice in the separation or power to avert its occurrence. STATEMENT, OCT. 10, 1886, IN *MESSAGES,* 3:72-91

doctrine

These four great God-given gifts are the unshakable cornerstones which anchor The Church of Jesus Christ of Latter-day Saints, as well as the individual testimonies and convictions of its members: (1) the reality and the divinity of the Lord Jesus Christ as the Son of God; (2) the sublime vision given the Prophet Joseph Smith of the Father and the Son, ushering in the dispensation of the fullness of times; (3) the Book of Mormon as the word of the God speaking in declaration of the divinity of the Savior; and (4) the priesthood of God divinely conferred to be exercised in righteousness for the blessing of our Father's children. GORDON B. HINCKLEY, "FIRST PRESIDENCY MESSAGE," *ENSIGN,* FEB. 2004

Who is to declare the doctrine? It is well established by revelation and practice that the current president of the Church and his counselors have the keys to declare the doctrine. The investiture of this authority comes from revelation. JAMES E. FAUST, "FIRST PRESIDENCY MESSAGE," *ENSIGN,* JULY 2000

There are four absolutes about which it is always appropriate for us to testify:

The first is that Jesus is the Christ, the Savior, the Mediator and Redeemer of the world.

The second is that Joseph Smith was a prophet of God and reestablished the Church of Christ upon the earth with its keys and authority.

The third is that all of the Presidents of the Church since Joseph Smith have been successors in that power and authority.

The fourth is that President Gordon B. Hinckley is the only prophet of God upon the earth, holding all of the keys, powers, and authorities of the Church in the earth today. JAMES E. FAUST, "FIRST PRESIDENCY MESSAGE," *ENSIGN,* MAR. 1997

We [First Presidency and Quorum of the Twelve] have the responsibility to preserve the doctrinal purity of the Church. We are united in this objective. *CHURCH NEWS,* OCT. 23, 1993

[F]ormal statements by the First Presidency are the definitive source of official Church positions. "EVOLUTION AND ORIGIN," 1992

At a meeting of the Council of the First Presidency and Quorum of the Twelve held on Thursday, March 17, 1983, it was decided that hereafter when a General Authority writes a book for publication, the preface of the book should contain a statement embodying the points or concepts contained in the following statement:

"The author wishes to make it clear that the opinions and views expressed in this publication are those for which he and he alone is responsible. This is not a Church publication and has not been written under assignment of or at the request of the First Presidency or the Quorum of the Twelve Apostles.

"Therefore, the views expressed in this book do not represent the official position of The Church of Jesus Christ of Latter-day Saints."

It is expected that the author will phrase the statement in the preface in his own language, but such a statement should, as indicated, embody all of the elements contained in the above quoted statement. FIRST PRESIDENCY TO ALL GENERAL AUTHORITIES, MAR. 22, 1983

The Lord has declared that we must always be on our guard against false teachings which destroy faith and lead the Church members into forbidden paths. It is particularly the obligation of those in positions of authority to be constantly watchful to see to it that men and women preaching false doctrines or belonging to groups or cults that teach and practice false principles will find no opportunity to spread their errors in the gatherings of our people. "DEAR BRETHREN," FEB. 22, 1972

The revelations of the Lord as set forth in the standard works constitute the law and the doctrine of the Church. *CHURCH HANDBOOK,* 1960

Our doctrines are open to the world. They are not secret or clothed in mystery. We proclaim the pure gospel of Christ as revealed from heaven in these last days through the great prophet of the nineteenth century, Joseph Smith. We invite all mankind to look into our teachings and promise all who obey them a witness of their truth by the power of the Holy Ghost, which makes men free indeed. *IMPROVEMENT ERA,* JUNE 1911, IN *MESSAGES,* 4:224-29

The theology of our Church is the theology taught by Jesus Christ and his apostles, the theology of scripture and reason. *IMPROVEMENT ERA,* MAY 1907, IN *MESSAGES,* 4:143-55

We refuse to be bound by the interpretations which others place upon our beliefs, or by what they allege must be the practical consequences of our doctrines. Men have no right to impute to us what they think may be the logical deduction from our beliefs, but which we ourselves do not accept. IBID.

[T]he theories, speculations, and opinions of men, however intelligent, ingenious, and plausible, are not necessarily doctrines of the Church or principles that God has commanded His servants to preach. No doctrine is a doctrine of this Church until it has been accepted as such by the Church, and not even a revelation from God should be taught to His people until it has first been approved by the presiding authority—the one through whom the Lord makes known His will for the guidance of the Saints as a religious body. The spirit of revelation may rest upon anyone, and teach him or her many things for personal comfort and instruction. But these are not doctrines of the Church, and however true, they must not be inculcated until proper permission is given. JOSEPH F. SMITH TO LILLIE GOLSAN, JULY 16, 1902

The nature of the work of the Lord, the spirit and genius of his Church, founded upon the rock of his revealed word, compels us to admonish the brethren to have great care, lest in giving expression to their private opinions they advance theories opposed to the revealed word and will of the Lord. In this is no man justified. No man is authorized to teach to the Church new or advanced doctrines except the presidency thereof. Light comes from the head, and to that point must the members of the Church look for knowledge and wisdom and doctrine and principle. *MILLENNIAL STAR,* APR. 15, 1878, IN *MESSAGES,* 2:311-13

It ought to have been known, years ago, by every person in the Church—for ample teachings have been given on the point—that no member of the Church has the right to publish any doctrines, as the doctrines of The Church of Jesus Christ of Latter-day Saints, without first submitting them for examination and approval to the First Presidency and the Twelve. There is but one man upon the earth, at one time, who holds the keys to receive commandments and revelations for the Church, and who has the authority to write doctrines by way of commandment unto the Church. And any man who so far forgets the order instituted by the Lord as to write and publish what may be termed new doctrines, without consulting with the First Presidency of the Church respecting them, places himself in a false position, and exposes himself to the power of darkness by violating his priesthood. *MILLENNIAL STAR*, OCT. 21, 1865, IN *MESSAGES,* 2:229-35

[I]f men believe a system, and profess that it was given by inspiration, certainly the more intelligibly they can present it, the better." STATEMENT, FEB. 17, 1835, IN *MESSAGES,* 1:47-48

dress and grooming

Prophets have always counseled us to dress modestly. This counsel is founded on the truth that the human body is God's sacred creation. Respect your body as a gift from God. Through your dress and appearance, you can show the Lord that you know how precious your body is.

Your clothing expresses who you are. It sends messages about you, and it influences the way you and others act. When you are well groomed and modestly dressed, you can invite the companionship of the Spirit and exercise a good influence on those around you. *TRUE TO FAITH,* 2004

How truly beautiful is a well-groomed young woman who is clean in body and mind. She is a daughter of God in whom her Eternal Father can take pride. How handsome is a young man who is well groomed. He is a son of God, deemed worthy of holding the holy priesthood of God. He does not need tattoos or earrings on or in his body. The First Presidency and the Quorum of the Twelve are all united in counseling against these things. GORDON B. HINCKLEY, "FIRST PRESIDENCY MESSAGE," *ENSIGN*, JAN. 2001

Prophets of God have always counseled His children to dress modestly. The way you dress is a reflection of what you are on the inside. Your dress and grooming send messages about you to others and influence the way you and others act. When you are well groomed and modestly dressed, you invite the companionship of the Spirit and can exercise a good influence on those around you. *STRENGTH OF YOUTH,* 2001

Worthy young men should not be denied a temple recommend because their hair is too long. Good grooming should be encouraged through love, kindness, persuasion, and understanding. Rigid rules must not be established that would prohibit those in this category from participation in sacred priesthood ordinances including ordinances of the temple. However, they should be counseled to keep their hair clean and presentable. *CHURCH HANDBOOK,* 1976

In itself, the wearing of long hair by men is not a sin. We feel, however, that those who prefer to have long hair and beards should keep themselves well groomed and conduct their lives in an irreproachable manner. FIRST PRESIDENCY TO TED E. MADSEN, JAN. 25, 1972

The Church has not attempted to indicate just how long women's or girls' dresses should be nor whether they should wear pant suits or other types of clothing. We have always counseled our members to be modest in their dress, maintaining such standards in connection therewith as would not be embarrassing to themselves and to their relatives, friends, and associates. "DEAR BRETHREN," APR. 12, 1971

It is difficult to make an over-all statement concerning

modest standards of dress because modesty cannot be determined by inches or fit, since that which looks modest on one person may not be so on another. *STRENGTH OF YOUTH*, 1968

The teachings of the Church of Jesus Christ set forth the fact that the human body is the temple of the spirit and should be kept sacred and not displayed to the public gaze, and particularly before those whose moral purpose may be questioned. HEBER J. GRANT TO BEN W. INFANGER, MAR. 30, 1935

Immodesty in dress should be frowned down by parents and all decent people. The shameless exhibitions of the human form purposely presented in modern styles of dress, or rather undress, are indications of that sensuous and debasing tendency toward moral laxity and social corruption which have hurried nations into irretrievable ruin. *DESERET NEWS*, DEC. 21, 1912, IN *MESSAGES*, 4:277-82

drugs, ***see*** **Word of Wisdom**

E

Easter, *see* resurrection

education

While the Church strongly encourages education, Church facilities are dedicated for the purpose of worship, religious instruction, and other Church-related activities. Church meetinghouses should not be used as home school or day care facilities, or for hosting home school activities. "DEAR BRETHREN," APR. 19, 2005

Study is an act of faith requiring the use of personal agency. *PREACH MY GOSPEL,* 2005

The Lord wants you to educate your minds and hands, whatever your chosen field. Whether it be repairing refrigerators, or the work of a skilled surgeon, you must train yourselves. Seek for the best schooling available. Become a workman of integrity in the world that lies ahead of you. GORDON B. HINCKLEY, "FIRST PRESIDENCY MESSAGE," *ENSIGN,* JAN. 2001

Be willing to work diligently and make sacrifices to obtain learning. Education is an investment that brings great rewards. *STRENGTH OF YOUTH,* 2001

The Church is neutral regarding home schooling. The manner of education of children is considered to be the parents' decision. "CLARIFICATION OF LDS CHURCH EDUCATIONAL SYSTEM SEMINARY POLICIES ON HOME SCHOOLS," NOV. 16, 2000

The Church has always had a vital interest in public education and encourages its members to participate in parent-teacher activities and other events designed to improve the education of our youth. THOMAS S. MONSON, "FIRST PRESIDENCY MESSAGE," *ENSIGN*, JUNE 2000

The Lord has said very plainly that His people are to gain knowledge of countries and kingdoms and of things of the world through the process of education, even by study and by faith. Education is the key which will unlock the door of opportunity for you. It is worth sacrificing for. It is worth working at, and if you educate your mind and your hands, you will be able to make a great contribution to the society of which you are a part, and you will be able to reflect honorably on the Church of which you are a member. GORDON B. HINCKLEY, "FIRST PRESIDENCY MESSAGE," *ENSIGN,* JUNE 1999

Education is the great conversion process under which abstract knowledge becomes useful and productive activity. It is something that need never stop. No matter how old we grow, we can acquire knowledge and use it. We can gather wisdom and profit from it. We can be entertained through the miracle of reading and exposure to the arts and add to the blessing and fulfillment of living. GORDON B. HINCKLEY, "FIRST PRESIDENCY MESSAGE," *ENSIGN,* AUG. 1992

The Church's university and colleges are founded on the gospel of Jesus Christ and exist to provide an environment of faith in which our young people can pursue serious study. "DEAR BRETHREN," SEPT. 15, 1986

Brigham Young University is designed to enlarge and develop the powers of the spirit and to educate you for eternity. Here you have the privilege of preparing yourself for life's vocation and at the same time combining theory and practice in preparation for eternal life. Here you prepare to make a living, but more important still, you prepare to live toward perfection, toward exaltation and godhood.

This institution has no justification for its existence unless it builds character, creates and develops faith, and makes men and women of strength and courage, fortitude, and service—men and women who will become stalwarts in the kingdom and bear witness of the restoration and the divinity of the gospel of Jesus Christ. It is not justified on an academic basis only, for your parents pay taxes to support state institutions to which you are eligible in every state of the Union and most foreign countries. This institution has been established by a prophet of God for a very specific purpose: to combine spiritual and moral values with secular education. SPENCER W. KIMBALL, "FIRST PRESIDENCY MESSAGE," *ENSIGN,* APR. 1979

The Church has long encouraged its members, and especially its youth, either to obtain a college education or to become well trained in some vocation in a trade school. In our fast growing industrial society, this becomes almost a necessity, for unless our young people are well educated, or well trained, they will not be able to obtain proper jobs or positions in the future. The jobs that require no education or training are decreasing from year to year and soon will be practically non-existent. "DEAR BRETHREN," APR. 1, 1966

The Church has long encouraged its members, and especially its youth, to study at institutions of higher education. We now reaffirm and emphasize that admonition. We suggest that you counsel the youth under your jurisdiction upon graduation from high school to seek the type of educational program for which they are best suited and which will best prepare them for service in the Church and the community. "DEAR BRETHREN," DEC. 28, 1964

Because of its combination of revealed and secular learning, Brigham Young University is destined to become, if not the largest, at least the most proficient institution of learning in the world, producing scholars with testimonies of the truth who will become leaders in science, industry, art, education, letters, and government. FIRST PRESIDENCY TO ALL STAKE PRESIDENTS, NOV. 4, 1957

The Church schools must, it is true, give instruction in secular fields of learning, but this instruction should be given in such manner and in such terms as will strengthen and build up the spiritual knowledge and experience of the students. Furthermore, in addition to this secular instruction *per se,* so taught, there must also be given instruction, encouragement, and support in matters essentially relating to the spirit—in the restored gospel defined and understood in the fullest sense of the term. Indeed, the spiritual element, as revealed in the restored gospel, should dominate all else in the Church school system. FIRST PRESIDENCY TO EXECUTIVE COMMITTEE, CHURCH BOARD OF EDUCATION, FEB. 21, 1945, IN *MESSAGES,* 6:220-23

To the Latter-day Saints, salvation itself, under the Atonement of Christ, is a process of education. *IMPROVEMENT ERA,* MAY 1907, IN *MESSAGES,* 4:143-55

[W]e wish it distinctly understood that we are not in favor of, but are emphatically opposed to, denominational teachings in our public schools. We are proud of that splendid system of schools, and do not desire that they should be interfered with in any way whatever. For religious and devotional training, other institutions are provided, by our Church as well as by other churches, and we cannot too strongly urge that the two systems continue to be kept entirely separate and apart. "DEAR BRETHREN," *IMPROVEMENT ERA,* FEB. 1905

The education of the mind and the education of the body should go hand in hand. A skillful brain should be joined with a skillful hand. Manual labor should be dignified among us and always be made honorable. STATEMENT, OCT. 10, 1887, IN *MESSAGES*, 3:133-55

We need educated men, and the more we have of them the better; they should be men of faith and good works. For all such there are grand opportunities offered to them in defending and advocating the principles of righteousness which God has revealed. We feel that if education is to be obtained at the cost of faith, the price is too great; and we should counsel no one to go away from home to obtain education if there is the least danger of their coming back infidels. JOHN TAYLOR TO KARL G. MAESER, DEC. 10, 1886

Elohim, *see* God the Father

endowment, *see* temple work

entertainment

Church members should seek out wholesome, appropriate entertainment. Such entertainment may include that which is provided by professional performing artists or theatrical groups who uphold Church standards of morality and decency. Performers who provide wholesome entertainment in accordance with Church standards should be encouraged and patronized. *BULLETIN*, NOV. 1982

eternal life, *see* exaltation

eternal progression

We bear witness that all men and women are sons and

daughters of God, each accountable to Him; that our lives here on earth are part of an eternal plan; that death is not the end, but rather a transition from this to another sphere of purposeful activity made possible through the Atonement of the Redeemer of the world; and that we shall there have the opportunity of working and growing toward perfection. *CHURCH NEWS,* APR. 12, 1980

The goal of our progression is to become like God. *PRINCIPLES,* 1976

To progress in eternity we must become worthy of exaltation in the celestial kingdom. IBID.

[A]s literal offspring of God, we have within ourselves the potential to become as He now is. Our bodies are patterned after His, and in the resurrection we will receive perfected, immortal bodies, as He has. And through faith and obedience to the principles, laws, and ordinances of the gospel, we will be able to develop the personal attributes of our Father in heaven so that we will be worthy of being exalted in the celestial glory to dwell with Him. IBID.

[T]he Church has never announced a definite doctrine on this point ["progression from one kingdom to another following the resurrection"]. Some of the brethren have held the view that it was possible in the course of progression to advance from one glory to another, invoking the principle of eternal progression; others of the brethren have taken the opposite view. But, as stated, the Church has never announced a definite doctrine of this point. FIRST PRESIDENCY TO WILFORD W. KIMBALL, OCT. 2, 1969

We believe there is no limit to man's progress. The mind, the intellect, of man has no bounds. *DESERET NEWS,* DEC. 15, 1962

[S]piritually we move onward or we recede, we never stand still. We must go forward every day, becoming a little stronger, a little more certain, a little nearer perfection. No truth is more deeply bedded in the restored gospel than that of eternal progression. That progression began in the life before this, is here on this earth and now, and will be with us throughout the eternities. It need not and does not wait for eternity for a beginning. "CHARGE TO PRESIDENT HOWARD S. MCDONALD," NOV. 14, 1945, IN *MESSAGES,* 6:228-38

We admonish every man of high or low degree, and in whatever land, to act and live in accordance with the revealed will of the Lord, and we promise to every one of God's children who does so live, not only a joy in life and in living that nothing else can bring, but also salvation in the world to come, with an eternity of service, of unspeakable happiness, and a progression that shall never end. *DESERET NEWS,* DEC. 17, 1938

Man is the child of God, formed in the divine image and endowed with divine attributes, and even as the infant son of an earthly father and mother is capable in due time of becoming a man, so the undeveloped offspring of celestial parentage is capable, by experience through ages and aeons, of evolving into a God. *DESERET NEWS,* JULY 18, 1925, QUOTING *IMPROVEMENT ERA,* NOV. 1909

We consider that God has created man with a mind capable of instruction and a faculty which may be enlarged in proportion to the heed and diligence given to the light communicated from heaven to the intellect and that the nearer man approaches perfection, the clearer are his views and the greater his enjoyments, till he has overcome the evils of his life and lost every desire for sin and, like the ancients, arrives at that point of faith where he is wrapped in the power and glory of his Maker, and is caught up to dwell with Him. STATEMENT, JAN. 22, 1834, IN *MESSAGES,* 1:23-44

euthanasia, *see* life, sanctity of

evolution (organic). *See also* Adam and Eve; creation

[T]here has never been a formal declaration from the First Presidency addressing the general matter of organic evolution as a process for development of biological species. "EVOLUTION AND ORIGIN," 1992

[Y]ou ask regarding the Church's position on the theory of evolution.

I have been directed to say that the Church has issued no official statement on this subject. It is a theory, and it is subject to and undergoing modification from time to time, at least in the differing interpretations of scientific people. Under these circumstances, any conflict which may seem to exist between the scientific theory and truth of revealed religion should be dealt with by suspending judgment as long as may be necessary to arrive at the facts and a complete understanding of the truth.

While the theory is subject to controversy and differences of opinion in the scientific world, the authorities of the Church rely upon the revelations of the Lord for information about the creation of man. CLARE MIDDLEMISS, SECRETARY TO DAVID O. MCKAY, LETTER DATED MAY 8, 1964

The Brethren feel very sure that serious reflection on the matter will persuade you of the problems and resulting difficulties that would come to the First Presidency from any announcement that they might make on this matter of "organic evolution." You will appreciate that any statement they might make on this subject would be presumed to meet the problem as it is now understood by the scientists and the people. They feel sure that you will also appreciate that the problem as it now exists under the theories of present scientists might well not be the problems that will exist 50 or 100 years from now any more than that an explanation made to meet the theories of 100 years ago would meet the problems of today. As the Brethren understand, science must never accept any alleged solution of the problems of science (and they are many and in different fields) as the final truth. As a matter of fact, some of the older Brethren know that the explanations made 50 years ago are quite inapplicable to what are virtually the same problems of today. For example, the character and structure of the atom and molecule, etc., etc. At that time the scientists told us there were 76 elements and they did not anticipate the discovery of any more. Now they advise us that there are more than 130 elements, and the end is not yet. Furthermore, you will appreciate that anything they might say to you in this personal letter that you request would not remain personal with you, nor with them, nor with your students. It would become a public document, and the Brethren say they would not wish to make any statement that might not be made public. We seem to be in an age of such great and fundamental scientific readjustments on many matters, which age we have come to speak of as the nuclear age, that to attempt to harmonize the spiritual truths of the gospel with the scientific theories would be futile, not because spiritual truths are not truths, because they are, but because the theories are admittedly largely hypothetical and subject to change. The Brethren sometimes say that this harmonizing of which so much is sometimes said should be harmonizing of science with spiritual truth, and not the harmonizing of spiritual truth with science, which latter can be accepted only when science comes to the ultimate truth, and nobody knows when that will be. JOSEPH ANDERSON, SECRETARY TO THE FIRST PRESIDENCY, TO HAROLD J. BISSELL, MAY 3, 1960

I am directed to say to you that, as you will perceive on a little reflection, until either the Lord speaks directly upon the matter [i.e., "certain theories which are being announced by different scientists regarding the earth, its age, creation, etc."], or until the scientists are able to say that they have the ultimate truth covering these matters, it would only be confusing for the First Presidency to make any statement regarding such things. JOSEPH ANDERSON, SECRETARY TO THE FIRST PRESIDENCY, TO ARMIN J. HILL, FEB. 25, 1959

The Church has issued no official statement on the subject of the theory of evolution.

Neither "Man, His Origin and Destiny" by Elder Joseph Fielding Smith, nor "Mormon Doctrine" by Elder Bruce R. McConkie, is an official publication of the Church.

Evolution is a theory. You say that biologists would agree on the general lines of what happened, although there may be less agreement about just how it happened. While scientific people themselves differ in their interpretations and views of the theory, any conflicts which may seem to exist between the theory and the truths of revealed religion can well be dealt with by suspending judgment as long as may be necessary to arrive at facts and at a complete understanding of the truth. DAVID O. MCKAY TO A. KENT CHRISTENSEN, FEB. 3, 1959

Upon the fundamental doctrines of the Church we are all agreed. Our mission is to bear the message of the restored gospel to the people of the world. Leave Geology, Biology, Archaeology, and Anthropology, no one of which has to do with the salvation of the souls of mankind, to scientific research, while we magnify our calling in the realm of the Church.

We can see no advantage to be gained by a continuation of the discussion to which reference is here made [i.e., human life before Adam], but on the contrary are certain that it would lead to confusion, division, and misunderstanding if carried further. Upon one thing we should all be able to agree, namely, that Presidents Joseph F. Smith, John R. Winder, and Anthon H. Lund were right when they said: "Adam is the primal parent of our race." STATEMENT, APR. 7, 1931

I believe and accept without reservation every fact that has been brought to light, and every truth that has been demonstrated, by Darwin or by any other person. I regard Charles Darwin as one of the most able and devoted students of Nature the world has known, and as an investigator whose labors have been of incalculable good to mankind. I do not accept, however, his hypotheses as facts, nor the many vagaries and unproved theories that less able men have tried to add to his teachings. JOSEPH F. SMITH TO ELMER KNEALE, MAR. 9, 1912

exaltation

The ordinances of baptism, confirmation, Melchizedek Priesthood ordination (for men), and the temple endowment and sealing are required for exaltation for all accountable persons. *CHURCH HANDBOOK 2,* 1998

As Latter-day Saints, we know that to obtain exaltation and eternal life in the celestial kingdom, where our Father and our Savior and the righteous of all ages dwell, we must comply with the principles and ordinances of the gospel of Jesus Christ. This requires honesty, integrity, purity, and righteousness. It requires us to avoid filth of every kind in thought and action. MARION G. ROMNEY, "FIRST PRESIDENCY MESSAGE," *ENSIGN,* SEPT. 1984

[T]here is a goal beyond the resurrection. That is exaltation in our Father's kingdom. It will be achieved by obedience to the commandments of God. It will begin with acceptance of

Him as our Eternal Father and of His Son as our living Redeemer. It will involve participation in various ordinances, each one important and necessary. The first of these is baptism by immersion in water, without which, according to the Savior, a man cannot enter into the kingdom of God. There must follow the birth of the Spirit, the gift of the Holy Ghost. Then in succession through the years will come, for men, ordination to the priesthood, followed by the blessings of the temple for both men and women who are worthy to enter therein. These temple blessings include our washings and anointings that we may be clean before the Lord. They include the instruction service in which we are given an endowment of obligations and blessings that motivate us to behavior compatible with the principles of the gospel. They include the sealing ordinances by which that which is bound on earth is bound for the continuity of the family. GORDON B. HINCKLEY, "FIRST PRESIDENCY MESSAGE," *ENSIGN*, FEB. 1982

[E]xaltation is available only to those who become righteous members of the kingdom of Jesus Christ, only to those who obtain their endowments and are sealed for eternity as well as time, and who then continue to live righteously. This is not man's interpretation. This is the program of our Heavenly Father and is made clear by the scriptures. It is not futile formality nor empty ritual. It we do not understand, it is an indication that we need to get close to our Heavenly Father so that we may fathom it, for the things of God are understood by the Spirit of God. SPENCER W. KIMBALL, "FIRST PRESIDENCY MESSAGE," *ENSIGN,* OCT. 1979

Eternal life, or life with God, is our goal. It is a great blessing to know that we can have an eternal family and eternal progression, with continuing opportunity and challenge. The doctrines of the Church should help us all to solve our problems and prepare for our declining years as we put forth the effort to study and live according to the teachings of the gospel. As we learn of the fatherhood of God, the brotherhood of man, intelligence, eternal progression, endurance, the resurrection, and eternal marriage and family, we are given hope, stability, and purpose for living. N. ELDON TANNER, "FIRST PRESIDENCY MESSAGE," *ENSIGN,* DEC. 1976

Only the faithful will receive the promised reward, which is eternal life. For one cannot receive eternal life without becoming a "doer of the word" (see James 1:22) and being valiant in obedience to the Lord's commandments. And one cannot become a "doer of the word" without first becoming a "hearer." And to become a "hearer" is not simply to stand idly by and wait for chance bits of information; it is to seek out and study and pray and comprehend. Therefore the Lord said, "Whoso receiveth not my voice is not acquainted with my voice, and is not of me" (D&C 84:52). SPENCER W. KIMBALL, "FIRST PRESIDENCY MESSAGE," *ENSIGN,* SEPT. 1976

An essential requirement for exaltation is celestial marriage, for exaltation depends upon the continuation of the family in eternity and the power to populate other worlds as our Father did this one. *PRINCIPLES,* 1976

Mankind may become exalted sons and daughters unto God as they learn celestial laws and ordinances and live in perfect harmony with them. "BASIC DOCTRINES," 1971

Exaltation means eternal life or godhood, the kind of life our Heavenly Father lives.

Priesthood ordinances, including celestial marriage, are essential for exaltation. IBID.

In the many mansions prepared for those who love Him, allocations will be made on the basis of depth and height and breadth and quality of love, heartfelt, soulful, mind-illuminating love. *CHURCH NEWS*, DEC. 21, 1968

So far as the stages of eternal progression and attainment have been made known through divine revelation, we are to understand that only resurrected and glorified beings can become parents of spirit offspring. Only such exalted souls have reached maturity in the appointed course of eternal life; and the spirits born to them in the eternal worlds will pass in due sequence through the several stages or estates by which the glorified parents have attained exaltation. *IMPROVEMENT ERA,* AUG. 1916, IN *MESSAGES,* 5:26-34

All the perfected beings who are rightly called gods, being, like the Savior, possessed of "the fullness of the Godhead bodily" [Col. 2:9], are ONE, just as the Father and the Son and the Holy Ghost are one. *IMPROVEMENT ERA,* APR. 1912, IN *MESSAGES,* 4:270-71

The highest glory, according to our view, is attainable only by those who receive the gospel here, and are valiant for it, enduring faithful to the end; or those who would have done these things had they been upon earth when the opportunity was afforded. *DESERET NEWS,* NOV. 4, 1911, IN *MESSAGES,* 4:231-51

The life of a saint is not simply a personal perfecting, it is also a factor in the entire scheme of Earth's redemption. No one can be saved alone, by himself or herself, unassisted by or unassisting others. The weight of our influence must be either for good or harm, be an aid or an injury to the work of human regeneration; and as we assume responsibilities, form ties, enter into covenants, beget children, accumulate families, so does the weight of our influence increase, so does its extent broaden, and deepen. STATEMENT, OCT. 10, 1886, IN *MESSAGES,* 3:72-91

[N]one but the pure in heart can see God, none but those who have sanctified all their affections and passions by entire and complete subservience to His laws and dwell in His eternal presence! *MILLENNIAL STAR,* MAY 17, 1886, IN *MESSAGES,* 3:46-71

Remember that it is the trifling things of this life which make up our existence, and that but a small number of great and important events transpire without them. They are, however small, the important little duties of life, upon the daily practice of which much depends to fit a people for the coming of the Lord Jesus, or to prepare them for an exaltation in the kingdom of our God. *MILLENNIAL STAR,* JAN. 26, 1856, IN *MESSAGES,* 2:177-87

[O]ur holy religion absorbs every feeling, desire, ambition, motive, and action of our nature, and renders every association in life tributary hereto; it forms the vitality of our very existence; it enters not only into our spiritual but also into our temporal organization, and controls us in all our affairs. This is true of every person who has tasted the good word of life, has received the Holy Ghost, and continues to walk in the light, and be led by its gentle influence. This is salvation in the kingdom of God, it is glory celestial, and exaltation. *MILLENNIAL STAR,* AUG. 11, 1855, IN *MESSAGES,* 2:159-71

Think not, O ye Elders of Israel! that your eternal heirship is won, and immutably secured, because you have attained to a portion of the holy priesthood, and few of its initiating ordinances, while as yet your life and the security of all your great and glorious blessings, in hope and prospect, are as a vapor before the sun; as yet depending wholly on your meekness, faithfulness, and perseverance to the *end,* in *everything good.* Think not that you are legally entitled to even *one life* while you live on this earth unless you are sealed up to *everlasting lives* by the will and *decree* of the *Eternal Father* and a knowledge of the fact has been communicated to you through the *proper source,* and not *direct* to *you* in *person.* And consider that the blessings you have hitherto received through the mercies of Him who loveth you, even your Father in Heaven, will all be *wrested* from you, like *David's* of old, should you err like him. *MILLENNIAL STAR,* JULY 9, 1853, IN *MESSAGES,* 2:110-19

God has in reserve a time, or period appointed in His own bosom, when He will bring all His subjects, who have obeyed His voice and kept His commandments, into His celestial rest. This rest is of such perfection and glory that man has need of a preparation before he can, according to the laws of that kingdom, enter it and enjoy its blessings. This being the fact, God has given certain laws to the human family, which, if observed, are sufficient to prepare them to inherit this rest. This, then, we conclude, was the purpose of God in giving His laws to us: if not, why, or for what were they given? STATEMENT, JAN. 22, 1834, IN *MESSAGES,* 1:23-44

excommunication. ***See also*** **Church discipline; disfellowshipment**

A person who is excommunicated is no longer a member of the Church. Excommunication is the most severe Church disciplinary action. *CHURCH HANDBOOK,* 1998

A person who is excommunicated does not enjoy any of Church membership. He may not wear temple garments or pay tithes and offerings. He may attend public Church meetings if his conduct is orderly, but his participation in such meetings is limited the same as for disfellowshipped membership. IBID.

[A] person who was excommunicated may be readmitted into the Church by baptism. IBID.

Endowed persons who were excommunicated and later re-admitted by baptism can receive their priesthood and temple blessings only through the ordinance of restoration of blessings. Such persons are not ordained to priesthood offices or endowed again, since all priesthood and temple blessings held at the time of excommunication are restored through the ordinance. IBID.

[T]he penalty of excommunication is not an instrument of coercion or control as you suggest, but is rather a means of giving official expression to a condition brought about by individuals who, through their own conduct, have estranged themselves from the Church. FRANCIS M. GIBBONS, SECRETARY TO THE FIRST PRESIDENCY, TO STERLING M. MCMURRIN, SEPT. 22, 1971

Members who have been disfellowshipped or excommunicated should not be avoided or persecuted by the members of the Church. They should be dealt with kindly and prayerfully, in the hope that they may turn from their mistakes and receive again the full privileges of Church membership. *CHURCH HANDBOOK,* 1960

F

faith

Divine favor will attend those who humbly seek it. THOMAS S. MONSON, "FIRST PRESIDENCY MESSAGE," ENSIGN, JAN. 2006

Faith is a gift from God, but you must nurture your faith to keep it strong. Faith is like the muscle of your arm. If you exercise it, it grows strong. If you put it in a sling and leave it there, it becomes weak. *TRUE TO FAITH*, 2004

Having faith in Jesus Christ means relying completely on Him—trusting in His infinite power, intelligence, and love. It includes believing His teachings. It means believing that even though you do not understand all things, He does. Remember that because He has experienced all your pains, afflictions, and infirmities, He knows how to help you rise above your daily difficulties (see Alma 7:11-12; D&C 122:8). He has "overcome the world" (John 16:33) and prepared the way for you to receive eternal life. He is always ready to help you as you remember His plea: "Look unto me in every thought; doubt not, fear not" (D&C 6:36). IBID.

How do we know the things of the Spirit? How do we know that it is from God? By the fruits of it. If it leads to growth and development, if it leads to faith and testimony, if it leads to a better way of doing things, if it leads to godliness, then it is of God. If it tears us down, if it brings us into darkness, if it confuses us and worries us, if it leads to faithlessness, then it is of the devil. GORDON B. HINCKLEY, "FIRST PRESIDENCY MESSAGE," *ENSIGN,* JULY 1998

The fundamental principle of our religion is faith in the Lord Jesus Christ. EZRA TAFT BENSON, "FIRST PRESIDENCY MESSAGE," *ENSIGN,* JUNE 1990

Faith in Jesus Christ consists of complete reliance on Him. As God, He has infinite power, intelligence, and love. There is no human problem beyond His capacity to solve. Because He descended below all things (see D&C 122:8), He knows how to help us rise above our daily difficulties. IBID.

Faith is not a theological platitude. It is a fact of life. Faith can become the very wellspring of purposeful living. There is no more compelling motivation to worthwhile endeavor than the knowledge that we are children of God, the Creator of the universe, our all-wise Heavenly Father! God expects us to do something with our lives, and He will give us help when help is sought. GORDON B. HINCKLEY, "FIRST PRESIDENCY MESSAGE," *ENSIGN,* AUG. 1988

Faith is based on truth and is preceded by a certain degree of knowledge; through the workings of the Holy Ghost, faith in the knowledge which we have received can enter our hearts. Once that faith is in our hearts, it works a change in us which manifests itself in our thoughts and actions. Thus, faith is a conviction of the truth which we have experienced not with our physical senses, but rather with our spirits, and which motivates us to a Christlike life. *PRINCIPLES,* 1976

family. ***See also*** **home life; parents**

It is always appropriate in all family relationships to ask, "What would Jesus do?" JAMES E. FAUST, "FIRST PRESIDENCY MESSAGE," *ENSIGN,* SEPT. 2006

We live in a world where the family is falling apart. We put great emphasis on the family. Keep your families close together, and love and honor your children. Raise them in truth and faith to love the Lord. GORDON B. HINCKLEY, "FIRST PRESIDENCY MESSAGE," *ENSIGN,* MAR. 2006

The only things you will take with you, when all is said and done, are your family relationships. IBID.

The purposes of home, family, and personal enrichment are to strengthen faith in Jesus Christ and to teach parenting and homemaking skills. *ENSIGN,* JAN. 2006

There is no fullness of joy in the next life without a family unit, including a husband, a wife, and posterity. "ISSUES RESOURCES," 2006

Because families are ordained of God, they are the most important social unit in time and in eternity. God has established families to bring happiness to His children, allow them to learn correct principles in a loving atmosphere, and prepare them for eternal life. *PREACH MY GOSPEL,* 2005

[T]he concept of a united family which lives and progresses forever is at the core of Latter-day Saint doctrine. *QUICK FACTS,* 2005)

The family is the fundamental unit in the Church, and home is the most important place for gospel learning. No other organization can take the place of the family. Even as the Church continues to grow, its purpose will always be to support and strengthen families and individuals in their efforts to live the gospel. *TRUE TO FAITH,* 2004

Life's greatest joys are found in the family. Strong family relationships require effort, but such effort brings great happiness in this life and throughout eternity. Even if you have not had a happy family life in the past, you can seek to have a happy eternal marriage and a loving relationship with family members. IBID.

Parents and teachers should help children learn what a testimony is and when it is appropriate for them to express it. It may be best to have younger children learn to share their testimonies at such times as family home evening or when giving talks in Primary until they are old enough to do so in a fast and testimony meeting. "DEAR BRETHREN," MAY 2, 2002

Not all families are the same, but each is important in Heavenly Father's plan. *STRENGTH OF YOUTH,* 2001

We counsel parents and children to give highest priority to family prayer, family home evening, gospel study and instruction, and wholesome family activities. However worthy and appropriate other demands or activities may be, they must not be permitted to displace the divinely appointed duties that only parents and families can adequately perform. *ENSIGN,* JUNE 1999

We call upon parents to devote their best efforts to the teaching and rearing of their children in gospel principles which will keep them close to the Church. The home is the basis of a righteous life, and no other instrumentality can take its place or fulfill its essential functions in carrying forward this God-given responsibility. FIRST PRESIDENCY TO MEMBERS OF THE CHURCH THROUGHOUT THE WORLD, FEB. 11, 1999, IN *CHURCH NEWS,* FEB. 27, 1999

As we strengthen families, we will strengthen the entire Church. IBID.

To follow the Savior, we must begin at home within the

family unit. Parents need to teach children the doctrine of Christ which includes unshaken faith in Him, repentance, baptism, the gift of the Holy Ghost, and faithfully enduring to the end in living gospel principles in their homes. *CHURCH NEWS,* APR. 4, 1998

The family is ordained of God. It is central to His plan for the eternal destiny of His children. God has established families to bring happiness to His children, to help them learn correct principles in a loving atmosphere, and to prepare them for eternal life. *CHURCH HANDBOOK 2,* 1998

The family is ordained of God. It is traditional for families to be together during the holiday season. Happy families are paramount among the blessings for which gratitude should be expressed to the Lord.

Husbands and wives have a solemn responsibility to love and care for each other and for their children. They have a sacred duty to rear their children in love and righteousness, to provide for their physical and spiritual needs, to teach them to love and serve one another, to observe the commandments of God, and to be law-abiding citizens wherever they live. *CHURCH NEWS,* NOV. 9, 1996

Life's deepest joys and lasting happiness come from our loving association and caring concern one for another as fathers, mothers, and children in the family. The Church of Jesus Christ of Latter-day Saints has long taught that the family is the basic unit of society and that the strength of any nation lies in the strength of its families. Successful families are established and maintained on principles of faith, prayer, repentance, forgiveness, respect, love, compassion, work, and wholesome recreational activities. Such families provide an example that all should emulate.

We encourage citizens and governments to do all they can

to promote and build strong and happy families which will act as a mighty fortress against the evils of our day. *CHURCH NEWS,* NOV. 18, 1995

[W]e warn that the disintegration of the family will bring upon the individuals, communities, and nations the calamities foretold by ancient and modern prophets. *CHURCH NEWS,* SEPT. 30, 1995

The primary emphasis of family home evening should be for families to be together to study the gospel. We remind all that the Lord has admonished parents to teach their children the gospel, to pray, and to observe the Sabbath Day. The scriptures are the most important resource for teaching the gospel. *CHURCH NEWS,* OCT. 1, 1994

[T]he family is divine. It was instituted by our Heavenly Father. It encompasses the most sacred of all relationships. Only through its organization can the purposes of the Lord be fulfilled. GORDON B. HINCKLEY, "FIRST PRESIDENCY MESSAGE," *ENSIGN,* JAN. 1994

We must recognize that the family is the cornerstone of civilization and that no nation will rise above the caliber of its homes. The family is the rock foundation of the Church. EZRA TAFT BENSON, "FIRST PRESIDENCY MESSAGE," *ENSIGN,* AUG. 1993

Every family has problems and challenges. But successful families try to work together toward solutions instead of resorting to criticism and contention. They pray for each other, discuss, and give encouragement. Occasionally these families fast together in support of one of the family members.

Successful families do things together: family projects, work, vacations, recreation, and reunions. IBID.

The strength of any nation lies in the strength of its families. Our Heavenly Father intends that the greatest happiness and deepest joys should come in our associations and our concerns for one another as fathers, mothers, and children. Strong family life comes of the perception that each of us is a child of God, born with a divine birthright and with unlimited potential. Strong family life comes from parents who love and respect one another and who teach and nurture their children in the ways of the Lord. *CHURCH NEWS*, NOV. 14, 1992

The Church of Jesus Christ of Latter-day Saints teaches that the family is most effective in instilling lasting values in its members. The family is a fortress against the evils of our day. Marriage and homes are established by divine plan to build a happy family where love and respect among family members are taught and exemplified. *CHURCH NEWS*, NOV. 18, 1989

No family can have peace, no life can be free from the storms of adversity unless that family and that home are built on foundations of morality, fidelity, and mutual respect. There cannot be peace where there is not trust; there cannot be freedom where there is not loyalty. The warm sunlight of love will not rise out of a swamp of immorality. GORDON B. HINCKLEY, "FIRST PRESIDENCY MESSAGE," *ENSIGN*, AUG. 1989

There is no better place than the family to teach fundamental values and virtues. It is the best place to teach each other how to become more Christlike in thought and action. The home is an ideal setting for sharing the virtues of love and respect for others and practicing the precepts of the gospel of Jesus Christ. The righteous influence of each caring individual within the family can have a great impact for good upon the other members of the household. *PLANNING CALENDAR*, 1986

The family is the basic organizational unit of the Church. No agency or institution can or should replace the family. By sacred covenant and eternal priesthood government, the eternal family unit is established. By virtue of the commitment made as a part of that covenant, husbands are obligated to provide for their families. MARION G. ROMNEY, "FIRST PRESIDENCY MESSAGE," *ENSIGN,* APR. 1981

Next to one's own self, the responsibility, the blessing, and great opportunity for lovingly sustaining an individual until he or she leaves mortality rests upon his or her family—parents for their children, children for their parents. The same covenant that obligates parents to care for their children also obligates children to care for their parents when they need it. The commandment to "honor thy father and thy mother" extends to modern Israel and is required for all who are faithful members of the Church. IBID.

We affirm the sanctity of the family as a divine creation and declare that God our Eternal Father will hold parents accountable to rear their children in light and truth, teaching them "to pray, and to walk uprightly before the Lord" [D&C 68:28]. *CHURCH NEWS,* APR. 12, 1980

Our spiritual progress, individually and as a Church, will largely be determined by how faithfully we live the gospel in our homes. *FAMILY HOME EVENING,* 1980

We urge parents and children both to come back home. Parents should not let social activities take precedence over time with their families. Young men and women should balance their involvement in school and other social activities by participating in family activities and spending appropriate time in the home. IBID.

May we all work together to make the home a place where we love to be, a place of listening and learning, a place where each member can find mutual love, support, appreciation, and encouragement. IBID.

In the gospel plan, families are forever. The greatest joys here and in the hereafter have their beginnings in happy homes where the gospel is taught and lived. *FAMILY HOME EVENING,* 1978

Our families should be more important to us than anything else in the world. To be complete, a family consists of father, mother, and children. The Lord established marriage for the purpose of multiplying and replenishing the earth. N. ELDON TANNER, "FIRST PRESIDENCY MESSAGE," *ENSIGN,* JUNE 1977

In our own dispensation, which the scriptures have identified as the dispensation of the fullness of times, the Lord has promised that He would "gather together in one all things, both which are in heaven, and which are on earth" (D&C 27:13; see also Eph. 1:10).

Certainly gathering "together in one all things" is related to the Apostle Peter's statement regarding the "time of restitution of all things, which God hath spoken by the mouth of all his holy prophets since the world began" (Acts 3:21). This very important prophecy refers especially to the return of those prophets of old who held the various priesthood keys of the kingdom.

Thus, the keys of the divine patriarchal order which were held by the fathers anciently were restored, saying, in effect, that the time had finally come for Abraham's great lineage to be restored to the gospel and the priesthood. Through this priesthood "shall all the families of the earth be blessed" (Abr. 2:11)–meaning in part that the blessings of the gospel are brought to individuals and also that, through the priesthood's new and everlasting covenant of marriage, all the elect children of God who are gathered together out of the earth may be sealed together in family units into the lineage of Abraham, or, in other words, into the organized, eternal family of God. SPENCER W. KIMBALL, "FIRST PRESIDENCY MESSAGE," *ENSIGN*, JAN. 1977

The Lord's government is patriarchal in nature, with the family as the center and the father as the head of the family. In the premortal existence, we lived in a patriarchal order with our Heavenly Father at the head. From Adam until Moses, the priesthood was organized as a patriarchal order, but administration of Church affairs is necessarily on a different basis in our day. However, when a person marries in the temple in the new and everlasting covenant of marriage, he inherits the blessings of Abraham, Isaac, and Jacob, and thereby enters into the patriarchal order of the Melchizedek Priesthood. This is the fullness of the priesthood, and it is necessary for exaltation in the celestial kingdom. If we enter and keep this eternal marriage covenant, we will receive the full blessings of the patriarchal order of the Melchizedek Priesthood in eternity. *PRINCIPLES,* 1976

The most important organization in the Church is the family. The Latter-day Saint home is bound together for eternity by the sealing power of the priesthood. A worthy bearer of the Melchizedek Priesthood should preside over each family and home. Thus, a primary responsibility of the Church today is to support and strengthen the home, and the Church's programs are intended to strengthen the father and help him lead the members of his family to exaltation. IBID.

The home and family have an important influence in the life of each individual, and the Church's purpose is to strengthen, unify, and exalt every family. IBID.

Fathers and mothers, your foremost responsibility is your family. By working together you can have the kind of home the Lord expects you to have. By showing love and consideration for one another and for your children, you can build a reservoir of spiritual strength that will never run dry.

Some families neglect to build that reservoir for their children, depending solely on runoff from other sources. They depend on the Sunday School or the seminary organizations; a dam built in such a manner is like a dam of rock and brush, full of cracks and leaks, which washes away when the torrents flood. The Church auxiliaries are very important, and we should all partake of the blessings they offer. But we should never, never allow them to replace parents, to relieve parents of the responsibility to teach their children the gospel of Jesus Christ. SPENCER W. KIMBALL, "FIRST PRESIDENCY MESSAGE," *ENSIGN,* JUNE 1975

Foremost in the family is the responsibility of the father who bears the priesthood, and therefore is designated as head of the household. This does not mean that mother love can ever be eclipsed, because she is the companion to the father and shares with him the blessings of the holy priesthood and the responsibility in the raising and the teaching of their children.

No Church organization can supplant the parents in discharging this obligation. The best the Church can do is to give every aid possible so that the parents will be left without excuse in discharging this most sacred and vital work of building a solid foundation in the home from which their children can learn lessons that will strengthen them to resist the temptations of the world. *FAMILY HOME EVENING,* 1974

The primary function of a Latter-day Saint home is to ensure that every family member works to create the climate and condition in which all can grow toward perfection. For the parents, this requires a dedication of time and energy far beyond the mere providing of their children's physical needs. For the children, this means controlling the natural tendency toward selfishness. *FAMILY HOME EVENING,* 1973

[T]he Church has no choice—and never has had—but to do more to assist the family in carrying out its divine mission, not only because that is the order of heaven, but also because that is the most practical contribution we can make to our youth—to help improve the quality of life in the Latter-day Saint homes. As important as our many programs and organizational efforts are, these should not supplant the home; they should support the home. HAROLD B. LEE, "FIRST PRESIDENCY MESSAGE," *ENSIGN,* MAR. 1971

There is no more appropriate place for teaching the gospel than the home. Only at home can children learn the nature of family life as authored by our Heavenly Father. *FAMILY HOME EVENING,* 1971

[I]n these times when so many conflicting demands and loyalties are fragmenting and submerging the importance of the family, we must do everything in our power to strength it. Aside from the family home evening, there is no more powerful tool available for this purpose than the family Church meeting—sacrament meeting. Let us use it as we ought and let us not permit anything to weaken or destroy its purpose either by unduly shortening the length of it or by losing the quality and spirit of it. "DEAR BRETHREN," DEC. 17, 1970

The importance of family unity—love and consideration for one another in the family—cannot be overemphasized. Spiritual solidarity in family relationships is the sure foundation upon which the Church and society itself will flourish. This fact is well known and appreciated by the adversary, and as never before, he is using every clever device, influence, and power within his control to undermine and destroy this eternal institution. Only the gospel of Jesus Christ applied in family relationships will thwart this devilish destructiveness. *FAMILY HOME EVENING,* 1970

We are members of the family of God our Eternal Father. He designed the plan of salvation and exaltation to enable us to become like Him, thus gaining eternal families of our own. The family is an important organization in time or in eternity. The Church helps us to create and perfect eternal family units; it serves the family and the individual. *CHURCH HANDBOOK,* 1968

It is our responsibility to do all possible to preserve the sanctity of the home, to safeguard our children, and strengthen their faith by a cultivation of gospel principles in the home. *CHURCH NEWS,* DEC. 19, 1964

We call upon the Latter-day Saints everywhere to strengthen family ties, to preserve the sanctity of the home, and to safeguard the faith of our children, ever bearing in mind that universal peace may best be achieved by cultivating peace in the homes of the people. *DESERET NEWS,* DEC. 14, 1955

There can never be a noble nation of ignoble households, nor a joyful nation of unhappy homes. *DESERET NEWS,* DEC. 12, 1951

The family is the foundation of eternal glory, the nucleus of a kingdom without end. The husband will have the wife, the wife her husband, parents their children, forever, provided they secure them in the manner prescribed by Him whose right it is to regulate all things pertaining to His kingdom. *DESERET NEWS,* NOV. 4, 1911, IN *MESSAGES,* 4:231-51

We sensibly feel that there is no greater field of labor connected with the work of God upon the earth today than that of seeking to uplift our young people morally and spiritually, and to throw around them safeguards against the prevailing evils of the world. WILFORD WOODRUFF AND JOSEPH F. SMITH TO WILLARD YOUNG AND THOMAS HULL, APR. 27, 1892

fasting

The Church designates one Sunday each month, usually the first Sunday, as a day of fasting. Proper observance of fast Sunday includes going without food and drink for two consecutive meals, attending fast and testimony meeting, and giving a fast offering to help care for those in need. *TRUE TO FAITH,* 2004

A proper fast day observance includes abstaining from food and drink for two consecutive meals, attending fast and testimony meeting, and giving a generous fast offering to help care for those in need. *CHURCH HANDBOOK,* 1998

Fasting, accompanied by prayer, is a form of worship. The Lord has commanded His people to fast to help them draw closer to Him, overcome worldliness, gain spiritual strength, increase their compassion, and prepare themselves for service. Fasting is fundamental to spiritual well-being and temporal welfare. *CHURCH HANDBOOK 2,* 1998

We ask all Latter-day Saints to observe the designated fast and to contribute to the Church a generous fast offering, for the blessing of both the needy and those who give. "DEAR BRETHREN," NOV. 15, 1989

Periodic fasting can help clear up the mind and strengthen the body and the spirit. The usual fast, the one we are asked to participate in for fast Sunday, is to abstain from food and drink for two consecutive meals. Some people, feeling the need, have gone on longer fasts of abstaining from food but have taken the needed liquids. Wisdom should be used, and this fast should be broken with light eating. To make a fast most fruitful, it should be coupled with prayer and meditation; physical work should be held to a minimum, and one should ponder on the scriptures and the reason for the fast. EZRA TAFT BENSON, "FIRST PRESIDENCY MESSAGE," *ENSIGN,* OCT. 1986

Fast offerings have long constituted the means from which the needs of the Lord's poor have been provided. It has been, and now is, the desire and objective of the Church to obtain from fast offerings the necessary funds to meet the cash needs of the welfare program, and to obtain from welfare production projects the commodity needs. If we give a generous fast offering, we shall increase our own prosperity both spiritually and temporally. SPENCER W. KIMBALL, "FIRST PRESIDENCY MESSAGE," *ENSIGN,* AUG. 1984

A *minimum* fast offering is defined as the value of two meals, but, in practice, members who can do so should make a generous charitable contribution. *CHURCH HANDBOOK,* 1983

1. Missionaries should not engage in excessive or lengthy fasting. Generally, once a month is sufficient for fasting. Occasionally there may be special matters for which missionaries might want to fast. If so, they may take another day during the month, but they should not extend the fast beyond one day.

2. Missionaries should not request friends, relatives, or members of their home wards or branches to participate with them in special fasts for investigators.

3. Missionaries should be encouraged to gain the full blessings of the law of the fast by paying fast offerings on fast Sunday to the bishop or branch president in the area where they are serving. "DEAR BRETHREN," MAR. 15, 1977

One Sunday a month, usually the first Sunday, the regular sacrament meeting consists of a special fast and testimony meeting in which the time is devoted to the performance of ordinances and the bearing of voluntary testimonies. *CHURCH HANDBOOK,* 1976

The purpose of the fast offering funds is to provide food, shelter, clothing, and medical care to those in need. IBID.

An effective fast must concentrate on spiritual matters as well as avoiding the physical; it must be purposeful and must be accompanied by prayer and thoughtfulness. Without prayer and a purpose, we lose many of the personal blessings of fasting. *PRINCIPLES,* 1976

Hypocrisy in fasting goes unrewarded by God. IBID.

There is nothing in the revelations indicating the duration of the fast, the accepted meaning of the fast being to abstain from eating and drinking. It has normally been considered that a proper fast consists of refraining from eating two meals on fast day, and in practice the fast is usually broken after the fast meeting. "DEAR BRETHREN," APR. 8, 1966

True observance of the fast consists of abstaining from food and drink for two consecutive meals, attending the fast and testimony meeting, and making a generous cash offering to the bishop for the care of those in need. The amount, equivalent of the value of the two meals from which they have abstained, should constitute the minimum amount of the fast offering. *CHURCH HANDBOOK,* 1963

The first Sunday of each month is a day of fasting and prayer on which a special testimony meeting is held.... Preachments, long drawn out narrations of experiences and routine repetitious statements by certain members should be discouraged, but every encouragement should be given to the bearing of brief, heartfelt testimonies and the relating of faith-promoting experiences. Every effort should be made to obtain the attendance and enjoy the participation of the children and other young people of the ward. *CHURCH HANDBOOK,* 1960

Fasting is a form of self denial for self mastery. It is a physical sacrifice for spiritual blessing. All Saints should be urged to observe the fast day and enjoy the blessings to be derived thereby. In general, fasting means abstaining from two consecutive meals and taking neither food nor drink into the body. *HELPS AND SUGGESTIONS,* 1956

The fast offering should be the equivalent of the total cash value of the two meals abstained from. Church members should be as conscientious in the computation and payment of their fast offerings as they are expected to be in the payment of tithing. IBID.

Testimony bearing is one of the great privileges and responsibilities of Church members. We consider the fast meeting as one of the most important meetings of the Church, and are anxious to have it so arranged that the highest possible spiritual benefits will flow to those who are privileged to attend and participate. "DEAR BRETHREN," MAR. 28, 1952

The fast meeting is primarily for the bearing of testimonies and the expression of faith and gratitude by members of the Church generally. *CHURCH HANDBOOK,* 1940

In general, fasting means taking nothing into the body. No direct instruction is given in the Doctrine and Covenants regarding abstaining from water while fasting; but in the Bible there are three references wherein the drinking of water was omitted during the period of the fast. These are: Exodus 34:28 and Deuteronomy 9:9-18, where it states that Moses "did neither eat bread nor drink water;" and Esther 4:16, where Esther asked the Jews to fast for her and to "neither eat nor drink." IBID.

The first Sunday in the month is set apart as a day of fasting and prayer. On this day members of the Church should remember the poor and make contributions for relieving their needs. Fasting is a form of self-denial for self-mastery. It is a physical sacrifice for spiritual blessing. Those who practice fasting with the desire to enjoy a greater portion of the spirit of the Lord can testify that their hopes have been realized. All Saints are urged to observe the fast day and enjoy the blessings that come therefrom. When fasting, members of the Church are advised to abstain from two meals each fast day and contribute as a donation the amount saved thereby for the support of the worthy poor; also, by prayer in connection with fasting, to develop spiritual power. The main thing to encourage is the spirit of fasting. Too much stress should not be laid on technical details, but the self-denial of food, striving for spiritual strength, and donating for the benefit of the poor should be kept constantly in mind. *CHURCH HANDBOOK,* 1934

The first Sunday in the month is set apart as a day of fasting and prayer. Upon this day the Saints should remember the poor and make contributions for relieving their necessities. It is the duty of the Saints to make their offerings even though there be no poor in the ward to which they belong. *CHURCH HANDBOOK,* 1913

A fast meeting should be held in every ward on the first Sunday of each month, when the Saints should remember the poor and donate for their benefit. Such donations should equal, at least, the amount saved by the person or family by fasting. All such offerings should be used exclusively for assisting the worthy poor. *CHURCH HANDBOOK,* 1909

Partaking of the sacrament is not breaking fast. The only way to break fast is to eat food with the intention to satisfy hunger or gratify the appetite. JOSEPH F. SMITH TO EDWARD ARTHUR SMITH, JAN. 30, 1897

The objects of fasting are twofold—and perhaps many-fold; but I have two great objects in view: 1st to draw nearer to the Lord and the better to enjoy the presence of His spirit. And 2d to remember the poor by making an offering of the cost of one or more meals, at least, for their good. JOSEPH F. SMITH TO HYRUM M. SMITH, OCT. 31, 1896

First Presidency. *See also* priesthood; revelation

The Church of Jesus Christ of Latter-day Saints is headed by the President of the Church and two Counselors, together known as the First Presidency. The First Presidency and Twelve Apostles are regarded by Latter-day Saints as prophets, receiving divine revelation and inspiration to guide the Church.

Together the Council of the First Presidency and the Twelve Apostles comprise the principal policy-making and administrative body of the Church. The apostles have the scriptural charge to be special witnesses of Jesus Christ throughout the world and to ensure the orderly and correct operation of the Church everywhere. At the death of the President of the Church, the senior Apostle (determined by length of service as an apostle, not by age) becomes President of the Church. *QUICK FACTS*, 2005

The President of the Church is the prophet, seer, and revelator. As the senior Apostle and president of the Melchizedek Priesthood, he presides over the entire Church (see D&C 107:8, 65-67, 91-91). He is the only person on Earth who may use (or authorize another person to use) the keys of the priesthood for governing the entire Church (43:1-4; 81:2; 132:7). He is also the only person on earth who is authorized to receive revelation for the entire Church (28:2; 132:7).

The Presidency's Counselors are also prophets, seers, and revelators. The President and his Counselors form a Quorum of the First Presidency of the Church (107:22). *CHURCH HANDBOOK,* 1998

The First Presidency has ultimate authority over all Church discipline. Decisions of the First Presidency take precedence despite any rules or procedures to the contrary. IBID.

We have been promised that the President of the Church, as the revelator for the Church, will receive guidance for all of us. Our safety lies in paying heed to that which he says and following his counsel. JAMES E. FAUST, "FIRST PRESIDENCY MESSAGE," *ENSIGN,* AUG. 1996

The President of the Church is the president of the high priesthood of the Church. He is assisted by his Counselors and the Council of the Twelve. The First Presidency and the Council of the Twelve have the responsibility for the supervision and direction of all priesthood, auxiliary, and other affairs of the Church. *CHURCH HANDBOOK,* 1986

The kingdom of God on Earth is presided over by the President of the Church, who is a prophet, seer, and revelator and who holds all of the keys for administering the work of the Church. He generally has two Counselors, and together they form the First Presidency, which is the highest presiding body of the Church. *PRINCIPLES,* 1976

In the Church of Jesus Christ of Latter-day Saints, the final authority, both temporal and spiritual, in all matters whatsoever—legislative, executive, and judicial—is vested in the President of the Church, who is prophet, seer, and revelator for the Church, and who is the presiding high priest. To assist him in the affairs of administration he has two Counselors, First and Second. They form the quorum of the First Presidency. *CHURCH HANDBOOK,* 1963

The First Presidency have the supreme control of Church affairs and not the Apostles. FIRST PRESIDENCY TO REED SMOOT, JAN. 20, 1904

First Vision. *See also* Smith, Joseph

We have a perfect knowledge of the nature of God that has come through the First Vision of the Prophet Joseph [Smith]. He saw God. He heard Him speak. He saw His Son. He heard Him speak, and he could speak to Them. There was no question in his mind about the true nature of God. What a tremendous thing that is. GORDON B. HINCKLEY, "FIRST PRESIDENCY MESSAGE," *ENSIGN*, FEB. 2007

For your testimony of the restored gospel to be complete, it must include a testimony of Joseph Smith's divine mission. The truthfulness of The Church of Jesus Christ of Latter-day Saints rests on the truthfulness of the First Vision and the other revelations the Lord gave to the Prophet Joseph. *TRUE TO FAITH,* 2004

The appearance of God the Father and His Son, Jesus Christ, to Joseph Smith is the greatest event that has occurred in this world since the resurrection of the Master. As the restored Church of Jesus Christ, we humbly and gratefully bear this witness to all men. It is the truth, intended for all of our Father's children. EZRA TAFT BENSON, "FIRST PRESIDENCY MESSAGE," *ENSIGN,* APR. 1993

We testify that this restored gospel was introduced into the world by the marvelous appearance of God the Eternal Father and His Son, the resurrected Lord Jesus Christ. That most glorious manifestation marked the beginning of the fulfillment of the promise of Peter, who prophesied of "the times of restitution of all things, which God hath spoken by the mouth of all his holy prophets since the world began," this in preparation for the coming of the Lord to reign personally upon the earth (Acts 3:21). *CHURCH NEWS,* APR. 12, 1980

foreordination. ***See also*** **premortal existence**

God foreordained (or called) certain spirits before this mortal life to perform certain acts and hold important offices during their lives upon the earth. *PRINCIPLES,* 1976

Although men were foreordained to hold positions and accomplish particular tasks during this life, they still have their free agency. If they choose to do otherwise, they may. IBID.

forgiveness. ***See also*** **repentance**

Pray for strength to forgive those who have wronged you. Abandon feelings of anger, bitterness, or revenge. Look for the good in others rather than focusing on their faults and magnifying their weaknesses. Allow God to be the judge of others' harmful actions. It may be difficult to let go of hurt feelings, but you can do it with the Lord's help. You will find that forgiveness can heal terrible wounds, replacing their poison of contention and hatred with the peace and love that only God can give. *TRUE TO FAITH,* 2004

Forgiveness is an important part of putting bad behavior behind us. As we make the necessary changes, we need to forgive ourselves. But we may also need to forgive others who have been traveling with us on the wrong path. Forgiveness will help us to let go of the bad behavior we are forsaking. JAMES E. FAUST, "FIRST PRESIDENCY MESSAGE," *ENSIGN,* MAR. 2001

A spirit of forgiveness and an attitude of love and compassion toward those who may have wronged us is of the very essence of the gospel of Jesus Christ. Each of us has need of this spirit. The whole world has need of it. The Lord taught it. He exemplified it as none other has exemplified it. GORDON B. HINCKLEY, "FIRST PRESIDENCY MESSAGE," *ENSIGN,* JUNE 1991

We encourage Church members to forgive those who may have wronged them. NEWS RELEASE, DEC. 20, 1985

The evidence that sins have been forgiven is peace of conscience and a desire to do good. *PRINCIPLES,* 1976

As we try to apply the Golden Rule, we must realize that love will not permit us to hold grudges or ill feelings. These canker the soul and crowd out love. We hurt ourselves by holding grudges and ill feelings. We hurt and sometimes destroy the person about whom we are bearing tales. We would not think of stealing from or injuring physically one of our associates, friends, or neighbors, but we do even worse by stealing his good name. N. ELDON TANNER, "FIRST PRESIDENCY MESSAGE," *ENSIGN,* OCT. 1971

fornication, *see* sexual relations

Founding Fathers, *see* Constitution of the United States

free agency, *see* agency; freedom

freedom. *See also* Constitution of the United States; politics

Citizens of this nation are free, of course, to participate in efforts designed to warn of the threat of any force or power, theory, or principle that would deprive them of their freedom or the individual liberties vouchsafed by the Constitution. "DEAR BRETHREN," UNITED STATES, JAN. 15, 1987

Among America's most precious assets is its religious heritage that teaches the supreme importance of the individual as a child of God, blessed with all the responsibility, opportunity, and freedom which that status implies. We can waste or lose this asset only at our grave peril. *DESERET NEWS,* NOV. 7, 1964

For nearly two thousand years the professed followers of Jesus Christ have associated with His birth the heavenly announcement of "peace on earth and good will toward men" [Luke 2:14]. Indeed, ever since man was placed on earth, peace has been among his noblest quests.

Associated with it has been his desire for freedom–freedom to express what he thinks; freedom to choose his work without dictatorial compulsion; freedom to worship without molestation; freedom to own a home into which dictators or usurpers may not enter unbidden–indispensable conditions to the enjoyment of peace. *DESERET NEWS,* DEC. 14, 1960

The same ethical and moral standards applied to individuals should find application in the judging of nations. No race or national government has a moral right to infringe upon the rights of other countries, and aggressive measures can be justified only for the protection of life, liberty, and the maintenance of peace and justice in the world. *DESERET NEWS,* DEC. 14, 1949

Individual freedom of conscience and the right to choose one's own beliefs and course of action (limited only by the overarching principle that in the pursuit of one's own chosen course he must not trespass upon the equivalent right in all others) are basic tenets of the Church. Out of a painful and tragic experience it learned the value of freedom under a rule of just laws and the degradation which flows from a ruthless violation of them. It knows that its own security and the very right to pursue the practice of Christian teachings and to be protected in an observance of the code of decency depend upon the preservation in civil governments of the guaranty to every individual of his God-given right to be free. "DEAR BRETHREN," JULY 8, 1948, IN *MESSAGES,* 6:275-77

The God we worship does not hold men responsible for opportunities that they do not possess. *DESERET NEWS,* DEC. 20, 1924, IN *MESSAGES,* 5:240-42

We are at liberty to believe what we please, but our acts must conform to the laws of the land. FIRST PRESIDENCY TO REED SMOOT, JAN. 20, 1904

We are filled with regret when we see steps taken by those in authority, who ought to know better, to shackle the human mind and thought, to bring American citizens into bondage, and to pass and maintain laws that are violative of every constitutional right. *DESERET NEWS,* JULY 25, 1885, IN *MESSAGES,* 3:18-22

G

gambling

The Church of Jesus Christ of Latter-day Saints is opposed to gambling, including lotteries sponsored by governments. *TRUE TO FAITH,* 2004

The Church opposes gambling in any form, including government-sponsored lotteries. Members are urged to join with others who have similar concerns in opposing the legalization and government sponsorship of any form of gambling. *CHURCH HANDBOOK,* 1998

The Church of Jesus Christ of Latter-day Saints opposes gambling in its various forms. Experience has clearly shown gambling to be harmful to the human spirit, financially destructive of individuals and families, and detrimental to the moral climate of communities. *CHURCH NEWS,* JAN. 11, 1992

There can be no question about the moral ramifications of gambling. As it has been in the past, The Church of Jesus Christ of Latter-day Saints stands opposed to gambling, including government-sponsored lotteries.

Public lotteries are advocated as a means of relieving the burden of taxation. It has been clearly demonstrated, however, that all too often lotteries only add to the problems of the financially disadvantaged by taking money from them and giving nothing of value in return. The poor and the elderly become victims of the inducements that are held out to purchase lottery tickets on the remote chance of winning a substantial prize. "DEAR BRETHREN," SEPT. 26, 1986

Church leaders must never permit games of chance in any form, including raffles and bingo, in connection with any Church function. *CHURCH HANDBOOK,* 1976

The Authorities of the Church have always advised the people against card games, that is, cards of the kind that are used by gamblers and others, with ace, king, jack, queen, etc. HEBER J. GRANT TO LEOLIN N. DICKEY, NOV. 27, 1934

The Church always has been and now is unalterably opposed to gambling in any form whatever. It is opposed to any game of chance, occupation, or so-called business which takes money from the person who may be possessed of it without giving value received in return. It is opposed to all practices the tendency of which is to encourage the spirit of reckless speculation, and particularly to that which tends to degrade or weaken the high moral standard which the members of the Church and of our community at large have always maintained.

We therefore advise and urge all members of the Church to refrain from participation in any activity which is contrary to the view herein set forth. *DESERET NEWS,* SEPT. 21, 1925

[N]o kind of chance game, guessing-contest, or raffling device can be approved in any entertainment under the auspices of our Church organizations.

The desire to get something of value for little or nothing is pernicious; and any proceeding that strengthens that desire is an effective aid to the gambling spirit, which has proved a veritable demon of destruction to thousands. Risking a dime in the hope of winning a dollar in any game of chance is a species of gambling.

Let it not be thought that raffling articles of value, offering prizes to the winners in guessing-contests, the use of machines of chance, or any other device of the kind is to be allowed or excused because the money so obtained is to be used for a good purpose. The Church is not to be supported in any degree by means obtained through gambling. *IMPROVEMENT ERA,* DEC. 1908, IN *MESSAGES,* 4:187-88

Gathering

[W]e wish to reiterate the long-standing counsel to members of the Church to remain in their homelands rather than immigrate to the United States.

Experience has shown that those who relocate to the United States often encounter language, cultural, and economic challenges, resulting in disappointment and personal and family difficulties.

As members throughout the world remain in their homelands, working to build the Church in their native countries, great blessings will come to them personally and to the Church collectively. Stakes and wards throughout the world will be strengthened, making it possible to share the blessings of the gospel with an even greater number of our Heavenly Father's children. *CHURCH NEWS,* DEC. 11, 1999

Generally, Church members are encouraged to remain in their native lands to build up and strengthen the Church. *CHURCH HANDBOOK,* 1998

Through the preaching of the gospel to the nations of the earth, Israel will be gathered. "BASIC DOCTRINES," MAR. 5, 1971

[P]eople who have fairly good positions in their homeland [should] remain where they are and help to build up the Church in the localities where they live. FIRST PRESIDENCY TO FRED TADJE, OCT. 18, 1929, IN *MESSAGES,* 5:268-69

We advise members of the Church who are located in well

established communities of Latter-day Saints to remain and assist in the development of the localities already occupied, rather than remove to new regions where the prospect for development is problematical and social environment and financial opportunity very uncertain. *DESERET NEWS,* APR. 25, 1923

The establishment of the latter-day Zion on the American continent occasions the gathering of the Saints from all nations. This is not compulsory, and, particularly under present conditions, is not urged, because it is desirable that our people shall remain in their native lands and form congregations of a permanent character to aid in the work of proselytizing. *MILLENNIAL STAR,* MAR. 2, 1911, IN *MESSAGES,* 4:221-23

The policy of the Church is not to entice or encourage people to leave their native lands; but to remain faithful and true in their allegiance to their governments, and to be good citizens. STATEMENT, DEC. 12, 1907, IN *MESSAGES,* 4:164-66

The God of Israel will communicate to His disciples all things necessary for the building up of His kingdom on the earth until Israel is gathered, yea even all the blood of Abraham scattered over all the earth, Zion established, Jerusalem rebuilt, and the whole earth be filled with the glory and knowledge of God. BRIGHAM YOUNG AND WILLARD RICHARDS TO ALL ELDERS AND SISTERS IN GREAT BRITAIN, AUG. 22, 1844, IN *MESSAGES,* 1:238-39

The greatest temporal and spiritual blessings which always flow from faithfulness and concerted effort never attended individual exertion or enterprise. The history of all past ages abundantly attests this fact. In addition, to all temporal blessings, there is no other way for the Saints to be saved in these last days, [than by the gathering,] as the concurrent testimony of all holy prophets clearly proves, for it is written—"They shall come from the east, and be gathered from the west; the north shall give up, and the south shall keep not back" [Ps. 107:3; 3 Ne. 10:13]. "The sons of God shall be gathered from far, and His daughters from the ends of the earth" [Isa. 43:6].

It is also the concurrent testimony of all the prophets that this gathering together of all the Saints must take place before the Lord comes to "take vengeance upon the ungodly" [D&C 29:17] and "to be glorified and admired by all those who obey the gospel" [2 Thes. 1:10]. STATEMENT, JAN. 15, 1841, IN *MESSAGES,* 1:125-32

gender. *See also* premortal existence

All human beings–male and female–are created in the image of God. Each is a beloved son or daughter of heavenly parents, and, as such, each has a divine nature and destiny. Gender is an essential characteristic of individual premortal, mortal, and eternal identity and purpose. *CHURCH NEWS,* SEPT. 30, 1995

Our designation as men or women began before this world was. JAMES E. FAUST, "FIRST PRESIDENCY MESSAGE," *ENSIGN,* SEPT. 1995

A correct understanding of the divinely appointed roles of men and women will fortify all against sinful practices. FIRST PRESIDENCY TO ALL MEMBERS, NOV. 14, 1981

Based upon ancient and modern revelation, The Church of Jesus Christ of Latter-day Saints gladly teaches and declares the Christian doctrine that all men and women are brothers and sisters, not only by blood relationship from common mortal progenitors but also as literal spirit children of an Eternal Father. "STATEMENT OF THE FIRST PRESIDENCY REGARDING GOD'S GUIDANCE TO ALL MANKIND," FEB. 15, 1978

We recognize men and women as equally important before

the Lord, but with differences biologically, emotionally, and in other ways. *DESERET NEWS,* OCT. 22, 1976

The bodies of men and the bodies of women were created differently so they complemented each other, so that the union of the two would bring a conception which would bring a living soul into the world, one of those numerous, uncountable spirits that Abraham saw when the Lord had pulled back the curtains.

Now we must emphasize here that the Lord made man and woman, male and female to reproduce after their kind, and in the billions of unions there has continued to come a male or a female. Their bodies are still so formed that they will continue to the end of time in producing male or female, the spirit children of God. SPENCER W. KIMBALL, "FIRST PRESIDENCY MESSAGE," *ENSIGN,* OCT. 1975

God the Father

Believe in God. Believe in God the Eternal Father. He is the great governor of the universe, but He is our Father and our God to whom we may go in prayer. We are His sons and daughters. Have you ever really thought that you were a child of God and that you have something of divinity with you? GORDON B. HINCKLEY, "FIRST PRESIDENCY MESSAGE," *ENSIGN,* MAR. 2006

God is our Heavenly Father. We are His children. He has a body of flesh and bone that is glorified and perfected. He loves us. He weeps with us when we suffer and rejoices when we do what is right. He wants to communicate with us, and we can communicate with Him through sincere prayer. *PREACH MY GOSPEL,* 2005

God the Father is the Supreme Being in whom we believe and whom we worship. He is the ultimate Creator, Ruler, and

Preserver of all things. He is perfect, has all power, and knows all things. He "has a body of flesh and bones as tangible as man's" (D&C 130:22). *TRUE TO FAITH,* 2004

In what shall we believe? In the first place, we shall believe in God our Eternal Father. He is the Father of each of us. He is the ruler and governor of the entire universe, and yet somehow He can hear us when we pray. What a marvelous thing that is, that the God of Heaven will hear your prayers and my prayers. We are His children. GORDON B. HINCKLEY, "FIRST PRESIDENCY MESSAGE," *ENSIGN,* JULY 1998

God revealed Himself and His beloved Son, Jesus Christ, our Redeemer, anew in this dispensation. He has revealed anew the way in which we must walk if we would know Him. First, we must seek Him in the manner He prescribed–namely, by prayer and by studying the word of God, modern and ancient, but particularly modern. Such prayer and study leads to faith in God, the Eternal Father, and in His Son, Jesus Christ. The next step is repentance. Such faith and true repentance is followed by baptism and the reception of the Holy Ghost. Accepting and obeying these first basic principles and ordinances, as they are prescribed by the gospel of Jesus Christ, and then continuing to conform to the commandments of God, gives one not only an intellectual concept of God, but a personal knowledge which is derived from "profound reverence," which is the beginning of wisdom. Wisdom, thus gained, will not only lead individuals to a solution of their personal problems, but if enough persons gain wisdom, it will lead mankind to a solution of the larger problems facing this generation. MARION G. ROMNEY, "FIRST PRESIDENCY MESSAGE," *ENSIGN,* JULY 1983

God is good. He is eager to forgive. He wants us to perfect

ourselves and maintain control of ourselves. He does not want Satan and others to control our lives. We must learn that keeping our Heavenly Father's commandments represents the *only* path to total control of ourselves, the only way to find joy, truth, and fulfillment in this life and in eternity. SPENCER W. KIMBALL, "FIRST PRESIDENCY MESSAGE," *ENSIGN,* OCTOBER 1982

The God we believe in is a living God with body, parts, and passions, in whose image we were made, who is the Father of the spirits of all mankind and under whose direction the world was created and all things therein. He created the earth solely for the purpose of having a place whereon man could dwell and prove himself worthy of coming back into His presence. He is a loving father who is interested in us and our welfare and who stands ready to answer our call if we will but go to Him. N. ELDON TANNER, "FIRST PRESIDENCY MESSAGE," *ENSIGN,* APR. 1982

We must always remember that God rules in the affairs of men, and that He is truly the Heavenly Father of all mankind. We are all brothers and sisters. *ENSIGN,* NOV. 1973

God is our Father; He is the being in whose image man is created. He has a body of flesh and bones as tangible as man's (D&C 130:22), and He is the literal and personal father of the spirits of all men. He is omnipotent and omniscient; He has all power and all wisdom; and His perfections consist in the possession of all knowledge, all faith or power, all justice, all judgment, all mercy, all truth, and the fullness of all godly attributes. JOSEPH FIELDING SMITH, "FIRST PRESIDENCY MESSAGE," *ENSIGN,* MAY 1971

The Gods who preside over this universe are our Heavenly Father, His Son Jesus Christ, and the Holy Ghost.

Our Heavenly Father is sovereign and supreme in this universe. God, our Heavenly Father, and His Son, Jesus Christ, are immortal, glorified, and exalted. Each has an eternal spirit inseparably connected with a body of flesh and bones.

The Father, the Son, and the Holy Ghost have all knowledge, virtue, and power. Their influence is everywhere present as they operate through the principles of eternal law.

The work and the glory of the Godhead is to bring to pass the immortality and eternal life of man.

Our Heavenly Father (God and Father)[:]

God is the greatest intelligence. He understands and lives in harmony with celestial law.

Our Heavenly Father is the Father of the spirit body of Jesus Christ and of the spirit bodies of all mankind, and He is also the Father of the physical body of Jesus Christ.

Our Heavenly Father presides over and administers the work of the Godhead. "BASIC DOCTRINES," 1971

To know God and thereby gain the promised eternal life, one must come to have adequate concepts of His personality in its various aspects—intellectual, social, moral, and spiritual: Accurate concepts will come only as God reveals them. The promise "... seek, and ye shall find ..." [Matt. 7:7] will bring fulfillment. In seeking, the heart and soul require the cooperation and guidance of the mind. Men must think about God if they would worship intelligently. But we must ever beware of the rank growth of mistaken speculation. We must ever seek this most precious knowledge by the light of revelation. We know God as we become like Him and to know Him is to love Him. To become like God, man must progressively understand Him. *CHURCH NEWS*, DEC. 21, 1968

[T]he Latter-day Saint Church has published nothing but what is broadcast to all people in the world, and the doctrine of God and the Godhead, as accepted by the Church, is found in the standard Church works, the Bible, Book of Mormon, Doctrine and Covenants, and Pearl of Great Price. HEBER J. GRANT TO MRS. J. M. AIME, DEC. 4, 1934

[T]he sole object of worship, God the Eternal Father, stands supreme and alone, and it is in the name of the Only Begotten that we thus approach Him, as Christ taught always. *IMPROVEMENT ERA,* APR. 1912, IN *MESSAGES,* 4:270-71

The Church of Jesus Christ of Latter-day Saints worships Him, and Him alone, who is the father of Jesus Christ, whom He worshipped, whom Adam worshipped, and who is God the Eternal Father of us all. FIRST PRESIDENCY TO SAMUEL O. BENNION, FEB. 20, 1912, IN *MESSAGES,* 4:266-67

[I]f the Son of God be the express image (that is, likeness) of His Father's person, then His Father is in the form of man; for that was the form of the Son of God, not only during His mortal life, but before His mortal birth and after His resurrection. It was in this form that the Father and the Son, as two personages, appeared to Joseph Smith, when, as a boy of fourteen years, he received his first vision. *IMPROVEMENT ERA,* NOV. 1909, IN *MESSAGES,* 4:200-206

The Father of Jesus is our Father also. IBID.

God Himself is an exalted man, perfected, enthroned, and supreme. By His almighty power He organized the earth, and all that it contains, from spirit and element, which exist co-eternally with Himself. He formed every plant that grows, and every animal that breathes, each after its own kind, spiritually and temporally—"that which is spiritual being the likeness of that which is temporal, and that which is temporal in the likeness of that which is spiritual" [D&C 77:2]. He made the tadpole and the ape, the lion and the elephant, but He did not make them in His own image, nor endow them with godlike reason and intelligence. Nevertheless, the whole animal creation will be perfected and perpetuated in the hereafter, each class in its "distinct ["destined"] order or sphere," and will enjoy "eternal felicity" [77:3]. IBID.

We are in the hands of our Heavenly Father, the God of Abraham and Joseph [Smith], who guided us to this land, who fed the poor Saints on the plains with quails, who gave His people strength to labor without bread, who sent the gulls of the deep as saviors to preserve (by devouring the crickets) the golden wheat for bread for His people, and who has preserved His Saints from the wrath of their enemies. He is our Father and our protector; we live in His light, are guided by His wisdom, protected by His shadow, and upheld by His strength. FIRST PRESIDENCY TO ORSON HYDE, JULY 28, 1850, IN *MESSAGES,* 2:50-51

We admit that God is the great source and fountain from whence proceeds all good; that He is perfect intelligence, and that His wisdom is alone sufficient to govern and regulate the mighty creations and worlds which shine and blaze with such magnificence and splendor over our heads, as though touched with His finger and moved by His almighty word. STATEMENT, JAN. 22, 1834, IN *MESSAGES,* 1:23-44

Godhead. *See also* God the Father; Jesus Christ; Holy Ghost

They [God the Eternal Father, His Son Jesus Christ, and the Holy Ghost] are distinct beings, but They are one in purpose and effort. They are united as one in bringing to pass the grand, divine plan for the salvation and exaltation of the children of God.

In His great, moving prayer in the garden before His betrayal, Christ pleaded with His Father concerning the Apostles, whom He loved, saying:

"Neither pray I for these alone, but for them also which shall believe on me through their word;

"That they all may be one; as thou, Father, are in me, and I in thee, that they also may be one in us" (John 17:20-21).

It is that perfect unity between the Father, the Son, and the Holy Ghost that binds these three into the oneness of the divine Godhead.

Miracle of miracles and wonder of wonders. They are interested in us, and we are the substance of Their great concern. They are available to each of us. We approach the Father through the Son, He is our intercessor at the throne of God. How marvelous it is that we may so speak to the Father in the name of the Son. GORDON B. HINCKLEY, "FIRST PRESIDENCY MESSAGE," *ENSIGN,* JULY 2006

godhood, *see* exaltation

gospel

The purpose of the gospel is to cleanse people of their sins so they can receive the Savior's mercy at the day of judgment. *PREACH MY GOSPEL,* 2005

As you learn gospel truths, you will increase in your understanding of Heavenly Father's eternal plan. With this understanding as a foundation for your life, you will be able to make wise choices, live in harmony with God's will, and find joy in living. Your testimony will grow stronger. You will remain true to the faith. *TRUE TO FAITH,* 2004

[T]hrough regular personal prayer and study of the scriptures and the doctrines of the gospel, you will be prepared to withstand evil influences that would deceive you and harm you. IBID.

The true gospel of Jesus Christ never led to bigotry. It never led to self-righteousness. It never led to arrogance. The true gospel of Jesus Christ leads to brotherhood, to friendship, to appreciation of others, to respect and kindness and love. GORDON B. HINCKLEY, "FIRST PRESIDENCY MESSAGE," *ENSIGN,* APR. 2002

An important part of the gospel message is that we not be too rigid: that we open our minds, develop some tolerance, and not be quick to render judgment. JAMES E. FAUST, "FIRST PRESIDENCY MESSAGE," *ENSIGN,* MAR. 2000

At the heart of the message of the Savior of the world is a single, glorious, wonderful, still largely untried concept. In its simplest terms the message is that we should seek to overcome the selfishness we all seem to be born with, that we should overcome human nature and think of others before self. We should think of God and serve Him, and think of others and serve them. JAMES E. FAUST, "FIRST PRESIDENCY MESSAGE," *ENSIGN,* DEC. 1999

Our main task is to declare the gospel and do it effectively. We are not obligated to answer every objection. Every man eventually is backed up to the wall of faith, and there he must make his stand. EZRA TAFT BENSON, "FIRST PRESIDENCY MESSAGE," *ENSIGN,* JAN. 1988

This principle of love is the basic essence of the gospel of Jesus Christ. Without love of God and love of neighbor, there is little else to commend the gospel to us as a way of life. GORDON B. HINCKLEY, "FIRST PRESIDENCY MESSAGE," *ENSIGN,* MAR. 1984

The gospel is not merely a moral code of living based on seeking to acquire the attributes of the Savior, but it is also the actual means essential to salvation. Thus, we believe that Christ willingly gave His life for you and me that we might be raised from the dead and go back into the presence of our Father in Heaven. N. ELDON TANNER, "FIRST PRESIDENCY MESSAGE," *ENSIGN,* APR. 1982

[T]he gospel always has been and always will be operated through families. Our whole system of genealogical research and of salvation for the dead centers around the concept of turning the hearts of the children to their fathers so that gospel blessings may be offered to Abraham's seed. *PATRIARCHS,* 1981

One cannot honestly study the scriptures without learning gospel principles because the scriptures have been written to preserve principles for our benefit.

Learning the gospel from the written word, however, is not enough. It must also be lived. As a matter of fact, getting a knowledge of the gospel and living it are interdependent. They go hand in hand. One cannot fully learn the gospel without living it. A knowledge of the gospel comes by degrees; one learns a little, obeys what he learns, learns a little more and obeys that. This cycle continues in an endless round. Such is the pattern by which one can move on to a full knowledge of the gospel. MARION G. ROMNEY, "FIRST PRESIDENCY MESSAGE," *ENSIGN,* SEPT. 1980

The gospel of Jesus Christ teaches that man is eternal—that he lived as a spirit before he came to Earth, and that after death he will be resurrected and will dwell in a place determined by how he kept his mortal estate. Every man may choose for himself whether or not he wishes to live forever with God, or be cast out of His presence.

One of the principles of the gospel is that the family will continue as an eternal unit. Where true love exists between husband and wife, it is most comforting to know that through a special ordinance in the holy temple a man and wife are sealed for time and all eternity, and the children born of that union will be with them forever. How glorious! N. ELDON TANNER, "FIRST PRESIDENCY MESSAGE," *ENSIGN,* OCT. 1978

We also declare that the gospel of Jesus Christ, restored to His Church in our day, provides the only way to a mortal life of happiness and a fullness of joy forever. For those who have not received this gospel, the opportunity will come to them in the life hereafter if not in this life. "STATEMENT OF THE FIRST PRESIDENCY REGARDING GOD'S GUIDANCE TO ALL MANKIND," FEB. 15, 1978

In general, the gospel may be said to consist of all truth secular and religious, for any truth can contribute to progression and improvement. In the sense in which it is used most frequently in the scriptures, however, the word *gospel* is "the power of God unto salvation to every one that believeth" (Rom. 1:16). It consists of all the principles, laws, covenants, ordinances, and truths that will secure exaltation in the celestial kingdom for those who believe and obey. *PRINCIPLES,* 1976

Regardless of country, clime, or condition, the gospel of Jesus Christ applies to every individual just the same. It is a way of life that each can accept, and if lived, will bring greater joy, success, and happiness than anything else in the world. In fact, it sets forth in all simplicity the principles of the gospel established by Jesus Christ while He was here upon the earth. And the Church is the same organization that Christ formed while heading the Church here in His life, with the same officers, namely, apostles, prophets, pastors, teachers, evangelists, etc. N. ELDON TANNER, "FIRST PRESIDENCY MESSAGE," *ENSIGN,* JULY 1974

The gospel offers us the only way to eternal life, and whenever accepted, a new era in life begins. N. ELDON TANNER, "FIRST PRESIDENCY MESSAGE," *ENSIGN,* FEBRUARY 1972

How fortunate we are to be members of The Church of Jesus Christ, wherein we are taught the gospel in its fullness as it has been revealed and restored in these latter days. What a great blessing it is for us to know that God is a real personage in whose image we are created; that we are His spirit children; that He loves us and is interested in us; that through His Son He has given us a blueprint of life that if followed will lead us back into His presence, where we can enjoy eternal progression with our families and loved ones. N. ELDON TANNER, "FIRST PRESIDENCY MESSAGE," *ENSIGN,* APRIL 1971

The eternal principles, laws, and ordinances by which mankind may obtain immortality and eternal life through the Atonement are known as the gospel of Jesus Christ.

The first principles and ordinances of the gospel, which must be received and obeyed by those who are accountable, are—

a. Faith in God the Father, in the Lord Jesus Christ, and in the Holy Ghost.

b. Repentance from all sins.

c. Baptism for the remission of sins.

d. Laying on of hands for the gift of the Holy Ghost.

Man must also prove faithful in giving willing obedience to all gospel principles and ordinances. "BASIC DOCTRINES," 1971

[The gospel] is a spiritual force which can crash and overcome all physical barriers. Surely we must put on the whole armor of God, consisting, as Paul said, of truth, righteousness, peace, faith, with the helmet of salvation and the sword of the spirit, which is the word of God. Because of our faith in a living, personal, and all powerful God, we do not fear the final outcome in our fight against the emissaries of Satan, though we must ever be alert, united, and on guard.

Nothing but the restored gospel of Jesus Christ—which we

gratefully proclaim—can save the world or the individual from the dangers that threaten us.

This is a gospel of character-building activity, of invincible faith and the courage that is born of faith; of repentance, the doorway to progress; of sanctification through baptism of water and of the Spirit; the doorway to the celestial kingdom. Let us take courage in the knowledge that Christ, the Prince of Peace, is at the helm. *CHURCH NEWS*, DEC. 21, 1968

The spirit of true brotherly love is a fundamental concept of the gospel of Jesus Christ. Fostering the spirit of brotherhood among all peoples of this nation could well aid in the solution of many of the social problems which foster riots and other disturbances. ... Deeds of true brotherhood are necessary for spiritual wholeness. *CHURCH NEWS,* FEB. 17, 1968

With the knowledge that the gospel of Jesus Christ if accepted and lived will bring love, peace, and joy to the world, we as members of His Church have the privilege and responsibility of living it and sharing it with the world. By doing this we become ambassadors of the Lord in helping Him to bring peace and joy to the world and immortality and eternal life to man. FIRST PRESIDENCY TO ALL MISSIONARIES AND SAINTS IN THE SOUTH AFRICAN MISSION, CHRISTMAS 1965

The gospel of Jesus Christ, properly understood, we believe, embraces all truth, provides sound bases in human understanding for the ultimate reconciliation of human and cultural differences, while preserving individuality, nationality, and freedom of group identity. In our Father's house are many mansions. We are mindful that our Lord and Master, Himself, was born, lived, and fulfilled His earthly mission in the "fertile crescent" which functions as a significant land bridge between the great continents of Europe, Africa, and

Asia. Certain common bonds which underlie Christendom, Islam, and Judaism, properly understood and examined, we feel, can be extended and broadened to assist mankind in acquiring a more tolerant attitude. The revelation inherent in His declaration, "I am the Way, the Truth, and the Life," can yet dawn in greater degree upon suffering mankind, we hope and pray, through the extension of religious liberty, and with it, peace and freedom. We must never cease to proclaim His message as Prince of Peace, of Peace on Earth, Good Will Toward Men—to all men everywhere. "A REPORT TO THE NATIONAL CITIZENS' COMMISSION ON INTERNATIONAL COOPERATION," ATTACHED TO FIRST PRESIDENCY TO DEAN RUSK, AUG. 6, 1965

Jesus said, "... I am come that they might have life, and that they might have it more abundantly" (John 10:10). As we contemplate our challenges and blessings, let us remember that Christ's gospel is the only true pattern for joyous, purposeful, and abundant living. Every principle he taught and every example he set were designed to help us meet the challenges and problems of this life and to lay the foundation for our personal growth, development and happiness here and in the hereafter. If we would have life and "have it more abundantly" we have but to seek and follow him. *CHURCH NEWS,* DEC. 21, 1963

The underlying genius of the restored gospel is, in a word, that everything known to man has a spiritual foundation. The earth was created spiritually before the temporal creation. Man himself is the spirit child of God, whose destiny is to return to the presence of the Lord whence he came. Family, health, property, government, brotherhood are, in the revealed interpretation of the gospel, concepts based on eternal spiritual properties. If a man would truly enjoy the blessing of life and living, let him gratefully recognize and acknowledge the source of all beneficence, the giver of every good and perfect gift. *DESERET NEWS,* DEC. 12, 1956

We bear solemn witness that Christ is the Lord of the earth, that the saving principles of his gospel are as essential for the happiness and peace of mankind here in mortal life as for salvation in the life to come. IBID.

[T]he gospel as believed and taught by The Church of Jesus Christ of Latter-day Saints does not consist in a mere passive assent to the validity of the principles it proclaims. These require deeds, active translation into terms of daily life. It is not an academic thing; it is a body of living principles which reach out into and permeate and give color and character to the daily course of individual conduct. But no one can escape entirely the effect of the predominating influence of the community or society in which he daily dwells. The Church, therefore, as part of its mission, has a vital concern with the atmosphere in which its people live and by which they are inevitably affected.

It conceives it to be its duty to throw the whole weight of its influence and marshal to the purpose all proper resources within its grasp to the end that prevailing conditions in our communities (including civic influences) shall be such as are conducive to the fostering of the high standards of honor and morality its teachings enjoin. "DEAR BRETHREN," JULY 8, 1948, IN *MESSAGES,* 6:275-77

[T]he social side of the restored gospel is only an incident of it; it is not the end thereof. FIRST PRESIDENCY TO LOWRY NELSON, JULY 17, 1947

Ethics are man-made and vary with man's concepts and development; the gospel is God's truth and is unchanging through the eternities. FIRST PRESIDENCY TO JOSEPH FIELDING SMITH,

JOHN A. WIDTSOE, HAROLD B. LEE, AND MARION G. ROMNEY, AUG. 9, 1944, IN *MESSAGES,* 6:209-15

The principles of the gospel are all-embracing—they are everlasting, unchangeable, ultimate truth. They will fit every situation, every problem, every contingency that may arise in the life of man. *IMPROVEMENT ERA,* NOV. 1942, IN *MESSAGES,* 6:170-85

The gospel of Christ is a gospel of love and peace, of patience and long suffering, of forbearance and forgiveness, of kindness and good deeds, of charity and brotherly love. Greed, avarice, base ambition, thirst for power, and unrighteousness dominion over our fellow men can have no place in the hearts of Latter-day Saints nor of God-fearing men everywhere. *IMPROVEMENT ERA,* MAY 1942, IN *MESSAGES,* 6:148-63

The gospel of Jesus Christ is the very essence of simplicity and truth. The Church which bears His name must resist the introduction of formalities that may lead to ritualistic and imposing ceremonies. In every Church gathering, it is important to consider whether any particular formalities may develop an attitude that might detract from the worship of the Lord. Whatever detracts from a particular ordinance being performed or the true worship of the Lord will tend toward formalism. *CHURCH HANDBOOK,* 1940

[T]he gospel teachings touch this life not only, but the life that is to come, with its salvation and exaltation as the final goal. *DESERET NEWS,* AUG. 13, 1938, IN *MESSAGES,* 6:44-58

The restoration of priesthood and gospel in their fullness have poured out upon the peoples of the earth a divine bounty of saving spiritual truth—a gift free as air to every man, no matter how high or how low he might be, who would in humility seek and receive it, a gift that has brought courage to him that faltered, a living hope to him that was downtrodden and oppressed, the joy of a full life here, of exaltation and eternal progression hereafter to him that lived the word. The Lord has blessed His people beyond measure and beyond price. *IMPROVEMENT ERA,* APR. 1935, IN *MESSAGES,* 6:4-5

The gospel is a plan for the guidance of men in their minglings together here as mortals, and for their direction in their spiritual lives to the end that they may be saved and exalted in the world to come. The gospel is not a social program, though its living on this earth involves one if greed and avarice, covetousness, and selfishness be trodden under foot and if ambition, envy, and love of earthly power and dominion be cast out. The gospel is eternal truth, existent from eternity to eternity; it is all truth. *DESERET NEWS,* DEC. 15, 1834

Our gospel is that of peace and good will, of happiness and harmony, of physical, mental, and spiritual enjoyment and common sense. *DESERET NEWS,* DEC. 20, 1913, IN *MESSAGES,* 4:293-99

The doctrines taught by the Latter-day Saints are not a mere imitation of the teachings of the apostles as contained in the New Testament. It is the same gospel preached by them and possesses the same sanctifying, life-giving power, and the same spiritual gifts and powers have followed the believers in our day as anciently. *LIAHONA,* APR. 6, 1907, IN *MESSAGES,* 4:155-57

The gospel has made us free, and has placed in our possession the means to make others free. Truth is liberty, and we have the truth. Let not this assurance, however, lull you to sleep. "Eternal vigilance is the price of safety." Because peace and prosperity, spiritual and temporal, are yours, do not allow yourselves to imagine that Christ and Belial are friends or ever can be. *DESERET NEWS,* DEC. 20, 1902

In regard to our religion, or our eternal covenants, we have no compromise to make, nor principles to barter away; they emanate from God and are founded upon the rock eternal ages; they will live and exist when empires, powers, and nations shall crumble and decay; and with the help of the Almighty we will guard sacredly our covenants and maintain our interests and be true to our God, while time exists or eternity endures. STATEMENT, AUG. 29, 1882, IN *MESSAGES,* 2:342-47

government. *See also* **freedom; politics; Socialism**

Elected officials who are Latter-day Saints make their own decisions and may not necessarily be in agreement with one another or even with a publicly stated Church position. While the Church may communicate its views to them, as it may to any other elected official, it recognizes that these officials still must make their own choices based on their best judgment and with consideration of the constituencies whom they were elected to represent. "ISSUES RESOURCES" 2006

We wish to reiterate the divine counsel that members "should be anxiously engaged in a good cause, and do many things of their own free will, and bring to pass much righteousness" (D&C 58:27) while using gospel principles as a guide and while cooperating with other like-minded individuals.

Through such wise participation as citizens, we are then in better compliance with this scripture: "Governments were instituted of God for the benefit of man; and ... he holds men accountable for their acts in relation to them" (134:1).

Therefore, as in the past, we urge members of the Church to be full participants in political, governmental, and community affairs. Members of the Church are under special obligations to seek out and then uphold those leaders who are wise, good, and honest (98:10).

Thus, we strongly urge men and women to be willing to serve on school boards, city and county councils and commissions, state legislatures, and other high offices of either election or appointment, including involvement in the political party of their choice. *ENSIGN,* APR. 1998

Church members should obey, honor, and sustain the laws in any country where they reside or travel (see D&C 58:21-22). This includes laws that prohibit proselyting. *CHURCH HANDBOOK,* 1998

Members should study political issues and candidates carefully and vote for individuals whom they believe will act with integrity and in ways conducive to good communities and good government. Members of the Church are under special obligation to seek out and uphold leaders who are honest, good, and wise (see D&C 98:10).

Church members are urged to be willing to serve in elected and appointed public offices in local and national government.

Members should do their civic duty by supporting measures that strengthen society morally, economically, and culturally. Members are urged to be actively engaged in worthy causes to improve their communities and make them wholesome places in which to live and rear families. However, members should not give the impression that they represent the Church as they work for solutions to city or community problems. IBID.

There is far too much immorality, dishonesty, and lack of integrity in the lives of those who are leading and guiding the affairs of our nations, our schools, and our communities. Somehow we must get back to the lofty ideals and high-minded principles which characterized the lives of those who fought and died for truth, religion, and freedom. N. ELDON TANNER, "FIRST PRESIDENCY MESSAGE," *ENSIGN,* JAN. 1983

[A]s citizens of this great nation, we are accountable for the kind of leaders and lawmakers we elect. *DESERET NEWS,* NOV. 4, 1977

Good, law-abiding citizenship is a key to more abundant, joyful living. *CHURCH NEWS,* APR. 15, 1977

The workings of our government should be an example to the world—in uncompromising integrity, in wise and prudent stewardship of public funds, in personal morality, including fidelity in marriage, and in an openness on activities which will build the confidence of the electorate. The citizenry should expect no less. NEWS RELEASE, JUNE 3, 1976

The voter should study and make up his mind as to what he wishes his government to be, and then, if he is so minded, vote for the one he believes will most nearly carry out his ideas about government and its free institutions. *DESERET NEWS,* OCT. 26, 1970

We affirm that this is indeed a land choice above all others. And we would remind all of the prophetic warnings centuries ago that it will stay free and strong only as long as its people serve the Lord.

For much of its history, America's leaders have indeed served the Almighty and invoked His blessings. A sense of dependence on God runs through the crucial years of our nation's birth and its growth to greatness. A nation built on the concept that man is a son of God is a nation of individual morality, dignity, and responsibility. Only as America supports these principles of citizenship can it remain strong and free. *DESERET NEWS*, NOV. 11, 1967

We believe that all men are bound to sustain and uphold the respective governments in which they reside, while protected in their inherent and inalienable rights by the laws of such governments; and that sedition and rebellion are unbecoming every citizen thus protected, and should be punished accordingly; and that all governments have a right to enact such laws as in their own judgments are best calculated to secure the public interest, at the same time, however, holding sacred the freedom of conscience.

We believe that rulers, states, and governments have a right and are bound to enact laws for the protection of all men in the free exercise of their religious belief; but we do not believe that they have a right in justice to deprive any man of his property, or prescribe men in their opinions, so long as a regard and reverence are shown to the laws and such religious opinions do not justify sedition nor conspiracy. "DESIRABLE OBJECTIVES," MAY 14, 1965

Our efforts to continue to inspire in all men a love of our country and a love of God, closely associated as they are, are to be encouraged. *DESERET NEWS,* JUNE 28, 1963

The same ethical and moral standards applied to individuals should find application in the judging of nations. No race or national government has a moral right to infringe upon the rights of other countries, and aggressive measures can be justified only for the protection of life, liberty, and the maintenance of peace and justice in the world. *DESERET NEWS,* DEC. 14, 1949

We exhort men in the service of government everywhere, ever to have in mind the life and teachings of the Master; hour by hour to keep out from their hearts, in the camp and on the battle field itself, all cruelty, hate, and murder; always to have in their thoughts the few short years of time as against the unnumbered cycles of eternity; never to forget that the gross pleasures of the flesh lead always to destruction, while the lofty joys of the spirit build everlasting joy and progression. *DESERET NEWS,* DEC. 13, 1941, IN *MESSAGES,* 6:140-41

No man and no group may destroy divine rights and escape the punishments that follow. A society where the right to work is denied is a society of anarchy and chaos. *DESERET NEWS,* SEPT. 26, 1941, IN *MESSAGES,* 6:130-33

The Church is so firmly committed to the maintenance and support of the governments in which its members have citizenship that it must regard violations of the law of the land as serious infractions of its own discipline and principles of Church government. We believe that any other position is untenable, either for ourselves as Church members or for other citizens of the Republic. We believe also that there is no better way to adequately test the value and ultimate worth of a law or principle than by strict and universal enforcement. *IMPROVEMENT ERA,* SEPT. 1932, IN *MESSAGES,* 5:309-10

Laws which are enacted for the protection of society have no value except when they are administered in righteousness and justice, and they cannot be so administrated if dishonest men occupy administrative offices. STATEMENT, JAN. 1928, IN *MESSAGES,* 5:258-59

In promoting the benefit of others, self-preservation ought to be paramount. This applies to nations as well as to individuals. Therefore, in extending to foreign governments similar liberties to those enjoyed under our heaven-inspired Constitution, care must be taken that the powers executed and the rights secured to us by the "supreme law of the land" are not invaded or abridged or weakened in any degree. We should not forfeit a single national prerogative or principle in endeavoring to break down rampant militarism and overthrow tyrannical monarchism. Let us have peace, but not at the price of our country's freedom. *DESERET NEWS,* DEC. 23, 1919, IN *MESSAGES,* 5:164-67

We think it is wrong, contrary to our religion, and contrary to good citizenship, for men to combine together in any organization to prevent their fellowmen from working because they do not join them or work for such an amount as they think workmen ought to have. STATEMENT DATED JULY 9, 1896, IN *MESSAGES,* 3:278-79

Criticism of the acts of United States officials was not considered then [1870s], neither is it now, as treason against the nation nor as hostility to the government. *DESERET NEWS WEEKLY,* DEC. 21, 1889, IN *MESSAGES,* 3:184-8)

No people or government can defy the sound principles of law which are essential to the correct administration of justice and to the maintenance of the rights of its citizens, without calling into existence forces which are calculated to lead to its destruction. STATEMENT, APR. 8, 1887, IN *MESSAGES,* 3:109-29

[T]he condition of a community, as a whole, depends upon the condition of the individuals composing it; as are its components parts, so is it in its entirety. If the individual members of a people are wise, just, intelligent, honest, honorable, and pure, that community will be distinguished among its fellows by those peculiar virtues. STATEMENT, MAR. 1886, IN *MESSAGES,* 3:46-71

Ye shepherds of Israel, feed the flock of God; seek His pleasure, and not your own, in all things; and teach the Saints to be subject to the powers that be, wherever they are. *DESERET NEWS,* OCT. 16, 1852, IN *MESSAGES,* 2:101-109

Sustain the government of the nation wherever you are, and speak well of it, for this is right, and the government has a right to expect it of you, so long as that government sustains you in your civil and religious liberty, in those rights which inherently belong to every person born on the earth; and if you are persecuted in your native land, and denied the privilege of worshipping the true God in spirit and in truth, flee to the land of Zion, to America—to the United States, where Constitutional rights and freedoms are not surpassed by any nation—where God saw fit, in these last days, to renew the dispensation of salvation, by revelations from the heavens, and where all, by the Constitution and laws of the land, when executed in righteousness, are protected in all the civil and religious freedom that man is capable of enjoying on earth; and our national institutions will never fail, unless it be through the wickedness of the people and the designs of evil men in brief authority; for those rights were ordained of God on this land, for the establishment of the principles of truth on the earth; and our national organization originated in the heavens. *MILLENNIAL STAR,* JULY 17, 1852, IN *MESSAGES,* 2:91-100

Amid all the revolutions that are taking place among the nations, the elders will ever pursue an undeviating course in being subject to the government wherever they may be, and sustain the same by all their precepts to the Saints, having nothing to do with political questions which engender strife, remembering that the weapons of their war are not carnal but spiritual, and that the gospel which they preach is not of man but from heaven; and if they persecute you beyond measure in one city, country, or kingdom, leave the testimony which Jesus has given for a witness unto your Father in Heaven, that you are free from their blood, and flee to other cities, countries, or kingdoms where they will receive you and believe your testimony. *DESERET NEWS,* APR. 8, 1851, IN *MESSAGES,* 2:62-73

It is a part of our religion to support any government, wherever we may be, that will protect us in common with other citizens; for, to this end governments are instituted; and as England has ever been true and faithful to us as a people, in common with others, the elders cannot be too particular to enjoin on all the Saints to yield obedience to the laws and respect every man in his office, letting politics wholly, entirely, and absolutely alone, and preach the principles of the gospel of salvation; for to this end were they ordained and sent forth.
TWELVE APOSTLES TO WILFORD WOODRUFF, MAY 8, 1845, IN *MESSAGES,* 1:267-68

The laws of men may guarantee to a people protection in the honorable pursuits of this life and the temporal happiness arising from a protection against unjust insults and injuries; and when this is said, all is said that can be in truth, of the power, extent, and influence of the laws of men, exclusive of the law of God. The law of heaven is presented to man, and as such guarantees to all who obey it a reward far beyond any earthly consideration; though it does not promise that the believer in every age should be exempt from the afflictions and troubles arising from different sources in consequence of the acts of wicked men on earth. Still, in that it is the law of heaven, which transcends the law of man, as far as eternal life the temporal; and as the blessings which God is able to give are greater than those which can be given by man, then certainly, if the law of man is binding upon man when acknowledged, how much more must the law of heaven be! And as much as the law of heaven is more perfect than the law of man, so much greater must be the reward if obeyed. The law of man promises safety in temporal life; but the law of God promises that life which is eternal, even an inheritance at God's own right hand, secure from all the powers of the wicked one.
STATEMENT, JAN. 22, 1834, IN *MESSAGES,* 1:23-44

H

happiness. ***See also*** **eternal progression; service; wealth**

The joy we seek is not a temporary emotional high, but a habitual inner joy learned from long experience and trust in God. JAMES E. FAUST, "FIRST PRESIDENCY MESSAGE," *ENSIGN,* JUNE 2006

Happiness does not consist of a glut of luxury, the world's idea of a "good time." Nor must we search for it in faraway places with strange-sounding names. Happiness is found at home. THOMAS S. MONSON, "FIRST PRESIDENCY MESSAGE," *ENSIGN,* OCT. 2001

Happiness in family life is most likely to be achieved when founded upon the teachings of the Lord Jesus Christ. *CHURCH NEWS,* NOV. 18, 2000

The more faithfully we keep the commandments of God, the happier we will generally be. JAMES E. FAUST, "FIRST PRESIDENCY MESSAGE," *ENSIGN,* OCT. 2000

[O]ur search for happiness largely depends on the degree of righteousness we attain, the degree of selflessness we acquire, the amount and quality of service we render, and the inner peace that we enjoy. We also have some external sources of happiness, including those loved ones and friends whose smiles and regard mean so much to us. Our destinies are bound by ties of common interest and sympathy to a host of others, unknown to us personally, within and without the Church. IBID.

"The way of the Lord is the way of happiness" (Alma 41:10). Transgression never was happiness. Sin never was happiness. Disobedience never was happiness. The way of happiness is following the way of the Lord. GORDON B. HINCKLEY, "FIRST PRESIDENCY MESSAGE," *ENSIGN,* AUGUST 1997

The Lord has not left mankind without clear guidance on matters that affect our happiness. That guidance is chastity before marriage, total fidelity in marriage, abstinence from all homosexual relations, avoidance of illegal drugs, and reverence and care for the body, which is the "temple of God" (1 Cor. 3:16)." NEWS RELEASE, MAY 27, 1988

[O]bedience to law, respect for others, mastery of self, joy in service—these constitute the *abundant life.* THOMAS S. MONSON, "FIRST PRESIDENCY MESSAGE," *ENSIGN,* MAR. 1988

Happiness abounds when there is genuine respect for one another. IBID.

There is no happiness or peace of mind except through obedience to the commandments of God. There is no salvation or eternal life except through acceptance of the gospel and living according to its teachings. There are no problems facing the nations of the world or individuals for which answers cannot be found in the gospel of Jesus Christ. He came to Earth for that purpose—to give us a plan of life and salvation through which we could enjoy happiness and eternal life. N. ELDON TANNER, "FIRST PRESIDENCY MESSAGE," *ENSIGN,* DEC. 1979

The sure way to peace and happiness in this life and life hereafter is to serve the Lord *today* and every day. MARION G. ROMNEY, "FIRST PRESIDENCY MESSAGE," *ENSIGN,* JUNE 1979

The main objective of most people is to find happiness and an inner peace which will help them to get the most out of living and to meet the problems and trials which come to all. As the philosophers say, it is not what happens to us, but how we meet it that spells the difference. And that is where religion plays an important part in our lives. N. ELDON TANNER, "FIRST PRESIDENCY MESSAGE," *ENSIGN,* OCT. 1978

[I]t is by serving that we learn how to serve. When we are engaged in the service of our fellowmen, not only do our deeds assist them, but we put our own problems in a fresher perspective. When we concern ourselves more with others, there is less time to be concerned with ourselves. In the midst of the miracle of serving, there is the promise of Jesus, that by losing ourselves, we find ourselves (see Matt. 10:39).

Not only do we "find" ourselves in terms of acknowledging guidance in our lives, but the more we serve our fellowmen in appropriate ways, the more substance there is to our souls. We become more significant individuals as we serve others. We become more substantive as we serve others–indeed, it is easier to "find" ourselves because there is so much more of us to find! SPENCER W. KIMBALL, "FIRST PRESIDENCY MESSAGE," *ENSIGN,* DEC. 1974

God does notice us, and He watches over us. But it is usually through another person that He meets our needs. Therefore, it is vital that we serve each other in the kingdom. IBID.

To remain strong, we must cherish chastity and fidelity, love of work, personal integrity, and the desire to serve our fellow men. *ENSIGN,* NOV. 1973

Real joy and happiness consists of being healed spiritually. It comes from inside. MARION G. ROMNEY, "FIRST PRESIDENCY MESSAGE," *ENSIGN,* SEPT. 1973

Few factors are more likely to lead to success in any endeavor than a singleness of purpose. The ability to concentrate on an objective and to work unceasingly toward its realization will make fruitful the labors of any man. FIRST PRESIDENCY TO "DEAR MISSIONARIES," MAR. 10, 1960

We admonish the members of the Church to remain steadfast in their faith and testimony of the truth, to render dutiful service, to seek knowledge, and to be temperate and considerate in judgment; to be not swerved in thought or conduct by philosophies that do not have foundation and support in revealed truth; to be composed in feelings when beset by the fears, apprehensions, and anxieties which conditions in the world provoke; to realize that he who has the truth about life and its meaning, who has complied with the requirements of the Lord, is entitled to the blessings of faith, confidence, and assurance regarding things of eternal value. *DESERET NEWS,* DEC. 12, 1956

[T]here is no enduring happiness except in goodness. *DESERET NEWS,* DEC. 12, 1951

The source of happiness is within one's soul; so springs faith in Jesus Christ as our Lord and Savior. *DESERET NEWS,* DEC. 15, 1948

He who gives happiness to others, subjugating his own personal desires, finds happiness in his own soul. *DESERET NEWS,* DEC. 15, 1945

The rising sun can dispel the darkness of night, but he cannot banish the blackness of malice, hatred, bigotry, selfishness, and greed from the hearts of humanity. Nor will happiness and peace come to earth until the light of love and human compassion enters the souls of men. *DESERET NEWS,* DEC. 19, 1936

It is far better to forego even the most promising pursuit of pleasure than to reap a harvest of barren regrets. *DESERET NEWS,* FEB. 8, 1916

If the Latter-day Saints lived as they should do, and as their religion teaches them to do, there would be no feeling in any breast but that of brotherly and sisterly affection and love. Backbiting and evil-speaking would have no existence among us; but peace and love and good will would reign in all our hearts and habitations and settlements. We would be the happiest people on the face of the earth, and the blessing and peace of Heaven would rest upon us and upon all that belongs to us. STATEMENT, OCT. 10, 1887, IN *MESSAGES,* 3:133-55

healing

The Church believes in the same manifestations of the Spirit, including healing, that existed in the Church organized by the Savior during His earthly ministry (see D&C 42:44). Church members should not go to so-called faith healers or seek other bizarre or unusual healings or cures. *CHURCH HANDBOOK,* 1983

The Lord is the one who heals the sick, not the individual elder who may officiate in the administration. HEBER J. GRANT TO MRS. T. WILLIAM RHOADES, SEPT. 14, 1935

The administration of the ordinances of the gospel to the sick is for the purpose of healing them, that they may continue lives of usefulness until the Lord shall call them hence. This is as far as we should go. If we adhere strictly to that which the Lord has revealed in regard to this matter, no mistake will be made. *IMPROVEMENT ERA,* OCT. 1922, IN *MESSAGES,* 5:220

history

The Church today is greatly blessed because of the excellent historical accounts of the testimonies, cultural development, and lives maintained by our ancestors. This important process, including the keeping of personal journals, is expected to continue. "DEAR BRETHREN," APR. 2, 1984

Journals (diaries) of members of the Church are one of the best sources of history. *CHURCH HANDBOOK,* 1968

Holy Ghost. *See also* revelation

The Holy Ghost stands as the third member of the Godhead, the Comforter promised by the Savior who would teach His followers all things and bring all things to their remembrance, whatsoever He had said unto them (see John 12:26).

The Holy Ghost is the testifier of truth, who can teach men things they cannot teach one another. GORDON B. HINCKLEY, "FIRST PRESIDENCY MESSAGE," *ENSIGN,* JULY 2006

In answer to our prayers, the Holy Ghost will teach us truth through our feelings and thoughts. Feelings that come from the Holy Ghost are powerful, but they are also usually gentle and quiet. *PREACH MY GOSPEL,* 2005

Those who receive the gift of the Holy Ghost and remain worthy can enjoy His companionship throughout their lives. The Holy Ghost has a sanctifying, cleansing effect upon us. The Holy Ghost testifies of Christ and helps us recognize the truth. He provides spiritual strength and helps us do what is right. He comforts us during times of trial or sorrow. He warns us of spiritual or physical danger. IBID.

We can recognize when the Holy Ghost is teaching us the truth. Our minds will be filled with inspiring and uplifting thoughts. We will be enlightened, or given new knowledge. Our hearts will have feelings of peace, joy, and love. We will want to do good and be helpful to others. These feelings are hard to describe but can be recognized as we experience them. IBID.

The Holy Ghost is also referred to as the Holy Spirit of Promise (see D&C 88:3). To be sealed by the Holy Spirit of Promise means that the Holy Ghost confirms that righteous acts, ordinances, and covenants are acceptable to God. The Holy Spirit of Promise testifies to the Father that the saving ordinances have been performed properly and that the covenants associated with them have been kept. Those who are sealed by the Holy Spirit of Promise receive all that the Father has (76:51-60; Eph. 1:13-14). All covenants and performances must be sealed by the Holy Spirit of Promise if they are to be valid after this life (D&C 132:7, 18-19). Breaking covenants may remove the sealing. IBID.

The Holy Ghost is the third member of the Godhead. He is a personage of spirit, without a body of flesh and bones (see D&C 130:22). He is often referred to as the Spirit, Holy Spirit, the Spirit of God, the Spirit of the Lord, or the Comforter. *TRUE TO FAITH,* 2004

After you were baptized into The Church of Jesus Christ of Latter-day Saints, one or more Melchizedek Priesthood holders laid their hands on your head and, in a sacred priesthood ordinance, confirmed you a member of the Church. As part of this ordinance, called confirmation, you were given the gift of the Holy Ghost.

The gift of the Holy Ghost is different from the influence of the Holy Ghost. Before your baptism, you could feel the influence of the Holy Ghost from time to time, and through that influence you could receive a testimony of the truth. Now that you have the gift of the Holy Ghost, you have the right to the constant companionship of that member of the Godhead if you keep the commandments.

Full enjoyment of the gift of the Holy Ghost includes receiving revelation and comfort, serving and blessing others through spiritual gifts, and being sanctified from sin and made fit for exaltation in the celestial kingdom. These blessings depend on your worthiness; they come a little at a time as you are ready for them. As you bring your life in harmony with God's will, you gradually receive the Holy Ghost in great measure. IBID.

Latter-day Saints, having received the gift of the Holy Ghost by the laying on of hands, are entitled to personal inspiration in the small events of life as well as when they are confronted with the giant Goliaths of life. If worthy, we are entitled to receive revelations for ourselves, parents for their children, and members of the Church in their callings. But the right of personal revelation for others does not extend beyond our own stewardship. JAMES E. FAUST, "FIRST PRESIDENCY MESSAGE," *ENSIGN,* MAR. 2002

The Holy Ghost stands as the third member of the Godhead, the Comforter promised by the Savior who would teach His followers all things and bring all things to their remembrance, whatsoever He had said unto them (see John 14:26).

The Holy Ghost is the testifier of truth, who can teach men things they cannot teach one another. In those great and challenging words of Moroni, a knowledge of the truth of the Book of Mormon is promised "by the power of the Holy Ghost." Moroni then declares, "And by the power of the Holy Ghost ye may know the truth of all things" (Moro. 10:4-5). GORDON B. HINCKLEY, "FIRST PRESIDENCY MESSAGE," *ENSIGN,* MAR. 1998

It is possible for all of us, through the power of the Holy Ghost, to have a personal witness. It is a personal source of information and revelation. JAMES E. FAUST, "FIRST PRESIDENCY MESSAGE," *ENSIGN,* OCT. 1997

The gift of the Holy Ghost, however, in distinction from the Spirit of God, does not come to all men and women. The ministrations of the Holy Ghost are, however, limited without receiving the gift of the Holy Ghost. JAMES E. FAUST, "FIRST PRESIDENCY MESSAGE," *ENSIGN*, APR. 1996

The gift of the Holy Ghost comes after one repents and becomes worthy. It is received after baptism by the laying on of hands by those who have the authority. IBID.

The comforting spirit of the Holy Ghost can abide with us twenty-four hours a day: when we work, when we play, when we rest. Its strengthening influence can be with us year in and year out. That sustaining influence can be with us in joy and sorrow, when we rejoice as well as when we grieve. IBID.

[T]he Holy Spirit of Promise ... is the sealing and ratifying power of the Holy Ghost. To have a covenant or ordinance sealed by the Holy Spirit of Promise is a compact through which the inherent blessings will be obtained, provided those seeking the blessing are true and faithful (see D&C 76:50-54). IBID.

To have a covenant or ordinance sealed by the Holy Spirit of Promise means that the compact is binding on Earth and in heaven. IBID.

The people of the world have the Light of Christ to help guide them, but we also are entitled to the gift of the Holy Ghost. For the Holy Ghost to be fully operative in our lives, we must keep our channels clear of sin. The clearer our channels, the easier it is for us to receive God's message. And the more of His promptings we receive and follow, the greater will be our joy. If our channels are not clear of sin, then we may think we have received inspiration on a matter when it is really promptings from the devil. EZRA TAFT BENSON, "FIRST PRESIDENCY MESSAGE," *ENSIGN,* SEPT. 1988

The Holy Ghost causes our feelings to be more tender. We feel more charitable and compassionate with each other. We are more calm in our relationships. We have a greater capacity to love each other. People want to be around us because our very countenances radiate the influence of the Spirit. We are more godly in our character. As a result, we become increasingly more sensitive to the promptings of the Holy Ghost and thus able to comprehend spiritual things more clearly. IBID.

Often when the Holy Ghost is mentioned, the reference is to His power or gift, not to Himself as a distinct personage. The Holy Ghost is also known as the Spirit of the Lord (or of God). *PRINCIPLES,* 1976

We speak of receiving the Holy Ghost after baptism, at the time we are confirmed members of the Church. We mean that we are given the right to receive the gift of the Holy Ghost. IBID.

Any person who is worthy can receive the influence and enlightenment of the Holy Ghost; however, in order to have Him as a constant companion, to receive the spiritual gifts, we must obey the principles and ordinances of the gospel and have the right to His companionship given to us when we are confirmed members of the Church. IBID.

The Holy Ghost is a personage of spirit and is the witness and messenger of the Father and the Son.

Through the Holy Ghost, revelations are given.

The Holy Ghost is a cleansing and purifying agent to all who receive Him, His gifts, and blessings. "BASIC DOCTRINES," 1971

[T]he divine essence called the Spirit of God, or Holy Spirit, or Holy Ghost by which God created or organized all things and by which the prophets wrote and spoke, was bestowed in former ages and inspired the Apostles in their ministry long before the day of Pentecost. The words "Ghost" and "Spirit" are often used synonymously, and this causes some confusion, when the difference between the "personage of spirit" and the spirit "poured out from on high" is not taken into consideration. There is a universally diffused essence which is the light and life of the world, which proceedeth forth from the presence of God throughout the immensity of space, the light and power of whom God bestows in different degrees to "them that ask Him," according to their faith and obedience; but the Holy Ghost, which Christ said he would send to His Apostles from the Father (John 14:26), was and is a "personage of spirit" and was not to come until Christ went away (16:7). Also the endowment from that divine being, the third person in the Holy Trinity, called "the gift of the Holy Ghost," is a special blessing sealed upon baptized repentant believers in Jesus Christ and is "an abiding witness." The spirit of God may be enjoyed as a temporary influence by which divine light and power come to mankind for special purposes and occasions. But the gift of the Holy Ghost, which was received by the Apostles on the day of Pentecost and is bestowed in confirmation, is a permanent witness and higher endowment than the ordinary manifestations of the Holy Spirit. *DESERET NEWS,* FEB. 26, 1916

The Holy Ghost does not contradict its own revealings. Truth is always harmonious with itself. *DESERET NEWS,* AUG. 2, 1913, IN *MESSAGES,* 4:285-86

[T]he Holy Ghost is a personage of spirit, He constitutes the third person in the trinity of the Godhead. The gift of the

Holy Ghost is the authoritative act of conferring Him upon man. The Holy Ghost in person may visit a man and will visit those who are worthy and bear witness to their spirit of God and Christ, but may not tarry with them. The Spirit of God which emanates from Deity may be likened to electricity which fills the earth and the air and is everywhere present. It is the power of God, the influence that He exerts throughout all His works by which He can effect His purposes and execute His will, agreeable to the laws of free agency which He has conferred upon man. JOSEPH F. SMITH TO JOSEPH R. SMITH, SEPT. 13, 1899

The Spirit of God which lighteth all men into the world—is that power from the Great Creator bestowed upon the creatures, which gives consciousness of good or ill, right and wrong, light and darkness and will not cease to strive with man until he is brought into possession of the greater light, received through obedience to the laws of God by the laying on of hands—even the Holy Ghost. But when men who have received the greater light rebel against it—by committing sin and transgression, then both the Spirit of God—which prompts to do good—and the Holy Ghost, which gives a knowledge of truth and confirms all good upon the mind, withdraw themselves. JOSEPH F. SMITH TO JOSEPH R. SMITH, AUG. 8, 1899

Only those who are "born again" can see the kingdom of heaven, and not always are those "born of the water" also "born of the Spirit." In other words, not everyone who is baptized receives the Holy Ghost, notwithstanding the "gift" may be bestowed. JOSEPH F. SMITH TO HYRUM M. SMITH, SEPT. 4, 1896

In conferring the Holy Ghost, the words "receive ye the Holy Ghost" should be used, not "receive ye the gift of the Holy Ghost." GEORGE REYNOLDS TO HENRY S. TANNER, JAN. 23, 1895

Through the Holy Ghost a knowledge of things past, present, and to come is communicated and the mind and will of the Father made known. In this way the Almighty reveals His purposes to those who obey His commandments and whose lives are pure and acceptable before Him, so that they can be prepared for all the events and trials that may lie in their pathway.

If there are any members of the Church who do not know by their own experience that this is true, they may be assured that they do not live up to their privileges. All Saints should be in close communion with the Holy Ghost, and, through it, with the Father, or there is danger of their being overcome of evil and falling by the wayside. *WOMAN'S EXPONENT,* APR. 15, 1888, IN *MESSAGES,* 3:156-63

It ["gift of the Holy Spirit"] shall bring things past to your understanding and remembrance, and shall show you things to come.

It shall also import unto you many great and glorious gifts, such as the gift of healing the sick, and of being healed, by the laying on of hands in the name of Jesus; and of expelling demons; and even of seeing visions and conversing with angels and spirits from the unseen world.

By the light of this Spirit, received through the ministration of the ordinances–by the power and authority of the holy apostleship and priesthood, you will be enabled to understand, and to be the children of light; and thus be prepared to escape all the things that are coming on the earth, and so stand before the Son of Man. STATEMENT, APR. 6, 1845, IN *MESSAGES,* 1:252-66

home life. ***See also*** **family; parents**

It is in the home that we form our attitudes, our deeply held beliefs. It is in the home that hope is fostered or destroyed. Our homes are to be more than sanctuaries; they should also be places where God's Spirit can dwell, where the storm stops at the door, where love reigns and peace dwells. THOMAS S. MONSON, "FIRST PRESIDENCY MESSAGE," *ENSIGN,* APR. 2006

For us to have successful homes, values must be taught, and there must be rules, there must be standards, there must be absolutes. JAMES E. FAUST, "FIRST PRESIDENCY MESSAGE," *ENSIGN,* OCT. 2005

Our homes are the laboratories of our lives. What we do there determines the course of our lives when we leave home. THOMAS S. MONSON, "FIRST PRESIDENCY MESSAGE," *ENSIGN,* JUNE 2000

We have heard that the greatest service we can render will be within the walls of our own homes. It is also true that no nation is stronger than its homes. For a man, there is no calling as great as being a righteous patriarch who is married in the house of the Lord and who presides over his family. Even God is pleased when we address Him as "our Father who art in Heaven." For a woman there is no calling as great as that of a righteous mother who is married in the house of the Lord and who rears a worthy posterity. EZRA TAFT BENSON, "FIRST PRESIDENCY MESSAGE," *ENSIGN,* SEPT. 1988

Selfishness is a destructive, gnawing, corrosive element in the lives of most of us. It lies at the root of much of the tension between parents and children, and it leads to strain in well-meaning parents who sometimes nurture harmful selfishness in children by indulging with extravagance their wishes for costly and unneeded things.

The antidote of selfishness is service, a reaching out to those about us—those in the home and those beyond the walls of the home. A child who grows in a home where there is a selfish, grasping father is likely to develop those tendencies in his own life. On the other hand, a child who sees his father and mother forego comforts for themselves as they reach out to those in distress, will likely follow the same pattern when he or she grows to maturity. GORDON B. HINCKLEY, "FIRST PRESIDENCY MESSAGE," *ENSIGN,* JUNE 1985

The home should be a place where reliance on the Lord is a matter of common experience, not reserved for special occasions. One way of establishing that is by regular, earnest prayer. It is not enough just to pray. It is essential that we really speak to the Lord, having faith that He will reveal to us as parents what we need to know and do for the welfare of our families. It has been said of some men that when they prayed, a child was likely to open his eyes to see if the Lord were really there, so personal and direct was the petition. SPENCER W. KIMBALL, "FIRST PRESIDENCY MESSAGE," *ENSIGN,* JAN. 1984

A true Latter-day Saint home is a haven against the storms and struggles of life. Spirituality is born and nurtured by daily prayer, scripture study, home gospel discussions and related activities, home evenings, family councils, working and playing together, serving each other, and sharing the gospel with those around us. Spirituality is also nurtured in our actions of patience, kindness, and forgiveness toward each other and in our applying gospel principles in the family circle. Home is where we become experts and scholars in gospel righteousness, learning and living gospel truths together. SPENCER W. KIMBALL, "FIRST PRESIDENCY MESSAGE," *ENSIGN,* JAN. 1982

If the trouble in the world is to be corrected, it will have to begin in the home where the future leaders are trained. What greater contribution can be made than for women to bear children who, through the mother's influence, can be instrumental in righting some of the wrongs in the world. N. ELDON TANNER, "FIRST PRESIDENCY MESSAGE," *ENSIGN,* JUNE 1978

An ideal Latter-day Saint home is presided over by parents who have been sealed together by the power of the priesthood, and children not born under the covenant have been sealed to their parents.

Such a home has been acquired, that is, purchased or rented, with tithed money; and the income of all family members has been tithed.

In a true Latter-day Saint home, each day begins and closes with prayer, both family and secret prayer.

The gospel of Jesus Christ is taught and practiced by precept and by example.

In such a home the priesthood is honored.

The members of a true Latter-day Saint home are loyal to each other. They love, honor, and sustain one another. MARION G. ROMNEY, "FIRST PRESIDENCY MESSAGE," *ENSIGN,* DEC. 1977

Every Latter-day Saint home should be a model home, where the father is the head of the household, but presiding with love, and in complete harmony with the righteous desires of the mother. Together they should be seeking the same goals for the family, and the children should feel the love and harmony that exists. N. ELDON TANNER, "FIRST PRESIDENCY MESSAGE," *ENSIGN,* JUNE 1977

Our homes and buildings are the showcases of what we believe. They should be attractive and give every indication of cleanliness, orderliness, and self-esteem. *CHURCH NEWS,* SEPT. 28, 1974

There is no better place than in the home to teach and learn about marriage, love, and sex as these can properly combine in a sanctified temple marriage. There is no better place to deal with the doubts of our young than where there is love—at home. Love can free our youth to listen to those whom they know they can trust. Our curricula, quorums, and classes should supplement the home, and where homes are seriously defective, we will have to compensate as best we can. HAROLD B. LEE, "FIRST PRESIDENCY MESSAGE," *ENSIGN,* MAR. 1971

homosexuality, *see* sexual relations

humanitarian work, *see* welfare

hymns, *see* music

hypnosis

The use of hypnosis under competent, professional medical supervision for the treatment of diseases or mental disorders is a medical question to be determined by competent medical authorities. Members should not participate in hypnosis for purposes of demonstration or entertainment. *CHURCH HANDBOOK,* 1998

I

immigration, *see* Gathering

immunization

Immunization is such a simple, yet vital, matter and such a small price to pay for protection against these destroying diseases. *DESERET NEWS,* MAY 6, 1978

incest. *See also* child abuse

[I]ncest refers to sexual relations between a parent and a natural, adopted, or foster child or stepchild. A grandparent is considered the same as a parent. Incest also refers to sexual relations between brothers and sisters. It almost always requires excommunication. *CHURCH HANDBOOK,* 1998

Incest is an extremely serious transgression. *CHURCH HANDBOOK,* 1985

infallibility

[T]he General Authorities of this Church will never lead you in paths that will take you down. They will lead you in a trail that leads upward if you will follow in faith and faithfulness. GORDON B. HINCKLEY, "FIRST PRESIDENCY MESSAGE," *ENSIGN,* MAR. 2006

[T]he Lord will not permit any man to lead His Church astray. His are the powers of life and death. It is His Church, not the church of any man. He will see to it that it is cared for, that it moves forward, that its members are nurtured with the good word of God, and that it will go on to its destined mission. GORDON B. HINCKLEY, "FIRST PRESIDENCY MESSAGE," *ENSIGN,* JUNE 1996

inspiration, *see* revelation

intellectualism. *See also* knowledge; science

We encourage members of the Church to never teach or pass on such statements [i.e., which have been attributed to the leaders of the Church] without verifying that they are from approved Church sources, such as official statements, communications, and publications. Any notes made when General Authorities, Area Authority Seventies, or other general Church officers [were] speaking at regional and stake conferences or other meetings should not be distributed without the consent of the speaker. Personal notes are for individual use only. "DEAR BRETHREN," MAY 13, 2004, IN *CHURCH NEWS,* MAY 29, 2004

Reading is one of the true pleasures of life. In our age of mass culture, when so much that we encounter is abridged, adapted, adulterated, shredded, and boiled down, it is mind-easing and mind-inspiring to sit down privately with a congenial book. THOMAS S. MONSON, "FIRST PRESIDENCY MESSAGE," *ENSIGN,* OCT. 2001

As a means of coming to truth, people in the Church are encouraged by their leaders to think and find out for themselves. They are encouraged to ponder, to search, to evaluate, and thereby to come to such knowledge of the truth as their own consciences, assisted by the Spirit of God, lead them to discover. JAMES E. FAUST, "FIRST PRESIDENCY MESSAGE," *ENSIGN,* SEPT. 1998

The Church warns its members against symposia and similar gatherings that include presentations that (1) disparage, ridicule, make light of, or are otherwise inappropriate in their treatment of sacred matters or (2) could injure the Church, detract from its mission, or jeopardize its members' well-being. Members should not allow their position or standing in the Church to be used to promote or imply endorsement of such gatherings. *CHURCH HANDBOOK,* 1998

Members who have questions concerning Church doctrine, policies, or procedures have been counseled to discuss those concerns confidentially with their local leaders. These leaders are deeply aware of their obligation to counsel members wisely in the spirit of love in order to strengthen their faith in the Lord and in His great latter-day work. *CHURCH NEWS,* AUG. 22, 1992

We appreciate the search for knowledge and the discussion of gospel subjects. However, we believe that Latter-day Saints who are committed to the mission of their church and the well-being of their fellow members will strive to be sensitive to those matters that are more appropriate for private conferring and correction than for public debate. Jesus taught that when a person has trespassed against us, we should "go and tell him his fault between thee and him alone," and if he will "neglect to hear" this private communication we should "tell it unto the church" (Matt. 18:15, 17). Modern revelation tells us that this last step "shall be done in a meeting, and that not before the world" (D&C 42:89). There are times when public discussion of sacred or personal matters is inappropriate. *ENSIGN,* NOV. 1991

With the abundance of books available today, it is a mark of a truly educated man to know what *not* to read. Of the making of books there is no end. In our reading, we would do well to follow the counsel of John Wesley's mother: "Avoid whatever weakens your reason, impairs the tenderness of your conscience, obscures your sense of God, takes off your relish for spiritual things, ... increases the authority of the body over the mind."

The fact that a book or publication is popular does not necessarily make it of value. The fact that an author wrote one good work does not necessarily mean that all his books are worthy of our reading. Many novels, and modern publications, are corrupters of morals or distorters of truth. EZRA TAFT BENSON, "FIRST PRESIDENCY MESSAGE," *ENSIGN,* SEPT. 1988

The humanists who criticize the Lord's work, the so-called intellectualists who demean, speak only from ignorance of spiritual manifestation. They have not heard the voice of the Spirit. They have not heard it because they have not sought after it and prepared themselves to be worthy of it. Then, supposing that knowledge comes only of reasoning and of the workings of the mind, they deny that which comes by the power of the Holy Ghost. GORDON B. HINCKLEY, "FIRST PRESIDENCY MESSAGE," *ENSIGN,* APR. 1986

As a Church, we encourage gospel scholarship and the search to understand all truth. Fundamental to our theology is belief in individual freedom of inquiry, thought, and expression. Constructive discussion is a privilege of every Latter-day Saint. GORDON B. HINCKLEY, "FIRST PRESIDENCY MESSAGE," *ENSIGN,* SEPT. 1985

We have nothing to fear when we walk by the light of eternal truth. But we had better be discerning. Sophistry has a way of masking itself as truth. Half truths are used to mislead under the representation that they are whole truths. Innuendo is often used by enemies of this work as representing truth. Theories and hypotheses are often set forth as if they were confirmed truth. Statements taken out of context of time or circumstance or the written word are often given as truth, when as a matter of fact such procedure may be the very essence of falsehood. GORDON B. HINCKLEY, "FIRST PRESIDENCY MESSAGE," *ENSIGN,* OCT. 1984

We must remember that neither God nor His gospel can be found and understood through research alone. The skeptic will some day learn to his sorrow that his egotism robbed him of much joy and growth. The things of God—and often the things of His earth—cannot be understood by the spirit of man, but are understood only through the Spirit of God (see 1 Cor. 2:11). SPENCER W. KIMBALL, "FIRST PRESIDENCY MESSAGE," *ENSIGN,* SEPT. 1983

If any person will read the word of the Lord, if any person will talk in prayer with Him, if any person will live His teachings and serve in His cause, his or her doubts will leave; and shining through all of the confusion of the philosophy, the so-called higher criticism, and the negative theology of our day will come the witness of the Holy Spirit that Jesus is in very deed the Son of God, born in the flesh, the Redeemer of the world, resurrected from the grave, the Lord who shall come to reign as King of Kings. It is our opportunity and blessing so to know. It is our obligation so to find out. GORDON B. HINCKLEY, "FIRST PRESIDENCY MESSAGE," *ENSIGN,* APR. 1983

Anyone who, with an open mind and a prayerful heart, will give as much attention to the teachings of Jesus Christ as to scientific and academic studies will keep his faith. Doubt, skepticism, and unbelief are weapons of the adversary, enemies of righteousness, and barriers that stand in the way of growth and progress. Do not be afraid or ashamed to learn of God and the teachings of Jesus Christ. N. ELDON TANNER, "FIRST PRESIDENCY MESSAGE," *ENSIGN,* OCT. 1973

[I]f we would accept what the Lord has given us plainly in the revelations and leave what we don't know to the future revelations of the Lord, we would be far wiser than we would otherwise be. Someone has well said "one has knowledge when he knows what he knows, but one has wisdom when he knows what he doesn't know." HAROLD B. LEE TO TRENT D. STEPHENS, JAN. 4, 1973

Throughout all ages the Lord has called upon the Saints to study and to learn the gospel through individual effort. "DEAR BRETHREN," UNITED STATES, APR. 3, 1970

Wisdom should be exercised in choosing gospel texts for personal study. All books, except the four standard works, contain only such wisdom as their authors have, and generally are not approved by the First Presidency unless they are to be used as gospel texts. There are many sound gospel texts, however, which should be studied by Church members. IBID.

We feel that the right to know, to inquire, to communicate and exchange ideas is fundamental to human well-being and an essential concomitant of freedom of conscience; that to extend by peaceful means the boundaries within which may occur the free exchange of ideas, without incitement to contempt or violence, should be an important objective of current efforts at international cooperation. "DESIRABLE OBJECTIVES," 1965

[T]he Church does not have a list of approved books, nor does it have a list of books that are not approved. The standard works of the Church are, of course, approved, and those books which are printed and issued by the Church itself are reliable. All other publications are issued by private individuals, and express the views of the individuals who wrote them.

Books issued by persons that are made from excerpts of writings or prophecies of the Brethren are frequently compiled to represent the ideas of the compilers, and are not always to be relied upon, since the quotations made have been removed from their context and so, by themselves, fail to express the true views of those quoted, and furthermore, in some cases, express views of the writers or speakers, which views are not endorsed by the Church. FIRST PRESIDENCY TO PRESIDENTS OF MISSIONS, SEPT. 12, 1952

[I]t is our divinely imposed duty to teach the truth, not error, and in carrying this out we must not provide pulpits and congregations to those who teach error. This must be mandatory upon all of us.

In this view we must call attention to the hazardous practice of some who teach and who present error on the theory that the learner may choose between the error and truth. You do not teach a false multiplication table in order that the learner may choose between the true table and the false. There is not available time and opportunity enough to teach young minds enough of truth to enable them successfully to reason and rationalize against well entrenched error. A living testimony of the restored gospel will withstand all error, and nothing but a testimony will successfully wage a conflict with error. "DEAR BRETHREN," JUNE 30, 1952

[W]e urge the Saints to refrain from the discussion of mysteries and to refrain from asking questions about matters and principles concerning which the Lord has made no definite statement. "DEAR BRETHREN," DEC. 19, 1951

[W]hile we do not expect people to come here to make

studies and to write their accounts to be propagandists for us nor to violate their own convictions in order to be kind in their statements concerning us, we think we have a right to expect that they should be fair and honest and not distort the truth in order to provide sensation and thus increase the saleability of their product. FIRST PRESIDENCY TO JOSEPH H. WESTON, APR. 19, 1946, IN *MESSAGES,* 6:251-52

"Rationalizing" may be most destructive of faith. That the Finite cannot fully explain the Infinite casts no doubt upon the Infinite. FIRST PRESIDENCY TO JOSEPH FIELDING SMITH, JOHN A. WIDTSOE, HAROLD B. LEE, AND MARION G. ROMNEY, AUG. 9, 1944, IN *MESSAGES,* 6:209-15

[Y]ou cannot rationalize the things of the spirit, because first, the things of the spirit are not sufficiently known and comprehended, and secondly, because finite mind and reason cannot comprehend nor explain infinite wisdom and ultimate truth. *DESERET NEWS,* AUG. 13, 1938, IN *MESSAGES,* 6:44-58

It is suggested that any members or officers of the Church in doubt regarding any matters or questions should be encouraged to consult with the ward bishopric or stake presidency. If, for any reason, these brethren should find it necessary to secure further information, they could then submit the question to the General Authorities. *CHURCH HANDBOOK,* 1934

There are questions relating to doctrine and principle that are proper subjects for class discussion, when that is conducted for the purpose of gaining information. There are topics, however, that are of no particular moment, or on which no definite conclusion can be authoritatively reached, and these ought to be avoided, as a waste of time and a cause of endless dispute. Let the light shine and be sought for in faith, but let contention have no place among the Latter-day Saints! *IMPROVEMENT ERA,* APR. 1912, IN *MESSAGES,* 4:270-71

Dogmatic assertions do not take the place of revelation, and we should be satisfied with that which is accepted as doctrine and not discuss matters that, after all disputes, are merely matters of theory. *IMPROVEMENT ERA,* MAR. 1912, IN *MESSAGES,* 4:264-65

[T]hat the Church relies upon duplicity in the propagation of her doctrines, and shuns enlightened investigation, is contrary to reason and fact. Deceit and fraud in the perpetuation of any religion must end in failure. A system of religion, ethics, or philosophy, to attract and hold the attention of men, must be sincere in doctrine and honest in propaganda. *IMPROVEMENT ERA,* MAY 1907, IN *MESSAGES,* 4:143-55

The labor of mind is not less labor than that of hand and body! JOSEPH F. SMITH TO JESSE W. CROSBY, MAY 30, 1881

A fanciful and flowery and heated imagination beware of; because the things of God are of deep import; and time, and experience, and careful and ponderous and solemn thought can only find them out. Thy mind, O man! if thou wilt lead a soul unto salvation, must stretch as high as the utmost heavens, and search into and contemplate the darkest abyss, and the broad expanse of eternity—thou must commune with God. How much more dignified and noble are the thoughts of God than the vain imaginations of the human heart! None but fools will trifle with the souls of men. STATEMENT, MAR. 25, 1839, IN *MESSAGES,* 1:88-104

We deem it a just principle, and it is one the force of which we believe ought to be duly considered by every individual, that all men are created equal, and that all have the privilege of thinking for themselves upon all matters relative to conscience. STATEMENT, JAN. 22, 1834, IN *MESSAGES,* 1:23-44

Islam

As the Church grows around the world, Latter-day Saints find themselves in increasingly frequent contact with members of the Islamic faith. Islam teaches much that is inspiring, noble, and worthy of the highest respect. Missionaries and other Church members must be sensitive and respectful toward the deeply held beliefs of Muslims and endeavor to avoid offending them. Latter-day Saints must be ever mindful of the need to obey, honor, and sustain the law in whatever county they find themselves, including those where the laws may prohibit proselyting activities. *BULLETIN,* 1992-1

Israel, house of. *See also* patriarchal blessings

It does not matter if your lineage in the house of Israel is through bloodlines or by adoption. As a member of the Church, you are counted as a descendant of Abraham and so heir to all the promises and blessings contained in the Abrahamic covenant ... *TRUE TO FAITH,* 2004

1. Israel consists of the blood descendants of Jacob.
2. Israel was scattered among all nations, in all lands, and over all the earth.
3. Israel has now intermixed with Gentile nations so that a large proportion of the inhabitants of the earth have Israelitish blood.
4. The tribes of Ephraim and of Manasseh are now being gathered, with occasional members of some of the other tribes.
5. The general gathering of the other tribes is yet future.
6. The term Gentile has had various definitions in vari-

ous ages. Using the name to mean those who are not of or are not intermixed with the blood of Israel, the seed of Cain may properly be classified as Gentiles. ...

7. When faithful Gentiles join the Church, they are accounted as the seed of Abraham and become adopted members of his family. All worthy males may receive the priesthood; therefore no gospel blessing is denied them. *PATRIARCHS,* 1981

Every individual born on this earth comes into a lineage according to a pre-earth-life determination. "BASIC DOCTRINES," 1971

J

Jesus Christ

[N]o member of this Church must ever forget the terrible price paid by our Redeemer, who gave His life that all men might live–the agony of Gethsemane, the bitter mockery of His trial, the vicious crown of thorns tearing at His flesh, the blood cry of the mob before Pilate, the lonely burden of His heavy walk along the way to Calvary, the terrifying pain as great nails pierced His hands and feet, the fevered torture of His body as He hung that tragic day, the Son of God crying out, "Father, forgive them; for they know not what they do" (Luke 23:34). GORDON B. HINCKLEY, "FIRST PRESIDENCY MESSAGE," *ENSIGN,* APR. 2005

Jesus Christ, the Son of God, is the greatest figure of time and eternity. He is Jehovah of the Old Testament. He is the Messiah of the New Testament. He died and was resurrected and lives in glory with our Eternal Father. He is our Savior and Redeemer. *CHURCH NEWS,* MAR. 26, 2005

The Savior defined His gospel to include some very vital and basic doctrines. He came into the world to do His Father's will, and His Father sent Him into the world to be lifted up on the cross. By His Atonement and Resurrection, all men will be lifted up to stand before Christ to be judged of their works, whether they be good or evil. Those who exercise faith in Christ, repent of their sins, and are baptized in Christ's name can be sanctified by the Holy Ghost. If they endure to the end, they will stand spotless before Christ at the last day and will enter into the rest of the Lord. Christ will hold them guiltless before the Father. He will be their Mediator and Advocate. Those who do not endure in faithfulness to the end will be "cast into the fire ... because of the justice of the Father" (see 3 Ne. 27:13-22; cf. 2 Ne. 31:10-21; 3 Ne. 11:31-41; D&C 76:40-42, 50-53). *PREACH MY GOSPEL,* 2005

It is His holy influence that stirs mankind to acts of mercy and kindness. He who has "borne our griefs, and carried our sorrows" (Isa. 53:4) inspires each of us to reach out with love to the poor, the lonely, and the downtrodden. *CHURCH NEWS,* DEC. 6, 2003

Jesus is our King, our Lord, our Master, the living and resurrected Christ, who stands on the right hand of His Father. He lives! He lives, resplendent and wonderful, the living Son of the living God. *CHURCH NEWS,* APR. 19, 2003

Jesus was in very deed the great Jehovah of the Old Testament, who left His Father's royal courts on high and condescended to come to Earth as a babe born in the most humble of circumstances. GORDON B. HINCKLEY, "FIRST PRESIDENCY MESSAGE," *ENSIGN,* DEC. 2002

[W]e solemnly testify that Jesus Christ was appointed and foreordained to be our Redeemer before the world was formed. With His divine sonship, His exemplary life, His suffering in the Garden of Gethsemane and on the cross of Calvary, and subsequent Resurrection from the grave, He became the author of salvation for all mankind. *CHURCH NEWS,* MAR. 23, 2002

Born in a stable, cradled in a manger, He came forth from heaven to live on Earth as mortal man and to establish the kingdom of God. During His earthly ministry, He taught men the higher law. His glorious gospel reshaped the thinking of the world. He blessed the sick; He caused the lame to walk, the blind to see, the deaf to hear. He even raised the dead to life. *CHURCH NEWS,* DEC. 2, 2000

He was the Great Jehovah of the Old Testament, the Messiah of the New. Under the direction of His Father, He was the creator of the earth. "All things were made by him; and without him was not any thing made that was made" (John 1:3). Though sinless, He was baptized to fulfill all righteousness. He "went about doing good" (Acts 10:23), yet was despised for it. His gospel was a message of peace and goodwill. He entreated all to follow His example. He walked the road of Palestine, healing the sick, causing the blind to see, and raising the dead. He taught the truths of eternity, the reality of our premortal existence, the purpose of life on earth, and the potential for the sons and daughters of God in the life to come.

He instituted the sacrament as a reminder of His great atoning sacrifice. He was arrested and condemned on spurious charges, convicted to satisfy a mob, and sentenced to die on Calvary's cross. He gave His life for the sins of all mankind. His was a great vicarious gift in behalf of all who would ever live upon the earth.

We solemnly testify that His life, which is central to all human history, neither began in Bethlehem nor concluded on Calvary. He was the Firstborn of the Father, the Only Begotten Son in the flesh, the Redeemer of the world.

He rose from the grave to "become the first fruits of them that slept" (1 Cor. 15:20). As Risen Lord, He visited among those He had loved in life. He also ministered among His "other sheep" (John 10:16) in ancient America. In the modern world, He and His Father appeared to the boy Joseph Smith, ushering in the long-promised "dispensation of the fullness of times" (Eph. 1:10). *CHURCH NEWS,* JAN. 1, 2000

The influence of the Savior, His matchless example of goodness and mercy, and His incomparable teachings have filtered down through the ages to become the catalyst which brings acts of kindness and love to mankind. *CHURCH NEWS,* DEC. 4, 1999

While Jesus' body lay in the tomb after His Crucifixion, His spirit went to the spirit world, where He preached the gospel to the spirits of the just (see 1 Pet. 3:18-20; 4:6; D&C 138:11-19). While there, the Savior organized missionaries among those righteous spirits to preach the gospel to those in spirit prison. *CHURCH HANDBOOK 2,* 1998

Jesus showed us the way to peace by His example. Out of the abundance of His heart, He spoke to the poor, the downtrodden, the widows, the little children. He blessed the lame, the blind, the deaf. He taught lessons of love and repeatedly demonstrated unselfish service to others.

In like manner, members of the Church are called upon to change our hearts, to make our outward actions conform to what we say we believe. We are asked to be kinder with one another, more gentle and forgiving. We are asked to be slower to anger and more prompt to help. We are asked to extend the hand of friendship and resist the hand of retribution. We are called upon to be true disciples of Christ, to love one another with genuine compassion, for that is the way Christ loved us. *CHURCH NEWS,* APR. 15, 1995

Of all things of heaven and earth of which we bear testimony, none is so important as our witness that Jesus, the Christmas child, condescended to come to Earth from the realms of His Eternal Father, here to work among men as healer and teacher, our Great Exemplar. And further, and most important, He suffered on Calvary's cross as an atoning sacrifice for all mankind. GORDON H. HINCKLEY, "FIRST PRESIDENCY MESSAGE," *ENSIGN,* DEC. 1992

[W]e affirm that Jesus Christ is the literal Son of God, the Savior of the world. By His infinite Atonement, which comprehended the suffering for all mankind, the blessings for eternal life are opened to those who serve Him and comply with the laws and ordinances of His gospel. *CHURCH NEWS,* APR. 14, 1990

The Lord works from the inside out. The world works from the outside in. The world would take people out of the slums. Christ takes the slums out of people, and then they take themselves out of the slums. The world would mold men by changing their environment. Christ changes men, who then change their environment. The world would shape human behavior, but Christ can change human nature. EZRA TAFT BENSON, "FIRST PRESIDENCY MESSAGE," *ENSIGN,* JULY 1989

Jesus was a God in the pre-earthly existence. Our Father in heaven gave Him a name above all others–the Christ. EZRA TAFT BENSON, "FIRST PRESIDENCY MESSAGE," *ENSIGN,* MAR. 1986

How poor indeed would be our lives without the influence of the Savior's teachings and his matchless example. The lessons of the turning of the other cheek, going the second mile, the return of the prodigal, and scores of other incomparable teachings have filtered down the ages to become the catalyst to bring kindness and mercy out of much of man's inhumanity to man. NEWS RELEASE, DEC. 15, 1983

Brutality reigns where Christ is banished. Kindness and forbearance govern where Christ is recognized and His teachings are followed. GORDON B. HINCKLEY, "FIRST PRESIDENCY MESSAGE," *ENSIGN,* DEC. 1983

Our position is that Jesus Christ is the key figure of our faith. The official name of the Church is The Church of Jesus Christ of Latter-day Saints. We worship Him as Lord and Savior. The Bible is our scripture. We believe that the prophets of the Old Testament who foretold the coming of the Messiah spoke under divine inspiration. We glory in the accounts of Matthew, Mark, Luke, and John, setting forth the events of the birth, ministry, death, and resurrection of the Son of God, the Only Begotten of the Father in the flesh. Like Paul of old, we are "not ashamed of the gospel of Christ; for it is the power of God unto salvation" (Rom. 1:16). And like Peter, we affirm that Jesus Christ is the only name "given among men, whereby we must be saved" (Acts 4:12). GORDON B. HINCKLEY, "FIRST PRESIDENCY MESSAGE," *ENSIGN,* APR. 1983

Is a belief in the divinity of our Lord out of date in the twentieth century? We say that the great scientific and technological age of which we are a part does not demand a denial of the miracle that is Jesus. Rather, there was never a time in all of the history of man that made more believable that which in the past might have been regarded as supernatural and impossible.

How can anyone today regard anything as impossible? IBID.

Our faith is centered in the living Christ, whom we seek to serve. Our prayers of gratitude ascend to God, our Eternal Father, for the great work of redemption wrought by His Son, Jesus Christ, the promised Messiah who shall come again.

We believe, and proclaim to the world, that "there is none other name under heaven given among men, whereby we must be saved" (Acts 4:12). We know He is God's almighty Son and invite all men and women, young and old, to come unto Christ and be perfected in Him. NEWS RELEASE, DEC. 15, 1982

Every teaching [Jesus Christ] espoused was designed to

make men happier and their lives fuller and richer, with the ultimate promise of eternal life in the presence of God. N. ELDON TANNER, "FIRST PRESIDENCY MESSAGE," *ENSIGN,* DEC. 1982

We urge all people to search the Savior's life for truths that will guide and give meaning to their own lives. And especially as we commemorate His great gifts to us, we urge all to follow His example, that they may be able to enjoy the abundant blessings of God. *CHURCH NEWS,* APR. 3, 1982

We believe that Jesus Christ is literally the Son of God, the Only Begotten in the flesh, that He was born of a mortal mother, that He dwelt among men, that He gave man the plan of life and salvation, and that He was crucified. We believe that He had power of death, that He willingly gave His life, and that He was literally resurrected so that man might be saved and resurrected from the dead and enjoy eternal life. N. ELDON TANNER, "FIRST PRESIDENCY MESSAGE," *ENSIGN,* APR. 1982

When in a quiet moment we think of the humble circumstances associated with Jesus' birth and of His life and teachings, we remember that the gifts of the Spirit are the most important ones of all. For it was the Savior Himself who set the supreme example of giving. He permitted His life to be sacrificed so that everyone, no matter who they are, will have an opportunity to return to our Heavenly Father if they live good lives and are obedient to Jesus' teachings. What a magnificent and generous gift! *FRIEND,* DEC. 1978

Jesus perfected His life and became our Christ. Priceless blood of a God was shed, and He became our Savior; His perfected life was given, and He became our Redeemer; His Atonement for us made possible our return to our Heavenly Father, and yet how thoughtless, how unappreciative are most beneficiaries! Ingratitude is a sin of the ages. SPENCER W. KIMBALL, "FIRST PRESIDENCY MESSAGE," *ENSIGN,* FEB. 1971

Jesus Christ is the spiritual and physical Son of the Father. He was the Firstborn of the Father, chosen before this world to be its Creator (see Col. 1:15-19). *PRINCIPLES,* 1976

As the Creator and foreordained Redeemer of this world, Jesus Christ became the God of this world, under the presiding authority of God the Father (see John 12:49). Because of these positions, He was the God of the Old Testament, Jehovah. IBID.

We encourage the Christian spirit so emulated by our Lord and Savior as He dwelt among men. He taught us to love one another, to bless the children, to provide for the poor, to comfort the distressed, to visit the widowed and fatherless, and to forgive those who trespass against us. *CHURCH NEWS,* DEC. 20, 1975

Jesus Christ is the Firstborn Son of God in the spirit and is the Only Begotten Son in the flesh.

Jehovah, the Creator, known in mortality as Jesus Christ, was the Lawgiver to Moses and other Old Testament prophets.

Jesus Christ was foreordained to become the Savior and Redeemer of mankind.

Because of His divine sonship and His perfect, sinless life, Jesus Christ was able to redeem mankind from spiritual death upon the condition of repentance by the individual sinner.

Because of His great love for us and because He wanted to be obedient to all the commandments of God, Jesus Christ was willing to redeem mankind from both the physical and spiritual deaths which resulted from the Fall of Adam. This act of love is called the Atonement.

Jesus Christ is the Mediator between God the Father and mankind. No man can come unto the Father except through Christ. "BASIC DOCTRINES," 1971

The most important thing that Jesus Christ taught when He was on Earth is that we must love one another. He told us that "love is of God" and commanded us to "love one another" (1 Jn. 4:7). N. ELDON TANNER, "FIRST PRESIDENCY MESSAGE," *ENSIGN,* JAN. 1971

As all other Christians, members of the Church accept and love to contemplate the life and ministry of Jesus as recorded in the four Gospels. From the birth in Bethlehem, where He was cradled in a manger, to the death in Jerusalem, where He was crucified upon a cross. We of the Church love to linger with Him to learn of His wisdom, to share His humanity, and to stir to His divinity. To us He is the Son of God come to earth to show us how to live–how to face death–and then–the glory of it all–to redeem us!

It is wonderful that God would give His Son to ransom us–it is likewise wonderful that the Son would die that we may live eternally. *DESERET NEWS,* DEC. 11, 1957

If men ever reject the fact that Christ is our Lord and Savior; that His mission is to redeem man from the sordid, animal life of selfish indulgence and sin and lift him into a realm shown only by Him of self-sacrifice, generosity, beauty, and love; if the majority of nations fail to recognize Him as the only "name under Heaven given among men, whereby we must be saved" [Acts 4:12]; if doubting men reject the possibility of obtaining that spiritual assurance of Christ's divinity disclosed by Thomas when he reverently exclaimed: "My Lord, and my God" [John 22:28]; if men's acts be in accordance with such rejections rather than in accordance with their acceptance of Him as the One divine, then this world will continue to be torn by contention, made miserable by hideous warfare, and ignominiously wrecked on the shoals of materialism, selfish indulgence, and disbelief.

Without Jesus of Nazareth, the crucified Christ, the risen Lord, the world cannot survive. *DESERET NEWS,* DEC. 15, 1948

We humbly proclaim our testimony that the Son was in the beginning with the Father; that the Son was the Creator of the world and all that in it is; that He was made flesh, the very Son of God, and dwelt among men; that He moved among men in the flesh doing mighty miracles; that He is the bread of life, none hungering who eats thereof and none thirsting who believe on him; that He is the way, the truth, and the life; that there is no other name under heaven given among men whereby men must be saved; that He made the great Atonement for the Fall of Adam and thereby made it possible for all of God's children to come back finally into His presence; that He died and was resurrected, the first fruits of the resurrection; that by and through His Resurrection all men will be resurrected in due time of the Lord. *DESERET NEWS,* DEC. 20, 1947

Fundamental in all Christ's teachings was the crime of wrong thinking. He condemned avarice, enmity, and jealousy in the mind almost as vehemently as He did the results that avarice, enmity, and jealousy produce. Can anyone in this modern world truthfully gainsay the practicability of such teaching? Equally applicable to present conditions are His teachings regarding the value and sacredness of human life, the virtue of forgiveness, the necessity of fair dealing, the crime of hypocrisy, the sin of covetousness, the saving power of love, universal brotherhood, the immortality of men, and many other vital principles. *IMPROVEMENT ERA,* JAN. 1938, IN *MESSAGES,* 6:37-40

The message of peace and good will which He brought to the house of Israel was rejected by His own people. He suffered persecution, and was finally crucified, because the new truths which He revealed were in conflict with the old law by which Israel, from the time of their deliverance from the Egyptian captivity under the leadership of the prophet Moses, had been governed. *DESERET NEWS,* DEC. 21, 1929

[T]he Lord Jehovah took upon Himself a body of flesh, to carry into effect the foreordained plan whereby redemption would be assured and salvation made possible to all humankind. *DESERET NEWS,* DEC. 22, 1928, IN *MESSAGES,* 5:264-66

The birth of Christ our Lord was more than an incident, it was an epoch in the history of the world to which prophets had looked forward, of which poets had sung, and in which angels joined their voices with mortals in praise to God. It was the day decreed and foreordained by our Father who is in heaven when He would manifest Himself to His children who are here upon Earth, in the person of His Only Begotten Son. *DESERET NEWS,* DEC. 19, 1925, IN *MESSAGES,* 5:245-48

The Holy Ghost came upon Mary, and her conception was under that influence, even of the Spirit of Life; our Father in Heaven was the Father of the Son of Mary, to whom the Savior prayed, as did our earthly father Adam. FIRST PRESIDENCY TO SAMUEL O. BENNION, FEB. 2, 1920, IN *MESSAGES,* 4:266-67

He came that man might see and know God as He is, for He bore witness that whoever had seen Him had seen the Father, for He was the express image of His person. IBID.

Jesus, however, is the Firstborn among all the sons of God—the first begotten in the spirit, and the only begotten in the flesh. He is our elder brother, and we like Him, are in the image of God. *DESERET NEWS,* JULY 18, 1925, QUOTING *IMPROVEMENT ERA,* NOV. 1909

Among the spirit children of Elohim, the firstborn was and is Jehovah or Jesus Christ, to whom all others are juniors. *IMPROVEMENT ERA,* AUG. 1916, IN *MESSAGES,* 5:26-34

Jesus Christ is the Son of Elohim both as spiritual and bodily offspring; that is to say, Elohim is literally the Father of the spirit of Jesus Christ and also of the body in which Jesus Christ performed His mission in the flesh, and which body died on the cross and was afterward taken up by the process of resurrection, and is now the immortalized tabernacle of the eternal spirit of our Lord and Savior. IBID.

Jesus Christ is not the Father of the spirits who have taken or yet shall take bodies upon this earth, for He is one of them. He is the Son, as they are sons or daughters, of Elohim. IBID.

Whether viewed as Deity embodied or as mortal deified, He shines out in the history of the earth as the one effulgent sun that is the light and glory of the world, compared to whom all mundane luminaries are but as glittering satellites. *DESERET NEWS,* DEC. 19, 1914, IN *MESSAGES,* 4:318-26

We bow to Him as the veritable Son of the living God in the fullest sense of the hallowed term. As Mary was His saintly mother, so the mighty God was His everlasting and literal Father. He was "the Only Begotten" of Deity, in the flesh, to die that man may live. IBID.

[I]f God made man–the first man–in His own image and likeness, he must have made him like unto Christ, and consequently like unto men of Christ's time and of the present day. That man was made in the image of Christ is positively stated in the Book of Moses: "And I, God, said unto mine Only Begotten, which was with me from the beginning, Let us make man in our image, after our likeness; and it was so.... And I, God, created man in mine own image, in the image of mine Only Begotten created I him, male and female created I them" (2:26, 27). *IMPROVEMENT ERA,* NOV. 1909, IN *MESSAGES,* 4:200-06

Jesus Christ, the Son of God, is "the express image" of His Father's person (Heb. 1:3). He walked the earth as a human being, as a perfect man, and said, in answer to a question put to Him: "He that hath seen me hath seen the Father" (John 14:9). This alone ought to solve the problem to the satisfaction of every thoughtful, reverent mind. IBID.

As members of His Church–the body of Christ–we recognize Him as the head and not only as the Great Teacher but as the veritable Son of God. *DESERET NEWS,* DEC. 17, 1904, IN *MESSAGES,* 4:92-98

Christ Himself is the Great High Priest, and President of this Universe. JOSEPH F. SMITH TO JOHN T. NATTRESS, FEB. 24, 1900

Judaism

We think that generally speaking the Mormon people have understood the Jews, and have probably been more friendly to them than any other people, and with our concept of universal brotherhood it is untenable that as a people we should entertain prejudice and ill will against any of our Father's children. FIRST PRESIDENCY TO PRESIDENTS OF STAKES AND STAKE MISSION PRESIDENTS, MAR. 2, 1959

We have a message for the Jews. We shall be most happy to give it to them if they will listen. IBID.

The Church for which we speak and its members individually reverently acknowledge an over-ruling power in the rich and marvelous history of the Jewish race, and are united in confident assurance of yet greater achievements, the consummation of which shall be the realization of all that has been predicted by holy prophets, who have voiced the beneficent plan of Israel's God in the destiny of His chosen people.

We rejoice in every development whereby the Jewish people are brought nearer the full attainment of their promised blessings, nearer the rehabilitation of the race as a unified nation and their establishment in the land of blessed promise, with enduring autonomy and assured solidarity even surpassing their ancient status.

Though for tens of centuries they have been scattered, dispersed among the nations, yet shall they be gathered within the fold of divine protection and nurturing—for theirs is a heritage of unfailing promise and assured redemption.

We regard ourselves as belonging to other divisions of the house of Israel, and therefore as brothers to the Jews, whose near futurity is closely involved with our own. *JEWISH TRIBUNE,* JUNE 29, 1932

The Book of Mormon leads us to believe that very many of the Jews will receive the gospel and acknowledge Christ as the Messiah before He comes again. JOHN TAYLOR AND GEORGE Q. CANNON TO JAMES H. HART, OCT. 15, 1885

[T]he Jews among all nations are hereby commanded, in the name of the Messiah, to prepare, to return to Jerusalem in Palestine, and to rebuild that city and temple unto the Lord:

And also to organize and establish their own political government, under their own rulers, judges, and governors in that country. STATEMENT, APR. 6, 1845, IN *MESSAGES,* 1:252-66

judgment

Judgment is an important use of your agency and requires

great care, especially when you make judgments about other people. All your judgments must be guided by righteous standards. Remember that only God, who knows each individual's heart, can make final judgments of individuals (see Rev. 20:12; 3 Ne. 27:14; D&C 137:9). *TRUE TO FAITH,* 2004

If we want mercy as part of our own final Judgment, we need to be merciful and loving in our attitudes toward others. *PRINCIPLES,* 1976

We will not be forgiven unless we are willing to forgive others (see Matt. 18:21-35). IBID.

Individuals are judged according to the light and knowledge received. All men are held accountable for their attitudes, thoughts, and works. "BASIC DOCTRINES," 1971

By the voice of the Lord, spoken through his servants, and by signs and wonders which are constantly manifested, He is calling His children to repentance. He pleads with them to forsake sin and return to His service, that they may be delivered from the tragic judgment which their own wicked acts will bring upon them. *DESERET NEWS,* DEC. 21, 1929

Men judge their fellows by the narrow gauge of their own conceptions of right and wrong, but God will judge in righteousness. JOSEPH F. SMITH TO WILLIAM BUDGE, APR. 28, 1906

[I]n all cases where charity can cover as a mantle a sin or even a multitude of sins, without harm occurring to others, the mantle of charity is the right thing. JOSEPH F. SMITH TO ALVIN F. SMITH, JULY 22, 1905

Always lean towards mercy, but remember there is no forgiveness or remission of sin without repentance. IBID.

According to the light we receive, so shall we be judged; the Lord will not hold us responsible for what we have had no opportunity of learning and His mercies will be extended to those who do not know the law. JOSEPH F. SMITH TO WILLIAM A. SMITH, JAN. 23, 1903

When the earth is purified by fire, it will be known whose works have been like gold, silver, and precious stone, and whose will be like wood, hay, and stubble; and until that day, the war between the kingdom of God and the kingdoms of the world (of Satan) will wax hotter and hotter, with occasional slight intervals of rest ... FIRST PRESIDENCY TO THOMAS L. KANE, SEPT. 15, 1851

[T]here is to be a day when all will be judged of their works, and rewarded according to the same; that those who have kept the faith will be crowned with a crown of righteousness, be clothed in white raiment, be admitted to the marriage feast, be free from every affliction, and reign with Christ on the earth, where, according to the ancient promise, they will partake of the fruit of the vine new in the glorious kingdom with Him; at least we find that such promises were made to the ancient Saints. STATEMENT, JAN. 22, 1834, IN *MESSAGES,* 1:23-44

K

King James Version, *see* Bible

kingdom of God. *See also* Church; government

[W]ithout doubt the time will ultimately come when every man-made institution will be arrayed against the Church and kingdom of God–the only institution of divine origin on the earth, and the only institution that will stand and remain unmoved, while all others will fall, disintegrate, and decay. "DEAR BRETHREN," DEC. 16, 1907, IN *MESSAGES,* 4:167-71

[W]e want to ponder well the path of our feet, and be very careful in regard to every step that we take, lest we adopt principles which are at variance with the broad and comprehensive views of our Heavenly Father, pertaining to our liberty and to the liberty and rights of all men; and, while we seek to accord certain rights and privileges to individuals, that we be very careful that we do not trammel nor fetter others who have like privileges with us. We must ever remember, as the sun shines for all, and the breath of heaven is free to all, that the earth, air, and water should be as free to and within the reach of all, and that we should do nothing that will circumscribe the universal liberty of universal man. But while we accord to all this perfect liberty, which is granted freely by our Heavenly Father, we must never forget that this general liberty is subject to principles, rules, and government; that it is under the guidance and direction of our Heavenly Father, and of those to whom He commits His authority and who are His legitimate representatives, and that if He introduces principles and develops theories, ideas, and laws, He has a perfect right to claim the honor of such organization, such principles, and such developments. If the Lord is to be our judge, our king, and our lawgiver, He looks for and has a right to expect an acknowledgment of His prescience, wisdom, and intelligence, as well as a cheerful and unwavering submission to His will and law, and an acknowledgment of His authority. If as the cycles of time roll on, the nations, governments, and rulers are weighed in the balance and found wanting; and if, in the overthrow of nations and the dissolution of existing systems and dynasties, the Lord introduces a system of laws, governments, and organizations, He will expect to dictate in all matters pertaining to the welfare of His people on Earth and the building up and establishment of a righteous kingdom, namely, the kingdom of God. STATEMENT, MAY 1, 1882, IN *MESSAGES,* 2:334-41

The kingdom of God consists in correct principles; and it mattereth not what a man's religious faith is; whether he be a Presbyterian, or a Methodist, or a Baptist, or a Latter-day Saint or "Mormon," or a Campbellite, or a Catholic, or Episcopalian, or Mahometan, or even pagan, or any thing else, if he will bow the knee and with his tongue confess that Jesus is the Christ, and will support good and wholesome laws for the regulation of society, we hail him as a brother, and will stand by him while he stands by us in these things; for every man's religious faith is a matter between his own soul and his God alone; but if he shall deny the Jesus, if he shall curse God, if he shall indulge in debauchery and drunkenness, and crime; if he shall lie, and swear, and steal; if he shall take the name of the Great God in vain, and commit all manner of abominations, he shall have no place in our midst, for we have long sought to find a people that will work righteousness, that will distribute justice equally, that will acknowledge God in all their ways, that will regard those sacred laws and ordinances which are recorded in that sacred book called the Bible, which we verily believe, and which we proclaim to the ends of the earth.

We ask no pre-eminence; we want no pre-eminence; but where God has placed us, there we will stand, and that is to be one with our brethren, and our brethren are those that keep the commandments of God, that do the will of our Father who is in heaven, and by them we will stand, and with them we will dwell in time and eternity. *MILLENNIAL STAR,* MAR. 14, 1848, IN *MESSAGES,* 1:323-35

knowledge. ***See also*** **education; intellectualism; science; truth**

Members of the Church are counseled to study, learn, and teach things both spiritual and temporal. Learning is essential to eternal progress (see D&C 88:77, 118-19, 125). *CHURCH HANDBOOK 2,* 1998

The Lord has commanded His people to gain knowledge (see D&C 88:77-80, 118; 93:53; 130:18-19; 131:6). With knowledge and wisdom, they are able to discern truth from error and make better choices. They also are better able to understand God and others, and they have a deeper love for them. IBID.

Wisdom is the proper application of true knowledge. Not all knowledge has the same worth—nor are all truths equally valuable. The truths upon which our eternal salvation rest are the most crucial truths that we must learn. No man is truly educated unless he knows where he came from, why he is here, and where he can expect to go in the next life. He must be able to adequately answer the question Jesus posed, "What think ye of Christ? [Matt. 22:42]." EZRA TAFT BENSON, "FIRST PRESIDENCY MESSAGE," *ENSIGN,* SEPT. 1988

There is incumbent upon each of us as members of The Church of Jesus Christ of Latter-day Saints the responsibility to observe the commandment to study and to learn. Said the Lord: "Seek ye out of the best books words of wisdom; seek learning, even by study and also by faith" (D&C 88:118).

He further made it clear that our search for truth must be broad, that we are to learn "of things both in heaven and in the earth, and under the earth; things which have been, things which are, things which must shortly come to pass; things which are at home, things which are abroad; the wars and the perplexities of the nations, and the judgments which are on the land; and a knowledge also of countries and of kingdoms" (88:79).

What a charge has been laid upon us to grow constantly toward eternity! None of us can assume that he has learned enough. As the door closes on one phase of life, it opens on another, where we must continue to pursue knowledge.

Ours ought to be a ceaseless quest for truth. That truth must include spiritual and religious truth as well as secular. As we go forward with our lives and our search for truth, let us look for the good, the beautiful, the positive. GORDON B. HINCKLEY, "FIRST PRESIDENCY MESSAGE," *ENSIGN,* APR. 1986

There has never been a day such as now in all of earthly history when secular learning was so far advanced and widespread as it is today. Yet so many of those around us do not enjoy the truths and the freedom those truths bring of which the Master taught. Rather, to so many people, it seems that truth and true freedom elude their grasp.

The central core of the Father's plan of salvation is that to obtain these truths and the peace, happiness, security, and freedom these truths bring to their righteous adherents, we must draw upon a source of knowledge that lies above and beyond the reach of ordinary learning processes.

The road to this sure knowledge is a sincere and honest desire to obtain truth from God, seeking such truth through sustained prayer, through devoted study of God's scriptures, and through righteous, charitable behavior in our daily lives. MARION G. ROMNEY, "FIRST PRESIDENCY MESSAGE," *ENSIGN,* FEB. 1984

[S]ecular knowledge can be most helpful to the children of our Father in Heaven who, having placed first things first, have found and are living those truths which lead one to eternal life. These are they who have the balance and perspective to seek all knowledge—revealed and secular—as a tool and servant for the blessing of themselves and others. They know that preeminent among all activities in this life is preparing themselves for eternal life by subjugating the flesh, subjecting the body to the spirit, overcoming weaknesses, and so governing themselves that they may give leadership to others. Important, but of second priority, comes the knowledge associated with life in mortality. SPENCER W. KIMBALL, "FIRST PRESIDENCY MESSAGE," *ENSIGN,* SEPT. 1983

As a people, we Latter-day Saints have been encouraged by the Lord to progress in the learning of God as well as in the sound learning of the earth. Too many of us spend far too much time watching the television or in habits and activities that do not enlarge ourselves or bless others. Would that we might lift ourselves to higher visions of what we could do with our lives! There should be no people who have a higher desire to obtain truth, revealed and secular, than Latter-day Saints. IBID.

The Church of Jesus Christ of Latter-day Saints has always

taught that the glory of God is intelligence and that a man can be saved no faster than he gains knowledge. It also encourages its members to "seek ... first the kingdom of God, and His righteousness" (Matt. 6:33), with the understanding that all things for their good will be added unto them. N. ELDON TANNER, "FIRST PRESIDENCY MESSAGE," *ENSIGN,* OCT. 1973

We glory in the advancement of knowledge and achievement as seen in man's efforts to conquer space and the landing of men on the moon. This represents important advances in man's understanding of the universe about him, all of which is the handiwork of God. Acquiring such knowledge is in full harmony with gospel principles. All truth, whether it pertains to the universe, to this earth, or to the individual and his environment, is a part of the gospel of Jesus Christ. *CHURCH NEWS,* DEC. 20, 1969

[T]he Lord has made clear that the members of His Church should constantly seek wisdom and learning in every field. This is basic to our faith.

Words of wisdom are to be sought in the best books, and we are to seek learning by study and by faith. All truth is ours, but we shun and throw away all evil, from whatever source and in whatever guise. "DEAR BRETHREN," JUNE 30, 1952

[G]od made clear that the gaining of knowledge is not to be like the commonplace work of earning a living. He who invades the domain of knowledge must approach it as Moses came to the burning bush; he stands on holy ground; he would acquire things sacred; he seeks to make his own the attributes of Deity, the truth which Christ declared He was (John 14:6), and which shall make us free (8:32), free of the shackles of time and space, which shall be no more. We must come to this quest of truth—in all regions of human knowledge whatsoever—not only in reverence, but with a spirit of worship. "CHARGE TO PRESIDENT HOWARD S. MCDONALD," NOV. 14, 1945, IN *MESSAGES,* 6:228-38

In all His promises and commandments about gaining knowledge, the Lord has never withheld from our quest any field of truth. Our knowledge is to be coterminous with the universe and is to reach out and to comprehend the laws and the workings of the deeps of the eternities. All domains of all knowledge belong to us. In no other way could the great law of eternal progression be satisfied. IBID.

[W]orldly knowledge has its place, but it may not be substituted for revealed truth, nor the inspired utterance of God's prophets. FIRST PRESIDENCY TO JOSEPH FIELDING SMITH, JOHN A. WIDTSOE, HAROLD B. LEE, AND MARION G. ROMNEY, AUG. 9, 1944, IN *MESSAGES,* 6:209-15

If men would be great in goodness, they must be intelligent, for no man can do good unless he knows how; therefore seek after knowledge, all knowledge, and especially that which is from above, which is wisdom to direct in all things, and if you find any thing that God does not know, you need not learn that thing; but strive to know what God knows, and use that knowledge as God uses it, and then you will be like Him; will see as you are seen, and know as you are known; and have charity, love one another, and do each other good continually and forever, even as for yourselves.

But if a man have all knowledge, and does not use it for good, it will prove a curse instead of a blessing as it did to Lucifer, the Son of the Morning. *MILLENNIAL STAR,* JAN. 15, 1852, IN *MESSAGES,* 2:76-91

It is a gentile custom to sell knowledge. This principle is utterly opposed to the principles of salvation—by it no person would ever be able to enter the celestial gate. Had the Savior of the world required remuneration for disclosing His knowledge of the way to obtain eternal life made manifest by His words and atoning blood at the hands of the children of men, who could have been saved? FIRST PRESIDENCY TO IRON COUNTY SAINTS, OCT. 1851

L

labor unions. ***See also*** **government**

The Church ... is not opposed to labor organizations, but it is opposed to the attempts made by some of them to tyrannize over their fellow workers. It is essentially wrong for any organization to prevent by force, or by other improper means to compel working men or women to join a Union or any other society, or to prevent non-Union workers from obtaining employment. The Church as a body, as represented by its elders, is against all forms of oppression, tyranny, and injustice. The Church also holds that it is better for its members to put their standing in the Church first, and not to permit themselves to be drawn aside from their whole duty to God and the gospel, by affiliation with organizations that interfere with their full freedom to act as Church members and Saints of God. Working people have the right and liberty to unite for good purposes affecting them as individuals and societies, but not to compel others to join them in their organized endeavors. When any kind of "unions" use their powers to force people into their ranks or measures for the accomplishment of union purposes, the Church does not favor them, for the principle on which they act is fundamentally wrong and subversive of the freedom of mankind. FIRST PRESIDENCY TO FRED L. W. BENNETT, MAR. 8, 1918

We believe in the liberty of labor and the right of working people to combine for their own protection and advancement when it does not infringe upon the rights of other people, organizations, or associations. *DESERET EVENING NEWS,* DEC. 17, 1910

Lamanites, *see* American Indians

Last Days, *see* Second Coming

law

We affirm the historic principles set forth in the "Declaration of Belief regarding Governments and Laws in General," adopted at a general assembly of the Church in Kirtland, Ohio, August 17, 1835. Included is the belief that religion is instituted of God, and that men are amenable to Him, and to Him only, for the free exercise of it, unless their religious opinions prompt them to infringe upon the rights and liberties of others. Under such circumstances, governments may intervene by lawful means to safeguard the rights thus jeopardized. But we do not believe that human law has a right to interfere in prescribing rules of worship to bind the consciences of men, nor dictate forms for public or private devotion. The civil magistrate should restrain crime, but never control conscience; should punish guilt, but never suppress the freedom of the soul. "DESIRABLE OBJECTIVES," MAY 14, 1965

All rules and regulations, in fact all laws, especially the laws of God, are made for the benefit of the people. It is, of course, of the utmost importance that we become familiar therewith and conform thereto that we may have the blessings which were intended. *STRENGTH OF YOUTH,* 1965

[L]aw is, or should be, neither more nor less than a rule of action founded in justice for the proper regulation of the human family in their social intercourse, and written with the utmost plainness. *DESERET NEWS,* SEPT. 21, 1854, IN *MESSAGES,* 2:154-56

life, sanctity of

Life, even our own, is so precious that we are accountable to the Lord for it, and we should not trifle with it. Once gone, it cannot be called back. JAMES E. FAUST, "FIRST PRESIDENCY MESSAGE," *ENSIGN,* JUNE 2006

The Church of Jesus Christ of Latter-day Saints believes in the sanctity of human life, and is therefore opposed to euthanasia. Euthanasia is defined as deliberately putting to death a person who is suffering from an incurable condition or disease. Such a deliberate act ends the life immediately through, for example, so-called assisted suicide. Ending a life in such a manner is a violation of the commandments of God.

The Church of Jesus Christ of Latter-day Saints does not believe that allowing a person to die from natural causes by removing a patient from artificial means of life support, as in the case of long-term illness, falls within the definition of euthanasia. When dying from such an illness or an accident becomes inevitable, it should be seen as a blessing and a purposeful part of eternal existence. Members should not feel obligated to extend mortal life by means that are unreasonable. These judgments are best made by family members after receiving wise and competent medical advice and seeking divine guidance through fasting and prayer. "ISSUES RESOURCES," 2006

We affirm the sanctity of life and its importance in God's eternal plan. *CHURCH NEWS,* NOV. 24, 2001

A person who participates in euthanasia, including so-called assisted suicide, violates the commandments of God. *CHURCH HANDBOOK,* 1998

We declare the means by which mortal life is created to be divinely appointed. We affirm the sanctity of life and of its importance in God's eternal plan. *CHURCH NEWS,* SEPT. 30, 1995

Because of its belief in the dignity of life, the Church opposes euthanasia. *CHURCH HANDBOOK,* 1985

The Church does not look with favor upon any form of mercy killing. It believes in the dignity of life and that faith in the Lord and medical science should be appropriately called upon and applied to reverse conditions that are a threat to life. There comes a time when dying becomes inevitable, when it should be looked upon as a blessing, and a purposeful part of mortality. "ATTITUDES," 1974

Light of Christ. ***See also*** **revelation**

In the scriptures, the Light of Christ is sometimes called the Spirit of the Lord, the Spirit of God, the Spirit of Christ, or the Light of Life.

The Light of Christ should not be confused with the Holy Ghost. It is not a personage, as the Holy Ghost is. Its influence leads people to find the true gospel, be baptized, and receive the gift of the Holy Ghost (see John 12:46; Alma 26:14-15).

Conscience is a manifestation of the Light of Christ, enabling us to judge good from evil. *TRUE TO FAITH,* 2004

At birth each of us receives the Light of Christ, which encourages us to do what is right. *PRINCIPLES,* 1976

lotteries, ***see*** **gambling**

Lucifer, ***see*** **Satan**

M

marriage. ***See also*** **sealings, husband and wives**

[T]he marriage of a man and a woman is the only acceptable marriage relationship. *DESERET NEWS,* MAY 27, 2006

God loves all of His children. He has provided a plan for His children to enjoy the choicest blessings that He has to offer in eternity. Those choicest blessings are associated with marriage between a man and a woman by appropriate priesthood authority to bring together a family unit for creation and happiness in this life and in the life to come. "ISSUES RESOURCES," 2006

As a doctrinal principle, based on sacred scripture, we affirm that marriage between a man and a woman is essential to the Creator's plan for the eternal destiny of His children. The powers of procreation are to be exercised only between a man and a woman lawfully wedded as husband and wife. NEWS RELEASE, OCT. 19, 2004

In our Heavenly Father's plan of happiness, a man and a woman can be sealed to one another for time and all eternity. Those who are sealed in the temple have the assurance that their relationship will continue forever if they are true to their covenants. They know that nothing, not even death, can permanently separate them.

The covenant of eternal marriage is necessary for exaltation. *TRUE TO FAITH,* 2004

Remember that marriage, in its truest sense, is a partnership of equals, with neither person exercising dominion over the other, but with each encouraging, comforting, and helping the other. IBID.

A good marriage requires time. It requires effort. You have to work at it. You have to cultivate it. You have to forgive and forget. You have to be absolutely loyal to one another. GORDON B. HINCKLEY, "FIRST PRESIDENCY MESSAGE," *ENSIGN,* FEB. 1999

Only a marriage that has been sealed in the temple and confirmed by the Holy Spirit of Promise can be eternal (see D&C 132:7). *CHURCH HANDBOOK,* 1998

Marriage is ordained of God, marriage between a man and a woman. It is the institution under which He designed that children should come into the world. Sexual relationships under any other circumstances become transgression and are totally at odds with the teachings of the gospel of Jesus Christ. GORDON B. HINCKLEY, "FIRST PRESIDENCY MESSAGE," *ENSIGN,* JUNE 1996

We, the First Presidency and the Council of the Twelve Apostles, of The Church of Jesus Christ of Latter-day Saints, solemnly proclaim that marriage between a man and a woman is ordained of God and that the family is central to the Creator's plan for the eternal destiny of His children. *CHURCH NEWS,* SEPT. 30, 1995

The family is ordained of God. Marriage between man and woman is essential to His eternal plan. Children are entitled to birth within the bonds of matrimony, and to be reared by a father and a mother who honor marital vows with complete fidelity. Happiness in family life is most likely to be achieved when founded upon the teachings of the Lord Jesus Christ. Successful marriages and families are established and maintained on principles of faith, prayer, repentance, forgiveness, respect, love, compassion, work, and wholesome recreational activities. IBID.

Marriage between a man and a woman is ordained of God to fulfill the eternal destiny of His children. The union of husband and wife assures perpetuation of the race and provides a divinely ordained setting for the nurturing and teaching of children. This sacred family setting, with father and mother and children firmly committed to each other and to righteous living, offers the best hope for avoiding many of the ills that afflict society. *ENSIGN,* APR. 1994

Marriage, in its truest sense, is a partnership of equals, with neither exercising dominion over the other, but, rather, with each encouraging and assisting the other in whatever responsibilities and aspirations he or she might have. GORDON B. HINCKLEY, "FIRST PRESIDENCY MESSAGE," *ENSIGN,* AUG. 1992

The secret of a happy marriage is to serve God and each other. The goal of marriage is unity and oneness, as well as self-development. Paradoxically, the more we serve one another, the greater is our spiritual and emotional growth. EZRA TAFT BENSON, "FIRST PRESIDENCY MESSAGE," *ENSIGN,* JULY 1992

We teach that the most sacred of all relationships, those family associations of husbands and wives and parents and children, may be continued eternally when marriage is solemnized under the authority of the holy priesthood exercised in temples dedicated for these divinely authorized purposes. *CHURCH NEWS,* APR. 12, 1980

Honorable, happy, and successful marriage is surely the principal goal of every normal person. Marriage is designed of the Lord to make strong and happy homes and posterity. Anyone who would purposely avoid marriage is not only not normal, but is frustrating his own program. SPENCER W. KIMBALL, "FIRST PRESIDENCY MESSAGE," *ENSIGN,* OCT. 1979

In selecting a companion for life and for eternity, certainly the most careful planning and thinking and praying and fasting should be done to be sure that of all the decisions, this one must not be wrong. In true marriage there must be a union of minds as well as of hearts. Emotions must not wholly determine decisions, but the mind and the heart, strengthened by fasting and prayer and serious consideration, will give one a maximum chance of marital happiness. It brings with it sacrifice, sharing, and a demand for great selflessness. SPENCER W. KIMBALL, "FIRST PRESIDENCY MESSAGE," *ENSIGN,* MAR. 1977

Marriage is ordained of God. It is not merely a social custom. Without proper and successful marriage, one will never be exalted. IBID.

In our day, the restraints and control thrown around the marital relationship by law have so much changed the conditions about which the Savior spoke [Matt. 5:32; 19:9] that the following rule governing the Church in these matters [divorce and remarriage] has been followed: "There is no sin in honorable marriage."

In the Church, marriage performed by the properly authorized priesthood is an eternal sacrament and couples so married are united for time and for all eternity. In marriages of this type, only the binding power can loose the bond, and where the bond is loosed, couples are at liberty, of course, to remarry. FIRST PRESIDENCY TO ROBERT A. MADSEN, MAR. 28, 1975

It was never intended by the Lord that a large portion of one's life should be spent in the unmarried state. At a reasonable time in life, it was intended that each young man should find that young woman who is best for him, and she should find the young man who would be her best companion. Long-delayed marriages are certainly not approved of the Lord. SPENCER W. KIMBALL, "FIRST PRESIDENCY MESSAGE," *ENSIGN,* FEB. 1975

We hope that young people will be willing to sacrifice the pomp and show and pageantry of the civil weddings so that they, and generally their parents with them, can go to the holy temple for their marriages. Often the cost of a reception or a holiday or expensive gifts would more than pay for a temple wedding. IBID.

Eternal marriage was known to Adam and others of the prophets, but the knowledge was lost from the earth for many centuries. SPENCER W. KIMBALL, "FIRST PRESIDENCY MESSAGE," *ENSIGN,* AUG. 1974

Civil marriage is an earthly contract, completed in the death of either party. Eternal celestial marriage is a sacred covenant between man and woman, consecrated in the holy temple by servants of God who hold authoritative keys. It bridges death; it includes both time and eternity. IBID.

It should be made perfectly clear to couples and their families that the chapel marriage is not in anywise a substitute for, nor does it carry with it either the mortal or the eternal blessings and benefits and hopes which flow from a sealing of husband and wife in the temples of the Lord by those who have the authority to bind on earth and have the covenants thus entered into bind the union in heaven. JOSEPH ANDERSON, SECRETARY TO THE FIRST PRESIDENCY, LETTER DATED APR. 29, 1969

[M]arried couples should seek inspiration and wisdom from the Lord that they may exercise discretion in solving their marital problems, and that they may be permitted to rear their children in accordance with the teachings of the gospel. "DEAR BRETHREN," APR. 14, 1969

Marriage is one of the most sacred ordinances of the Church. It should not be performed before the gaze of the world. When couples are not to be married in the temple, a little discreet counsel from bishops (and chaplains) might lead them to have the ceremony performed in the home of one or the other of those being married. A good home is the next most sacred place to the temple. *SERVICEMEN'S PROGRAM,* 1961

To make a marriage achieve its divine purpose—to bring the spirit children of our Father into the world, nurture them through life, and then return them to his celestial presence in virtue and strength—is at once the highest ambition and the most acceptable contribution made by man or woman. It is the transcendent contribution our good homes may make to the broken, misguided family life of the world, to neglected, sorrowing, and delinquent children, to wholesome respect for law and order, and the elevation of the race. *DESERET NEWS,* DEC. 12, 1951

Every married couple, young and old, should understand, and the husband particularly should know that the wife is queen of her own body; that marriage does not give man the right to prostitute such a relation. Marriage is for the building of the home, and the rearing of children, the most sacred obligation therein. It should not be used as a cover for the mere gratification of personal or selfish desires. DAVID O. MCKAY TO "DEAR BROTHER," NOV. 4, 1947

[N]o change has been made to the rules, regulations, and doctrines of the Church which have been in force since the Church was organized that marriage to non-members is considered not wise. JOSEPH ANDERSON, SECRETARY TO THE FIRST PRESIDENCY, TO J. LELAND ANDERSON, SEPT. 17, 1945

The Church of Jesus Christ of Latter-day Saints stands for the highest and purest ideals in family life. By revelation we know that marriage is ordained of God, the paramount purpose of which is to bring into the world immortal spirits to be reared in honor and nobility of character to fulfill the measure of their mortal existence. Married couples who by inheritance and proper living have themselves been blessed with moral and physical vigor are recreant to their duty if they refuse to meet the rightful and natural responsibility of parenthood. DAVID O. MCKAY TO "DEAR BROTHER," MAR. 6, 1942

It is, of course, primarily the responsibility of parents to teach their sons and daughters the importance and sanctity of the marriage covenant. *CHURCH HANDBOOK,* 1940

Couples who have associated together illicitly should not be recommended to the Temple until they have satisfied their bishops that they have thoroughly repented, and have shown their repentance by living righteously for a prolonged period of time. Mere sorrow is not repentance. It is urged that the desirability of Temple marriages be continually emphasized. IBID.

In a country in which the common law marriage is recognized as legal, and the children resulting from such a marriage are recorded as legitimate offspring, the Church will recognize such marriage under the conditions attaching to recognition by the law of the land. However, in a country such as Holland, for instance, where conditions are as presented by President Lyon of the Netherlands Mission, where the children of such unions are registered in the records as "bastard children and the mother as a prostitute, the father recorded as unknown," a couple so living are certainly not living in honorable wedlock, and therefore cannot be recognized by the Church as married people.

With reference to the case of the German sister called ... to do local missionary work, who, it has since developed, has been living with a man to whom she is not legally married, obviously the proper course would be for this couple to marry. It appears this cannot be done because the man with whom she is living cannot get a legal divorce from his former wife. In this alternative the woman must of course be immediately released as a missionary.

We are keenly aware of the difficulties that such a situation presents in countries where not only the State but the established church and society wink at such irregularities. Where such relations are of very long standing, particularly if the relation existed at the time the people joined the Church, the Church should urge the legalizing of this union and should refrain from putting its stamp of approval upon such unions by placing in positions persons so living. Every effort should be made so to treat such cases that the Church is understood as not sanctioning illicit sexual relations. The Church must always stand for sexual purity.

However, it is our view that persons should not be taken into the Church who are living in such relations, and that every effort should be made to learn before baptism whether such relations exist. After persons become members of the Church, illicit sexual relations should no more be tolerated among Church members in Europe than in America, and they must be dealt with there as they are dealt with here. FIRST PRESIDENCY TO JOSEPH F. MERRILL, FEB. 11, 1935

Marriage presupposes parenthood, and parenthood involves the responsibility of husband to wife, wife to husband, parents to children, and children to parents.

Marriage is fraught with greater possibilities for good or

evil, happiness or despair, prosperity or penury, exaltation or condemnation, than any other relationship upon which a man or woman may embark. FIRST PRESIDENCY TO PRESIDENTS OF STAKES AND COUNSELORS, JUNE 17, 1933, IN *MESSAGES,* 5:315-30

Celestial marriage—that is, marriage for time and eternity—and polygamous or plural marriage are not synonymous terms. Monogamous marriages for time and eternity, solemnized in our temples in accordance with the word of the Lord and the laws of the Church, are celestial marriages. IBID.

We believe in the eternity of the marital covenant and conditions, when it is solemnized according to former divine commandment, revealed anew in the present generation, being for time and eternity instead of merely until death. *MILLENNIAL STAR,* MAR. 2, 1911, IN *MESSAGES,* 4:221-23

To the Latter-day Saints, marriage is not designed by our Heavenly Father to be merely an earthly union, but one that shall survive the vicissitudes of time, and endure for eternity, bestowing honor and joy in this world, glory and eternal lives in the worlds to come. *IMPROVEMENT ERA,* MAY 1907, IN *MESSAGES,* 4:143-55

No community can prosper and maintain a high standard of morality where there is a large percentage of unmarried young men and young women. STATEMENT, OCT. 10, 1887, IN *MESSAGES,* 3:133-55

We never have believed or taught that the doctrine of celestial [i.e., plural] marriage was designed for universal practice. *MILLENNIAL STAR,* NOV. 9, 1885, IN *MESSAGES,* 3:23-41

The Lord has revealed to us by His special revelations, as clearly and positively as He ever did to any of the ancient prophets, certain principles associated with the eternity of the marriage covenant, has given definite commands pertaining thereto, and made them obligatory upon us to carry out. He has made manifest to us those great and eternal principles which bind woman to man and man to woman, children to parents and parents to children, and has called upon us in the most emphatic and pointed manner to obey them. These glorious principles involve our dearest interests and associations in time and throughout the eternities that are to come. We are told that this is His everlasting covenant, and that it has existed from eternity; and furthermore, that all covenants that relate only to time shall be dissolved at death and be no longer binding upon the human family. STATEMENT, APR. 4, 1885, IN *MESSAGES*, 3:4-12

The eternity of the marriage covenant depends upon the faithful observance by both parties of all the laws, rites, and ceremonies pertaining to that condition in the new and everlasting covenant, failing in which forfeiture follows. JOSEPH F. SMITH TO J. E. BOOTH, SEPT. 18, 1881

The Lord has taught us how important it is that our marriages should be solemnized according to the laws He has given, in holy places, where wives can be joined to husbands for time and all eternity. FIRST PRESIDENCY, LETTER DATED OCT. 25, 1876, IN *MESSAGES,* 2:278-81

Melchizedek Priesthood, *see* priesthood

mentally challenged individuals, *see* accountability

Michael, *see* Adam and Eve

military service. *See also* conscientious objection; peace; war

We believe our young men should hold themselves in readiness to respond to the call of their government to serve in the armed forces when called upon, and again we repeat, we believe in honoring, sustaining, and upholding the law. *DAILY UNIVERSE*, BRIGHAM YOUNG UNIVERSITY, MAY 19, 1969

Millennium, *see* Second Coming

missionary work

The most powerful missionary message you can send is your own example of living a happy Latter-day Saint life. Remember that people do not join the Church only because of gospel principles they learn. They join because they feel something that begins to satisfy their spiritual needs. If you are sincere in your friendship with them, they will be able to feel the spirit of your testimony and happiness. *TRUE TO FAITH,* 2004

Full-time missionary service is a privilege for those who are called through inspiration by the President of the Church. "STATEMENT ON MISSIONARY WORK FROM THE FIRST PRESIDENCY AND THE QUORUM OF THE TWELVE APOSTLES," DEC. 11, 2002

Prospective missionaries need to be spiritually prepared and know how to respond to the whisperings of the Spirit. Individuals are not to be sent on a mission to be reactivated or reformed. They need to be filled with "faith, hope, charity and love, with an eye single to the glory of God" (D&C 4:5), and have a desire to serve. IBID.

Our purpose is to teach the message of the restored gospel in such a way as to allow the Spirit to direct both the missionaries and those being taught. It is essential to learn the concepts of the standard missionary discussions, but these should not be taught by rote presentation. The missionary should feel free to use his own words as prompted by the Spirit. He should not give a memorized recitation, but speak from the heart in his own terms. He may depart from the order of the lessons, giving that which he is inspired to do, according to the interest and needs of the investigator. Speaking out of his own conviction and in his own words, he should bear testimony of the truth of his teachings. IBID.

Every worthy young man should go on a mission. And each one of us, though we may not be called to active missionary service, can be on a mission and be involved in a cause that is greater than we are, the greatest cause of all in the world: the salvation of each of our Father's children. JAMES E. FAUST, "FIRST PRESIDENCY MESSAGE," *ENSIGN,* JULY 1997

Full-time missionary service is not a right, but a privilege for those who are called through inspiration by the First Presidency. Missionary service is for the benefit of the Lord and His Church to fulfill His purposes. Its objective is not primarily the personal development of an individual missionary, although righteous service invariably produces that result. "DEAR BRETHREN," MAR. 4, 1993

If there were no converts, the Church would shrivel and die on the vine. But perhaps the greatest reason for missionary work is to give the world its chance to hear and accept the gospel. SPENCER W. KIMBALL, "FIRST PRESIDENCY MESSAGE," *ENSIGN,* APR. 1984

Sharing the gospel brings peace and joy into our own lives, enlarges our own hearts and souls in behalf of others, increases our own faith, strengthens our own relationship with the Lord, and increases our own understanding of gospel truths. Perhaps almost more comes to us than to those to whom we introduce the gospel. SPENCER W. KIMBALL, "FIRST PRESIDENCY MESSAGE," *ENSIGN,* FEB. 1983

Our great need, and our great calling, is to bring to the people of this world the candle of understanding to light their way out of obscurity and darkness and into the joy, peace, and truths of the gospel. IBID.

It is the individual responsibility of each of us to so live that we may extend our influence to others, who, seeing our good works, will be led to glorify our Father in Heaven. N. ELDON TANNER, "FIRST PRESIDENCY MESSAGE," *ENSIGN,* DECEMBER 1982

[E]very man, woman, and child–every young person and every little boy and girl–should serve a mission. This does not mean that they must serve abroad or even be formally called and set apart as full-time missionaries. But it does mean that each of us is responsible to bear witness of the gospel truths that we have been given. We all have relatives, neighbors, friends, and fellow workmen, and it is our responsibility to pass the truths of the gospel on to them, by example as well as by precept. SPENCER W. KIMBALL, "FIRST PRESIDENCY MESSAGE," *ENSIGN,* OCT. 1977

Every gospel teaching experience is a spiritual experience for all parties, regardless of whether it leads to baptism or not. Our goal should be to identify as soon as possible which of our Father's children are spiritually prepared to proceed all the way to baptism into the kingdom. One of the best ways to find out is to expose your friends, relatives, neighbors, and acquaintances to the full-time missionaries as soon as possible. Don't wait for long fellowshipping nor for the precise, perfect moment. What you need to do is find out if they are the elect. "[My] elect hear my voice and harden not their hearts" (D&C 29:7). If they hear and have hearts open to the gospel, it will be evident immediately. If they won't listen and their hearts are hardened with skepticism or negative comments, they are not ready. In this case, keep loving them and fellowshipping them and wait for the next opportunity to find out if they are ready. You will not lose their friendship. They will still respect you. IBID.

[M]issionary work is not limited to proclaiming the gospel to every nation, kindred, tongue, and people now living on the earth. Missionary work is also continuing beyond the veil among the millions and even billions of the children of our Heavenly Father who have died either without hearing the gospel or without accepting it while they lived on the earth. Our great part in this aspect of missionary work is to perform on this earth the ordinances required for those who accept the gospel over there. The spirit world is full of spirits who are anxiously awaiting the performance of these earthly ordinances for them. SPENCER W. KIMBALL, "FIRST PRESIDENCY MESSAGE," *ENSIGN,* JAN. 1977

[B]ecause of the special role we play as members of the Lord's Church, it is our responsibility to take the gospel to all living persons and to try to bring them to a knowledge of the truth and to introduce them to the blessings of the Church through baptism and confirmation. However, no one should attempt to convert that broad mandate into a goal of a specific percentage of increase in the number of baptisms. We have learned through experience that the use of such an arbitrary goal often leads to faulty teaching, done merely to achieve the goal, rather than to bring understanding and, hopefully, salvation to those being taught. "DEAR BRETHREN," JAN. 14, 1976

[E]ven though a prospective missionary may have a working knowledge of a non-English language, his mission call will not be tailored to his foreign language ability, but as the Spirit of the Lord directs. FIRST PRESIDENCY TO ALL STAKE AND MISSION PRESIDENTS, UNITED STATES AND CANADA, SEPT. 30, 1974

It would be hoped that no missionary, motivated by his desire to increase his number of baptisms, would baptize individuals who have not experienced genuine conversion. FIRST PRESIDENCY TO ALL MISSION PRESIDENTS, DEC. 1962

We ask that you constantly keep in mind that each missionary is a personal ambassador of the Lord Jesus Christ, that cleanliness in thought, speech, and manner are essential, and that dedication to the work and a desire to serve are indispensable.

The demands of the work are such as to require mental alertness and emotional balance, the ability to read, physical capacity, pleasing appearance, neatness in dress, and propriety in deportment, and also faith in the gospel and a testimony of its truth. FIRST PRESIDENCY TO ALL STAKE PRESIDENTS AND MISSION PRESIDENTS, AUG. 22, 1962

We are convinced that our local Church officers must exercise more care and discrimination in recommending young men for missions. These young men must have a desire to serve as missionaries, and must be willing to put in the time and effort required of those who are now serving in the mission field. They likewise should have been well trained in the program of the Church and know enough of the doctrine to go into the world and teach it. "DEAR BRETHREN," JULY 21, 1960

Latter-day Saints should be taught that the most successful operation of the referral system [of proselytizing] occurs when members invite their non-member friends to their homes where the missionaries can be invited in to teach them the gospel.

The next most productive method is to introduce the missionaries to the non-members.

The next most productive method is to submit a written

referral card giving all the information available about the non-member and having the Latter-day Saint's name used as reference.

The least productive, though still beneficial, method is to hand to missionaries the names of non-members. *STAKE MISSIONS,* 1960

A sincere desire to do missionary work is one of the most important qualifications of a prospective missionary. Unwilling persons do not make good missionaries. Bishops should make certain, independent of the family, that the individual himself desires to go on a mission before he recommends him for a call. *CHURCH HANDBOOK,* 1960

Every missionary should realize that when he undertakes a mission, he goes as a representative of The Church of Jesus Christ of Latter-day Saints and as an ambassador of our Lord. While so engaged, he owes it to the cause he represents, to the people to whom he is sent, and to himself, not only to conduct himself in a manner befitting his calling, but also to make his appearance conform to his calling. He must ever bear in mind that the impression which he makes upon the people to whom he is sent in both his public and private appearances is of vital importance in his presentation of the gospel message. In the impression he makes, clothes are an important and sometimes a determining factor. *CHURCH HANDBOOK,* 1944

[W]hile men must be susceptible to truth in order to receive truth, the missionaries must likewise be susceptible to the operations of the Holy Spirit and render themselves capable of being directed and guided in the ways of the honest in heart. To be thus qualified, they must labor devotedly, with an eye single to the honor and glory of God. *LIAHONA,* DEC. 27, 1910, IN *MESSAGES,* 4:219-20

[W]e do not object to men being called [to missionary work] who in earlier years may have done wrong, have been rough or wayward in their youth, if in later years they have lived a godly life and brought forth the fruits of repentance. But we do not want men of bad moral character, habitual users of tobacco, or those whose conduct in any way would render them unworthy of this high calling recommended for missions, under the impression or with the hope that they will repent and change their lives when they get in the missionary field. Let them repent of their sins at home and reform their lives here, and then perhaps they may be called as ambassadors for Christ to the nations of the earth. We desire it to be esteemed as a high honor to be thus called, as a stamp of the approval of the Lord. Nor do we wish those selected to regard the call in the light of a conscription that they must meet whether willing or not, as men are compelled to serve in the German or other armies of the continent of Europe. "DEAR BRETHREN," NOV. 20, 1897, IN *MESSAGES,* 3:288-90

It is as much our duty to preach the gospel to warn the wicked and rebellious, as to save the sheep, for even the wicked cannot be condemned except they reject the truth, and how can they do that except they hear? and how can they hear except they are warned? And to this end are we sent out, that the righteous and the repentant sinner who proves worthy may be saved and the wicked and rebellious condemned. JOSEPH F. SMITH TO M. L. SHEPHERD, JAN. 31, 1882

A cause involving the salvation of mankind is of paramount importance to the whole world. Those who hold the keys of power to unlock the door of salvation, temporal and spiritual —present and eternal, to the betrayed, deceived, benighted, and misguided people of this world, wield in their hands a scepter of life and death which like a two-edged sword cuts both ways. They are called to be watchmen on the towers and battlements of Zion, not only to defend her cause but to give warning unto all. JOSEPH F. SMITH TO JOSEPH H. PARRY ET AL., JAN. 25, 1878

Should any of the elders indulge in the practice of drinking ale, beer, or any other intoxicating beverages, we wish you, if they do not abstain therefrom, to release them and send them home. Elders indulging in this habit are of no profit to themselves or to others, and their influence and example are injurious to the Saints. We also earnestly recommend to elders who may be in the habit of using tobacco, either by chewing or smoking, to refrain therefrom and to strictly observe the Word of Wisdom.

We wish the elders who are sent out not to depend upon the Saints or to spend all their time with them; but to move around among those who have not received the gospel and raise up new branches of the Church. "ADDITIONAL INSTRUCTIONS FOR PRESIDENT JOSEPH FIELDING SMITH, WHO HAS BEEN APPOINTED TO PRESIDE OVER THE EUROPEAN MISSION AND OTHER MISSIONS CONNECTED THEREWITH," MAY 11, 1877

modesty. *See also* dress and grooming

If we ourselves act in ways inappropriate for members of the Church or copy the immodest fashions of the world or are continually in the company of those who do, we show that we value the things of this world more than the things of the Spirit. Sloppiness and extremes of dress, such as "mod" hairstyles or clothes that deliberately reveal as much as possible of the body, detract from and destroy the proper spirit and modesty of those who adopt them or approve them. Loud laughter and irresponsible behavior also destroy modesty and drive out the Spirit of the Lord. *PRINCIPLES,* 1976

motherhood. ***See also*** **family; parents; women**

In all the world, there is no higher or greater honor or responsibility than motherhood. JAMES E. FAUST, "FIRST PRESIDENCY MESSAGE," *ENSIGN,* SEPT. 2006

[T]he leaders of the Church have consistently taught that mothers who have young children in the home should devote their primary energies to the companionship and training of their children and care of their families and should not seek employment outside the home unless there is no other way that the family's basic needs can be provided. As we view the distressing conditions in our society, many of which we attribute to the weakening of influences of the home, we earnestly desire that all members of The Church of Jesus Christ of Latter-day Saints–as well as all persons everywhere–would follow this counsel. FIRST PRESIDENCY TO NEAL A. MAXWELL AND DALLIN H. OAKS, CA. MAY 17, 1973

[T]here is no substitute for the care and love of a mother for a young son. *IMPROVEMENT ERA,* FEB. 1946, IN *MESSAGES,* 6:239-42

Motherhood is near to divinity. It is the highest, holiest service to be assumed by mankind. It places her who honors its holy calling and service next to the angels. *IMPROVEMENT ERA,* NOV. 1942, IN *MESSAGES,* 6:170-85

murder. ***See also*** **life, sanctity of; suicide**

[M]urder refers to the deliberate and unjustified taking of human life. It requires excommunication. Abortion is not defined as murder for this purpose. If death was caused by carelessness or by defense of self or others, or if mitigating circumstances prevail (such as deficient mental capacity or wartime conditions), the taking of a human life might not be defined as murder. *CHURCH HANDBOOK,* 1998

There is no forgiveness for murder. Murderers should be excommunicated from the Church. *CHURCH HANDBOOK,* 1963

There is not a Latter-day Saint living but what believes that the murderer has not eternal life, and to hire somebody to murder is just as bad as committing murder yourself. HEBER J. GRANT TO J. C. CHRISTENSEN, JAN. 21, 1935

music

Singing our beautiful, worshipful hymns is food for our souls. We become of one heart and one mind when we sing praises to the Lord. Among other influences, worshipping in song has the effect of spiritually unifying the participants in an attitude of reverence. JAMES E. FAUST, "FIRST PRESIDENCY MESSAGE," *ENSIGN,* JULY 2005

Music is an important and powerful part of life. It can be an influence for good that helps you draw closer to Heavenly Father. However, it can also be used for wicked purposes. Unworthy music may seem harmless, but it can have evil effects on your mind and spirit. *STRENGTH OF YOUTH,* 2001

Music ... can be used to educate, edify, inspire, and unite. However, music may be used for wicked purposes. Music can, by its tempo, beat, intensity, and lyrics, dull your spiritual sensitivity. You cannot afford to fill your minds with unworthy music. Music is an important and powerful part of life. *STRENGTH OF YOUTH,* 1990

Inspiring music may fill the soul with heavenly thoughts, move one to righteous action, or speak peace to the soul. EZRA TAFT BENSON, "FIRST PRESIDENCY MESSAGE," *ENSIGN,* OCT. 1986

Music has boundless powers for moving families toward greater spirituality and devotion to the gospel. Latter-day

Saints should fill their homes with the sound of worthy music. *HYMNS,* 1985

Teach your children to love the hymns. Sing them on the Sabbath, in home evening, during scripture study, at prayer time. Sing as you work, as you play, and as you travel together. Sing hymns as lullabies to build faith and testimony in your young ones. IBID.

Hymns can lift our spirits, give us courage, and move us to righteous action. They can fill our souls with heavenly thoughts and bring us a spirit of peace. IBID.

Hymns can also help withstand the temptations of the adversary. We encourage you to memorize your favorite hymns and study the scriptures that relate to them. Then, if unworthy thoughts enter your mind, sing a hymn to yourself, crowding out the evil with the good. IBID.

Music should play a very important part in the meetings of the Church. Hymns can be a source of great strength and inspiration and can teach and reinforce important gospel truths. They are also a means of prayer and praise to our Father in Heaven. *BULLETIN,* JUNE 1983

Inspirational music contributes greatly to the spirituality of sacrament meetings and other Church meetings. "DEAR BRETHREN," SEPT. 6, 1974

Through music, man's ability to express himself extends beyond the limits of the spoken language in both subtlety and power. Music can be used to exalt and inspire or to carry messages of degradation and destruction. It is therefore important that as Latter-day Saints we at all times apply the principles of the gospel and seek the guidance of the Spirit in selecting the music with which we surround ourselves. *PRIESTHOOD BULLETIN,* AUG. 1973

We feel it our responsibility to warn our people against the present day wave of musical performances which are aimed at the destruction of sacred principles, which form the very foundations upon which we stand. *DESERET NEWS,* OCT. 9, 1971

Music is a most important part of our religious services and our recreational activities. The highest standards in music literature and musical performance must be maintained. Musical numbers for religious services should be sung or played at such moderate tempo as to instill faith and devotion in the singers and hearers, and teach the doctrines of the restored gospel.

Love songs, popular ballads, spirituals, and songs not in harmony with the doctrine of the Church are not to be used. *CHURCH HANDBOOK,* 1960

Music in Church meetings should follow the general pattern set in the general conference of the Church, and any musical innovations that precede or follow the prayers in Church meetings are not approved. IBID.

O

obedience. *See also* agency

The distinction between feelings or inclinations on the one hand, and behavior on the other, is very clear. It's no sin to have inclinations that if yielded to would produce behavior that would be a transgression. The sin is in yielding to temptation. Temptation is not unique. Even the Savior was tempted. "ISSUES RESOURCES," 2006

[W]e do not accept the fact that conditions that prevent people from attaining their eternal destiny were born into them without any ability to control. That is contrary to the plan of salvation, and it is contrary to the justice and mercy of God. It's contrary to the whole teaching of the gospel of Jesus Christ, which expresses the truth that by or through the power and mercy of Jesus Christ we will have the strength to do *all* things. That includes resisting temptation. That includes dealing with things that we're born with, including disfigurements, or mental or physical incapacities. None of these stand in the way of our attaining our eternal destiny. The same may be of a susceptibility or inclination to one behavior or another which if yielded to would prevent us from achieving our eternal destiny. IBID.

God has given us no commandment that He will not give us the strength and power to observe. That is the plan of salvation for His children, and it is our duty to proclaim that plan, to teach its truth, and to praise God for the mission of His son Jesus Christ. IBID.

[L]et us remember that the wisdom of God may not be easily understandable by mortals, but the greatest single lesson we can learn is that when God speaks and a man obeys, that man will always be right. THOMAS S. MONSON, "FIRST PRESIDENCY MESSAGE," *ENSIGN*, JUNE 2005

The satisfying thing is that obedience brings happiness. It brings peace; it brings growth—all of these to the individual—and his or her good example brings respect for the institution of which he or she is a part. GORDON B. HINCKLEY, "FIRST PRESIDENCY MESSAGE," *ENSIGN*, JAN. 2005

The Lord has given us counsel and commandment on so many things that no member of this Church need ever equivocate. He has established our guidelines concerning personal virtue, neighborliness, obedience to law, loyalty to government, observance of the Sabbath day, sobriety and abstinence from liquor and tobacco, the payment of tithes and offerings, the care of the poor, the cultivation of home and family, the sharing of the gospel—to mention only a few. IBID.

Obedience to Jesus Christ is a lifelong commitment. *PREACH MY GOSPEL*, 2005

God gives us commandments for our benefit. They are instructions from a loving Father in Heaven to help us have happy lives. He also gives us agency, or the ability and opportunity to choose between good and evil. When we obey God, we follow the influence of the Spirit and choose to conform to His will. Obedience to the commandments brings us peace in this life and eternal life in the world to come. Obedience shows our love for God. Disobedience brings us sorrow. IBID.

Our obedience to the commandments is an expression of our love for Heavenly Father and Jesus Christ. *TRUE TO FAITH*, 2004

Let us remember that the wisdom of God may appear as foolishness to men, but the greatest single lesson we can learn in mortality is that when God speaks and we obey, we will always be right. Some foolish persons turn their backs on the wisdom of God and follow the allurement of fickle fashion, the attraction of false popularity, and the thrill of the moment. Their course of conduct so resembles the disastrous experience of Esau, who exchanged his birthright for a mess of pottage. THOMAS S. MONSON, "FIRST PRESIDENCY MESSAGE," *ENSIGN,* FEB. 2001

Some people knowingly break God's commandments, expecting to repent before they go to the temple or serve a mission. Such deliberate sin mocks the Savior's Atonement and invites Satan to influence your life. Repentance for such behavior is difficult and can take a long time. *STRENGTH OF YOUTH,* 2001

The Lord can't bless those who aren't obedient. GORDON B. HINCKLEY, "FIRST PRESIDENCY MESSAGE," *ENSIGN,* AUG. 2000

Many people expend far too much precious energy in protesting the rules. Since they did not make the rules, some feel that they should not be restricted by them. Others make a game of testing the fences to see what they can get away with. Some think that by breaking the rules they somehow become stronger or independent. Those who fight the rules spend much time and energy trying to express independence in their quest to find identity. And having traveled far down this road, they find that this is not the road to freedom but to slavery. JAMES E. FAUST, "FIRST PRESIDENCY MESSAGE," *ENSIGN,* MAR. 2000

Obedience is a hallmark of prophets, but it should be realized that this source of strength is available to us today. THOMAS S. MONSON, "FIRST PRESIDENCY MESSAGE," *ENSIGN,* JULY 1997

If we do not sustain the living prophet, whoever he may be, we die spiritually. JAMES E. FAUST, "FIRST PRESIDENCY MESSAGE," *ENSIGN,* AUG. 1996

[W]hen we try in faith to walk in obedience to the requests of the priesthood, the Lord opens the way, even when there appears to be no way. GORDON B. HINCKLEY, "FIRST PRESIDENCY MESSAGE," *ENSIGN,* JULY 1995

The ability to stand by one's principles, to live with integrity and faith according to one's belief—that is what matters. That devotion to true principle—in our individual lives, in our homes and families, and in all places that we meet and influence other people—that devotion is what God is ultimately requesting of us. It requires commitment—whole-souled, deeply held, eternally cherished commitment to the principles we know to be true in the commandments God has given. HOWARD W. HUNTER, "FIRST PRESIDENCY MESSAGE," *ENSIGN,* OCT. 1994

Any system dealing with the eternal consequences of human behavior must set guidelines and adhere to them, and no system can long command the loyalties of men and women which does not expect of them certain measures of discipline, and particularly self-discipline. The cost in comfort may be great. The sacrifice may be real. But this very demanding reality is the substance of which comes character and strength and nobility. Permissiveness never produced greatness. Integrity, loyalty, and strength are virtues whose sinews are developed through the struggles that go on within as we practice self-discipline under the demands of divinely spoken truth. GORDON B. HINCKLEY, "FIRST PRESIDENCY MESSAGE," *ENSIGN,* JULY 1993

In matters of religion, when an individual is motivated by great and powerful convictions of truth, then he disciplines himself not because of demands made by the Church, but because of the knowledge within his heart that God lives; that he is a child of God with an eternal and limitless potential; that there is joy in service and satisfaction in laboring in a great cause. IBID.

Through a faithful observance of all of our Heavenly Father's commandments, we can draw upon His promise: "I, the Lord, am bound when ye do what I say; but when ye do not what I say, ye have no promise" (D&C 82:10). THOMAS S. MONSON, "FIRST PRESIDENCY MESSAGE," *ENSIGN,* FEB. 1993

Our only real safety, physically and spiritually, lies in keeping the Lord's commandments. LETTER TO ALL MEMBERS OF THE CHURCH OF JESUS CHRIST OF LATTER-DAY SAINTS, NOV. 14, 1991

You cannot do wrong and feel right. It is impossible! Years of happiness can be lost in the foolish gratification of a momentary desire for pleasure. Satan would have you believe that happiness comes only as you surrender to his enticement to self-indulgence. We need only to look at the shattered lives of those who violate God's laws to know why Satan is called the "father of all lies" (2 Ne. 2:18).

You can avoid the burden of guilt and sin and all of the attending heartaches if you will but heed the standards provided you through the teachings of the Lord and His servants. *STRENGTH OF YOUTH,* 1990

One of Satan's most frequently used deceptions is the notion that the commandments of God are meant to restrict freedom and limit happiness. Young people especially sometimes feel that the standards of the Lord are like fences and chains, blocking them from those activities that seem most enjoyable in life. But exactly the opposite is true. The gospel plan is *the* plan by which men are brought to a fullness of joy. EZRA TAFT BENSON, "FIRST PRESIDENCY MESSAGE," *ENSIGN,* OCTOBER 1989

Our voices must be united in defense of those virtues that when practiced in the past made men and nations strong and when neglected brought them to decay. *CHURCH NEWS,* OCT. 22, 1988

One who rationalizes that he or she has a testimony of Jesus Christ but cannot accept direction and counsel from the leadership of His Church is in a fundamentally unsound position and is in jeopardy of losing exaltation. EZRA TAFT BENSON, "FIRST PRESIDENCY MESSAGE," *ENSIGN,* FEB. 1987

When we resist the counsel of the Lord, we manifest stubbornness and rejection of His inspired guidance. MARION G. ROMNEY, "FIRST PRESIDENCY MESSAGE," *ENSIGN,* AUG. 1985

Ours or any society will be put in order only when, by precept and example, parents teach and inspire in their children a willing resolution to live the principles of the gospel of Jesus Christ. For when one receives a witness of their divinity and glimpses the joy of their promise, he will pray fervently, work diligently, and strictly obey the commandments of God, which of course include the laws of the land. IBID.

Every commandment that God has given to His servants is for the benefit of those who receive and obey it. It is man who profits by the careful and strict observance; it is man who suffers by the breaking of the laws of God. SPENCER W. KIMBALL, "FIRST PRESIDENCY MESSAGE," *ENSIGN,* JAN. 1978

In this day of rising permissiveness, we commend to people everywhere the truism that we cannot break the Ten Commandments. We can only break ourselves against them. *CHURCH NEWS,* APR. 15, 1977

Let us teach our children more respect for the law. To do so is a precious investment in their freedom in the challenging tomorrows ahead. IBID.

When men place anything else above the love of God, they are practicing false worship, the worship of something other than God, and in this way they deny Him (see J.S.-H 2:19). *PRINCIPLES,* 1976

When we make a covenant or agreement with God, we must keep it at whatever cost. Let us not be like the student who agrees to live by certain standards of conduct and who then breaks his oath and tries to see how long he can get away with his deceit. Let us not be like the missionary who agrees to serve the Lord for two years, then wastes his time with laziness and rationalization. Let us not be like the Church member who partakes of the sacrament in the morning, then defiles the Sabbath that afternoon by cleaning the house or by watching television or by choosing an afternoon of sleep over an afternoon of service. Instead, let us have integrity like Abraham did, observing with all soberness the solemn contracts we have made with God. SPENCER W. KIMBALL, "FIRST PRESIDENCY MESSAGE," *ENSIGN,* JUNE 1975

Though we believe in "obeying, honoring, and sustaining the law," many keep the laws of the land in order to be free from punishment which they are sure will follow any violation. God's punishment will surely follow disobedience to His commandments, but we should keep His laws and commandments because of His love and sacrifice for us and for the blessings He has promised. N. ELDON TANNER, "FIRST PRESIDENCY MESSAGE," *ENSIGN,* APR. 1974

How blessed are Latter-day Saints to be assured by the revealed word of God that there will be no capriciousness in the world to come; that the rule of law is irrevocable; that every soul will be rewarded according to the law he has obeyed; that all divine law is as immutable as the law of gravity; that it is the same yesterday, today, and forever; that judgment will be mercifully administered, but that it will be administered pursuant to law, and that it will not rob justice. Not only are Latter-day Saints blessed by having this knowledge concerning "the rule of law," they are twice blessed by having both a knowledge and an understanding of the laws by which they are to be judged. MARION G. ROMNEY, "FIRST PRESIDENCY MESSAGE," *ENSIGN,* FEB. 1973

The blessings flowing from the observance of covenants are sufficiently great to recompense for all mere inconvenience. "DEAR BRETHREN," MAR. 17, 1969

All rules and regulations, in fact all laws, especially the laws of God, are made for the benefit of the people. It is, of course, of the utmost importance that we become familiar therewith and conform thereto that we may have the blessings which were intended. *STRENGTH OF YOUTH,* 1968

Section 130 of the Doctrine and Covenants, verses 18-21, state a fundamental principle which indicates that through diligence and obedience we gain our blessings. It is presumed that from premortal existence we came into this life having gained certain of the advantages and blessings we enjoy here, and "if a person gains more knowledge or intelligence in this life through his diligence and faithfulness than another, he will have so much the advantage in the world to come." "When we obtain any blessings from God, it is by obedience to the law upon which it is predicated." This law is regarded as universal and eternal, and as applicable in the premortal existence as it is here, and will be hereafter. The blessings of obedience are available to all men. A. HAMER REISER, ASSISTANT SECRETARY TO THE FIRST PRESIDENCY, TO JOHN W. FITZGERALD, JAN. 12, 1959

We recognize that many of the oppressed and destitute of the world would regard this simple formula [obedience] as a poor substitute for bread and liberty. That is because many do not, and many will not, understand. If they did understand, they would know that the acquisition of bread and liberty, based on any principle other than compliance with the laws of the Lord, must at best be but temporary, and in the end disappointing. *DESERET NEWS,* DEC. 12, 1956

Our understanding that the Lord's purposes must be accomplished, and our submission to His will, will enable us to stand and endure where weaker faith and imperfect vision fail. IBID.

Every day if men would but open their eyes they would see that compliance with Christ's will brings blessings; rejection of it, disquietude, misery, death. *DESERET NEWS,* DEC. 15, 1954

Only by adherence to fundamental principles of righteousness can peace come, either to individuals or to nations. *DESERET NEWS*, DEC. 17, 1952

We declare that men, peoples, and nations must turn to Him [Jesus Christ] and acknowledge His divine sonship and keep His commandments if they are to be saved from destruction. We solemnly affirm there is no other way. *DESERET NEWS,* DEC. 13, 1950

In the early days of the Church the Lord announced that where men prevented His Saints from carrying out the commandments He had given them, the Lord would relieve the Saints from rendering obedience to the commandment, and would visit the iniquity and transgression involved in such disobedience upon the heads of those who "hindered" His work. The Lord said this rule was given for the consolation of the

Saints "who have been commanded to do a work and have been hindered by the hands of their enemies, and by oppression" (D&C 124:49ff). "DEAR BRETHREN," OCT. 2, 1950, IN *MESSAGES,* 6:287-88

The Prophet Joseph Smith's method was to teach the people correct principles, and let them govern themselves. It has always been the disposition of people to take license from the fact that they feel that the Church is not doing certain things the way they feel they should be done. If I should be guilty of theft, it would never be charged to anyone else's account, and if the leaders of the Church are doing wrong, as some people suppose, you do not need to worry about it, they will have to pay the penalty. If you and others keep the commandments of the Lord, you and they will get the reward for so doing, and no one can take from you any particle of that reward. HEBER J. GRANT TO O. N. ANDERSON, APR. 30, 1935

God will pour out His richest blessings upon all His faithful people; and we bless you with comfort, and with peace, and joy in mind and spirit in the measure that you keep His commandments. *DESERET NEWS,* DEC. 15, 1834

Without beneficent laws, righteously administered, the foundations of civilization crumble, anarchy reigns, decay and dissolution follow. *LIAHONA,* NOV. 13, 1928, IN *MESSAGES,* 5:258-59

Your question is: "Which is heaven's first law, order or obedience?" I might say neither, but I will not attempt to decide what is or is not "heaven's first law." I think it very unwise to contend among ourselves on such questions. All of the laws of God are essential and it matters not which is first or which is last. The greatest of all the commandments, as defined by our Savior, is this: "Thou shalt love the Lord thy God with all thy heart, and with all thy soul, and with all thy mind. This is the first and great commandment, and the second is like unto it, thou shalt love thy neighbor as thyself" (Matt. 22:37). Now, if a commandment of God is a law of heaven, then here you have Christ's testimony as to which is the "first law of heaven," and of earth too, for that matter. JOSEPH F. SMITH TO J. H. WELLING ET AL., NOV. 26, 1897

[I]n general, God blesses and punishes on natural principle for obedience or disobedience to His laws. JOSEPH F. SMITH TO HYRUM M. SMITH, FEB. 18, 1897

In the striving after compliance with the apparently weightier matters of the law, there is a possibility that the importance of this spirit of love and kindness and charity may be underestimated. STATEMENT, MAR. 18, 1893, IN *MESSAGES,* 3:241-44

The Lord does not permit His enemies, nor the enemies of His people, to prevail over them for any length of time when they are living near unto Him and complying strictly with His will. STATEMENT, APR. 8, 1887, IN *MESSAGES,* 3:109-29

Know this, that God, in giving us the previous blessings we possess, demands from us a suitable return. By receiving them, we are placed under obligations. If these are not discharged, condemnation inevitably follows. *MILLENNIAL STAR,* NOV. 9, 1885, IN *MESSAGES,* 3:23-41

If God commands us to obey a law, we must do so or we will come under condemnation for disobedience thereto. JOSEPH F. SMITH TO PHILIP H. BOYER, DEC. 26, 1881

It is important that we be obedient and passive in the hands of the servants of God, and when we have embraced the truth, and placed ourselves with all we have upon the altar, to so remain, regardless alike of friend or foe, sunshine or shade, peace or plenty, of war, famine, and pestilence. It is our duty not only to profess and be believers, but to work out our salvation, continuing faithful in all things, even unto the end. *MILLENNIAL STAR*, JAN. 26, 1856, IN *MESSAGES*, 2:177-87

How much better to do what is proper, and necessary to be done, under the most favorable circumstances than to wait until stern necessity compels. *MILLENNIAL STAR,* AUG. 11, 1855, IN *MESSAGES,* 2:159-71

Inasmuch as the spirits of men have wisely been organized as diverse in power and peculiarities as their number, it is not expected, possible, or desirable that the thoughts and actions of mankind be run in the same mould, but it is positively necessary for one who wishes salvation under a celestial law to abide that law. *DESERET NEWS,* SEPT. 14, 1854, IN *MESSAGES,* 2:149-53

Do we not offer violence to the Supreme Intelligence of heaven when we admit the truth of its teachings and do not obey them? STATEMENT, JAN. 22, 1834, IN *MESSAGES,* 1:23-44

occult

Members should not engage in forms of so-called Satan worship or affiliate in any way with the occult. *CHURCH HANDBOOK,* 1998

It is not good practice to become intrigued by Satan and his mysteries. No good can come from getting close to evil. Like playing with fire, it is too easy to get burned: "The knowledge of sin tempteth to its commission." The only safe course is to keep well distanced from him and from any of his wicked activities or nefarious practices. The mischief of devil worship, sorcery, casting spells, witchcraft, voodooism, black magic, and all other forms of demonism should be avoided like the plague. JAMES E. FAUST, "FIRST PRESIDENCY MESSAGE," *ENSIGN*, SEPT. 1995

We caution all members of the Church not to affiliate in any way with the occult or those mysterious powers it espouses. Such activities are among the works of darkness spoken of in the scriptures. They are designed to destroy one's faith in Christ, and will jeopardize the salvation of those who knowingly promote this wickedness. These things should not be pursued as games, be topics in Church meetings, or be delved into in private, personal conversations. "DEAR BRETHREN," SEPT. 18, 1991

ordinances, ***see*** **priesthood ordinances**

organ donations

The decision to will or donate one's own body organs or tissue for medical purposes, or the decision to authorize the transplant of organs or tissue from a deceased family member, is made by the individual or the deceased member's family.

The decision to receive a donated organ should be made after receiving competent medical counsel and confirmation through prayer. *CHURCH HANDBOOK,* 1998

Each individual must determine from deep within his conscience whether to will his bodily organs to be used for transplants or for research. The Church advises those who seek counsel on the subject to review the advantages and disadvantages, to implore the Lord for inspiration and guidance, and then to take the action that gives them a feeling of peace and comfort. *CHURCH HANDBOOK,* 1983

[T]he question of whether one wills his bodily organs to be used as transplants, or for research after death, must be answered from deep within the conscience of the individual involved. Those who seek counsel from the Church on this subject are encouraged to review the advantages and disadvantages of doing so, to implore the Lord for inspiration and guidance, and then to take the course of action which will give them a feeling of peace and comfort. FIRST PRESIDENCY TO JACK MCDONALD, APR. 14, 1982

[W]e feel that if a man or woman should desire to will parts or all of his or her body to any medical institution in the interest of medical research, that is a matter for the individual personally to decide. We have, however, advised against this in cases where people have been through the temple and received their endowments. FIRST PRESIDENCY TO W. DEAN BELNAP, FEB. 12, 1970

organic evolution, ***see*** **evolution**

P

parents. ***See also*** **family**

It is important to remember that in this Church, the husbands and fathers, and members of the family through them, enjoy a power and influence ["priesthood of God"] in their lives far beyond the natural gifts of the intellect and character of the father. JAMES E. FAUST, "FIRST PRESIDENCY MESSAGE," *ENSIGN,* SEPT. 2006

Let every mother understand that if she does anything to diminish her children's father or the father's image in the eyes of the children, it may injure and do irreparable damage to the self-worth and personal security of the children themselves. How infinitely more productive and satisfying it is for a woman to build up her husband rather than tear him down. You women are so superior to men in so many ways that you demean yourselves by belittling masculinity and manhood. IBID.

While few human challenges are greater than that of being good parents, few opportunities offer greater potential for joy. Surely no more important work is to be done in this world than preparing our children to be God-fearing, happy, honorable, and productive. Parents will find no more fulfilling happiness than to have their children honor them and their teachings. It is the glory of parenthood. JAMES E. FAUST, "FIRST PRESIDENCY MESSAGE," *ENSIGN,* OCT. 2005

To be a good father and mother requires that the parents

defer many of their own needs and desires in favor of the needs of their children. As a consequence of this sacrifice, conscientious parents develop a nobility of character and learn to put into practice the selfless truths taught by the Savior Himself. IBID.

It is useless to debate which parent is most important. No one would doubt that a mother's influence is paramount with newborns and in the first years of a child's life. The father's influence increases as the child grows older. However, each parent is necessary at various times in a child's development. Both fathers and mothers do many intrinsically different things for their children. Both are equipped to nurture children, but their approaches are different. Mothers seem to take a dominant role in preparing children to live within their families, present and future. Fathers seem best equipped to prepare children to function in the environment outside the family. JAMES E. FAUST, "FIRST PRESIDENCY MESSAGE," *ENSIGN,* AUG. 2004

Parents have a sacred responsibility to look after the physical and spiritual welfare of their children. As children grow older, they become more responsible for their own welfare. Parents should teach them basic principles of welfare, helping them prepare to be self-reliant and provide for their own families in the future. Parents can also give children opportunities to help care for the poor and the needy. *TRUE TO FAITH,* 2004

We counsel parents and children to give highest priority to family prayer, family home evening, gospel study and instruction, and wholesome family activities. However worthy and appropriate other demands and activities may be, they must not be permitted to displace the divinely appointed duties that only parents and families can adequately perform. FIRST PRESI-

DENCY TO MEMBERS OF THE CHURCH THROUGHOUT THE WORLD, FEB. 11, 1999; *CHURCH NEWS,* FEB. 27, 1999

By divine design, fathers are to preside over their families in righteousness. *CHURCH HANDBOOK 2,* 1998

Parents have primary responsibility for the welfare of their children (see D&C 68:25-28). The bishop and other ward leaders support but do not replace them in this responsibility. IBID.

There is no need in any land for conflict between diverse groups of any kind. Let there be taught in the homes of people that we are all children of God, our Eternal Father, and that as surely as there is fatherhood, there can and must be brotherhood. Let there be taught respect for womanhood and manhood. Let every husband speak with respect, kindness, and appreciation for his wife. Let every wife look for and speak of the virtues of her husband. GORDON B. HINCKLEY, "FIRST PRESIDENCY MESSAGE," *ENSIGN,* SEPT. 1996

Husband and wife have a solemn responsibility to love and care for each other and for their children. "Children are an heritage of the Lord" (Ps. 127:3). Parents have a sacred duty to rear their children in love and righteousness, to provide for their physical and spiritual needs, to teach them to love and serve one another, to observe the commandments of God, and to be law-abiding citizens wherever they live. Husbands and wives–mothers and fathers–will be held accountable before God for the discharge of these obligations. *CHURCH NEWS,* SEPT. 30, 1995

By divine design, fathers are to preside over their families in love and righteousness and are responsible to provide the necessities of life and the protection of their families. Mothers are primarily responsible for the nurture of their children. In these sacred responsibilities, fathers and mothers are obligated to help one another as equal partners. Disability, death, or other circumstances may necessitate individual adaptation. Extended families should extend support when needed. IBID.

God established that fathers are to preside in the home. Fathers are to provide, love, teach, and direct.

A mother's role is also God-ordained. Mothers are to conceive, bear, nourish, love, and train. They are to be helpmates and are to counsel with their husbands.

There is no inequality between the sexes in God's plan. It is a matter of division of responsibility. EZRA TAFT BENSON, "FIRST PRESIDENCY MESSAGE," *ENSIGN,* AUG. 1993

The most important teachings in the home are spiritual. Parents are commanded to prepare their sons and daughters for the ordinances of the gospel: baptism, confirmation, priesthood ordinations, and temple marriage. They are to teach them to respect and honor the Sabbath day; to keep it holy. Most importantly, parents are to instill within their children a desire for eternal life and to earnestly seek that goal above all else. EZRA TAFT BENSON, "FIRST PRESIDENCY MESSAGE," *ENSIGN,* JULY 1992

We ask that parents begin early to train their children. Where there is family prayer, where there are family home evenings, where there is scripture reading, where the father and mother are active in the Church and speak with enthusiasm concerning the Church and the gospel, the children in such homes become imbued in a natural way with a desire to teach the gospel to others. There is usually a tradition of missionary work in such homes. Savings accounts are set up while children are small. Boys grow up with a natural expectation that they will be called to serve as missionaries for the Church.

A mission becomes as much a part of a boy's program for life as is an education. GORDON B. HINCKLEY, "FIRST PRESIDENCY MESSAGE," *ENSIGN,* OCT. 1987

Parents have a God-given duty to teach their children to understand the laws and ordinances of the gospel of Jesus Christ (D&C 68:25-28). Parents cannot properly shift this duty to other persons or organizations. "DEAR BRETHREN," ENGLISH-SPEAKING AREAS, JUNE 19, 1986

There is no guarantee, of course, that righteous parents will succeed always in holding their children, and certainly they may lose them if they do not do all in their power. The children have their free agency.

But if we as parents fail to influence our families and set them on the "strait and narrow way," then certainly the waves, the winds of temptation and evil, will carry the posterity away from the path. SPENCER W. KIMBALL, "FIRST PRESIDENCY MESSAGE," *ENSIGN,* JAN. 1984

A child leaving to go away to school or on a mission, a wife suffering stress, a family member being married or desiring guidance in making an important decision—all these are situations in which the father, in exercise of his patriarchal responsibility, can bless his family. IBID.

There is no greater responsibility, privilege, or blessing bestowed upon us than to be worthy parents. N. ELDON TANNER, "FIRST PRESIDENCY MESSAGE," *ENSIGN,* DEC. 1981

The most important calling of a priesthood holder is that of husband and father. The most divine station of a woman is that of wife and mother. *FAMILY HOME EVENING,* 1980

Home life, home teaching, parental guidance, father in

leadership–these are the panacea for the ailments of the world, a cure for spiritual and emotional diseases, a remedy for problems. Parents should therefore not leave the training of children to school teachers or to the Primary or the Relief Society or the Sunday School or Mutual. The father and the mother must undertake this great responsibility, using the Church programs to assist them. SPENCER W. KIMBALL, "FIRST PRESIDENCY MESSAGE," *ENSIGN*, APR. 1978

Remember that neither the wife nor the husband is the slave of the other. Husbands and wives are equal partners, particularly Latter-day Saint husbands and wives. They should so consider themselves and so treat each other in this life, and then they will do so throughout eternity. MARION G. ROMNEY, "FIRST PRESIDENCY MESSAGE," *ENSIGN,* MAR. 1978

Parents, draw your children around you and, with great love, teach them about the Savior and His commandments. Help them to develop individual strength and commitment to keep the laws of God. Build lasting family unity in a setting of learning and fun. *FAMILY HOME EVENING,* 1978

The Lord planned that men and women would find each other and have a happy family relationship, be true to each other, and remain clean and worthy.

The Lord could have organized His world without this propagation program; He could have filled the earth with physical human bodies in some other way than that which He designed, perhaps some incubator process, but it seems that merely filling the earth with human beings was not the great objective of our Lord, and therefore a father and a mother were designed to be given to every child that was born, and they should love and teach that child and prepare him to become like his Father in heaven, in righteousness and purity.

SPENCER W. KIMBALL, "FIRST PRESIDENCY MESSAGE," *ENSIGN,* FEB. 1975

We remind you of the responsibility which has been given by revelation from the Lord to you as parents to teach your children the principles of the gospel before they come to the age of accountability and afterwards, during their growing-up years, to teach these children to pray and to walk uprightly before the Lord and, furthermore, to keep the Sabbath day holy and see that they are taught habits of industry and thrift. *FAMILY HOME EVENING*, 1974

No priority should come before responsible parenthood. No unit needs continual strengthening more than the family. *ENSIGN,* NOV. 1973

Do you spend as much time making your family and home successful as you do in pursuing social and professional success? Are you devoting your best creative energy to the most important unit in society–the family; or is your relationship with your family merely a routine, unrewarding part of life?

Parents and children must be willing to put family responsibilities first in order to achieve family exaltation. *FAMILY HOME EVENING,* 1973

Love begins in the home. Sacrifice for one another. Make one another happy.

If there is love between the father and the mother, there will be love between the parents and the children, and among the children. One cannot overemphasize the importance and value of being courteous, kind, considerate, and polite in the home. Where there is true and perfect love in a family, there will be no need to be reminded of such other commandments as "Honor thy father and thy mother," "Thou shalt not steal," "Thou shalt not kill," and "Thou shalt not bear false witness."

They will be kept automatically. N. ELDON TANNER, "FIRST PRESIDENCY MESSAGE," *ENSIGN,* OCT. 1971

The Lord has admonished parents to teach their children to pray and to walk uprightly before Him (see D&C 68:28). This is our most important obligation to our children—to teach them that they are the spirit children of their Heavenly Father, that He is real, that He has great love for His children and wants them to succeed, that they should pray to Him expressing gratitude and asking for guidance, realizing that faith in Him will bring them greater strength and success and happiness than they can receive from any other source.

We as parents must teach by example and let the efficacy of prayer in our own lives show our children the value of faith in God. How sad to deprive a child of the great blessing of learning to know God and learning to depend on Him for the comfort and strength and guidance the child needs so badly in order to cope with the problems of the day. It is equally sad when children are not taught that everything they have comes from God and that they should express their gratitude and strive to be worthy of the blessings they receive. N. ELDON TANNER, "FIRST PRESIDENCY MESSAGE," *ENSIGN,* AUG. 1971

The Lord's program is one of living and teaching the gospel. The home is the basic unit in which this purpose is achieved. Parents have the chief responsibility to bring up their children in light and truth, to prepare them for missions, temple marriage, and righteous living, to be self-sustaining and to walk uprightly before the Lord. *CHURCH HANDBOOK,* 1968

Parents are under obligation most solemn to instruct, train, and provide for their children. If they are indifferent or negligent and the children become evil or wicked, the parents are held responsible.

Children are to honor their parents, obey them in righteousness, and comply with their just demands. FIRST PRESIDENCY TO PRESIDENTS OF STAKES AND COUNSELORS, JUNE 17, 1933, IN *MESSAGES,* 5:315-30

The responsibility resting upon the parents in providing for the spiritual as well as the temporal welfare of their children is of the utmost importance. They should teach them the principles of the gospel from their earliest childhood, impressing upon their minds the divinity of the mission of the Prophet Joseph Smith. They should be encouraged to do right, be virtuous, honest, truthful, and faithful to every obligation and covenant. This can best be impressed upon their minds by example on the part of the parents. They should themselves be what they would have their children to be; they should do what they would have them do, and avoid the evils that would grieve their own spirits should their children commit them. They should admonish them in kindness; encourage them in well-doing; instruct them in the home to keep the Word of Wisdom, to pray and give thanks to God for all His blessings, in the law of tithing, and in all virtuous deportment; and grant to them every opportunity to receive the benefits and instruction afforded them by the several organizations of the Church. *DESERET NEWS*, DEC. 18, 1909, IN *MESSAGES,* 4:206-11

Parents should take time—if not every day, at least as often as they can and not allow many days to elapse—to call their families together and interrogate them respecting their associations, their words, actions, &c., and teach them the principles of the gospel. STATEMENT, JULY 11, 1877, IN *MESSAGES,* 2:283-95

It is the duty of all parents to train up their children in the way they should go, instructing them in every correct principle so fast as they are capable of receiving and setting an example worthy of imitation; for the Lord holds parents responsible for the conduct of their children until they arrive at the years of accountability before him; and the parents will have to answer for all misdemeanors arising through their neglect. Mothers should teach their little ones to pray as soon as they are able to talk. *MILLENNIAL STAR,* MAR. 15, 1848, IN *MESSAGES,* 1:323-35

patriarchal blessings

Patriarchal blessings are given to worthy members of the Church by ordained patriarchs. Your patriarchal blessing declares your lineage in the house of Israel and contains personal counsel from the Lord to you. *TRUE TO FAITH*, 2004

While your patriarchal blessing contains inspired counsel and promises, you should not expect it to answer all your questions or to detail all that will happen in your life. If your blessing does not mention an important event, such as a full-time mission or marriage, you should not assume that you will not receive that opportunity.

Similarly, you should not assume that everything mentioned in your patriarchal blessing will be fulfilled in this life. A patriarchal blessing is eternal, and its promises may extend into the eternities. Be assured that if you are worthy, all promises will be fulfilled in the Lord's due time. Those that are not realized in this life will be fulfilled in the next. IBID.

Patriarchal blessings contemplate an inspired declaration of the lineage of the recipient. A patriarchal blessing also includes an inspired and prophetic statement of the life possibilities and mission of the recipient. It may include such blessings, promises, advice, admonitions, and warnings as the patriarch may be prompted to give. It should always be made clear that the realization of all promised blessings is conditioned upon faithfulness and the Lord's will. *PATRIARCHS,* 1981

To the extent that the Spirit directs, the patriarch should identify for the recipient work to be done, accomplishments to be realized, challenges to be overcome, and blessings to be received, reminding always that promises and gospel blessings from the Lord are contingent on faithful, worthy living.

Patriarchal blessings give encouragement to keep the commandments and to qualify for eternal life, and help to define responsibilities and goals.

A patriarch should avoid wordy, complicated language. He should speak in his own words, dignified and spiritual, but clear and simple. He should pronounce only those promises prompted by the Spirit. A patriarchal blessing should be fairly short. The patriarch should not let a blessing become overly long in preachment or exhortation.

The patriarch should give a blessing, not merely a prayer, nor a sermon of admonition or information. He should make clear that spiritual blessings come from the Lord, and that the patriarch is His agent of communication. IBID.

A vital part of every patriarchal blessing is the declaration of lineage. A patriarch should study the scriptures relating to the history and lineage of Abraham, Isaac, Jacob, and the twelve sons of Jacob, including Joseph and his sons Manasseh and Ephraim. It is not appropriate to designate one from the tribe of Joseph only. The patriarch should be responsive to the whisperings of the Spirit as he identifies lineage and the special promises and blessings attendant thereto. Patriarchs gain the inspiration to declare the lineage of the person receiving the blessing, naming the tribe of which the individual is a member. Many members of the Church are of the lineage of Ephraim, but some are of another lineage–Manasseh, Judah, or one of the other tribes of Israel. Occasionally, when giving a blessing to a member from some racial group, a patriarch may not be inspired to declare a lineage from a specific tribe, but to declare that the individual will receive his blessings through Israel. The declaration of lineage is to come by the promptings of the Holy Ghost. *This inspiration can come to the patriarch regardless of the race or nationality of the person receiving the blessing.* IBID.

A patriarchal blessing should be viewed from an eternal perspective. Sometimes blessings promised may not come in this life, but may be realized in eternity. IBID.

Certainly we should give new and additional emphasis to the role of the father in giving blessings to children in the family. We think we should generally leave to the ordained patriarchs in the stakes the responsibility of declaring lineage in connection with an official patriarchal blessing, but still we could leave unlocked the door so that any father who felt inspired to pronounce the lineage in connection with a father's blessing he was giving to his children should not be prevented from doing so.

We should urge and encourage fathers to give a father's blessing to their children on such occasions as their going into the military or away from home to school or on missions and on other appropriate occasions. *CHURCH HANDBOOK,* 1976

Should there be any questions relative to a blessing previously received, these questions should be discussed by the person with the patriarch who gave the blessing if he is available. IBID.

When giving blessings, patriarchs should—

1. Through a friendly visit learn about the candidate's life, background, and parentage; his Church devotion and experience; and his aims, attitudes, and goals in life.

2. Keep an open mind and rely upon the Spirit for guidance in what is said.

3. Gain the inspiration to declare the lineage blessings of the candidate.

4. Give wise counsel and direction relative to obedience to the whole gospel plan.

5. Use care in making unusual promises and be sure that what is said comes by the spirit of inspiration; avoid extravagant statements.

6. Impart blessings directly to the individual, rather than solicit the Lord to grant blessings as one would in prayer, for patriarchs are entitled to speak authoritatively for the Lord when they give patriarchal blessings. IBID.

The fact that the patriarch declares an individual to be of certain lineage does not mean that the person's blood may not be intermingled with the blood of other races. FIRST PRESIDENCY TO J. DUANE DUDLEY, MAY 17, 1974

Patriarchal blessings are the only blessings that patriarchs as such are specifically ordained to give. They may include a declaration of the lineage of the person blessed, as moved upon by the Spirit, and a statement of future goals and possibilities, gift or gifts of the Spirit, and such blessings, cautions, and admonitions as the patriarch may be prompted to give for the accomplishment of one's mission in life, it being always made clear that the realization of all blessings is conditioned upon faithfulness in the gospel. *CHURCH HANDBOOK,* 1968

Patriarchal blessings contemplate inspired declaration of the lineage of the recipient, and also, where so moved upon by the Spirit, an inspired and prophetic statement of the life mission of the recipient, together with such blessings, cautions, and admonitions as the patriarch may be prompted to give for the accomplishment of such life's mission, it being always made clear that the realization of all promised blessings is conditioned upon faithfulness to the gospel of our Lord, whose servant the patriarch is. "SUGGESTIONS FOR STAKE PATRIARCHS," MAY 25, 1943, IN *MESSAGES,* 6:194-96

Patriarchal Order, *see* family

patriarchs

One of the offices in the Melchizedek Priesthood is that of patriarch. Those so chosen and ordained are called to give patriarchal blessings to worthy members of the Church. *CHURCH HANDBOOK,* 1976

The patriarchal office is one of blessing, not of administration. Patriarchal blessings are the only blessings that patriarchs are specifically ordained and sustained to give. FIRST PRESIDENCY TO PRESIDENTS OF STAKES, JAN. 9, 1970

The patriarch is not a counselor to the people of the stake as are the presidency of the stakes and the bishoprics. It is the duty of the patriarchs ever to sustain these administrative officers in the policies adopted and the counsels given to the people. If patriarchs are solicited for counsel and advice relating to the conduct of members of the Church and decisions to be made in both temporal and spiritual matters, they should refer such persons to the administrative officers whose right it is to give attention to such matters. Patriarchs, as all others who hold the proper priesthood, may, when requested to do so, give blessings for the healing of the sick, but such blessings for the sick, or for the comfort of individuals, are of no higher order than, nor are they to be distinguished from, similar blessings by others who hold the proper priesthood. IBID.

Patriarchal service is gratuitous. *CHURCH HANDBOOK,* 1963

Patriarchs are not to be sought out for counsel, but Church

members should be encouraged to go to bishoprics and stake presidencies. IBID.

peace

Many people think of peace as the absence of war. But we can feel peace even in times of war, and we can lack peace even when no war is raging. The mere absence of conflict is not enough to bring peace to our hearts. Peace comes through the gospel—through the Atonement of Jesus Christ, the ministration of the Holy Ghost, and our own righteousness, sincere repentance, and diligent service. *TRUE TO FAITH,* 2004

World peace, though a lofty goal, is but an outgrowth of the personal peace each individual seeks to attain. THOMAS S. MONSON, "FIRST PRESIDENCY MESSAGE," *ENSIGN,* MAR. 2004

Peace may be found through adhering to the teachings of the Prince of Peace.

Comfort will come to those who mourn through their understanding of the purpose of life as taught by the Savior, who is well acquainted with grief. *CHURCH NEWS,* DEC. 4, 1993

We are persuaded that most men and women long for peace, and when there is a strong enough desire to bring it about, it may be achieved. The application of the Golden Rule as taught by the Savior of mankind will bring a resolution of almost any disagreement, whether in the home, the neighborhood, the marketplace, the state, the nation, or the world. IBID.

[I]t is our hope and prayer that people throughout the world will incorporate into their daily thoughts and actions the principles espoused by Jesus. To do so would most assuredly lead to less war and more peace, less turmoil and more serenity, less unrest and more stability, less crime and sin and more self-respect and happiness.

If greed and lust and the quest for power and dominion were to be replaced by commitments to pattern lives after the example of the Prince of Peace Himself, how blessed the world would be. *CHURCH NEWS*, MAR. 23, 1986

To those who yearn for peace, we announce that it may be found with the Prince of Peace. Even in these tumultuous times, the individual who turns to Christ can find the inner peace that surpasses understanding. NEWS RELEASE, DEC. 13, 1985

We encourage men and women throughout the world to contemplate the life and example of the Savior, to incorporate His teachings into their lives, and to teach their families about Him. Within His teachings and His life lie the answers to every problem which confronts humankind. War, hunger, family strife, despair, and sorrow could be remedied if the world would turn to His example. Only as we look to the Prince of Peace will we find true peace as individuals, as families, and as members of the world community. NEWS RELEASE, MAR. 29, 1985

[B]anishing Satan by living the gospel of Jesus Christ is the price of–and the only way to–peace. God, in His infinite solicitude for the welfare of His children, chartered for them this way to peace in the beginning of the world, and He has re-charted it in every dispensation since. He has just as consistently sounded warnings of disasters, which follow abandonment of that course. If a single person, yielding to Satan, is filled with the works of the flesh, he wars within himself. If two yield, they each war within themselves and fight with each other. If many people yield, a society flourishes with the harvest of great stress and contention. If the rulers of a country yield, there is world-wide contention, for as the prophet Isaiah says, "the wicked are like the troubled sea, when it cannot rest, whose waters cast up mire and dirt. There is no peace, saith my God, to the wicked" (Isa. 57:20-21). MARION G. ROMNEY, "FIRST PRESIDENCY MESSAGE," *ENSIGN*, OCT. 1983

[I]f we are to have peace in our hearts, we must learn how to preserve it in our hearts in the midst of trouble and trial. MARION G. ROMNEY, "FIRST PRESIDENCY MESSAGE," *ENSIGN*, JULY 1981

While recognizing the need for strength to repel any aggressor, we are enjoined by the word of God to "renounce war and proclaim peace" [D&C 98:16]. We call upon the heads of nations to sit down and reason together in good faith to resolve their differences. If men of good will can bring themselves to do so, they may save the world from a holocaust, the depth and breadth of which can scarcely be imagined. We are confident that when there is enough of a desire for peace and a will to bring it about, it is not beyond the possibility of attainment. NEWS RELEASE, DEC. 20, 1980

Ours is a diverse society, but we are persuaded that most men and women long for peace as they hunger for bread. Again, where there is a strong enough desire to bring it about, it may be achieved. The application of the Golden Rule laid down by the Savior of mankind will bring a resolution of almost any disagreement. This applies to the home, in the neighborhood, in the marketplace, the state, the nation, and the world. IBID.

[W]e express an urgent sense of rededication to the Savior and to His great work of bringing to pass the immortality and eternal life of man. This noble objective can be attained only by teaching and living the eternal principles of the gospel, by exercising faith in the Lord Jesus Christ, by repenting of our transgressions, by being baptized by immersion for the remission of sins, and by receiving and utilizing the great gift of the Holy Ghost by which we can testify of the divinity of the Savior and be guided and directed in the paths of truth and righteousness. It is only through teaching and living these principles that the peace "which passeth all understanding" spoken of in the scriptures can be attained [Philip. 4:7]. There is no other way. *CHURCH NEWS,* DEC. 16, 1972

One of the greatest essentials for peace is communications among men, hopefully resulting in better understanding and more tolerance. FIRST PRESIDENCY TO BISHOPS OF UTAH WARDS, OCT. 15, 1965

The mission of the Church is to establish peace–peace in individual hearts, peace and harmony in homes; cessation of war and discord among nations. *DESERET NEWS,* DEC. 17, 1952

We need not dwell on the world's needs. They are patent to all serious and honest observers, all summed up in the Savior's simple admonition to love one another. While progress for peace among the nations is so painfully slow, we urge our own and all other righteous people to seek for and promote peace within themselves, their families, and immediate communities. Out of righteous conduct and Christian behavior toward our fellowmen will come the peace the Savior designed for the world. He is the author of that peace. He prescribed the formula, and the only formula upon which it may be obtained. It is founded upon recognition of the sovereignty of God, and the divine sonship of man; that God is the Creator, the Lawgiver and the Supreme Judge, and the Author of Right, and that only those who seek the right will truly prosper the world. *DESERET NEWS,* DEC. 12, 1951

The responsibility of establishing peace in the world rests not alone upon a union of nations; it rests upon every individual, upon every home, upon every hamlet and city. *DESERET NEWS,* DEC. 15, 1948

Faith in God is the first essential to peace. It is folly for the United Nations now seeking ways and means to permanent peace to exclude the idea of God from their deliberations. Only through an acknowledgement of the Divine Being as Father can the sense of human brotherhood have potency. Only thus can life have purpose and humanity as a whole live in peace.

With faith in God must be associated the realization that peace springs from the individual heart. *DESERET NEWS,* DEC. 14, 1946

Peace, therefore, is an individual acquisition, a family duty, a community attainment, a national possibility, a world conquest. IBID.

What this country needs, and what the world needs, is a will for peace, not war. *IMPROVEMENT ERA,* FEB. 1946, IN *MESSAGES,* 6:239-42

We declare to all men that peace, the lasting peace which is the hope of the suffering peoples of the nations, will not come to the earth except men shall follow the laws revealed and proclaimed by the Christ. *DESERET NEWS,* DEC. 18, 1943

Before peace can reign, there must be manifest in human hearts more compassion and less hatred; more generosity, and less greed; more sanctity in the home, fewer divorces; more guardianship, less neglect of children; more temperance, less drunkenness; more chastity, less debauchery–in a word, there must be more seeking first "the kingdom of God and His righteousness" [Matt. 6:33]. *IMPROVEMENT ERA,* JAN. 1943, IN *MESSAGES,* 6:188-91

[T]here will be no lasting peace until it is built upon the foundation of faith in God and upon adherence to the principles of the gospel of Jesus Christ. *DESERET NEWS,* DEC. 14, 1940

How infinitely greater it is to lead nations to peace, than to subdue a nation to chains. Let America put her house in order, forsake selfishness, greed, and avarice, abolish unrighteousness, wipe hate from her heart, hold in loyal friendship the good and upright of all nations and peoples. Then to her shall come the high destiny of the peacemaker. *IMPROVEMENT ERA,* DEC. 1940, IN *MESSAGES,* 6:115-17

[P]eace [has] the price of eternal vigilance and constant righteous effort. Forces of evil and misery are still rampant in the world and must be resisted. *DESERET NEWS,* DEC. 19, 1936

The great need of the world today is peace–the "first of human blessings." *DESERET NEWS,* DEC. 21, 1935

[W]e appeal to Latter-day Saints and to sincere men and women the world over to live for peace, for the brotherhood of man and the fatherhood of God. To achieve this, each one will cherish in his or her soul the ideal of truth. Honor, integrity, fair dealing will be manifest in daily activities and duties; kindness and generosity will replace cruelty and selfishness; reverence for God and all things sacred will supplant disbelief and cynicism, which shrivel the spirit and make sordid the soul; each will cherish as his life's ideal the divine sonship of Jesus Christ, will acknowledge His creature power, His perfect character, and supreme leadership, and accept what a distracted world must some day inevitably accept as a fact, that only through Him and by obedience to the principles of His gospel can there be established peace on earth and good will toward men. IBID.

If the people of the world will turn to God, and acknowledge His Son, our Redeemer; if each citizen of our country will put away selfishness, strife, and bitterness; if men who enact our laws will be governed by the necessities of all of the people, and not of a favored few; if every citizen will pledge himself to rigidly observe the laws, and uphold the men who frame and execute them, the clouds of adversity will roll away, the sun of prosperity will shine again, and peace and plenty will prevail "from the rivers to the end of the earth." *DESERET NEWS,* DEC. 19, 1931

To bring peace and good will among men is the mission of the Church. It constitutes the very essence of our message to the world. *DESERET NEWS,* NOV. 7, 1929

We appeal to all people to come unto Christ and to accept him as the creator and controller of the world. The salvation of the world depends upon their acknowledgement of the Savior and obedience to His commandments. In this way only can they secure lasting safety and peace. *DESERET NEWS,* DEC. 18, 1926, IN *MESSAGES,* 5:252-54

We are for peace, and not for strife or animosity. We deplore dissension and abhor abuse. Though we submit to misrepresentation, it is nonetheless repellant to our sense of fairness and right, and we oppose retaliation and counter crimination. We counsel forbearance, being willing to leave our cause and our course in His hands who declares that He will repay. We prefer the olive branch to the sword, and silence when slandered to hasty rejoinder. *DESERET EVENING NEWS,* DEC. 17, 1910

While an inevitable result of the introduction of the gospel among men in all ages has been division—a division between Christ and Belial, between good and evil, right and wrong—peace nevertheless, and unity and love in their broadest and best significance, are the spirit, purpose, and ultimate achievement of all God's dealings with man. The Saints and servants of the Lord should be peace makers and peace promoters wherever they dwell and in whatsoever capacity they are called to minister. They should be worthy followers of the Prince of Peace, for whose reign of righteousness and brotherly love they are here to prepare the way. *DESERET NEWS*, DEC. 20, 1902

philosophy, *see* intellectualism; knowledge; revelation; truth

pioneers

Theirs was a vision, transcendent and overriding all other considerations. When they came west, they were a thousand miles, a thousand tedious miles, from the nearest settlements to the east and eight hundred miles from those to the west. A personal and individual recognition of God their Eternal Father to whom they could look in faith was of the very essence of their strength. They believed in that great scriptural mandate: "Look to God and live" (Alma 37:47). With faith they sought to do His will. With faith they read and accepted divine teaching. With faith they labored until they dropped, always with a conviction that there would be an accounting to Him who was their Father and their God. GORDON B. HINCKLEY, "FIRST PRESIDENCY MESSAGE," *ENSIGN*, JULY 1984

That which made the Utah Pioneers truly worthy of the homage now paid them, and which will enhance their greatness in future years, is not the mere fact that they endured persecution, suffered privations, subsisted in a wilderness, and that the vanguard made a thousand-mile journey across the plains without a death or even a serious mishap—achievements, it is true, worthy the praises of posterity—but what made them truly great is the fact that no matter how intense their suffering or how dark their forebodings, they ever cherished as beacon lights unchanging truths fundamental to human peace and progress. *DESERET NEWS*, JULY 24, 1947

If our colonial and national history be examined, it will be found that in no other part of the continent have so many new settlements been formed, extending over such a breadth of territory as we now occupy, with so little loss of life and property as has been experienced by our people since our residence here. This can only be attributed to the blessing of God on our labors, and to the wisdom which He has bestowed upon us to take care of ourselves. In the midst of our difficulties with the Indians, suffering as we have, from repeated provocations and aggressions we have never forgotten that they are human beings and the descendants of Abraham. To this feeling must a considerable portion of the success we have had in settling among them be attributed. We have borne more than any other people would have endured at their hands, through the knowledge which we have had revealed unto us of their origin and the Lord's purposes concerning their future. FIRST PRESIDENCY TO ORSON HYDE AND BISHOPS AND SAINTS IN SANPETE, SEVIER, PIUTE, AND SUMMIT COUNTIES AND ERASTUS SNOW AND SAINTS IN IRON, KANE, AND WASHINGTON COUNTIES, APR. 28, 1866

plan of salvation. *See also* gospel

In a very real sense, we are builders of eternal houses. We are apprentices to the trade–not skilled craftsmen. We need divine help if we are to build successfully. THOMAS S. MONSON, "FIRST PRESIDENCY MESSAGE," *ENSIGN,* JAN. 2006

The plan of salvation is the fullness of the gospel. It includes the Creation, the Fall, the Atonement of Jesus Christ, and all the laws, ordinances, and doctrines of the gospel. Moral agency, the ability to choose and act for ourselves, is also essential in Heavenly Father's plan. Because of this plan, we can be perfected through the Atonement, receive a fullness of joy, and live forever in the presence of God. Our family relationships can last throughout the eternities. *TRUE TO FAITH,* 2004

Your entire lives on earth are intended to give you the opportunity to learn to choose good over evil, service over selfishness, kindness and thoughtfulness over self-indulgence and personal gratification. *STRENGTH OF YOUTH,* 1990

The plan of salvation includes all the commandments, principles, laws, ordinances, and doctrines in the gospel of Jesus Christ. Obedience to these is necessary for exaltation in the celestial kingdom. God brought forth the plan of salvation to bless mankind, helping us progress and become like God Himself. *PRINCIPLES,* 1976

In its general sense, salvation will be given to all men (except the sons of perdition) because Christ broke the bands of death and bore the sins of the world (see D&C 76:40-48).

Salvation is also used in the Church to mean exaltation in the celestial kingdom. This type of salvation comes only to those who accept and obey all the laws and ordinances of the gospel. IBID.

Salvation means a man's being placed beyond all enemies, including the powers of death and hell. After the death of the mortal body, the spirits of all men go into the postmortal spirit world.

Every person who has lived or who will live upon this earth will be resurrected and receive a degree of glory (except the sons of perdition) according to his faithfulness in keeping the commandments of God. The order of body received will be determined by the type of life lived upon this earth. "BASIC DOCTRINES," 1971

plural marriage, *see* polygamy

politics. *See also* government

[N]o member occupying an official position in any organization of the Church is authorized to speak in behalf of the Church concerning the Church's stand on political issues. NEWS RELEASE, OCT. 19, 2006

We encourage Church members to study the issues and candidates carefully and prayerfully and then vote for those they believe will act with integrity and will most nearly carry out ideals of good government.

While the Church does not endorse political candidates, platforms, or parties, members are urged to be full participants in political, governmental, and community affairs. *CHURCH NEWS,* JUNE 24, 2006

Because national campaigns on moral, social, or political issues often become divisive, the Church urges those who participate in public debate–including its own members–to be respectful of each other. While disagreements on matters of principle may be deeply held, an atmosphere of civility and mutual respect is most conducive to the strength of a democratic society. NEWS RELEASE, APR. 24, 2006

Principles compatible with the gospel may be found in the platforms of all major political parties. *DESERET NEWS,* MAR. 15, 2006

The Church's mission is to preach the gospel of Jesus Christ, not to elect politicians. The Church of Jesus Christ of Latter-day Saints is neutral in matters of party politics. This applies in all of the many nations in which it is established. "ISSUES RESOURCES" 2006

The Church of Jesus Christ of Latter-day Saints cannot be committed, as an institution, except on those issues which are determined by the First Presidency and Twelve to be of such a nature that the Church should take an official position concerning them.

We believe that to do so otherwise would involve the Church, formally and officially, on a sufficient number of issues [where] the result would be to divert the Church from its basic mission of teaching the restored gospel to the world. "ISSUES RESOURCES," 2006

While affirming its Constitutional right of expression on political and social issues, the Church reaffirms its long-standing policy of neutrality regarding political parties, political platforms, and candidates for political office. *CHURCH NEWS,* JULY 31, 2004

As a Latter-day Saint, you should understand your place and position in the land in which you live. Learn about the history, heritage, and laws of the land. If you have the opportunity to vote and to participate in the affairs of government, be actively engaged in supporting and defending the principles of truth, righteousness, and freedom. *TRUE TO FAITH,* 2004

Latter-day Saints are under special obligation to seek out and then uphold leaders who will act with integrity and are "wise," "good," and "honest" (see D&C 98:10). *CHURCH NEWS,* OCT. 5, 2002

Candidates for public office should not imply that their candidacy is endorsed by the Church or its leaders, and Church leaders and members should avoid statements or conduct that may be interpreted as Church endorsement of any political party or candidate. In addition, members who hold public office should not give the impression they represent the Church as they work for solutions to social problems. *CHURCH NEWS*, OCT. 28, 2000

As personal circumstances allow, we encourage men and women in the Church to serve in public offices of either election or appointment–including school boards, city and county councils and commissions, state legislatures, and national offices. IBID.

There are times when each of us has to have some gumption to take a stand as to what we wish to preserve or change in order to maintain our self-respect and not be as "a reed shaken with the wind" (Matt. 11:7). We need to take our great stands in life on moral issues and not kick against insignificant matters, appearing to be eccentric or unbalanced or immature. We lose much credibility and strength, and we risk being weighed on an uneven balance, when, Don Quixote-like, we go around "tilting windmills." JAMES E. FAUST, "FIRST PRESIDENCY MESSAGE," *ENSIGN,* MAR. 2000

While the Church does not endorse political candidates, platforms, or parties, members are counseled to study the candidates carefully and vote for those individuals they believe will act with integrity and in ways conducive to good communities and good government. *ENSIGN,* APR. 1998

The Church is politically neutral. It does not endorse political parties, platforms, or candidates. *CHURCH HANDBOOK*, 1998

The Church does not endorse political candidates or parties in elections.

The Church does not advise its members how to vote.

Church facilities are not used for political purposes. FIRST PRESIDENCY, LETTER DATED MAY 6, 1996

Members are encouraged to participate as responsible citizens in supporting measures that strengthen society morally, economically, and culturally. They are urged to be actively engaged in worthy causes to improve their communities and make them more wholesome places in which to live and rear families. IBID.

We have no candidates for political office and we do not undertake to tell people how to vote. "DEAR BRETHREN," UNITED STATES, JUNE 9, 1988

The Church does not favor one political party over another. The Church has no candidates for political office; we do not undertake to tell people how to vote. NEWS RELEASE, MAR. 13, 1984

We need to be supportive of one another, instead of backbiting and maligning and resorting to malicious gossip. Particularly in the areas of local and national politics do we need to select good, honest representatives who will espouse the cause of righteousness, and then we should forget partisanship and work together for the common good of all. N. ELDON TANNER, "FIRST PRESIDENCY MESSAGE," *ENSIGN,* DEC. 1982

[N]o announcements should ever be made in Church meetings about organizations which are not endorsed or approved by the First Presidency, nor should Church facilities or Church stationery be used to advertise their events. Moreover, tickets to such events should not be sold or promoted by local Church leaders in such a way as would wrongly imply official endorsement. "DEAR BRETHREN," UNITED STATES, MAY 14, 1980

We repeat the scriptural injunction that honest, wise, and

good men and women should be sought for diligently and upheld in the performance of their civic duty.

It is incumbent, therefore, upon Church members and all citizens, to study the issues, carefully consider the candidates, and to exercise their right to vote after prayerful and intelligent consideration. This will insure support for such candidates and measures as will protect freedom and justice and strengthen the moral fiber of our communities and nation.

In urging this devotion to good citizenship, we reaffirm that we take no partisan stand as to candidates or political parties, and exercise no constraint on the freedom of individuals to make their own choices in these matters. "DEAR BRETHREN," UNITED STATES, MAR. 5, 1980

Only the First Presidency and Twelve can declare a particular issue to be a moral issue worthy of full institutional involvement. Absent such a declaration, Church members should exercise great care and caution to distinguish between what they may do as citizens in exercising their full Constitutional rights and what the Church might do as an institution. "DEAR BRETHREN," UNITED STATES, JUNE 29, 1979

Support honest, able candidates and measures which will insure freedom and justice, and strengthen the moral fiber of our communities. *DESERET NEWS,* NOV. 4, 1977

Satan is trying more than ever before to weaken and destroy our free agency. The members of the Church must not complacently stand by and allow their freedoms to be slowly destroyed. As members of The Church of Jesus Christ of Latter-day Saints, we must be involved. We must maintain a high level of integrity and morality and help others to do so. We must support the laws to maintain the freedoms this country offers. *PRINCIPLES,* 1976

Members of the Church are, of course, free to affiliate with any non-Church group or association of their choice. However, members are not free to use their Church membership or Church meetings to encourage others to affiliate with non-Church groups or to solicit subscriptions to their publications. FIRST PRESIDENCY TO W. CLEON SKOUSEN, DEC. 15, 1975

We earnestly urge every citizen to exercise his or her franchise under the law to not only vote, but work toward better law making and law observing. *DESERET NEWS,* MAY 1, 1974

We have not in the past, nor do we now seek to bring coercion or compulsion upon the membership of the Church as to their political actions. On the contrary, we have urged and do now urge that all citizens, men and women, vote according to their honest convictions. *DESERET NEWS,* OCT. 26, 1970

On any issue presented for vote where there are differences of opinion, we encourage all to study both sides of the question thoroughly and then vote according to their own best judgment. IBID.

We urge all members of the Church to wield their influence in the matter of encouraging the introduction of proper legislation that will, when enacted into law, combat evil of the kind mentioned ["drinking, gambling, immorality and other vices"], and safeguard the morals of members and non-members alike. Latter-day Saints must always be alert and united in contending against any influence which tends to break down the moral and spiritual strength of the people. "DEAR BRETHREN," UNITED STATES AND CANADA, JAN. 27, 1969

The historic position of the Church has been one which is concerned with the quality of man's contemporary environment as well as preparing him for eternity. In fact, as social and political conditions affect man's behavior now, they obviously affect eternity.

The revelations in this dispensation place a sobering responsibility on us as individuals in seeking out and supporting political candidates who are "wise," "good," and "honest." Likewise, the health of our cities and communities is as genuine a concern now as it was in the planning and establishment of Nauvoo or Salt Lake City.

The growing world-wide responsibilities of the Church make it [in]advisable for the Church to seek to respond to all the various and complex issues involved in the mounting problems of the many cities and communities in which members live. But this complexity does not absolve members as individuals from filling their responsibilities as citizens in their own communities.

We urge our members to do their civic duty and to assume their responsibilities as individual citizens in seeking solutions to the problems which beset our cities and communities.

With our wide ranging mission so far as mankind is concerned, Church members cannot ignore the many practical problems that require solution if our families are to live in an environment conducive to spirituality.

Where solutions to these practical problems require cooperative action with those not of our faith, members should not be reticent in doing their part in joining and leading in those efforts where they can make an individual contribution to those causes which are consistent with the standards of the Church.

Individual Church members cannot, of course, represent or commit the Church, but should, nevertheless, be "anxiously engaged" in good causes, using the principles of the gospel of Jesus Christ as their constant guide. *DESERET NEWS,* SEPT. 7, 1968

Members of the Church are at perfect liberty to act according to their own consciences in the matter of safeguarding our way of life. They are, of course, encouraged to honor the highest standards of the gospel and to work to preserve their own freedoms. They are free to participate in non-Church meetings which are held to warn people of the threat of Communism or any other theory or principle which will deprive us of our free agency or individual liberties vouchsafed by the Constitution of the United States. CLARE MIDDLEMISS, SECRETARY TO DAVID O. MCKAY, LETTER DATED DEC. 8, 1965

[S]trive to support good and conscientious candidates, of either party, who are aware of the great dangers inherent in Communism, and who are truly dedicated to the Constitution in the tradition of our Founding Fathers.

They should also pledge their sincere fealty to our way of liberty–a liberty which aims at the preservation of both personal and property rights. *DESERET NEWS,* OCT. 23, 1964

We believe in a two-party system, and all our members are perfectly free to support the party of their choice. *SALT LAKE TRIBUNE,* JAN. 4, 1963

Strictly political matters should be left in the field of politics where they belong. However, on moral issues, the Church and its members take a positive stand.

Latter-day Saints must ever be alert and united in fighting any influence which tends to break down the moral and spiritual strength of the people. FIRST PRESIDENCY TO PRESIDENTS OF STAKES, UNITED STATES, SEPT. 25, 1962

[I]t is the duty of every citizen to exercise the voting franchise in accordance with his or her convictions. We have not in the past, nor do we now seek to bring coercion or compulsion upon the membership of the Church as to their political actions. On the contrary, we have urged and do now urge that all citizens, men and women, vote according to their honest convictions. The voter should study this government and make up his mind as to what he wishes his government to be, and then, if he is so minded, vote for the one he believes will most nearly carry out his ideas about our government and its free institutions. *DESERET NEWS*, AUG. 23, 1962

It is contrary to our instructions to have any use made of our meeting places, either stake, ward, or branch, for the holding of political rallies or for other political purposes, directly or indirectly, by any candidate prior to the primaries or by any party nominee selected by the primaries. We should under no circumstances open our buildings to one candidate or nominee without opening them to all. We should under any circumstances be entirely impartial as between candidates or nominees, regardless of party affiliation. Therefore, it is doubly important that we do not make any such use of our buildings for the benefit of or in the interest of any candidate or political party. FIRST PRESIDENCY TO "DEAR PRESIDENT," MAY 23, 1960

Our pulpits must not be available to those preaching error or seeking to advance purely or largely selfish personal interests, political or otherwise. The promotion of the work of the Lord, which embraces all truth, is the sole object of all of our Church activities. This is the sacred trust of all of us. Everything that hampers or delays that work is to be cast aside. "DEAR BRETHREN," JUNE 30, 1952

The Church stands for the separation of church and state. The church has no civil political functions. As the church may not assume the functions of the state, so the state may not assume the functions of the church. *IMPROVEMENT ERA,* MAY 1942, IN *MESSAGES,* 6:148-63

The Church does not interfere, and has no intention of trying to interfere, with the fullest and freest exercise of the political franchise of its members, under and within our Constitution, which the Lord declared, "I established ... by the hands of wise men whom I raised up unto this very purpose," and which, as to the principles thereof, the Prophet [Joseph Smith], dedicating the Kirtland [Ohio] Temple, prayed should be "established forever" [D&C 101:80; 109:54]. *DESERET NEWS*, JULY 3, 1936, IN *MESSAGES*, 6:17-18

We offer no counsel to members of the Church which may be considered partisan in its nature. We urge all to a dispassionate, intelligent, and honest use of the ballot, but we do not attempt to influence the choice of any voter. *DESERET NEWS*, OCT. 29, 1932

[W]hile the First Presidency of the Church recognize the right of its members to affiliate with the political party of their own choice, at the same time our own personal experience, together with the light in us, suggests the wisdom of our people remaining with one or the other of the two national parties, and not permit themselves to be drawn away by extremists in an endeavor to set up a third party. This advice we believe to be good for them as individuals, and good for us as a community. FIRST PRESIDENCY TO W. T. JACK, APR. 23, 1912

Obedience to law, human and divine, is to be rendered by all people. Governments and their appointed authorities must be respected in their respective spheres, and the rights of individuals must also be maintained with due regard for the regulations of society as established by the majority in each nation or part thereof. This includes political liberty to the fullest lawful extent. Endeavors to suppress it or to use coercion for its restriction are wrong and contrary to both civil and religious law. As the Presidency of the Church of Jesus Christ of Latter-day Saints, we take opportunity once more to proclaim our adherence to these principles.

We claim no authority, and have no desire, to use the power of the priesthood which we hold, to dictate or compel any member of the Church, or other human being, to unite with or oppose any political party or faction or to interfere with the freedom of the citizen, as frequently charged against us, nor do we believe in or attempt the restraint of trade and commerce or the suppression of enterprise, corporate or personal. We do not favor the establishment of monopolies, but believe in the freedom of capital within lawful limits and desire the promotion of such organizations as aid in the development of natural resources and the production of anything and everything that lend to the improvement of mankind socially, nationally, and universally. *DESERET EVENING NEWS*, DEC. 17, 1910

The religion of the Latter-day Saints stands for the rights of all men, whatever their standing may be in society. It teaches tolerance to those of all other religions or no religion. It inculcates obedience and subjection to presidents, kings, and rulers; its adherents look upon the Constitution of our land as an inspired document, and they teach their children to uphold and revere it. *LIAHONA,* APR. 6, 1907, IN *MESSAGES,* 4:155-57

The Mormon people are as well posted on politics as the people of any other state, and when it is remembered that nearly all of their men have traveled all over the world, we can say this without fear of successful contradiction. They have strong views on the burning questions of the day, and will not brook interference with their politics, and are really more free in this regard than the people of the East, for as yet they have not come under the rule of bossism. FIRST PRESIDENCY TO REED SMOOT, JAN. 20, 1904

[W]e sustain the laws and institutions of the country where we go, and find that good results follow, for so the Lord has revealed to us. FIRST PRESIDENCY TO "BELOVED BRETHREN AND SISTERS IN TURKEY," SEPT. 7, 1897, IN *MESSAGES*, 3:284-87

[T]he members of this Church are entirely and perfectly free in all political affairs. But they should not indulge in ill feeling or personalities. *DESERET NEWS WEEKLY,* MAR. 25, 1892, IN *MESSAGES,* 3:233

[T]his Church, while offering advice for the welfare of its members in all conditions of life, does not claim or exercise the right to interfere with citizens in the free exercise of social or political rights and privileges. *DESERET NEWS WEEKLY,* DEC. 21, 1889, IN *MESSAGES,* 3:184-87

[M]ingle as little as possible with the politics of the day, and above all *never* use the priesthood or the influence thereof to promote party questions or designs; it is condescending far too low to bring the authority of the high heaven's King to mingle in the party strifes which agitate the political world in this degenerate age. BRIGHAM YOUNG TO ORSON HYDE, MAY 7, 1855, IN *MESSAGES,* 2:173

All the cliques, parties, divisions, and subdivisions of the age, in politics, are easily cast in two grand molds, *truth* and *falsehood;* and so far as it may be possible that we diverge from the first, or embrace the second, we are not Mormons. And so far as we are Mormons, we embrace the first and despise the second. FIRST PRESIDENCY TO THOMAS L. KANE, SEPT. 15, 1851

polygamy. *See also* marriage

Polygamy was officially discontinued by The Church of Jesus Christ of Latter-day Saints in 1890. Any Church member adopting the practice today is excommunicated. Those groups which continue the practice in Utah and elsewhere have no association whatever with The Church of Jesus Christ of Latter-day Saints, and most of their practitioners have never been among our members. "DEAR BRETHREN," UNITED STATES AND CANADA, FEB. 17, 2006

Some early leaders and members of the Church entered into plural marriages during the latter half of the nineteenth century. After receiving a revelation, Church President Wilford Woodruff declared the practice should be discontinued in 1890. That position has been reaffirmed by every President of the Church since. Members of the Church who enter into plural marriage today face Church disciplinary action, including excommunication. *QUICK FACTS,* 2005

The Church of Jesus Christ of Latter-day Saints discontinued the practice of polygamy more than a century ago. No members of the Church today can enter into polygamy without being excommunicated. Groups that practice polygamy have nothing to do whatsoever with the Church and should not be referred to as Mormons. NEWS RELEASE, FEB. 12, 2002

prayer

The passport to peace is the practice of prayer. The feelings of the heart, humbly expressed rather than a mere recitation of words, provide the peace we seek. THOMAS S. MONSON, "FIRST PRESIDENCY MESSAGE," *ENSIGN*, DEC. 2006

When we remember that each of us is literally a spirit son or daughter of God, we will not find it difficult to approach our Heavenly Father in prayer. He appreciates the value of this raw material which we call life. THOMAS S. MONSON, "FIRST PRESIDENCY MESSAGE," *ENSIGN,* JAN. 2006

Of all that we might do to find solace, prayer is perhaps the most comforting. We are instructed to pray to the Father, in the same of His Son, the Lord Jesus Christ, and by the power of the Holy Ghost. The very act of praying to God is satisfying to the soul, even though God, in His wisdom, may not give what we ask for. JAMES E. FAUST, "FIRST PRESIDENCY MESSAGE," *ENSIGN*, JULY 2005

In prayer we speak openly and honestly with our loving Father in Heaven. We express gratitude and thanksgiving for our blessings. We may acknowledge our love for Him. We also ask for help, protection, and direction according to our needs.

As we pray with faith, sincerity, and real intent, we will see God's influence in our lives. He will guide us in our daily lives and help us make good decisions. He will bless us with feelings of comfort and peace. He will warn us of danger and strengthen us to resist temptation. He will forgive our sins. We will feel closer to Him. We must learn to recognize His influence in our lives. We must learn to listen to the still, small voice of the Spirit. *PREACH MY GOSPEL,* 2005

As you make a habit of approaching God in prayer, you will come to know Him and draw ever nearer to Him. Your desires will become more like His. You will be able to secure for yourself and for others blessings that He is ready to give if you will but ask in faith. *TRUE TO FAITH,* 2004

When you pray, you should use words that appropriately convey a loving, worshipful relationship with God. You may have some difficulty learning the language of prayer, but you will gradually become more comfortable with it as you pray and read the scriptures. IBID.

Remember that prayer is a two-way communication. As you close your prayers, take time to pause and listen. At times,

Heavenly Father will counsel, guide, or comfort you while you are on your knees. IBID.

Heavenly Father hears your prayers. He may not always answer as you expect, but He does answer—in His own time and according to His will. Because He knows what is best for you, He may sometimes answer no, even when your petitions are sincere. IBID.

You are a child of God. He is your Heavenly Father. He loves you and cares about you. He wants you to have faith in Him and pray to Him often—anytime, anywhere. *FAITH IN GOD,* 2003

Family prayer is the greatest deterrent to sin, and hence the most beneficent provider of joy and happiness. The old saying is yet true: "The family that prays together stays together." THOMAS S. MONSON, "FIRST PRESIDENCY MESSAGE," *ENSIGN,* OCT. 2001

Prayer is the passport to spiritual power. IBID.

Always use the names of God and Jesus Christ with reverence and respect. Misusing their names is a sin. *STRENGTH OF YOUTH,* 2001

Pray about the important things of your life—about attending school, about going on a mission, about the girl you will marry or the boy you will marry. The Lord will bless and guide you. GORDON B. HINCKLEY, "FIRST PRESIDENCY MESSAGE," *ENSIGN,* AUG. 2000

A fervent, sincere prayer is a two-way communication that will do much to bring the Spirit flowing like healing water to help with the trials, hardships, aches, and pains we all face. What is the quality of our secret prayers? As we pray, we should think of our Heavenly Father as being close by; full of knowledge, understanding, love, and compassion; the essence of power; and having great expectations of each of us. JAMES E. FAUST, "FIRST PRESIDENCY MESSAGE," *ENSIGN,* JAN. 1999

Men and women may offer prayers in Church meetings. Prayers should be brief and simple and should be spoken as directed by the Spirit. Members should use the pronouns *Thee, Thy, Thine,* and *Thou* when addressing Heavenly Father. All members should say an audible *amen* at the end of the prayer. *CHURCH HANDBOOK,* 1998

Prayer unlocks the powers of heaven in our behalf. Prayer is the great gift which our Eternal Father has given us by which we may approach Him and speak with Him in the name of the Lord Jesus Christ. GORDON B. HINCKLEY, "FIRST PRESIDENCY MESSAGE," *ENSIGN,* AUG. 1997

Most of the time there are no flags waving or bands playing when prayer is answered. His [God's] miracles are frequently performed in a quiet and natural manner. THOMAS S. MONSON, "FIRST PRESIDENCY MESSAGE," *ENSIGN,* AUG. 1995

Prayer is the channel to our Heavenly Father for personal inspiration and is the way to ascertain His will concerning our daily behavior and challenges.

The act of prayer itself can change and purify both individuals and societies. As far as the individual is concerned, prayer also has positive and practical consequences. For example, recent medical research has documented that people who pray and are prayed for are more likely to deal positively with illness and the challenges of their lives than those who do not pray or who are not prayed for.

Prayer in the family can be a meaningful way of binding family members together in love and mutual purpose. Regular family prayer has proven to be a tool that parents can use to direct their children in making correct and positive choices, and in bringing the love of the Savior, Jesus Christ, into the lives of family members. *CHURCH NEWS,* APR. 30, 1994

As we offer unto God our family prayers and our personal prayers, let us do so with faith and trust in Him. If we have been slow to hearken to the counsel to pray always, there is no finer hour to begin than now. Those who feel that prayer might denote a physical weakness should remember that individuals never stand taller than when they are upon their knees.
THOMAS S. MONSON, "FIRST PRESIDENCY MESSAGE," *ENSIGN,* OCT. 1991

We encourage daily personal and family prayers which express gratitude for past blessings and which seek guidance for future decisions and activities. CHURCH NEWS, APR. 20, 1991

For what should we pray? We should pray about our work, against the power of our enemies and the devil, for our welfare and the welfare of those around us. We should counsel with the Lord regarding all our decisions and activities (see Alma 37:36-37). We should be grateful enough to give thanks for all we have (see D&C 59:21). We should confess His hand in all things. Ingratitude is one of our great sins.

The Lord has declared in modern revelation: "And he who receiveth all things with thankfulness shall be made glorious; and the things of this earth shall be added unto him, even an hundred fold, yea, more" (D&C 78:19).

We should ask for what we need, taking care that we not ask for things that would be to our detriment (see James 4:3). We should ask for strength to overcome our problems (see Alma 31:31-33). We should pray for the inspiration and well-being of the President of the Church, the General Authorities, our stake president, our bishop, our quorum president, our home teachers, family members, and our civic leaders. Other suggestions could be made, but with the help of the Holy Ghost we will know about what we should pray (see Rom. 8:26-27). EZRA TAFT BENSON, "FIRST PRESIDENCY MESSAGE," *ENSIGN,* FEB. 1990

When the burdens of life become heavy, when trials test one's faith, when pain, sorrow, and despair cause the light of hope to flicker and burn low, communication with our Heavenly Father provides peace. THOMAS S. MONSON, "FIRST PRESIDENCY MESSAGE," *ENSIGN,* JUNE 1989

Nothing is better designed to keep the attention of humankind centered on God and righteousness than prayer. Every thought, word, and act is influenced or governed by the nature and extent of one's communion with Deity. *CHURCH NEWS,* APR. 23, 1988

We commend the practice of daily prayer to people everywhere. May we all, regardless of any particular religious affiliation, express daily gratitude to the Father of us all. And, to paraphrase a familiar hymn, when sore trials come upon us, when our souls are full of sorrow, when our hearts are filled with anger, let us think to pray and, in so doing, seek guidance and comfort and forgiveness from Him who gave us life. *CHURCH NEWS,* APR. 20, 1986

What a wonderful thing it is to remember before the Lord those who are sick and in sorrow, those who are hungry and destitute, those who are lonely and afraid, those who are in bondage and sore distress. When such prayers are uttered in sincerity, there will follow a greater desire to reach out to those in need. GORDON B. HINCKLEY, "FIRST PRESIDENCY MESSAGE," *ENSIGN,* JUNE 1985

Let prayer, night and morning, as a family and as individuals, become a practice in which children grow while yet young.

It will bless their lives forever. No parent in this Church can afford to neglect it. IBID.

From time immemorial, righteous and contrite men and women have instinctively knelt to acknowledge the majesty, wisdom, and goodness of God, to implore His forgiveness, and to seek His blessing on their honorable desires. NEWS RELEASE, APR. 23, 1985

Daily secret and family prayer is particularly imperative in this day when latter-day cultures seem to be trying to eliminate God and His righteousness from the daily lives and affairs of men.

No wise Latter-day Saint parent, with an understanding of the power of prayer and the irreligious trend of our society, will fail to train his or her children to pray. No person has a stronger weapon against the power of evil than he who, with unbroken regularity, goes night and morning on bended knee before our Heavenly Father in sincere and humble secret prayer. MARION G. ROMNEY, "FIRST PRESIDENCY MESSAGE," *ENSIGN,* JAN. 1985

Daily prayers, alone and with our loved ones, open our hearts and souls to the promptings of divine love and inspiration by which we fashion lives of compassion and courage, service, and selflessness. NEWS RELEASE, MAR. 16, 1984

Prayer, family prayer in the homes of people in all lands, is one of the simple medicines that would check the dread disease that robs men and women of honesty, character, and integrity. In generations past, individual and family prayers in the homes of people throughout the world were as much a part of the day's activity as was eating. As the practice of prayer has diminished, moral decay has increased.

The inclination to be holy, to be thankful, is increased as

family members kneel together and thank the Lord for life and peace and all that they may become under His guidance. In remembering before the Lord the poor, the needy, the oppressed, there is developed, unconsciously but realistically, a love for others above self, a respect for others, a desire to serve the needs of others. One cannot ask God to help a neighbor in distress without being motivated to do something toward helping that neighbor. NEWS RELEASE, NOV. 25, 1982

We need to kneel before the Lord daily, to thank Him for our well-being and for His blessing of all mankind. *CHURCH NEWS,* MAY 1, 1982

[I]f we pray fervently and righteously, individually and as a family, when we retire at night and when we arise in the morning, and around our tables at mealtime, we will not only knit together as loved ones but we will grow spiritually through communion with our Heavenly Father. SPENCER W. KIMBALL, "FIRST PRESIDENCY MESSAGE," *ENSIGN,* OCT. 1981

Learning the language of prayer is a joyous, lifetime experience. Sometimes ideas flood our mind as we listen after our prayers. Sometimes feelings press upon us. A spirit of calmness assures us that all will be well. But always, if we have been honest and earnest, we will experience a good feeling–a feeling of warmth for our Father in Heaven and a sense of His love for us. IBID.

[W]e should remember in our prayers all of those everywhere who are the victims of man's inhumanity to man. NEWS RELEASE, JAN. 28, 1981

As we seek the Lord in prayer and keep His commandments, we shall understand the meaning and purpose of life. N. ELDON TANNER, "FIRST PRESIDENCY MESSAGE," *ENSIGN,* OCT. 1978

No person ever called upon God in vain, if he truly prayed in faith. MARION G. ROMNEY, "FIRST PRESIDENCY MESSAGE," *ENSIGN*, AUG. 1976

Prayer is the key that unlocks the door to communion with Deity. MARION G. ROMNEY, "FIRST PRESIDENCY MESSAGE," *ENSIGN*, JAN. 1976

Not every prayer brings a spectacular response, but every sincere and earnest prayer is heard and responded to by the Spirit of the Lord. IBID.

Prayer is both an obligation, being a commandment, and a blessing or gift in that we can communicate with our Father. *PRINCIPLES*, 1976

Prayer should be part of family life, both morning and evening. *CHURCH NEWS*, DEC. 20, 1975

The Savior has assured us that if we ask, it shall be given; if we seek, we shall find; and if we knock, it shall be opened unto us (Matt. 7:7). This is an open invitation to all people to call upon Him in prayer. For answers in the field of science, go to the best authority in the field in which you are interested; but for answers to such vital questions as "Who am I and why am I here?" go to an authority in the field of religion and study the word of the Lord as recorded in the scriptures. Go to God through prayer, and listen to the prophet's voice. N. ELDON TANNER, "FIRST PRESIDENCY MESSAGE," *ENSIGN*, OCT. 1973

Our Father in Heaven knows our needs better than we. He knows what is for our good and the things we need to overcome in order to further our development and progression. We must learn to accept His will in all things, with the faith and assurance that in the end everything He does for us will redound to our good. N. ELDON TANNER, "FIRST PRESIDENCY MESSAGE," *ENSIGN,* AUG. 1971

Prayers in all Church meetings should be brief, simple, and given as led by the Spirit by the one who is voice. Their content should pertain to the particular matter at hand. *CHURCH HANDBOOK,* 1968

Group prayers in which those participating, sometimes kneeling and sometimes standing, arrange themselves in a circle and then hold each other's hands while the prayer is being offered should not be held. Where groups are assembled together for prayers, these should be offered in the ordinary way in which we offer prayers in our public services. This ruling does not exclude groups from kneeling in prayer, but it is intended to exclude all simulations of the sacred prayer circle taught in sacred places. IBID.

All prayers in all Church meetings should be *brief,* simple, and given as the one who is voice is led by the Spirit. Their content should pertain to the particular matter at hand.

Those praying should always use the sacred form of the personal pronoun (e.g., *Thee, Thine, Thou*) in addressing the Lord. *CHURCH HANDBOOK,* 1963

Who knows but what the Lord has already answered the prayers that have been offered in your behalf, but as is the case frequently with earthly parents, the answer may be a negative one. HEBER J. GRANT TO MRS. T. WILLIAM RHOADES, SEPT. 14, 1935

No earnest, righteous prayer has ever gone unheard or unanswered. *IMPROVEMENT ERA,* DEC. 1932, IN *MESSAGES,* 5:311

Much praying or praying at great length should not be indulged in, and to form a circle for this purpose would be an innovation. It is the prayer of faith, not of many words, that avails, and wisdom ofttimes suggests brevity in prayer, and especially is this the case when a delicate or weak patient is the subject of administration. FIRST PRESIDENCY TO PHILEMON C. MERRILL, MAR. 21, 1916

The too frequent use of the name of Deity, even in our prayers, is to be avoided; that name is holy, and the Lord will not hold guiltless one who uses His name lightly or in vain. *LIAHONA,* FEB. 23, 1914, IN *MESSAGES,* 4:303-304

By using the methods that God has appointed if He chooses to hear us, all well; if not, we must submit to the dispensations of our Heavenly Father. JOHN TAYLOR TO S. M. LARSON, MAR. 23, 1883

premortal existence. ***See also*** **foreordination**

All people on the earth were members of God's family in the premortal life (see Acts 17:26-29; Heb. 12:9). We are part of God's family in this life and can enjoy even greater blessings as members of His family in the life to come. We are all brothers and sisters in the family of God. *PREACH MY GOSPEL,* 2005

Before you were born on earth, you lived in the presence of your Heavenly Father as one of His spirit children. In this premortal existence, you attended a council with Heavenly Father's other spirit children. At that council, Heavenly Father presented His great plan of happiness (see Abr. 3:22-26). *TRUE TO FAITH,* 2004

You are a literal child of God, spiritually begotten in the premortal life. As His child, you can be assured that you have divine, eternal potential and that He will help you in your sincere efforts to reach that potential. IBID.

You are a spirit child of Heavenly Father, and you existed as a spirit before you were born on the earth. During your life on the earth, your spirit is housed in your physical body, which was born of mortal parents. IBID.

Throughout your premortal life, you developed your identity and increased your spiritual capabilities. Blessed with the gift of agency, you made important decisions, such as the decision to follow Heavenly Father's plan. These decisions affected your life then and now. You grew in intelligence and learned to love the truth, and you prepared to come to the earth, where you could continue to progress. IBID.

In the premortal spirit world, God appointed certain spirits to fulfill specific missions during their mortal lives. This is called foreordination.

Foreordination does not guarantee that individuals will receive certain callings or responsibilities. Such opportunities come in this life as a result of the righteous exercise of agency, just as foreordination came as a result of righteousness in the premortal existence. IBID.

In the premortal realm, spirit sons and daughters knew and worshiped God as their Eternal Father and accepted His plan by which His children could obtain a physical body and gain earthly experience to progress toward perfection and ultimately realize his or her divine destiny as an heir to eternal life. *CHURCH NEWS*, SEPT. 30, 1995

We are not chance creations in a universe of disorder. We lived before we were born. We were God's sons and daughters who shouted for joy (see Job 38:7). We knew our Father; He planned our future. We graduated from that life and matriculated in this. The statement is simple; the implications are profound. Life is a mission, not just the sputtering of a candle between a chance lighting and a gust of wind that blows it out forever. GORDON B. HINCKLEY, "FIRST PRESIDENCY MESSAGE," *ENSIGN,* JAN. 1994

In our premortal state, we shouted for joy as the plan of salvation was unfolded to our view (see Job 38:7).

It was there our elder brother Jesus, the firstborn of our Father's children in the spirit, volunteered to redeem us from our sins. He became our foreordained Savior, the Lamb "slain from the foundation of the world" (Moses 7:47). EZRA TAFT BENSON, "FIRST PRESIDENCY MESSAGE," *ENSIGN,* DEC. 1993

Every creature upon the earth existed spiritually before it was created physically (see Moses 3:5). Man, the greatest of God's creations, is no exception. Before coming to Earth, we lived with God as His spirit children. *PRINCIPLES,* 1976

One of the most important events in our eternal existence occurred in the premortal world. A council was held to decide the conditions of our life on the earth. Lucifer proposed to bring all of us back to our Father's presence, but he would have deprived us of our free agency. When his offer was rejected, he rebelled and was cast out of heaven with his followers. Christ was foreordained to redeem us from the sins we would commit while in mortality (see Abr. 3:24-28; Rev. 12:7-9). IBID.

Although we do not know how long we existed as spirits before coming to the earth, we know that it must have been a place of growth and testimony, where we had the power to make our own decisions and to progress. IBID.

[W]e have no revealed word to the effect that when we were in the pre-existent state we chose our parents and our husbands or wives. FIRST PRESIDENCY TO JOE J. CHRISTENSEN, JUNE 14, 1971

All mankind were (as intelligences) in the beginning with God.

All mankind are literal spirit sons and daughters of Heavenly Parents and dwelt with them before coming to this earth. All mankind are spirit brothers and sisters. "BASIC DOCTRINES," 1971

As all of us, Jesus lived spiritually in the pre-existent world before there was an earth. He was with the Father in the Great Council which deliberated earth life and man's part in it—his birth, his fall, and his redemption. *DESERET NEWS,* DEC. 11, 1957

[T]he conduct of spirits in the pre-mortal existence has some determining effect upon the conditions and circumstances under which these spirits take on mortality, and ... while the details of this principle have not been made known, the principle itself indicates that the coming to this earth and the taking on mortality is a privilege so great that it is given to those who kept their first estate; ... the worth of the privilege is so great that spirits are willing to come to Earth and take on bodies no matter what the handicaps may be as to the kind of bodies they are to secure, or as to the inhibitions that may follow because of the bodies they may secure; and that among the handicaps may be the failure of the right to enjoy, during mortality, the blessing of the priesthood. This is a handicap which spirits are willing to assume in order that they may come to Earth. FIRST PRESIDENCY TO THE URUGUAYAN MISSION, JAN. 15, 1952

[S]ome of God's children were assigned to superior positions before the world was formed. We are aware that some Higher Critics do not accept this, but the Church does. FIRST PRESIDENCY TO LOWRY NELSON, JULY 17, 1947

We of this Church have been told of the Lord that before

we came to this earth we had a life running back to the remotest stretches of eternity; that as spirits we lived out an existence before we came here, in which we prepared ourselves for life on the earth; that then, having kept our first estate, we came to this earth to obtain knowledge, wisdom, and experience, to learn the lessons, suffer the pains, endure the temptations, and gain the victories of mortality; that when our mortal bodies give up life, our spirits return to take up again the spirit life which we left to come to earth life, and we thereafter go on, building upon the achievements of our first spirit-life, our first estate, and of our mortal life, or second estate, progressing through the endless eternities that follow, until we reach the goal the Lord set: "Be ye perfect, even as your Father which is in heaven is perfect" [Matt. 5:48]. STATEMENT, MAY 30, 1937, IN *MESSAGES,* 6:30-36

The doctrine of pre-existence pours a wonderful flood of light upon the otherwise mysterious problem of man's origin. It shows that man, as a spirit, was begotten and born of Heavenly Parents, and reared to maturity in the eternal mansions of the Father, prior to coming upon the earth in a temporal body to undergo an experience in mortality. *DESERET NEWS,* JULY 18, 1925, QUOTING *IMPROVEMENT ERA,* NOV. 1909

All men and women are in the similitude of the universal Father and Mother, and are literally sons and daughters of Deity. IBID.

[A]ll people who come to this earth and are born in mortality had a pre-existent, spiritual personality as the sons and daughters of the Eternal Father. *IMPROVEMENT ERA,* MAR. 1912, IN *MESSAGES,* 4:264-65

A spirit born of God is an immortal being. IBID.

The doctrine of the pre-existence, revealed so plainly, particularly in latter days, ... teaches that all men existed in the spirit before any man existed in the flesh, and that all who have inhabited the earth since Adam have taken bodies and become souls in like manner. *IMPROVEMENT ERA,* NOV. 1909, IN *MESSAGES,* 4:200-06

We believe in the pre-existence of man as a spirit and in a future state of individual existence in which every soul shall find its place, as determined by justice and mercy, with opportunities of endless progression in the varied conditions of eternity. *IMPROVEMENT ERA,* MAY 1907, IN *MESSAGES,* 4:143-55

Presiding Bishopric. *See also* priesthood

The Presiding Bishopric is the presidency of the Aaronic Priesthood of the Church (see D&C 107:15). Under the direction of the First Presidency, the Presiding Bishopric administers the temporal affairs of the Church (107:68). *CHURCH HANDBOOK,* 1998

pride

We would say, beware of pride also; for well and truly hath the wise man said that pride goeth before destruction, and a haughty spirit before a fall. And again, outward appearance is not always a criterion by which to judge our fellow man; but the lips betray the haughty and overbearing imaginations of the heart; by his words and his deeds let him be judged. Flattery also is a deadly poison. A frank and open rebuke provoketh a good man to emulation, and in the hour of trouble he will be your best friend; but on the other hand, it will draw out all the corruptions of corrupt hearts. And lying and the poison of asps is under their tongues, and they do cause the pure in heart to be cast into prison because they want them out of their way. STATEMENT, MAR. 25, 1839, IN *MESSAGES,* 1:88-104

priesthood. ***See also*** **Church**

There are forces that will save us from the ever-increasing lying, disorder, violence, chaos, destruction, misery, and deceit that are upon the earth. Those saving forces are the everlasting principles, covenants, and ordinances of the eternal gospel of the Lord Jesus Christ. These same principles, covenants, and ordinances are coupled with the rights and powers of the priesthood of Almighty God. We of this Church are the possessors and custodians of these commanding powers that can and do roll back much of the power of Satan on the earth. We believe that we hold these mighty forces in trust for all who have died, for all who are now living, and for the yet unborn. JAMES E. FAUST, "FIRST PRESIDENCY MESSAGE," *ENSIGN*, JAN. 2007

It is through the power of the priesthood that marriage and the family unit can extend into and continue throughout all eternity. JAMES E. FAUST, "FIRST PRESIDENCY MESSAGE," *ENSIGN*, SEPT. 2006

The priesthood is the authority to act in God's name. The Church emphasizes that authority to act for God cannot simply be assumed by a person because he or she feels a sense of "call." Joseph Smith, first Prophet and President of the Church, taught: "A man must be called of God, by prophecy, and by the laying on of hands by those who are in authority, to preach the gospel and administer in the ordinances thereof" (AofF 1:5). *QUICK FACTS*, 2005

It is the priesthood power by which the world was created and the plan of salvation and happiness was put in place to bless our lives eternally if we are true to our covenants. It is the power that was magnified by His [Christ's] agony on the cross, bringing the single most important blessing to mankind. JAMES E. FAUST, "FIRST PRESIDENCY MESSAGE," *ENSIGN*, DEC. 2004

Many people do not understand our belief that God has wisely established a guiding authority for the most important institutions in the world. This guiding authority is called the priesthood. The priesthood is held in trust to be used to bless all of God's children. Priesthood is not gender; it is blessings from God for all at the hands of the servants He has designated. Within the Church this authority of the priesthood can bless all members through the ministration of home teachers, quorum presidents, bishops and branch presidents, fathers, and all other righteous brethren who are charged with the administration of the affairs of the kingdom of God. Priesthood is the righteous power and influence by which boys are taught in their youth and throughout their lives to honor chastity, to be honest and industrious, and to develop respect for and stand in the defense of womanhood. Priesthood is a restraining influence. Girls are taught that through its influence and power to bless, they can fulfill many of their desires. JAMES E. FAUST, "FIRST PRESIDENCY MESSAGE," *ENSIGN,* AUG. 2004

The priesthood is the eternal power and authority of God. Through the priesthood God created and governs the heavens and the earth. Through this power He redeems and exalts His children, bringing to pass "the immortality and eternal life of man" (Moses 1:39). *TRUE TO FAITH,* 2004

The offices of the Melchizedek Priesthood are apostle, seventy, patriarch, high priest, and elder. The President of the High Priesthood is the President of the Church (see D&C 107:64-66). IBID.

This greater [Melchizedek] priesthood was given to Adam and has been on the earth whenever the Lord has revealed His gospel. It was taken from the earth during the Great Apostasy, but it was restored in May 1829, when the Apostles Peter,

James, and John conferred it upon Joseph Smith and Oliver Cowdery. IBID.

When a man receives the Melchizedek Priesthood, he enters into the oath and covenant of the priesthood. He covenants to be faithful, magnify his calling, "give diligent heed to the words of eternal life," and "live by every word that proceedeth forth from the mouth of God." Those who keep this covenant will be sanctified by the Spirit and receive "all that [the] Father hath" (See D&C 84:33-44). IBID.

In the Church today, worthy male members may receive the Aaronic Priesthood beginning at age twelve. They receive many opportunities to participate in the sacred priesthood ordinances and give service. As they worthily fulfill their duties, they act in the name of the Lord to help others receive the blessings of the gospel. IBID.

The Aaronic Priesthood is "an appendage to the greater, or the Melchizedek Priesthood" (D&C 107:4). It is often called the preparatory priesthood. As a priesthood holder serves in the Aaronic Priesthood, he prepares to receive the Melchizedek Priesthood, to receive the blessings of the temple, to serve a full-time mission, to be a loving husband and father, and to continue in lifelong service to the Lord. IBID.

Although the authority of the priesthood is bestowed only on worthy male members of the Church, the blessings of the priesthood are available to all—men, women, and children. We all benefit from the influence of righteous priesthood leadership, and we all have the privilege of receiving the saving ordinances of the priesthood. IBID.

The priesthood is here. It has been conferred upon us. We act in that authority. We speak as sons of God in the name of

Jesus Christ and as holders of this divinely given endowment. We know, for we have seen, the power of this priesthood. We have seen the sick healed, the lame made to walk, and the coming of light and knowledge and understanding to those who have been in darkness. GORDON B. HINCKLEY, "FIRST PRESIDENCY MESSAGE," *ENSIGN,* FEB. 2004

The stake president and bishop are entitled to the discernment and inspiration necessary to be spiritual advisers and temporal counselors to ward members who need such help. They should prepare spiritually before counseling a member, seeking the power of discernment and the guidance of the Spirit. This guidance usually comes as impressions, thoughts, or feelings. The Spirit often prompts leaders to remember teachings from the scriptures and from latter-day prophets. *CHURCH HANDBOOK,* 1998

God gives priesthood authority to worthy male members of the Church so they can act in His name for the salvation of the human family. Through the priesthood they can be authorized to preach the gospel, administer the ordinances of salvation, and govern the kingdom of God on earth. *CHURCH HANDBOOK 2,* 1998

The priesthood should be exercised in a spirit of love with a desire to serve and bless others. The Lord revealed that "no power or influence can or ought to be maintained by virtue of the priesthood, only by persuasion, by long-suffering, by gentleness and meekness, and by love unfeigned" (D&C 121:41). IBID.

The exercise of priesthood authority is governed by those who hold its keys (see D&C 65:2; 124:123). These keys are the right to preside over and direct the Church within a jurisdiction.

The Lord Jesus Christ holds all the keys of the priesthood. He has given His Apostles the keys that are necessary for governing His Church. Only the senior Apostle, the President of the Church, may use (or authorize another person to use) these keys for governing the entire Church (43:1-4; 81:2; 132:7). IBID.

Every man who lives and honors the priesthood will be a better husband, will be a better father, will be a better man. GORDON B. HINCKLEY, "FIRST PRESIDENCY MESSAGE," *ENSIGN,* AUG. 1997

The Lord has so organized His Church that there is accessible to every member–man, woman, and child–a priesthood leader who serves as a spiritual adviser and a temporal counselor. We refer, of course, to the bishop or branch president and stake or mission president. A priesthood leader should know his flock personally and know the circumstances and conditions out of which their problems arise. By reason of his ordination, he is entitled to an endowment from our Heavenly Father of the necessary discernment and inspiration to enable him to counsel and advise members concerning their questions. "DEAR BRETHREN," JULY 15, 1987

The First Presidency and the Quorum of the Twelve are responsible for establishing and approving all Church policies and procedures. FIRST PRESIDENCY TO GENERAL AUTHORITIES AND HEADS OF CHURCH DEPARTMENTS AND ORGANIZATIONS, JUNE 30, 1987

Men are ordained to offices of the priesthood when their calling requires it and by inspiration and according to their worthiness. *BULLETIN,* NOV. 1983

The strength of Zion, according to the Prophet Joseph Smith, is the *power* and *authority* of the priesthood (see D&C

113:7-8). The authority of the priesthood comes when one is ordained. But each one given this sacred authority must cultivate carefully the power of the priesthood by faith, service, and righteous living. *PRIESTHOOD STUDY GUIDE,* 1980

In a revelation to the Prophet Joseph Smith in 1831, the Lord admonished, "Prepare ye the way of the Lord, make his paths straight" (D&C 65:1). This challenge has come to everyone who bears the priesthood. We are called to assist in the work of this dispensation, to stand as witnesses of the Savior, and to labor to prepare the way for the establishment of the kingdom of God upon the earth at His second coming. *PRIESTHOOD STUDY GUIDE,* 1978

Every bearer of the holy priesthood has an "errand from the Lord" [Jacob 1:17]. He is called to be the Lord's agent in every responsibility and duty assigned him. He is to stand as the Lord's witness at all times and in all places (see Mosiah 18:9). He is instructed to "live by every word that proceedeth forth from the mouth of God" (D&C 84:44). *PRINCIPLES,* 1976

It is by the ordinances administered by this [Melchizedek] priesthood that the power of godliness is manifest and that man can see the face of God. IBID.

Brethren, we have the rights and privileges that are associated with the greatest power for good in the universe–the priesthood of God. IBID.

The priesthood is the presiding authority of the Church. IBID.

On all levels of Church activity, in the quorums and auxiliary organizations, Church members preside through the authority of the priesthood they bear or under the direction of the priesthood. IBID.

The priesthood line of authority begins with the Lord and descends from the First Presidency and the Council of the Twelve to the stake president, to the Melchizedek Priesthood quorums and bishop; from the Melchizedek Priesthood quorum to the father, as head of his family; from the bishop to the Aaronic Priesthood quorums, and thus to the family or individual member. All other Church organizations not presided over by officers on this priesthood line of authority are supervised by appropriate priesthood officers. IBID.

The Melchizedek Priesthood quorums are the basic organizations of the Church for (1) teaching the priesthood holder the doctrine of the Church and his duties as a priesthood holder, (2) providing individual and group opportunities for service, (3) providing opportunities for each priesthood holder to enjoy brotherhood with fellow priesthood bearers, and (4) providing for an effective system of watching over the Church (home teaching). IBID.

The word *priesthood* has many different meanings and is used to refer to many different functions. Most specifically, however, it is the power of God, by which He created the earth and all things pertaining to it; by which He creates, governs, and controls the universe and worlds without number; and by which the plan of salvation and exaltation operates. IBID.

Those who receive the priesthood receive the right to exercise great power. However, we must be schooled in the use of this power, and this training is acquired only as we learn to live according to the principles of righteousness. IBID.

If a priesthood holder will magnify his priesthood calling, all that the Father has shall be given him (D&C 84:33-39). *PRIESTHOOD STUDY GUIDE,* 1975

The priesthood bearer's first and greatest responsibility is to bless and teach those of his own household. He is to serve as a loving husband and as an example of righteousness to his children. He is also called to be a strength to his quorum, his church, and his community in building the kingdom of God. *PRIESTHOOD STUDY GUIDE,* 1974

The priesthood is for the blessing of all—men, women, and children. Through the priesthood we receive and administer the ordinances of the gospel, which include baptism, confirmation, the sacrament, all temple ordinances, including sealings for time and all eternity, and work for the dead. By the power of the priesthood the sick are healed, the lame made to walk, the blind to see, and the deaf to hear, according to their faith and the will of our Father in Heaven. Blessings of the priesthood comfort those who mourn, and give aid to the stricken. N. ELDON TANNER, "FIRST PRESIDENCY MESSAGE," *ENSIGN*, JUNE 1973

Ordination to the priesthood is an eternal endowment, lost only through transgression and subsequent excommunication from the Church. FIRST PRESIDENCY TO WAYNE B. HALES, MAR. 23, 1972

The priesthood was first given to Adam. He is the head of all gospel dispensations. Through the priesthood, the kingdom of God (the Church) was established on Earth in order to help man govern himself properly. "BASIC DOCTRINES," 1971

The power of the priesthood, through the divine patriarchal order, aids the home in fulfilling its function as the basis of the righteous life. IBID.

Priesthood, when it is conferred on any man, comes as a blessing from God, not of men. FIRST PRESIDENCY TO ALL STAKE AND MISSION PRESIDENTS, DEC. 15, 1969

Holders of the priesthood are ordained representatives of the Savior on Earth. When the priesthood bearer represents Jesus worthily, he becomes a light unto the world. *PRIESTHOOD STUDY GUIDE,* 1967

The Lord has placed upon parents the obligation of teaching the gospel to their children. Thus a father has a major responsibility to his family. A priesthood member, as a father, can render no greater service than to influence his family to walk uprightly before the Lord through understanding and adopting the total priesthood program of the Church. *PRIESTHOOD STUDY GUIDE*, 1965

Since the priesthood is the authority of the Lord to man to officiate in His name, it is clearly His right to bestow it or to withhold it according to His will, and it is no man's right or prerogative to complain. A. HAMER REISER, ASSISTANT SECRETARY TO THE FIRST PRESIDENCY, TO JOHN W. FITZGERALD, JAN. 12, 1959

The quorums of the priesthood provide organizations through which the purposes of the Lord with respect to the priesthood may be more completely accomplished. Objectively, the quorum has two chief purposes: (1) To help every individual member of the quorum, and his family, to attain a condition of thorough well-being in body, mind, and spirit. Every need of a man holding the priesthood should be the concern of the quorum to which he belongs. (2) To help the Church itself in the accomplishment of the divine duties imposed upon it by training and developing quorum members to understand and perform the work in which the Church is engaged.

This means that in all quorum activities a quorum of priesthood must keep in mind the threefold duty resting upon the Church, namely:

1. To keep the members of the Church in the way of their full duty.

2. To teach the gospel to those who have not yet heard it or accepted it.

3. To provide for the dead, through the ordinances of the temple, the means by which the dead, if obedient, may participate in the blessings that are enjoyed by those who have merited citizenship in the kingdom of God.

A priesthood quorum, to magnify its opportunities and to justify its existence, must develop its members for greater fitness to aid in these three great divisions of Church activity.

The four primary objectives of quorums should be:

1. To become better acquainted, through careful study, with the doctrines of the gospel and their applications to life.

2. To render regularly some service to the Church.

3. To care for the personal welfare of every quorum member, temporally, intellectually, and spiritually.

4. To engage in varied activities, such as socials, outings, athletics, etc., through which quorum members may be provided means to meet adequately their social needs individually and as a family, and to extend a feeling of fellowship, faith, and love that shall meet all the needs of membership.

If the quorum thus assumes responsibility for the welfare of its members, it follows that each member must dedicate himself to the task imposed upon the quorum. A man who accepts the priesthood accepts the obligations of the priesthood and is expected to be loyal and faithful to the Church, the quorum, the priesthood which he holds, to his family, and to every principle of divine truth. *PRIESTHOOD HANDBOOK,* 1948

Physical defects should not ordinarily bar a person from receiving the priesthood, provided he is mentally alert, capable of being instructed, and able to understand the duties and responsibilities that pertain to the priesthood. IBID.

Persons who are mentally deficient should not be ordained to the priesthood. IBID.

For a long time, the General Authorities of the Church have felt that not enough care has been exercised in ordaining men to offices in the priesthood. There are in the Church thousands of men holding the Melchizedek Priesthood who are inactive. Many of these men never understood the full meaning of priesthood, nor the obligation they accepted to magnify their callings, when they were ordained. The Lord has made very clear in several revelations, notably sections 20:38-66; 84:32-42; and the entire revelation known as section 107, the importance of faithfulness and cleanliness of life on the part of those who are ordained to the priesthood.

This laxity in ordaining has resulted in many men, who have received the priesthood and were not really worthy, returning to their evil habits and indifferent ways, if these were ever forsaken. Because of this condition, presiding officers of stakes are asked to use care and discretion in approving candidates for ordination and be sure that they are living in full accord with the principles of the gospel and the doctrines of the Church. Moreover, presiding officers should faithfully impress upon all candidates for ordination the seriousness and responsibility which ordination to the priesthood entails and the dreadful consequences of disobedience or the violation of the covenants which are received when offices in the priesthood are conferred (see D&C 84:32-42). CHURCH HANDBOOK, 1944

The authority of Church government is vested in the holy priesthood of which there are two divisions—the Melchizedek Priesthood, which deals primarily with spiritual affairs, and the Aaronic Priesthood, which derives its authority from the Melchizedek Priesthood and deals with temporal affairs. *CHURCH HANDBOOK,* 1934

Any ceremony, pretending to bind man and woman together beyond the period of mortal life, which is not solemnized by one who has been commissioned and authorized by the man who holds the keys of authority to bind upon earth with a covenant which will be binding in heaven is of no efficacy or force when people are out of the world.

There is but one person on the earth at a time upon whom the keys of this sealing ordinance are conferred. That man is the presiding high priest, the President of the Church. He is the bearer of this authority, which he may exercise personally or he may commission others to exercise it under his jurisdiction, for such time, long or short, up to the end of his life, as he may desire. *DESERET NEWS*, JUNE 17, 1933, IN *MESSAGES*, 5:315-30

One of the specific duties of the priesthood is to teach. *IMPROVEMENT ERA,* DEC. 1920, IN *MESSAGES,* 5:184

Priesthood is not given for the honor or aggrandizement of man but for the ministry of service among those for whom the bearers of that sacred commission are called to labor. *LIAHONA,* FEB. 24, 1914, IN *MESSAGES,* 4:303-304

Everyone called to hold any office in the priesthood, whether of Aaron or Melchizedek, must be called by prophecy and by the laying on of hands to such ordination and be accepted and sustained as such by the proper order of the Church of Christ. FIRST PRESIDENCY TO BEN E. RICH, MAY 1, 1912

Priesthood and people are inseparable and, vindicated or condemned, stand together. *IMPROVEMENT ERA,* MAY 1907, IN *MESSAGES,* 4:143-55

The Lord has given us no particular form for ordination to the priesthood, and the Church recognizes none. FIRST PRESIDENCY TO JAMES R. MOFFETT, JAN. 6, 1905

It is our understanding that when a person is ordained a deacon, with all that pertains to that office sealed upon you, it is tantamount to conferring upon him the Aaronic Priesthood and ordaining him to the office of deacon, and so also in regard to the ordination of an elder. When a man is ordained an elder, it is understood that the Melchizedek Priesthood is conferred upon him whether the officiating elder expressed the fact or not in the ordination; and it is by virtue and authority of this priesthood that the elder performs the duties of his office. IBID.

The leading fact to be remembered is that the priesthood is greater than any of its offices and that any man holding the Melchizedek Priesthood may, by virtue of its possession, perform any ordinance pertaining thereto, or connected therewith, when called upon to do so by one holding the proper authority, which proper authority is vested in the President of the Church or in any whom he may designate. Every officer in the Church is under his direction, and he is directed of God. He is also selected of the Lord to be the head of the Church, and so becomes when the priesthood of the Church (which includes its officers) and its members shall have so accepted and upheld him (D&C 107:22). No man can justly presume to have authority to preside merely by virtue of his priesthood, ... for in addition, he must be chosen and accepted by the Church.... An office in the priesthood is a calling, like apostle, high priest, seventy, elder, and derives all its authority from that priesthood; these officers hold different callings but the same priesthood. *IMPROVEMENT ERA,* MAY 1902, IN *MESSAGES,* 4:42-44

[I]t has once in a while been found that men have been ordained to the priesthood who are unworthy of it or who cannot honor it but yet do nothing that would render them liable to excommunication. We can easily imagine a cause where a man, by weakness of mind, might bring disrepute upon the priesthood, yet be a faithful Saint according to miscellaneous intelligence. In other cases, men have done evil to an extent that they were considered unworthy to hold the priesthood, but the spirit of mercy suggested that they be permitted to retain a standing as members in the Church, and it has been so decided. WILFORD WOODRUFF AND GEORGE Q. CANNON TO MATTHEW NOALL, NOV. 19, 1892

[T]he eternal and everlasting priesthood is bestowed upon us for the purpose alone of administering in the ordinances of life and salvation, both for the living and the dead, and no man on Earth can use that priesthood for any other purpose than for the work of the ministry, the perfecting of the Saints, edifying the body of Christ, establishing the kingdom of heaven, and redeeming Zion. If we attempt to use it for unrighteous purposes, like lightning from heaven, our power, sooner or later, falls and we fail to accomplish the designs of God. *MILLENNIAL STAR,* AUG. 29, 1887, IN *MESSAGES,* 3:130-32

The written word alone never was, is not now, and never will be the only and sole guide of the Church.

God's revelation to Adam was not sufficient for Enoch or Noah; nor that [which was revealed] to either of the [antediluvian] patriarchs for Abraham; nor these [as given] to them, or to any who had gone before him, for Moses or the prophets; nor that which they received sufficient for Jesus and the apostles, nor the word given to the apostles for Joseph Smith; nor that to Joseph Smith for the present. A living priesthood has always been needed, which priesthood has guided, directed, and manipulated the officers in their day, they being guided in the past by former revelations and in the truth by the living word. JOHN TAYLOR TO I. F. ATWOOD, JAN. 10, 1883

This high priesthood, or apostleship, holds the keys of the kingdom of God and power to bind on earth that which shall be bound in heaven and to loose on earth that which shall be loosed in heaven. And, in fine, to do, and to administer in, all things pertaining to the ordinances, organizations, government, and direction of the kingdom of God. STATEMENT, APR. 6, 1845, IN *MESSAGES,* 1:252-66

priesthood ordinances

In the Church, an ordinance is a sacred, formal act performed by the authority of the priesthood. Some ordinances are essential to our exaltation. These ordinances are called saving ordinances. They include baptism, confirmation, ordination to the Melchizedek Priesthood (for men), the temple endowment, and the marriage sealing. With each of these ordinances, we enter into solemn covenants with the Lord.

Other ordinances, such as naming and blessing children, consecrating oil, and administering to the sick and afflicted, are also performed by priesthood authority. While they are not essential to our salvation, they are important for our comfort, guidance, and encouragement. *TRUE TO FAITH,* 2004

An ordinance is a sacred act, such as baptism, that is performed by the authority of the priesthood. The ordinances of baptism, confirmation, Melchizedek Priesthood ordination (for men), and the temple endowment and sealing are required for exaltation for all accountable persons. These are called the saving ordinances. As part of each saving ordinance, the recipient makes covenants with God. *CHURCH HANDBOOK,* 1998

When contemplating ordinances for a person who has a mental disability, priesthood leaders and parents prayerfully consider the person's wishes and degree of understanding.

Ordinances should not be withheld if the person is worthy, wants to receive them, and demonstrates an appropriate degree of responsibility and accountability. Living persons whose disabilities cause them to have the mental capacity of little children may not be accountable (see D&C 29:46-50). The saving ordinances do not need to be performed for these persons. IBID.

If an ordinance is to be valid, there are certain requirements that must be met in its performance. The one performing the ordinance should have prepared himself to be guided by the Holy Spirit and the ordinance must–

1. Be authorized by the person holding the proper keys of the priesthood.
2. Be performed by the authority of the priesthood.
3. Be performed in the name of Jesus Christ.
4. Entail the essential features of its performance, such as using appropriate words, laying on of hands, and using consecrated oil in anointing the sick.

All members of the priesthood should know how to perform ordinances they are authorized to perform. *CHURCH HANDBOOK,* 1976

When we participate in any priesthood ordinance, we need to prepare ourselves so that we are worthy of calling upon the Lord and representing Him. Often this may require repentance on the part of each of us participating in the ordinance. And the result of a worthily performed ordinance will be an outpouring of the Holy Spirit. *PRINCIPLES,* 1976

Outside of temple ordinances, the Church has but three fixed prayers in its ordinance work–two for the sacrament and one for baptism. The Church has always carefully refrained from using prescribed forms in prayers because our rules and doctrines require that we rely upon the direction of the Spirit to guide us in such matters. *CHURCH NEWS*, FEB. 6, 1954

Those who hold the priesthood in The Church of Jesus Christ of Latter-day Saints are divinely commissioned with the authority to perform holy ordinances that are essential to the happiness and eternal welfare of our Father's children.

There are few set forms in the Church. The Holy Spirit directs the priesthood.

Rather than following set forms, the brethren should live so that they may have the inspiration of the Spirit of God when called upon to officiate in the ordinances. Then their prayers will be simple, direct, appropriate, and effective in the sight of God.

The only forms, either for prayers or ordinances outside the temple, in which the wording is specifically prescribed are those pertaining to baptism and the administration of the sacrament. These may be found in the twentieth section of the Doctrine and Covenants and in chapters four and five of the Book of Moroni in the Book of Mormon.

No set forms have been revealed in our day pertaining to the blessing of children, confirmation and bestowal of the Holy Ghost, conferring the priesthood, consecration of oil, administering to the sick, and dedication of graves. The two essential elements in all of the foregoing are that each ordinance shall be performed by the authority of the priesthood and in the name of Jesus Christ. In confirmation it is essential that the Holy Ghost is bestowed. ...

Brethren officiating in ordinances should not repeat memorized prayers, except in the two cases referred to above, but exercise the privilege of blessing people and performing other ordinances under the inspiration of the Lord. It follows that faith, humility, and purity of life should rule the lives of all bearing the priesthood that "the vessels of the Lord" might be pure and receptive to the inspiration and direction of the Almighty. *CHURCH NEWS,* DEC. 27, 1947, QUOTING *INSTRUCTIONS IN ORDINANCE WORK*

Common sense, under peculiar circumstances, guided by the influence and wisdom of the good Spirit, will always prove acceptable to the Lord in the performance of every duty required at the hands of the priesthood, while technicalities will always prove a stumbling block in the path of the people and an impediment to the true progress of the work of God. JOSEPH F. SMITH TO ALMA L. SMITH, DEC. 21, 1875

probation. *See also* Church discipline

Formal probation is an action taken by a disciplinary council to restrict or suspend some of a transgressor's privileges of Church membership in ways that the council specifies. These restrictions could include or go beyond those imposed by informal probation. Positive conditions similar to those imposed by informal probation could also be prescribed. *CHURCH HANDBOOK,* 1998

Informal probation is a means for a presiding officer to restrict some of a transgressor's privileges of Church membership in ways that the officer specifies. Such restrictions may include suspending the right to partake of the sacrament, hold a Church position, exercise the priesthood, and enter a temple. IBID.

procreation

The first commandment that God gave to Adam and Eve pertained to their potential for parenthood as husband and wife. We declare that God's commandment for His children to multiply and replenish the earth [Gen. 1:28] remains in force. We further declare that God has commanded that the sacred powers of procreation are to be employed only between man and woman, lawfully wed as husband and wife.

We declare the means by which mortal life is created to be divinely appointed. *CHURCH NEWS,* SEPT. 30, 1995

Parents should teach their children the sacred nature of procreative powers and instill in them a desire to be chaste in thought and deed. FIRST PRESIDENCY TO ALL MEMBERS OF THE CHURCH OF JESUS CHRIST OF LATTER-DAY SAINTS, NOV. 14, 1991

The Lord has told us that it is the duty of every husband and wife to obey the command given to Adam to multiply and replenish the earth [Gen. 1:28], so that the legions of choice spirits waiting for their tabernacles of flesh may come here and move forward under God's great design to become perfect souls, for without these fleshly tabernacles they cannot progress to their God-planned destiny. Thus, every husband and wife should become a father and a mother in Israel to children born under the holy, eternal covenant. *IMPROVEMENT ERA,* NOV. 1942, IN *MESSAGES*, 6:170-85

profanity

How can anyone who regards himself or herself as a child of God stoop to the use of foul and filthy language concerning the body which is made in the image of God and which, as He has declared, is the temple of the spirit? GORDON B. HINCKLEY, "FIRST PRESIDENCY MESSAGE," *ENSIGN,* JUNE 1996

How you speak and the words you use tell much about the image you choose to portray. Use language to build and uplift those around you. Profane, vulgar, or crude language and inappropriate or off-color jokes are offensive to the Lord. They harm your spirit and degrade you. Don't lower yourself to use such language or jokes, even if people around you do. Never misuse the name of God or Jesus Christ. *STRENGTH OF YOUTH,* 1990

The seriousness of profanity should never be ignored simply because it is so widespread. *PRINCIPLES,* 1976

On the stage, on the telephone, sensitive ears and eyes are outraged daily by the unwarranted and blasphemous use of the names of the Lord our God. In the club, on the farm, in social circles, in business, and in every walk of life the names of the Redeemer are used presumptuously and sinfully. We who are thoughtless and careless, and we who are vicious and defiant, should remember that we cannot take the name of the Lord in vain with impunity. Are we not inviting eventual destruction as we desecrate all things holy and sacred, even to the common and irreverent use in our daily talk of the names of Deity? SPENCER W. KIMBALL, "FIRST PRESIDENCY MESSAGE," *ENSIGN,* FEBRUARY 1971

prophecy. ***See also*** **revelation**

As a messenger of God, a prophet receives priesthood authority, commandments, prophecies, and revelations from God. His responsibility is to make known God's will and true character to mankind and to show the meaning of His dealings with them. A prophet denounces sin and foretells its consequences. He is a preacher of righteousness. On occasion, a prophet may be inspired to foretell the future for the benefit of mankind. His primary responsibility, however, is to bear witness of Christ. *PREACH MY GOSPEL,* 2005

Those who listen to and follow the counsel of living prophets and apostles will not go astray. The teachings of living prophets provide an anchor of eternal truth in a world of shifting values and help us avoid misery and sorrow. The confusion and strife of the world will not overwhelm us, and we can enjoy the assurance of being in harmony with God's will. IBID.

Like the prophets of old, prophets today testify of Jesus Christ and teach His gospel. They make known God's will and true character. They speak boldly and clearly, denouncing sin and warning of its consequences. At times, they may be inspired to prophesy of future events for our benefit. *TRUE TO FAITH*, 2004

We testify that the spirit of prophecy and revelation is among us. "We believe all that God has revealed, all that He does now reveal; and we believe that He will yet reveal many great and important things pertaining to the kingdom of God" (AofF 1:9). The heavens are not sealed; God continues to speak to his children through a prophet empowered to declare his word, now as he did anciently. *CHURCH NEWS*, APR. 12, 1980

It is foolish to suppose that men can be left to their own devices and accomplish what God intended for them. That is just as unreasonable as it would be to leave a newborn babe on its own and expect it to learn to walk and talk and feed and clothe itself without assistance from those responsible for its care and training. A child so neglected and left alone would soon perish.

So it is with us. Without a knowledge and understanding of the gospel, or God's plan for His children, we cannot live according to the law which is necessary for our salvation; and therefore, those who neglect their spiritual training or fail to heed the warning voice of the prophets will suffer a spiritual death. N. ELDON TANNER, "FIRST PRESIDENCY MESSAGE," *ENSIGN*, AUG. 1979

Latter-day Saints should be able to accept the words of the

prophets without having to wait for science to prove the validity of their words. We are most fortunate to have a living prophet at the head of the Church to guide us, and all who heed his counsel will be partakers of the promised blessings which will not be enjoyed by those who fail to accept his messages. IBID.

[W]e take occasion to call the attention of our missionaries to the unwisdom of any attempt to set dates and times for the fulfillment of prophecy. As stated in the Ninth Article of Faith, "We believe all that God has revealed, all that He does now reveal, and we believe that He will yet reveal many great and important things pertaining to the Kingdom of God." We accept the revelations, we believe in the prophecies. The time of fulfillment is in the unfathomable wisdom of the Lord. It is well to teach all people to be prepared for the fulfillment of prophecy, and leave all else to Him. FIRST PRESIDENCY TO PRESIDENTS OF STAKES AND STAKE MISSION PRESIDENTS, MAR. 2, 1959

The reason why a prophet is not without honor, save in his own country, and among his own kin, is the want of faith and confidence among his countrymen. *MILLENNIAL STAR,* FEB. 15, 1851, IN *MESSAGES,* 2:51-61

Protestant reformers. *See also* religions (non-LDS)

The reformers were pioneers, blazing wilderness trails in a desperate search for those lost points of reference that they felt would lead mankind back to the truth Jesus taught.

Wycliffe, Luther, Hus, Zwingli, Knox, Calvin, and Tyndale all pioneered during the period of the Reformation. THOMAS S. MONSON, "FIRST PRESIDENCY MESSAGE," *ENSIGN,* AUG. 2006

Puritans. *See also* religions (non-LDS)

It was not by chance that the Puritans left their native land

and sailed away to the shores of New England and that others followed later. They were the advance guard of the army of the Lord, predestined to establish the God-given system of government under which we live and to make of America, which is the land of Joseph, the gathering place of Ephraim, an asylum for the oppressed of all nations and prepare the way for the restoration of the gospel of Christ and the re-establishment of His Church upon the earth. It was under these circumstances, and others of which the Lord was the author, that the stage was set for the raising of the curtain upon the opening scene of the dispensation of the fullness of times. *IMPROVEMENT ERA,* MAY 1930, IN *Messages,* 5:274-86.

R

race. *See also* Israel, house of

[T]he glories of salvation and eternal happiness and progress are secured to all the posterity of Adam, through obedience to the gospel of Jesus Christ, who died for all, no matter what their color or race may be. FIRST PRESIDENCY TO BEN E. RICH, MAY 1, 1912

So far as we know, there is no revelation, ancient or modern, neither is there any authoritative statement by any of the authorities of The Church of Jesus Christ of Latter-day Saints in support of that which many of our elders have advanced as doctrine, in effect that the negroes are those who were neutral in heaven at the time of the great conflict or war, which resulted in the casting out of Lucifer and those who were led by him, said to number about one-third of the hosts of heaven. FIRST PRESIDENCY TO MILTON H. KNUDSON, JAN. 13, 1912

rape, *see* sexual abuse

Relief Society, *see* women

religions (non-LDS). *See also* Islam; Judaism; Protestant reformers; Puritans; tolerance

You know and we know that there are many good people in other churches. There is much of good in them. GORDON B. HINCKLEY, "FIRST PRESIDENCY MESSAGE," *ENSIGN,* OCT. 2006

The great religious leaders of the world such as Mohammed, Confucius, and the Reformers, as well as philosophers including Socrates, Plato, and others, received a portion of God's light. Moral truths were given to them by God to enlighten whole nations and to bring a higher level of understanding to individuals.

The Hebrew prophets prepared the way for the coming of Jesus Christ, the promised Messiah, who should provide salvation for all mankind who believe in the gospel.

Consistent with these truths, we believe that God has given and will give to all peoples sufficient knowledge to help them on their way to eternal salvation, either in this life or in the life to come. "STATEMENT OF THE FIRST PRESIDENCY REGARDING GOD'S GUIDANCE TO ALL MANKIND," FEB. 15, 1978

repentance. *See also* confession; forgiveness

Repentance involves a change of heart and a desire to forsake sin and serve God. It involves humbly yielding to the Spirit and submitting to God's will. It requires that people increase their commitment to live in agreement with God's will. Repentance requires a sincere and lasting change of thoughts, desires, habits, and actions. *PREACH MY GOSPEL,* 2005

Repentance is one of the first principles of the gospel (see AofF 1:4). It is essential to your happiness in this life and throughout eternity. Repentance is much more than just acknowledging wrongdoings. It is a change of mind and heart that gives you a fresh view about God, about yourself, and about the world. It includes turning away from sin and turning to God for forgiveness. It is motivated by love for God and the sincere desire to obey His commandments. *TRUE TO FAITH,* 2004

[R]epentance means more than simply a reformation of behavior. Many men and women in the world demonstrate great willpower and self-discipline in overcoming bad habits and the weaknesses of the flesh. Yet at the same time they give no thought to the Master, sometimes even openly rejecting Him. Such changes of behavior, even if in a positive direction, do not constitute true repentance.

Faith in the Lord Jesus Christ is the foundation upon which sincere and meaningful repentance must be built. If we truly seek to put away sin, we must first look to Him who is the author of our salvation. EZRA TAFT BENSON, "FIRST PRESIDENCY MESSAGE," *ENSIGN,* OCT. 1989

Regardless of what we believe or how we live, we shall be resurrected, for through the Atonement of Christ redemption from the grave is granted to every soul unconditionally. This is not so, however, with respect to forgiveness and redemption from the effects of our own transgressions. The only persons who are thus forgiven and redeemed are those who accept and abide the terms prescribed by the Redeemer, thus bringing themselves, with respect to their own sins, within the reach of His atoning blood. MARION G. ROMNEY, "FIRST PRESIDENCY MESSAGE," *ENSIGN,* APR. 1985

That man who resists temptation and lives without sin is far better off than the man who has fallen, no matter how repentant the latter may be. The reformed transgressor, it is true, may be more understanding of one who falls into the same sin, and to that extent perhaps more helpful in the latter's regeneration. But his sin and repentance have certainly not made him stronger than the consistently righteous person. God will forgive—of that, we are sure. How satisfying it is to be cleansed from filthiness, but how much better it is never to have committed the sin! SPENCER W. KIMBALL, "FIRST PRESIDENCY MESSAGE," *ENSIGN,* MAR. 1982

Repentance is one of the basic principles of the gospel and

consists of a change of attitude and action away from worldly and sinful desires to spiritual desires. Repentance is a product of faith because when we learn of and believe in the divine mission of the Lord and His love toward men, we desire to serve Him and do His will. Repentance involves a feeling of guilt that prompts us to change our behavior, to replace error and wrong-doing with truth and righteousness. It must be more than a mere verbal acknowledgement of wrong-doing. *PRINCIPLES,* 1976

Repentance is not complete unless the sin is abandoned and a new path in the ways of the Lord is followed. Wanting to change is not repentance. There must be action. An actual change must take place, and much effort may be needed to make the change. Trying is not enough; the effort must be sincere and must result in a change in action and attitude. IBID.

resurrection

Each of us is a dual being of spiritual entity and physical entity. All know of the reality of death when the body dies, and each of us also knows that the spirit lives on as an individual entity and that at some time, under the divine plan made possible by the sacrifice of the Son of God, there will be a reunion of spirit and body. GORDON B. HINCKLEY, "FIRST PRESIDENCY MESSAGE," *ENSIGN,* JULY 2006

Of all the victories in human history, none is so great, none so universal in its effect, none so everlasting in consequences as the victory of the crucified Lord, who came forth in the Resurrection that first Easter morning. *CHURCH NEWS,* APR. 15, 2006

When our bodies and spirits are reunited through the resurrection, we will be brought into God's presence to be judged. We will remember perfectly our righteousness and our guilt. If we have repented, we will receive mercy. We will be rewarded according to our works and our desires. *PREACH MY GOSPEL,* 2005

Resurrection is the reuniting of the spirit with the body in a perfect immortal state, no longer subject to disease or death (see Alma 11:42-45). *TRUE TO FAITH,* 2004

When you die, your spirit will enter the spirit world and await the resurrection. At the time of the resurrection, your spirit and body will reunite, and you will be judged and received into a kingdom of glory. The glory you inherit will depend on the depth of your conversion and your obedience to the Lord's commandments ... IBID.

There are three kingdoms of glory: the celestial kingdom, the terrestrial kingdom, and the telestial kingdom. The glory you inherit will depend on the depth of your conversion, expressed by your obedience to the Lord's commandments. It will depend on the manner in which you have "received the testimony of Jesus" (D&C 76:51; see also vv. 74, 79, 101). IBID.

No event of human history carries a more compelling witness than does the reality of the Resurrection. His [Christ's] followers on two continents testified of it. Uncounted millions of men and women through the ages have suffered, even unto death, for the witness in their hearts that He lives, the Savior and Redeemer of all mankind, whose Atonement came as an act of grace for the entire world. How long and how great is the concourse of brave and humble people who have kept alive the name of Jesus and a testimony of His Redemption! GORDON B. HINCKLEY, "FIRST PRESIDENCY MESSAGE," *ENSIGN,* DEC. 2002

When all is said and done, when all of history is examined,

when the deepest depths of the human mind have been explored, nothing is so wonderful, so majestic, so tremendous as this act of grace when the Son of the Almighty, the Prince of His Father's royal household, He who had once spoken as Jehovah, He who had condescended to come to Earth as a babe born in Bethlehem, gave His life in ignominy and pain so that all of the sons and daughters of God of all generations of time, every one of whom must die, might walk again and live eternally. He did for us what none of us could do for ourselves. GORDON B. HINCKLEY, "FIRST PRESIDENCY MESSAGE," *ENSIGN,* DEC. 2000

This is the promise of the risen Lord. This is the relevance of Jesus to a world in which all must die. As He is the conqueror of death, so also is He the master of life. *CHURCH NEWS,* APR. 22, 2000

By virtue of His loving gift of life, each of us will rise from the grave, body and spirit joined together inseparably throughout eternity.

We proclaim that the "bands of death" (Mosiah 15:8) have, in very deed, been broken for the children of men. Each of us may lay aside all wonder, all fear of the darkness of death and rejoice, "having a perfect brightness of hope" (3 Ne. 31:20). *CHURCH NEWS,* MAR. 22, 1997

One of the most glorious announcements ever made to mortal man was spoken by the angels standing at the recently vacated sepulcher, "He is not here, but is risen" (Luke 24:6). These words bring a comforting assurance to all who ask the question posed so long ago by Job, "If a man die, shall he live again?" (Job 14:14). The witness of the angels and the image of the empty tomb answer this inquiry with a resounding "Yes!" Indeed, we shall all live again, blessed by the gift of the Resurrection. *CHURCH NEWS,* MAR. 30, 1996

The greatest events of history are those which affect the largest numbers for the longest periods. By this standard, no event could be more important to individuals or nations than the Resurrection of the Savior. Because of it, all of our Heavenly Father's children will be resurrected. *CHURCH NEWS,* MAR. 26, 1994

[T]he victory over death is not the only benefit arising from the resurrection of the Messiah; He not only freed all mankind from the bonds of eternal death but, through His Atonement, forgiveness of our individual sins may be obtained. He made it possible for all, through faith, repentance, and obedience to the ordinances and covenants of His gospel, to be forgiven of their sins. IBID.

The Lord's Resurrection completed the process of the Atonement that included His sinless life, His suffering in the Garden of Gethsemane, and His death on the cross. The Resurrection assured immortality for all, and the blessed Atonement provided a pathway to exaltation for those who will adhere to His gospel principles. *CHURCH NEWS,* APR. 3, 1993

The eventual resurrection of every soul who has lived and died on Earth is a scriptural certainty, and surely there is no event for which one should make more careful preparation. A glorious resurrection should be the goal of every man and woman, for it is a reality. Nothing is more absolutely universal than the resurrection. Every living being will be resurrected. "As in Adam all die, even so in Christ shall all be made alive" (1 Cor. 15:22). EZRA TAFT BENSON, "FIRST PRESIDENCY MESSAGE," *ENSIGN,* APR. 1993

The first Easter, the Resurrection of our Lord Jesus Christ, is the greatest and most significant miracle of all time.

We testify that the Resurrection was literal and real. He

brought to every person who ever lives on this earth the privilege of once again having a body, of living again. *CHURCH NEWS,* MAR. 23, 1991

Springtime is symbolic of the Savior's Resurrection. Just as spring inspires renewed hope and new life, so does the resurrection of Jesus Christ. *CHURCH NEWS,* APR. 2, 1988

When we speak of Jesus being resurrected, we mean that His premortal spirit, which animated His mortal body from His birth in the manger until He died on the cross, reentered that body; and the two, His spirit body and His physical body, inseparably welded together, arose from the tomb an immortal soul.

Our belief is, and we so testify, that Jesus not only conquered death for Himself and brought forth His own glorious resurrected body, but that in so doing He also brought about a universal resurrection. This was the end and purpose of the mission for which He was set apart and ordained in the great council in heaven, when He was chosen to be our Savior and Redeemer. MARION G. ROMNEY, "FIRST PRESIDENCY MESSAGE," *ENSIGN,* APR. 1985

Life is eternal. Death does not terminate the existence of man. He lives on and on. Man, whether good or evil, will be resurrected. His spirit will be reunited with his body from the grave, and if he has perfected his life and magnified his God-given opportunities, that spirit and body will be brought together in a new, fresh, never-ending immortality. SPENCER W. KIMBALL, "FIRST PRESIDENCY MESSAGE," *ENSIGN,* AUG. 1974

[S]omewhere in [the] after eternity of life, the body and the spirit will be re-united as an immortal soul in the glorious resurrection after the exact pattern of Him who was the first fruits of the resurrection. STATEMENT, MAY 30, 1937, IN *MESSAGES,* 6:30-36

We believe that by obedience to gospel requirements and standards, family relationships in the hereafter will be restored, that the mother who gave her son as a sacrifice upon the altar of liberty will have that son again hereafter and that the endearing relation of mother and son will continue; we believe that the wife and the children who gave their husband and father that we might have freedom will again join husband and father and that this family, happy and re-united, will as a family go on through eternity. IBID.

These dead shall rise again. Mother and son, wife and husband, father and child shall meet again in an actual life with resurrected bodies, conscious of their earth-life together, to live on forever in that state of joy for which they are willing to live and work. IBID.

[I]n the resurrection there will be no physical defects; and inasmuch as you are the mother of two children, you may rest assured that in the resurrected state you will have the mother instinct and affections, and your bodily organs will be normal. HEBER J. GRANT TO ALICE HALLADAY, SEPT. 7, 1935

As we think of Him, the sting of death is made more tolerable, the victory of the grave is swallowed up in the hope of a glorious resurrection. *DESERET NEWS,* DEC. 16, 1933

In His birth, His ministry and glorious Resurrection, and His ascension into heaven, He symbolized the story of our own lives. He taught us that those mortal bodies of ours shall put on immortality, and that we shall rise as He rose, to inherit the glory of everlasting life. This was the purpose for which He came to earth. *DESERET NEWS,* DEC. 17, 1932, IN *MESSAGES,* 5:312-13

The certainty of the persistence of man's spirit when the body has finished its earthly mission and the progress of the "better part" in worlds eternal, with the fond assurance of an actual resurrection and a reunion of family associations ordered under divine laws and covenants, robs death of its terrors and sheds light upon the darkness of sorrow or doubt. *DESERET NEWS,* DEC. 16, 1916, IN *MESSAGES,* 5:43-48

The second death is not a dissolution of the body, or a separation of the spirit from the body, but banishment from the presence of the Lord. JOSEPH F. SMITH TO H. D. ROPER, APR. 3, 1914

They [the dead] are rejoicing, with the hosts who have preceded them, in the progress of the work of salvation there and have a livelier hope and a more certain assurance even than we have of the rapid approach of the time for the second advent of the Lord and the glorious union of Saints with Him when He comes "the second time without sin unto salvation" [Heb. 9:28]. *DESERET NEWS,* DEC. 12, 1912, IN *MESSAGES,* 4:277-82

When the body dies, the spirit does not die. In the resurrected state the body will be immortal, as well as the spirit. *IMPROVEMENT ERA,* MAR. 1912, IN *MESSAGES,* 4:264-65

All temporal, vegetable, and mineral substances, and animal matter in mortal state, are subject to change or dissolution into other forms, but not so with the immortal spirit or beings who are the offspring of God. They cannot dissolve, nor be annihilated. There is no such doctrine as annihilation taught either in the Bible, Book of Mormon, or Doctrine and Covenants, nor in the teachings of Jesus Christ or Joseph Smith. JOSEPH F. SMITH TO JOSEPH R. SMITH, MAR. 24, 1901

We believe in death being swallowed up in victory, in "a new heaven and a new earth, wherein dwelleth righteousness"

[2 Pet. 3:13], in the resurrection of the just, both men and women, parents and children. *MILLENNIAL STAR,* MAY 17, 1886, IN *MESSAGES,* 3:46-71

revelation

[T]he language of the Spirit is gentle, quiet, uplifting to the heart, and soothing to the soul. THOMAS S. MONSON, "FIRST PRESIDENCY MESSAGE," *ENSIGN,* JUNE 2005

Revelation may come through the Light of Christ and the Holy Ghost by way of inspiration, visions, dreams, or visits by angels. Revelation provides guidance that can lead the faithful to eternal salvation in the celestial kingdom. The Lord reveals His work to His prophets and confirms to believers that the revelations to the prophets are true (see Amos 3:7). Through revelation, the Lord provides individual guidance for every person who seeks it and who has faith, repents, and is obedient to the gospel of Jesus Christ. *PREACH MY GOSPEL,* 2005

Individuals are entitled to divine revelation for meeting personal challenges. Parents are entitled to revelation for raising their families. *QUICK FACTS,* 2005

Revelation is communication from God to His children. This guidance comes through various channels according to the needs and circumstances of individuals, families, and the Church as a whole.

When the Lord reveals His will to the Church, He speaks through His prophet. The scriptures contain many such revelations–the world of the Lord through ancient and latter-day prophets. Today the Lord continues to guide the Church by revealing His will to His chosen servants.

Prophets are not the only people who can receive revelation. According to your faithfulness, you can receive revelation to help with your specific needs, responsibilities, and questions, and to help you strengthen your testimony. *TRUE TO FAITH,* 2004

Personal revelation comes as a testimony of truth and as guidance in spiritual and temporal matters. Latter-day Saints know that the promptings of the Spirit may be received upon all facets of life, including daily, ongoing decisions. Without seeking the inspiration of the Almighty God, how could anyone think of making an important decision such as "Who is to be my companion?" "What is my work to be?" "Where will I live?" "How will I live?" JAMES E. FAUST, "FIRST PRESIDENCY MESSAGE," *ENSIGN,* MAR. 2002

How do we recognize the promptings of the Spirit? That which is of Christ does edify, and if we have that feeling of edification, then we may know that the Holy Spirit, the Holy Ghost, is speaking to us. If we are in an attitude of prayer, if we are in an attitude of anxiously seeking the direction of the Spirit, we will receive it. GORDON B. HINCKLEY, "FIRST PRESIDENCY MESSAGE," *ENSIGN,* AUG. 2000

How can we receive the personal blessing of the Master's divine and exalting influence in our own lives? Since our own feelings are sacred to us and cannot be disputed by others, let us begin with those quiet assurances which occasionally can come to all of us and which we know are true. We cannot always prove these verities to others, yet they come as a form of knowledge. Is this part of the divine that ferments within us, reaching to its source? Is it not like the personal witness of truth flowing through the thin curtain that separates this world from another? Is there not a yearning to understand in your mind what is in your heart, a feeling that you cannot give utterance to because it is so unspeakably personal? In answer, the Master said that quiet reality can "speak peace to your mind concerning the matter" (D&C 6:23). JAMES E. FAUST, "FIRST PRESIDENCY MESSAGE," *ENSIGN,* JAN. 1999

Individual members, parents, and leaders have the right to receive revelation for their own responsibilities but have no duty nor right to declare the word of God beyond the limits of their own responsibilities. JAMES E. FAUST, "FIRST PRESIDENCY MESSAGE," *ENSIGN,* AUG. 1996

Frequently God's help comes silently—and though silently, occasionally with dramatic impact. THOMAS S. MONSON, "FIRST PRESIDENCY MESSAGE," *ENSIGN,* JUNE 1989

We hear the words of the Lord most often by a feeling. If we are humble and sensitive, the Lord will prompt us through our feelings. That is why spiritual promptings move us on occasion to great joy, sometimes to tears. EZRA TAFT BENSON, "FIRST PRESIDENCY MESSAGE," *ENSIGN,* APR. 1988

[W]hen we do not keep ourselves advised as to what the counsel of the Lord is, we are prone to substitute our own counsel for His. As a matter of fact, there is nothing else we can do but follow our own counsel when we do not know the Lord's instructions. MARION G. ROMNEY, "FIRST PRESIDENCY MESSAGE," *ENSIGN,* AUG. 1985

We know with certainty where the counsel of the Lord is to be found: (1) in the written word of the Lord, the scriptures; (2) in the counsel of the living prophets; and (3) through personal inspiration and revelation to each of us for guidance within the scope of our own assignments or circumstances. Drinking deeply from these springs of living water will bless each member of the Church. Don't let yourselves be too busy or too tired to so drink. The added strength, wisdom, and inspiration which comes therefrom will repay your efforts a thousandfold. IBID.

You may be sure if there is anything that has substance in regard to the safety and welfare of our people, we will see that the leaders of the Church are immediately advised so that we might act wisely and unitedly in order to not over-react to present situations.

The real danger lies in our people becoming confused and frustrated and looking elsewhere than to their Church leaders or to civil authorities in matters pertaining to their welfare. *CHURCH NEWS*, MAR. 30, 1970

The Church of Jesus Christ of Latter-day Saints owes its origin, its existence, and its hopes for the future to the principle of continuous revelation. FIRST PRESIDENCY TO ALL STAKE AND MISSION PRESIDENTS, DEC. 15, 1969

The Lord does not reveal to us at all times just what His purposes are–it may be doubted whether or not we could understand them even if He tried to reveal them. So whenever in this life we face a crisis, we must do so knowing that the Lord may not always reveal to man His will and that His all-wise will may not accord with what we believe to be wise. Therefore, we should approach the crisis with a determination to abide whatever He sends to us, whether or not it accords with our plans or with our desires. JOSEPH ANDERSON, SECRETARY TO THE FIRST PRESIDENCY, MAR. 2, 1946

Truth has but one source, and all revelations from heaven are harmonious one with the other. *DESERET NEWS,* JULY 18, 1925, QUOTING *IMPROVEMENT ERA,* NOV. 1909

The predictions of good things will come to pass, everything in its season. *DESERET NEWS,* DEC. 22, 1917

When visions, dreams, tongues, prophecy, impressions, or an extraordinary gift of inspiration conveys something out of harmony with the accepted revelations to the Church or contrary to the decisions of its constituted authorities, Latter-day Saints may know that it is not of God, no matter how plausible it may appear. Also, they should understand that directions for the guidance of the Church will come by revelation through the head. All faithful members are entitled to the inspiration of the Holy Spirit for themselves, their families, and for those over whom they are appointed and ordained to preside. But anything at discord with that which comes from God through the head of the Church is not to be received as authoritative or reliable. In secular as well as spiritual affairs, Saints may receive divine guidance and revelation affecting themselves, but this does not convey authority to direct others and is not to be accepted when contrary to Church covenants, doctrine or discipline, or to known facts, demonstrated truths, or good common sense. No person has the right to induce his fellow members of the Church to engage in speculations or take stock in ventures of any kind on the specious claim of divine revelation or vision or dream, especially when it is in opposition to the voice of recognized authority, local or general. The Lord's Church "is a house of order" [D&C 132:8]. It is not governed by individual gifts or manifestations but by the order and power of the holy priesthood as sustained by the voice and vote of the Church in its appointed conferences. *DESERET NEWS,* AUG. 2, 1913, IN *MESSAGES,* 4:285-86

The Lord has also appointed one man at a time on the earth to hold the keys of revelation to the entire body of the Church in all its organizations, authorities, ordinances, and doctrines. The spirit of revelation is bestowed upon all its members for the benefit and enlightenment of each individual receiving its inspiration, and according to the sphere in which he or she is called to labor. But for the entire Church, he who stands at the head is alone appointed to receive revelations by way of commandment and as the end of controversy. *IMPROVEMENT ERA,* APR. 1912, IN *MESSAGES,* 4:270-71

Man, by searching, cannot find out God. Never, unaided, will he discover the truth about the beginning of human life. The Lord must reveal Himself or remain unrevealed; and the same is true of the facts relating to the origin of Adam's race—God alone can reveal them. *IMPROVEMENT ERA,* NOV. 1909, IN *MESSAGES,* 4:200-206

[E]very individual member has the privilege of receiving revelation from the Lord for his guidance in his own affairs and to testify to him concerning the correctness of public teachings and movements. *WOMAN'S EXPONENT,* APR. 15, 1888, IN *MESSAGES,* 3:156-63

[U]pon true faith, repentance, baptism by the proper authority, and the laying on of hands for the reception of the Holy Ghost, it is not only the privilege but the duty of every individual to so live in accordance with the light and requirements of the gospel as to be able to ask and receive revelation from the Almighty at all times and under all circumstances, whenever necessary, to enable him to magnify his calling, roll forth salvation, and honor our Father in Heaven. *MILLENNIAL STAR,* NOV. 18, 1854, IN *MESSAGES,* 2:147-49

Ever remember, dear brethren, that if you would be righteous like your Heavenly Father, His righteousness comes by REVELATION, through your faith. Be content with nothing short of the revealed will of your Heavenly Father; for being built upon this foundation, the floods of error and temptation that must come upon all them that dwell upon the earth will not be able to overthrow you. *MILLENNIAL STAR,* JAN. 14, 1854, IN *MESSAGES,* 2:119-24

We believe that God condescended to speak from the heavens and declare His will concerning the human family, to give them just and holy laws, to regulate their conduct, and guide them in a direct way, that in due time He might take them to Himself and make them joint heirs with His Son. STATEMENT, JAN. 22, 1834, IN *MESSAGES,* 1:23-44

[I]f we have direct revelations given us from heaven, surely those revelations were never given to be trifled with, without the trifler's incurring displeasure and vengeance upon his own head, if there is any justice in heaven, and that there is must be admitted by every individual who admits the truth and force of God's teachings, His blessings and cursings, as contained in the sacred volume [of scripture]. IBID.

reverence

An atmosphere of reverence invites the Spirit of the Lord to be present in sacrament meetings. We see an urgent need to teach the members, young and old, to be reverent in all meetings, particularly those held in the chapel. "DEAR BRETHREN," JAN. 26, 1987

Reverence is the soul of true religion. Its seedbed is sincerity. Its quality is determined by the esteem in which one holds the object of his reverence, as evidenced by his behavior toward that object. When that object is *God,* the genuinely reverent person has a worshipful adoration coupled with a respectful behavior toward Him and all that pertains to Him. The want of such appreciation or behavior smacks of irreverence. MARION G. ROMNEY, "FIRST PRESIDENCY MESSAGE," *ENSIGN,* OCT. 1976

Reverence is the feeling and showing of deep respect, honor, and love. Reverence should accompany all our thoughts and actions relating to God, "before whose throne all things bow in humble reverence, and give him glory forever and ever" (D&C 76:92). We cannot worship God without reverence. *PRINCIPLES,* 1976

We believe the quality of reverence in stake meetings reflects the degree to which reverence is observed in ward and branch meetings. "DEAR BRETHREN," SEPT. 5, 1974

Reverence for God and for sacred things is fundamental in pure religion. "DEAR BRETHREN," MAY 2, 1946, IN *MESSAGES,* 6:252-53

S

Sabbath

Our Sabbath-day behavior is a reflection of our commitment to honor and worship God. By keeping the Sabbath day holy, we show God our willingness to keep our covenants. *PREACH MY GOSPEL,* 2005

When a community or nation grows careless in its Sabbath activities, its religious life decays and all aspects of life are negatively affected. The blessings associated with keeping the Sabbath day holy are lost. IBID.

Because the Sabbath is a holy day, it should be reserved for worthy and holy activities. Abstaining from work and recreation is not enough. In fact, it we merely lounge about doing nothing on the Sabbath, we fail to keep the day holy. *TRUE TO FAITH,* 2004

Observing the Sabbath will bring you closer to the Lord and to your family. It will give you needed rest and rejuvenation. *STRENGTH OF YOUTH,* 2001

Wherever possible, Sunday meetings, other than those under the three-hour schedule and perhaps council meetings on early Sunday mornings or firesides later in the evening, should be avoided so that parents may be with their children. FIRST PRESIDENCY TO MEMBERS OF THE CHURCH THROUGHOUT THE WORLD, FEB. 11, 1999; *CHURCH NEWS,* FEB. 27, 1999

Since the creation of the earth, the Sabbath day has been established by God for the spiritual well-being of His children. Throughout generations of time, the sacred law of the Sabbath has been upheld by the prophets of God as a holy observance to help sanctify and bring joy to those who would keep the commandments of the Lord. So important is this matter that the observance of the Sabbath was one of the Ten Commandments written by the finger of the Lord on Mount Sinai. *CHURCH NEWS*, OCT. 17, 1992

We sense that many Latter-day Saints have become lax in their observance of the Sabbath day. We should refrain from shopping on the Sabbath and participating in other commercial and sporting activities that now commonly desecrate the Sabbath.

We urge all Latter-day Saints to set this holy day apart from activities of the world and consecrate themselves by entering into a spirit of worship, thanksgiving, service, and family-centered activities appropriate to the Sabbath. As Church members endeavor to make their Sabbath activities compatible with the intent and Spirit of the Lord, their lives will be filled with joy and peace. IBID.

Many activities are appropriate for the Sabbath; however, it is not a holiday. You should avoid seeking entertainment or spending money on this day. *STRENGTH OF YOUTH,* 1990

Sunday should be a time for families to fulfill their Sunday duties, be together, and study the gospel. *BULLETIN,* FEB. 1982

We have become largely a world of Sabbath breakers. On the Sabbath the lakes are full of boats, the beaches are crowded, the shows have their best attendance, the golf links are dotted with players. The Sabbath is the preferred day for rodeos, conventions, family picnics; even ball games are played on the sacred day. "Business as usual" is the slogan for many, and our holy day has become a holiday. And because so many people treat the day as a holiday, numerous others cater to the wants of the fun-lovers and money-makers.

To many, Sabbath breaking is a matter of little moment, but to our Heavenly Father it is disobedience to one of the principal commandments. SPENCER W. KIMBALL, "FIRST PRESIDENCY MESSAGE," *ENSIGN,* JAN. 1978

The Sabbath calls for constructive thoughts and acts, and if one merely lounges about doing nothing on the Sabbath, he is breaking it. To observe it, one will be on his knees in prayer, preparing lessons, studying the gospel, meditating, visiting the ill and distressed, writing letters to missionaries, taking a nap, reading wholesome material, and attending all the meetings of that day at which he is expected. IBID.

Sabbath observance is the order of the Church and is one of the basic commandments of the Lord. Hiking and camping trips on Sunday are not approved. *CHURCH HANDBOOK,* 1976

The Church accepts the commandment given by the Lord that men are to rest from all temporal work and to worship the Lord one day each week. Sunday is the day set aside by the Church to observe the Sabbath. Rest on this day, though important, is incidental to the true purpose of the Sabbath which is to worship, to learn more about the Lord, to renew covenants with Him, and to feed our souls upon the things of the Spirit. "ATTITUDES," 1974

The attention of the young people, especially, should be directed frequently to the word of the Lord to His people and the teachings of the Church in relation to proper observance of the Sabbath day. With so many people making Sunday a day of pleasure and sport, some continuing their work the same as on other days, others engaging in fishing, hunting, resort parties, canyon trips, or attending moving picture shows and baseball games, and even some churches setting examples of activity clearly in violation of the commandments, young people are likely to become confused in their thinking and misled in their standards.

Latter-day Saints should be leaders of the world in observing both the letter and the spirit of the commandments to make Sunday a day of rest, worship, and religious devotion. Parents and leaders in the Church organizations should set examples as well as teaching proper observance of the Sabbath. The Lord has made His will known in language clear enough for all to understand. He has also promised glorious blessings to those who obey. It has been emphasized that immediate blessings of health of body and mind and of increased efficiency will come to those who follow His teachings.

Outdoor seasons present increased temptations to violate the Sabbath. Latter-day Saints should be on guard and make every effort to obey the law. There are six other days in which to secure recreation and to engage in relaxing and beneficial activities, but on Sunday we should "remember the Sabbath day, to keep it holy" [Ex. 20:8]. *CHURCH HANDBOOK,* 1940

[A]nything that tends to dull our sense of spirituality or makes us less responsive to the inspiration of the Lord should be avoided, and this applies particularly to men and women who have been called to positions of responsibility in the Church. DAVID O. MCKAY TO JESSE W. RICHINS, JUNE 25, 1935

[K]eeping the Sabbath day holy means resting from one's labors and worshipping the Lord. In the attainment of these purposes, there must be a cessation as far as practicable from one's daily occupation, and a turning of one's thoughts and actions to spiritual things. Nor is it sufficient to seek this spirituality as individuals alone; we are admonished to go to the house of prayer and there "offer sacraments to the Most High, and confess our sins unto our brethren before the Lord" [D&C 59:12]. "Offering sacraments" means to express devotion to God in songs of praise and thanksgiving, to partake of the sacrament in renewal of sacred covenants, and to increase love and fellowship one for another. HEBER J. GRANT TO MURCY NELSON, MAR. 29, 1935

The Lord's day is a holy day–not a holiday. It has been set apart as a day of rest and worship. A sacred Sabbath begets reverence for God. It is not pleasing in His sight that the day be given over to pleasure seeking in places of amusement or elsewhere. *LIAHONA,* OCT. 8, 1940, IN *MESSAGES,* 5:260

sacrament

Church members meet on the Sabbath to worship God and partake of the sacrament (see D&C 20:75; 59:9). During this holy ordinance, they partake of bread and water in remembrance of the Savior's flesh and blood and to renew their baptismal covenants (see Matt. 26:26-28; JST, Mark 14:20-25; Luke 22:15-20; 3 Ne. 18; Moro. 6:6). *CHURCH HANDBOOK,* 1998

Each time we partake of the sacrament, not only do we do it in remembrance of the sacrifice of the Son of God, who gave His life for each of us, but there is an added element that we take upon ourselves the name of Jesus Christ and pledge ourselves to keep His commandments, and He pledges with us that He will bless us with His Holy Spirit. We are a covenant people, and great are the obligations which go with that covenant. GORDON B. HINCKLEY, "FIRST PRESIDENCY MESSAGE," *ENSIGN,* AUG. 1997

Sacrament meeting is held for members to partake of the sacrament, worship reverently, and receive gospel instruction.

Families should be encouraged to attend as a family and to sit together.

Bishoprics plan all sacrament meetings and conduct them in a reverent and dignified manner. Bishoprics should not overprogram sacrament meetings and should be sure they end on time. *CHURCH HANDBOOK,* 1983

Sacrament meeting is a priesthood meeting held for the purpose of gathering families together to partake of the sacrament, to worship, and to be instructed in the gospel. *CHURCH HANDBOOK,* 1976

Sacrament meetings are for the entire membership of the ward, including children. Every effort should be made to have all of the young people of the ward attend. Attending and sitting together as family units should be encouraged. IBID.

On occasion there are families who find it almost impossible to attend sacrament meeting because they live a great distance from their ward. Since every member of the Church should have the spiritual blessings of partaking of the sacrament, it is permissible for a family in the above situation, when approved by the bishop, to hold a sacrament service in their home under the direction of the father, who must hold the appropriate priesthood to administer the sacrament. IBID.

Administration of the sacrament involves participation in one of the most sacred and holy ordinances in the Church. Those involved are placing before the Saints the sacramental emblems as a remembrance of the renewal of the covenants they have made with the Lord. Every young man participating should be taught that he is administering this ordinance to the Saints on behalf of the Lord and that it should be approached with a solemn, reverent attitude. Conduct at the sacrament table should be one of total dignity. IBID.

The sacrament is a priesthood ordinance through which the Saints worship Christ, witness to the Father their faith in Christ, and renew their covenants to obey His commandments and to serve Him. The sacrament consists of bread and water, symbolizing the flesh and the blood of the Savior and His sacrifice for us. *PRINCIPLES,* 1976

The sacrament meeting should be like a family gathering where as many as possible may participate in the exercises and all worship in love, reverence, and fellowship. *CHURCH HANDBOOK*, 1940

The sacramental meeting is the most important one held in the ward, and as such should receive first consideration. It is the duty of the bishopric to see that every meeting is made as instructive and interesting as possible to the people; that good speakers are secured; that appropriate music is provided; that all preparations for the administering and passing of the sacrament are made in advance to avoid confusion; and that the people are imbued with a sense of the importance of attendance at these meetings. Too much routine, especially in speaking, should be avoided. *CHURCH HANDBOOK,* 1928

The Saints should, if convenient, hold special meetings for the administration of the sacrament and not administer it in public meetings where the congregation is largely unbelievers. The sacrament is designed for members of the Church only, but if it has to be administered in the general meetings, where non-members are present, and they desire to partake, they should not be forbidden, but be allowed to do so on their own responsibility. The sacrament is a token of the new covenant, and any who understands it will scarcely partake unless they are in fellowship in that covenant. GEORGE REYNOLDS TO HENRY S. TANNER, FEB. 1, 1895

same-gender marriage, *see* marriage

Satan

It is not good practice to become intrigued by Satan and his mysteries. No good can come from getting close to evil. Like playing with fire, it is too easy to get burned ... The only safe course is to keep well distanced from him and any of his wicked activities or nefarious practices. The mischief of devil worship, sorcery, witchcraft, voodooism, casting spells, black magic, and all other forms of demonism should always be avoided. JAMES E. FAUST, "FIRST PRESIDENCY MESSAGE," *ENSIGN*, JAN. 2007

Satan became the devil by seeking glory, power, and dominion by force (see Moses 4:3-4). IBID.

[W]e need not become paralyzed with fear of Satan's power. He can have no power over us unless we permit it. He is really a coward, and if we stand firm, he will retreat. IBID.

Satan and his angels are not all-powerful. One of Satan's approaches is to persuade a person who has transgressed that there is no hope of forgiveness. But there is always hope. IBID.

Satan, also called the adversary or the devil, is the enemy of righteousness and those who seek to follow God. He is a spirit son of God, who was once an angel "in authority in the presence of God" (D&C 76:25; see also 26-27; Isa. 14:12). But in the premortal Council in Heaven, Lucifer, as Satan was then called, rebelled against Heavenly Father and the plan of salvation. *TRUE TO FAITH,* 2004

Because Satan "seeketh that all men might be miserable like unto himself" (2 Ne. 2:27), he and his followers try to lead us away from righteousness. He directs his most strenuous opposition at the most important aspects of Heavenly Father's plan of happiness. For example, he seeks to discredit the Savior and the priesthood, to cast doubt on the power of the Atonement, to counterfeit revelation, to distract us from the truth, and to contradict individual accountability. He attempts to undermine the family by confusing gender, promoting sexual relations outside of marriage, ridiculing marriage, and discouraging childbearing by married adults who would otherwise raise children in righteousness. IBID.

Satan is our greatest enemy and works night and day to destroy us. But we need not become paralyzed with fear of Satan's power. He can have no power over us unless we permit it. He is really a coward, and if we stand firm he will retreat. JAMES E. FAUST, "FIRST PRESIDENCY MESSAGE," *ENSIGN,* OCT. 2002

Satan is only interested in our misery, which he promotes by trying to persuade men and women to act contrary to God's plan. JAMES E. FAUST, "FIRST PRESIDENCY MESSAGE," *ENSIGN,* SEPT. 1995

We challenge the powers of darkness when we speak of the perfect life of the Savior and of His sublime work for all mankind through the Atonement. This supernal gift permits us, through repentance, to break away from Satan's grasping tentacles.

We please the devil if we argue that all roads lead to heaven and therefore it does not matter which road we take, for we will all end up in God's presence. And we also please the devil if we contend that since we are all God's children, it makes no difference to which church a person belongs, for we are all working for the same place. IBID.

The adversary is subtle. He is cunning. He knows that he cannot induce good men and women to do major evils immediately, so he moves slyly, whispering half-truths until he has his intended captives following him. SPENCER W. KIMBALL, "FIRST PRESIDENCY MESSAGE," *ENSIGN,* OCT. 1982

Satan, also called the adversary, the devil, and Lucifer, is a spirit son of God. In the council in heaven, Satan rebelled against God and drew away one third of God's spirit children with him. He claimed he would save all mankind, but at the expense of their free agency. *PRINCIPLES,* 1976

Lucifer was one of God's spirit sons having high status in the first estate. When he and his followers rebelled against God, he became Satan.

The rebellious spirits were cast out of heaven to this earth. They are allowed to tempt man, thus providing for opposition in all things. "BASIC DOCTRINES," 1971

The antithesis of love is hate. The forces of hate are sinister and their dangers relentlessly imbued with the satanic ideology that the fatherhood of God, the saviorhood of Christ, and the brotherhood of man are stupid myths, that religion is nothing but a tranquilizing opiate. They seek to deprive man of physical, mental, and spiritual freedom while they endow the state with monstrous supremacy. *CHURCH NEWS,* DEC. 21, 1968

[T]he enemy of all righteousness is also active. Wherever he discovers a weakness in the ranks of the faithful, he strikes and strikes hard, but his attacks are becoming more and more impotent. *DESERET NEWS,* DEC. 14, 1946

Satan is making war against all the wisdom that has come to men through their ages of experience. He is seeking to overturn and destroy the very foundations upon which society, government, and religion rest. He aims to have men adopt theories and practices which he induced their forefathers, over the ages, to adopt and try, only to be discarded by them when found unsound, impractical, and ruinous. He plans to destroy liberty and freedom—economic, political, and religious, and to set up in place thereof the greatest, most widespread, and most complete tyranny that has ever oppressed men. He is working under such perfect disguise that many do not recognize either him or his methods. There is no crime he would not commit, no debauchery he would not set up, no plague he would not send, no heart he would not break, no life he would not take, no soul he would not destroy. He comes as a thief in the night; he is a wolf in sheep's clothing. Without their knowing it, the people are being urged down paths that lead only to destruction. Satan never before had so firm a grip on this generation as he has now. *IMPROVEMENT ERA,* NOV. 1942, IN *MESSAGES,* 6:170-85

All that which exalts ease and pleasure and makes them the precious goal of this life is from evil. *DESERET NEWS*, DEC. 15, 1934

Slander, false witness, and the shafts of malice are arrayed against the Church and its authorities, as may be expected until Satan is bound and falsehood is [conquered] by divine truth. It is our duty to bear such things with patience, and not permit ourselves to be aroused to anger or retaliation. We should stand up for the right, and as far as possible ignore the wrong-doers. *DESERET NEWS,* DEC. 16, 1905, IN *MESSAGES,* 4:121-23

[T]he devil is not dead, neither is he sleeping. FIRST PRESIDENCY TO FRANCIS M. LYMAN, IN *MILLENNIAL STAR,* JUNE 11, 1903

Satan can enter any place where he is invited or permitted to enter by man. If wicked men enter the house of God or have dominion in it, Satan will have access there, but where the righteous rule and the righteousness of God prevails, there Satan cannot come, at least with power. JOSEPH F. SMITH TO JOSEPH FIELDING SMITH, APR. 3, 1900

Those who overcome evil in this life will be beyond the power of Satan in the life to come. In other words, Satan's power ends in this world so far as the righteous are concerned, for they rise above him and above his influence; and power is not given to him to tempt them in the spirit world, they having overcome him in this. So far then as the righteous are concerned, Satan is effectually bound, whether it is in this life or in the life to come. But as mortality is never free from its own weaknesses, there is no perfect safety in this sphere without the presence continually of the influence of the Holy Spirit. IBID.

Probably at no period in the world's history has Satan had such power over the hearts of the children of men as he appears to wield at the present. STATEMENT, OCT. 6, 1886, IN *MESSAGES,* 3:72-91

This is the work that makes angry the adversary, who fears the overthrow of his kingdom and power upon the earth, that causes Satan to rage and seek to destroy the Saints of the Most High, as he did in the day of Jesus and of his Apostles and followers. *MILLENNIAL STAR,* AUG. 11, 1855, IN *MESSAGES,* 2:159-71

science. *See also* intellectualism; knowledge

The accomplishments of science seem to be limitless. In many ways, it has made life more comfortable and beautiful, but it has also made life hideous. Though it brings into our homes the music of the spheres [i.e., heavenly music], at the same time it slays defenseless women and children indiscriminately. Manifestly, it cannot save mankind from wars, but it can annihilate the human race. The promise of science for human benefits, and particularly as an assurance of peace, is now questioned. *DESERET NEWS,* DEC. 14, 1946

[A]s to many matters—perhaps most matters—there are two or more points of view, and it is our understanding that this frequently happens even as to fundamental theories, and indeed, even as to certain so-called postulates, of science itself. We must, therefore, all have tolerance. FIRST PRESIDENCY TO STERLING B. TALMAGE, DEC. 2, 1935

God has given to His children a new universe of other and companion truths [to "spiritual truths"], the truths yielded by the realms of physical science, and these have come in a richness of measure never before equaled in the whole history of the world. The Lord has given these truths for the comfort, joy, and intellectual growth of His children while mortals, and for the upbuilding, perfection, and exaltation of their intelligences and souls in the world to come. These are the ends and purposes of all truth. *IMPROVEMENT ERA,* APR. 1935, IN *MESSAGES,* 6:4-5

Our message is one of love and mercy and light; not to deprive any sect or party or persons of the good they have, but to increase it and bring them nearer to God. Our religion is not hostile to real science. That which is demonstrated, we accept with joy; but vain philosophy, human theory, and mere speculations of men we do not accept, nor do we adopt anything contrary to divine revelation or to good common sense. But everything that tends to right conduct, that harmonizes with sound morality and increases faith in Deity, finds favor with us no matter where it may be found. *DESERET EVENING NEWS*, DEC. 17, 1910

scriptures

True spiritual growth is based on studying the scriptures, the teachings of the Brethren, and Church publications. "DEAR BRETHREN," IN *CHURCH NEWS*, MAY 29, 2004

The scriptures are the most important resource for teaching the gospel. *ENSIGN*, NOV. 1994

When a sacred text is translated into another language or rewritten into more familiar language, there are substantial risks that this process may introduce doctrinal errors or [may] obscure evidence of its ancient origin. *CHURCH NEWS*, FEB. 20, 1993

We counsel everyone to cultivate the influence of the scriptures by personal study of the word of the Lord contained therein. When this is done prayerfully, each who reads may know the truth of these sacred words by the power of the Holy Ghost (Moro. 10:5). IBID.

The more familiar you are with the scriptures, the closer you become to the mind and will of the Lord and the closer you become as husband and wife and children. You will find that by reading the scriptures the truths of eternity will rest on your minds. EZRA TAFT BENSON, "FIRST PRESIDENCY MESSAGE," *ENSIGN,* APR. 1988

We encourage people throughout a troubled world to read and re-read the divinely revealed scriptures, to ponder them, learn from them, and incorporate the teachings of the Savior into their lives so that, through their example, the influence of the gospel of peace and love and understanding will permeate every nation, culture, and society. NEWS RELEASE, NOV. 13, 1987

The word *search* indicates that your study of the scriptures should be more than a shallow reading of words. Your search should be an in-depth probe, a spiritual feast in which you come to know not only the gospel but also Him whose name it bears and the Father who sent Him to redeem us. *PRIESTHOOD STUDY GUIDE,* 1985

Within the scriptures is found an unfailing formula for peace and joy, especially in the words and teachings of the Lord Jesus Christ, our divine Savior, the Prince of Peace, the Redeemer of the world. NEWS RELEASE, NOV. 9, 1984

As we read the scriptures, we avail ourselves of the better part of this world's literature. *CHURCH NEWS,* MAR. 20, 1983

[I]t is a good thing for us to realize that we do not get the gospel of Jesus Christ out of the Bible only. We accept the doctrines of the gospel as taught in the Bible to be the word of God. The Bible teachings are the word of God wherever they have not been mutilated. But the teaching of the gospel as contained in the Bible is but a part of the teaching which the Lord and His prophets gave in past dispensations. MARION G. ROMNEY, "FIRST PRESIDENCY MESSAGE," *ENSIGN,* JANUARY 1981

The Old Testament, like other scriptures, is a handbook on how to proceed in times of threatened adversity. Because of the sharp and graphic contrasts that have been preserved in it, the lessons become unmistakable. MARION G. ROMNEY, "FIRST PRESIDENCY MESSAGE," *ENSIGN,* SEPTEMBER 1980

The scriptures are important as standards by which to measure all truth. Those ideas in harmony with the scriptures are true; those out of harmony are false. *PRINCIPLES,* 1976

Studying the scriptures and living according to the principles found in them can mean the difference between receiving exaltation and failing to do so. No Latter-day Saint can afford to neglect the scriptures. IBID.

The scriptures have been given to us as our guide, the blueprint of life. They give us a clear understanding that man is made in the image of God and that he has been placed here upon the earth as a mortal being with a body, to learn and prepare and prove himself to be worthy to go back into the presence of our Heavenly Father. We must accept and live according to the teachings of the scriptures if we want the promised blessings, or we can reject them and suffer the promised consequences. N. ELDON TANNER, "FIRST PRESIDENCY MESSAGE," *ENSIGN*, OCT. 1973

[W]e need to teach our people to find their answers in the scriptures. If only each of us would be wise enough to say that we aren't able to answer any questions unless we can find a doctrinal answer in the scriptures! And if we hear someone teaching something that is contrary to what is in the scriptures, each of us may know whether the things spoken are false–it is as simple as that. But the unfortunate thing is that so many of us are not reading the scriptures. We do not know what is in them, and therefore we speculate about the things that we ought to have found in the scriptures themselves. HAROLD B. LEE, "FIRST PRESIDENCY MESSAGE," *ENSIGN*, DEC. 1972

It is generally understood that Jonah was a real individual. However, it is barely possible that the story is one of those parables common in the writing of the time in which Jonah lived. It does not matter whether that is actually the case or not, the purpose and intent of the book are excellent and have several very grand lessons. These constitute the value of the work. It is of little significance as to whether Jonah was a real individual or one chosen by the writer of the book to write what is set forth therein. It is held by the Church that Job was a real character. It is barely possible that the book was one of the kind prevailing in olden times, setting forth certain principles in the form of a parable, as it was with the parables of Jesus Christ when in the flesh. That is not of very great importance so long as the doctrines contained in the work are correct. CHARLES W. PENROSE TO JOSEPH W. MCMURRIN, OCT. 31, 1921

[W]hen this fact is admitted, that the immediate will of heaven is contained in the scriptures, are we not bound as rational creatures to live in accordance to all its precepts? STATEMENT, JAN. 22, 1834, IN *MESSAGES*, 1:23-44

sealings, children to parents

Children born to parents who have been sealed in the temple are born in the covenant. These children automatically become part of an eternal family. Children who are not born in the covenant can also become part of an eternal family once their natural or adoptive parents have been sealed to one another. The ordinance of sealing children to parents is performed in the temple. *TRUE TO FAITH*, 2004

Children sealed to their parents have claim upon the blessings of the gospel beyond what others are entitled to receive. *CHURCH NEWS*, NOV. 8, 2003

Children who are born after their mother has been sealed to a husband in a temple are born in the covenant of that sealing. They do not need to receive the ordinance of sealing to parents. Being born in the covenant entitles children to an eternal parentage, depending on their faithfulness. However, it does not guarantee that children will be sealed to their natural parents if the parents are not faithful. *CHURCH HANDBOOK*, 1998

Children who were not born in the covenant can become part of an eternal family by being sealed to their natural or adoptive parents. These children receive the same right to blessings as if they had been born in the covenant.

A child may be sealed only to two parents—a husband and wife—and not to one parent only. IBID.

Living children who are born in the covenant or have been sealed to parents cannot be sealed to any other parents.

Living children who have been legally adopted and were neither born in the covenant nor sealed to former parents may be sealed to their adoptive parents after the adoption is final. IBID.

A deceased adopted person usually is sealed to his or her adoptive parents.

A deceased foster child usually is sealed to his or her natural parents. IBID.

A living child who was born out of wedlock may be sealed to both natural parents without special approval after the parents have been sealed in the temple.

A living child who was born out of wedlock may be sealed to one natural parent and a stepparent when at least one of the following conditions applies:

1. The child marries.
2. The child reaches the age of 21.
3. The child's other natural parent is deceased.
4. The other natural parent has given signed consent for the sealing.
5. The rights of the natural father or mother have been terminated by legal process, such as an adoption proceeding.

IBID.

Children conceived by artificial insemination or in vitro fertilization are born in the covenant if their parents are already sealed. If the children are born before their parents are sealed, they may be sealed to their parents after their parents are sealed to each other. IBID.

Children who are born in the covenant or sealed to their parents remain so even if the sealing of the parents is later (1) canceled or (2) revoked by the excommunication or name removal of either parent. Children who are born after their parents' sealing is canceled or revoked are not born in the covenant. IBID.

A living mentally retarded person is judged for temple work on his own behalf on the basis of his established mental age, based on the pattern prescribed for chronological age. A person with a mental age of less than eight years would not require baptism before sealing to parents. A person with a mental age of eight years or above would require baptism before being sealed to parents. *CHURCH HANDBOOK*, 1976

sealings, husband and wives. *See also* marriage

Time-only marriages in the temple are intended to be performed only for a couple where both the man and the woman are presently sealed to a deceased spouse. "DEAR BRETHREN," NOV. 12, 2003

Every man who truly loves a woman and every woman who truly loves a man hopes and dreams that their companionship will last forever. But marriage is a covenant sealed by authority. If that authority is of the state alone, it will endure only while the state has jurisdiction, and that jurisdiction ends with death. But add to the authority of the state the power of the endowment given by Him who overcame death, and that companionship will endure beyond life if the parties to the marriage live worthy of the promise. GORDON B. HINCKLEY, "FIRST PRESIDENCY MESSAGE," *ENSIGN*, JULY 2003

A living woman may be sealed to only one husband. If she is sealed to a husband and later divorced, she must receive a cancellation of that sealing from the First Presidency before she may be sealed to another man in her lifetime ... *CHURCH HANDBOOK,* 1998

A deceased woman may be sealed to all men to whom she was legally married during her life. However, if she was sealed to a husband during her life, all her husbands must be deceased before she can be sealed to a husband to whom she was not sealed during life. IBID.

If a husband and wife have been sealed and the wife dies, the man may have another woman sealed to him if she is not already sealed.

If a husband and wife have been sealed and later divorced, the man must receive a sealing clearance from the First Presidency before another woman may be sealed to him.... *A sealing clearance is necessary even if the previous sealing has been canceled.* IBID.

A deceased man may have sealed to him all women to whom he was legally married during his life if they are deceased or if they are living and not sealed to another man. IBID.

Deceased couples who were divorced may be sealed by proxy. IBID.

For sealing ordinances to be effective throughout eternity, those who receive them must be true and faithful to the covenants associated with the ordinances. *CHURCH HANDBOOK 2,* 1998

[I]t should be definitely understood that the authority to cancel temple sealings is vested in the President of the Church, and in him only, and that no sealing of the living or the dead can be authoritatively canceled except upon his personal authorization. FIRST PRESIDENCY TO PRESIDENTS OF TEMPLES, JAN. 4, 1966

Second Coming

When the Savior comes again, He will come in power and glory to claim the earth as His kingdom. His Second Coming will mark the beginning of the Millennium. *TRUE TO FAITH,* 2004

Do not concern yourself with the exact timing of the Savior's Second Coming. Instead, live so that you will be prepared whenever He comes. As you observe the calamities of these last days, remember that the righteous need not fear the Second Coming or the signs that precede it. IBID.

We testify that He will some day return to Earth. "And the glory of the Lord shall be revealed, and all flesh shall see it together" (Isa. 40:5). He will rule as King of Kings and reign as Lord of Lords, and every knee shall bend and every tongue shall speak in worship before Him. Each of us will stand to be judged of Him according to our works and the desire of our hearts. *CHURCH NEWS,* JAN. 1, 2000

Not many years hence, Christ will come again. He will come in power and might as King of Kings and Lord of Lords. And ultimately every knee shall bow and every tongue confess that Jesus is the Christ. EZRA TAFT BENSON, "FIRST PRESIDENCY MESSAGE," *ENSIGN,* DEC. 1993

Occasionally people claim to know the date of the Second Coming, but the Lord has not revealed exactly when He will come again. *PRINCIPLES,* 1976

Preceding the Second Coming of Jesus Christ, Zion must be established as a place and a people. The earth will again receive its paradisiacal glory.

Conditions of Zion will prevail during the millennial reign of the Savior on Earth. "BASIC DOCTRINES," 1971

[W]e have the sure word of prophecy, that Christ will come to Earth again to gather home God's children in a glorious redemption. *DESERET NEWS,* DEC. 11, 1957

The time is at hand when Jehovah shall again personally rule and reign among His people—when "out of Zion shall go forth the Law and the Word of the Lord from Jerusalem" [Isa. 2:3]. *JEWISH TRIBUNE,* JUNE 29, 1932

Oh, that mankind would recognize and heed these signs of the times in their real import as the fulfillment of prophecy made contingent on the persistent unrighteousness of the race! These are the last days, foretold in sacred writ, through the Lord's prophets of ancient times and of the present dispensation. *DESERET NEWS*, DEC. 20, 1930, IN *MESSAGES,* 5:286-89

We are nearer the time of the Second Advent than mankind have ever been, aye, nearer than mankind are willing to admit or believe. IBID.

During this period, the voice of the Lord, by his Spirit, has been constantly speaking to the pure in heart, while the voice of thunderings, and lightnings, of earthquakes, tempests, the sea heaving beyond its bounds, and the constant recurrence of war warn the people of the world that the day of the coming of the Lord is nigh. *DESERET NEWS,* DEC. 21, 1929

The hour and day of the Lord's future advent is withheld from the knowledge of both men and angels; yet the signs, so definitely specified as harbingers of His coming, are multiplying apace. The prevailing unrest among men and nations, the fury of the elements, widespread destruction by land and sea, the frequency and intensity of volcanic and earthquake disturbances—all tell to the well-tuned and listening ear that the gladsome yet terrible day of the Lord is nigh—aye, even at our doors! *DESERET NEWS,* DEC. 22, 1928, IN *MESSAGES,* 5:264-66

Each passing year brings us nearer the date of the Lord's coming in power and glory. True, the hour and the day when this great event is to take place no man knoweth, but all the promised signs indicate that it is not far distant. *DESERET NEWS,* DEC. 17, 1927, IN *MESSAGES,* 5:254-57

Despite the uneasiness and discontent in many parts of the earth, the suspicions and jealousies among the nations, the mounting wave of lawlessness and crime, and the seeming spread of the elements of destruction even in our own beloved country—despite these symptoms denoting the apparent growth of the power of evil, those who continue to stand in holy places can discern through it all the handworking of the Almighty in consummation of His own purposes and in furtherance of His will. That which, viewed with the natural eye, is portentous and dreadful, causes no apprehension to those who have faith that whatever happens, the Lord God omnipotent reigneth. IBID.

The conflicts and calamities of the times were foretold by Christ in plain and pointed language. They are among the signs of His Second Advent. They were to precede His appearance as the Prince of Peace. As they surely fulfill what He declared should herald His coming and kingdom, so certainly will that promise of His personal return in majesty be accomplished. *DESERET NEWS,* DEC. 16, 1916, IN *MESSAGES,* 5:43-48

We believe literally in the Second Advent of our Lord Jesus Christ, that He who was resurrected from the dead and ascended into heaven will come again to reign as King of Kings and Lord of Lords. "CHRISTMAS 1913," IN *MESSAGES,* 4:291-93

We look for His coming and His kingdom as certain verities, as much real as His nativity and His crucifixion. *DESERET NEWS,* DEC. 16, 1912, IN *MESSAGES,* 4:252-58

The many eruptions, earthquakes, and tidal waves which have occurred during the past year are signs which the Savior declared should foreshadow His Second Coming; although He said His advent should be as a thief in the night, still He gave certain signs which would indicate as surely His coming as the budding trees the coming of summer. *DESERET NEWS,* DEC. 15, 1906, IN *MESSAGES,* 4:128-32

Do not discuss the time of the coming of Christ in an unprofitable manner. There is a time appointed, and God only knows it. He has not revealed it. But the appointed time will surely come long before most people are prepared. This we know, it is not far distant, for the signs of His coming are now very plain. But there is yet much to do to prepare for that great event. Many of the honest have not yet heard of His great latter-day work. Zion must be fully established. Jerusalem must be rebuilt by the Jews, the ten tribes must return from the north, and American Indians, who are of the house of Israel, must be converted and become workers in His cause. And many more of the different branches of the House of Israel must return to the promised lands and be prepared to meet Him and to receive Him. He will be their king when He comes. God's works must all be fulfilled and we must wait patiently and labor in the fear of God that we may be with His holy company when He comes. For He will come in the clouds and save His Saints while His angels will reap the earth and cleanse it from sin. FIRST PRESIDENCY TO "BELOVED BRETHREN AND SISTERS IN TURKEY," SEPT. 7, 1897, IN *MESSAGES,* 3:284-87

The day is not far distant when our Lord and Savior will be revealed from the heavens, and we should live in constant expectation of this great event and seek, with all the energy and power that we can exercise and obtain, to prepare ourselves, our households, and, as far as we have influence, the inhabitants of the earth for His glorious appearing. STATEMENT, OCT. 10, 1887, IN *MESSAGES,* 3:133-55

All the signs which the Lord promised to send in the last days are making their appearance. They show that the day of the Lord is near. *MILLENNIAL STAR,* OCT. 15, 1877, IN *MESSAGES,* 2:297-303

The gathering of Israel has already commenced; Judea is receiving its ancient inhabitants, and the holy city is rebuilding, which is one prominent sign of the near approach of the Messiah. *DESERET NEWS,* APR. 8, 1851, IN *MESSAGES,* 2:62-73

The unparalleled spread of the gospel in so short a space of time and the rapid gathering of the Saints is another token of Messiah's near approach. IBID.

Of the day and the hour of the coming of Christ no man knoweth. It is not yet, neither is it far off; there are prophecies yet to be fulfilled before that event takes place; therefore, let no man deceive the Saints with vain philosophy and false prophecy; for false prophets will arise and deceive the wicked and, if possible, the good; but while the wicked fear and tremble at surrounding judgments, the Saints will watch and pray and, waiting the final event in patience, will look calmly on the passing scenery of a corrupted world and view transpiring events as confirmation of their faith in the holy gospel which they profess and rejoice more and more, as multiplied signs shall confirm the approach of the millennial day. IBID.

[W]e now bear witness that His coming is near at hand; and not many years hence, the nations and their kings shall see Him coming in the clouds of heaven with power and great glory. STATEMENT, APR. 6, 1845, IN *MESSAGES,* 1:252-66

We see that everything is being fulfilled, and that the time shall soon come when the Son of Man shall descend in the clouds of heaven. STATEMENT, MAR. 25, 1839, IN *MESSAGES,* 1:88-104

secret organizations

The Church advises its members strongly not to join any organization that (1) is antagonistic toward the Church, (2) is secret and oath-bound, (3) would cause members to lose interest in Church activities or violate Church standards, or (4) would interfere with members' performance of their Church duties. *CHURCH HANDBOOK,* 1983

Whether Church members who belong to secret, oath-bound organizations shall be ordained to or advanced in the priesthood or given the privileges of the temple depends upon their faithfulness in the Church and their compliance with the regulations governing these privileges. *CHURCH HANDBOOK,* 1976

[T]he counsel of the First Presidency of the Church in all cases has been and is against our people joining secret organizations for any purpose whatsoever, and that where any of them have already joined they are counseled to withdraw themselves from such organizations as soon as circumstances permit and wisdom dictates. The merits of the various orders are not considered at all; their aims may be ever so worthy and their objects ever so commendable. JOSEPH ANDERSON, SECRETARY TO THE FIRST PRESIDENCY, LETTER DATED JULY 25, 1967

Members of the Church are strongly advised not to join any

[secret oath-bound] organization ... which is antagonistic to the Church ... This does not apply to any association that is free from the conditions mentioned and that is organized for the commercial or general welfare of its members.... It should be understood that such individuals give their first allegiance and preference in time and service to the Church.

Church members who participate actively in secret oath-bound organizations will not have time to devote to Church positions of leadership and should not be appointed to them.
CHURCH HANDBOOK, 1963

self-awareness groups

There is increasing concern regarding Church members' involvement in groups that purport to increase self-awareness, raise self-esteem, and enhance individual agency. Many of these groups advocate concepts and use methods that can be harmful. Some falsely claim Church endorsement, actively recruit Church members, charge exorbitant fees, and encourage long-term commitments. Some intermingle worldly concepts with gospel principles in ways that can undermine spirituality and faith. Although participants may experience temporary emotional relief or exhilaration, old problems often return, leading to added disappointment and despair.

Church leaders and members should not become involved in self-awareness groups or any other groups that imitate sacred rites or ceremonies. Similarly, members should avoid groups that meet late into the night or encourage open confession or disclosure of personal information normally discussed only in confidential settings.

Church leaders are not to pay for, encourage participation in, or promote such groups or practices. Also, Church facilities are not to be used for these types of activities. Local leaders should counsel those desiring self-improvement to anchor themselves in gospel principles and to adopt wholesome practices that strengthen one's abilities to cope with challenges. *BULLETIN,* 1993-2

Many resources in the community provide effective help for members experiencing social or emotional problems. However, some questionable groups that purport to increase self-awareness, self-esteem, or self-actualization often use methods that may result in added stress, marital discord, and even divorce.

Members should avoid participation in groups that challenge religious and moral values or advocate unwarranted confrontation with spouse or family members in order to reach one's potential. Beware of groups that meet late into the evening or early morning hours over several days. This approach tends to lower inhibitions and encourage confession and disclosure of personal information in ways that may be damaging to the individual. It may foster unnecessary physical contact among participants. Groups advocating such techniques are often expensive. They tend to promise quick solutions to problems that normally require time and personal effort to resolve. Although participants may feel some initial relief, they often find their old problems returning.

Members should be reminded that the process of finding one's self comes through living gospel principles. Members experiencing social or emotional problems may wish to consult with priesthood leaders for guidance in identifying resources that are in harmony with gospel principles. *BULLETIN,* 1989-3

service. ***See also*** **welfare**

Without service we cannot receive exaltation because we are not developing that love and charity which will enable us to dwell in celestial glory. When we are unwilling to serve the Lord and our fellowmen or when we serve reluctantly, we are merely demonstrating our unwillingness to obey the two great commandments: to love the Lord and to love our neighbor. And when we have problems with these two basic commandments, other problems soon follow, for obedience to all the commandments depends on love of God and love of others. *PRINCIPLES,* 1976

seventy, quorums of. *See also* **priesthood**

Members of the quorums of the seventy are "called to preach the gospel, and to be especial witnesses unto the Gentiles and in all the world" (D&C 107:25). They work "under the direction of the Twelve ... in building up the church and regulating all the affairs of the same in all nations" (107:34). In their quorums, the Seventy are presided over by the Presidents of the Seventy (107:93-94). *CHURCH HANDBOOK,* 1998

sex education

Parents have primary responsibility for the sex education of their children. Teaching this subject honestly and plainly in the home will help young people avoid serious moral transgressions. *CHURCH HANDBOOK,* 1998

Where schools have undertaken sex education, it is appropriate for parents to seek to ensure that the instruction given their children is consistent with appropriate moral and ethical values. With encouragement from parents and other citizens, many schools that are currently offering sex education can be persuaded to include instruction on the importance of chastity, marriage at the appropriate time, the role of parents in prescribing moral standards for family members, and the moral and ethical responsibilities of family members to one another. Latter-day Saints should encourage and support the teaching of morality. "DEAR BRETHREN," ENGLISH-SPEAKING AREAS, JUNE 19, 1986

We believe that serious hazards are involved in entrusting to the schools the teaching of this vital and important subject [sex education] to our children. This responsibility cannot wisely be left to society, nor the schools; nor can the responsibility be shifted to the Church. It is the responsibility of parents to see that they fully perform their duty in this respect. *PRIESTHOOD BULLETIN*, JUNE 1971

sexual abuse

Victims of rape, incest, or other sexual abuse are not guilty of sin. If you have been a victim of any of these crimes, know that you are innocent and that God loves you. *STRENGTH OF YOUTH,* 2001

Victims of rape or sexual abuse frequently experience serious trauma and unnecessary feelings of guilt. Church officers should handle such cases with sensitivity and concern, reassuring such victims that they, as victims of the evil acts of others, are not guilty of sin, helping them to overcome feelings of guilt and to regain their self-esteem and their confidence in personal relationships.

Of course, a mature person who willingly consents to sexual relations must share responsibility for the act, even though the other participant was the aggressor. Persons who consciously invite sexual advances also have a share of responsibility for the behavior that follows. But persons who are truly forced into sexual relations are victims and are not guilty of any sexual sin. Whether a person was forced in this manner depends on so many individual circumstances that Church officers should normally refrain from assigning moral guilt to a victim who has been subject to significant force or credible threats, leaving final judgment to the omniscience of the Lord. "DEAR BRETHREN," FEB. 7, 1985

Persons threatened with rape or forcible sexual abuse should resist to the maximum extent possible or necessary under the circumstances. The extent of resistance required to establish that the victim has not willingly consented is left to the judgment of the victim, who is best acquainted with the total circumstances and their effect on his or her will. IBID.

The degree of resistance necessary to prevent a rape will, of course, vary with the circumstances. One attacker may be deterred by mere words of pleading or ridicule, while another may be so determined and violent that nothing short of death would deter him. We would be reluctant, therefore, to define precisely the form or degree of resistance which a woman should make to a threatened rape.

It is conceivable that a woman could be so terrified by mere threats of violence or death made by an attacker that her sense of agency would be overpowered, causing her to submit without making a real show of resistance. On this account, it would be difficult, even presumptuous, for another to judge the moral guilt or culpability of a person attacked, absent, of course, a confirmation through the Spirit that she is guilty or culpable.

Under these circumstances, we feel that the safe course is for leaders of the Church to urge sisters who are threatened with rape to resist to the maximum extent possible or necessary under the circumstances, leaving it to their own conscience and good judgment as to the degree of such resistance. Furthermore, because of lack of knowledge of the circumstances involved, which only the parties to the rape would know, we should not presume to judge a woman who has been raped and who survived, leaving such judgment to the omniscience of the Lord. FIRST PRESIDENCY TO B---- S. B---, NOV. 25, 1974; SEE ALSO "DEAR BRETHREN," JUNE 4, 1984

sexual relations. ***See also*** **birth control; marriage; procreation**

The Church does not have a position on the causes of ... susceptibilities or inclinations ... related to same-gender attraction. Those are scientific questions–whether nature or nurture–those are things the Church doesn't have a position on. "ISSUES RESOURCES," 2006

Physical intimacy between husband and wife is beautiful and sacred. It is ordained of God for the creation of children and for the expression of love within marriage. *TRUE TO FAITH*, 2004

[S]exual relations within marriage are divinely approved. While one purpose of these relations is to provide physical bodies for God's children, another purpose is to express love for one another–to bind husband and wife together in loyalty, fidelity, consideration, and common purpose. IBID.

All sexual relations outside of marriage violate the law of chastity and are physically and spiritually dangerous for those who engage in them. IBID.

The Brethren have counseled those who conduct worthiness interviews to avoid explicit questioning beyond the scope of what is contained in the temple recommend book. Persons who have been through the temple are aware of the responsibility to keep their thoughts and actions pure and, furthermore, have been counseled to avoid any unholy, unnatural, or impure practice. If a person is engaged in a practice which troubles him or her enough to ask about it, he or she should discontinue it. With this in mind, you can, through your personal supplication to our Father in Heaven, receive the guidance you may feel you need. F. MICHAEL WATSON, SECRETARY TO THE FIRST PRESIDENCY, LETTER, 2002

God has commanded that sexual intimacy be reserved for marriage. *STRENGTH OF YOUTH,* 2001

In God's sight, sexual sins are extremely serious because they defile the power God has given us to create life. IBID.

[S]exual relations within marriage are divinely approved not only for the purpose of procreation, but also as a means of expressing love and strengthening emotional and spiritual bonds between husband and wife. *CHURCH HANDBOOK,* 1998

The Lord's law of moral conduct is abstinence outside of lawful marriage and fidelity within marriage. Sexual relations are proper only between husband and wife appropriately expressed within the bonds of marriage. FIRST PRESIDENCY TO ALL MEMBERS OF THE CHURCH OF JESUS CHRIST OF LATTER-DAY SAINTS, NOV. 14, 1991

Can there be any reasonable doubt that in sowing the wind of a sex-saturated world, we are reaping the whirlwind of decay? GORDON B. HINCKLEY, "FIRST PRESIDENCY MESSAGE," *ENSIGN,* AUG. 1989

Licentiousness masquerades in the robes of liberty as profiteers prey upon young and old alike and loose a veritable flood of evil. NEWS RELEASE, MAY 31, 1985

In conducting worthiness interviews, ... you should never inquire into personal, intimate matters involving marital relations between a man and his wife. You should never deviate from or go beyond the specific questions contained in the temple recommend book. If in the course of such interviews a member asks questions about the propriety of specific conduct, you should not pursue the matter but should merely suggest that if the member has enough anxiety about the propriety of the conduct to ask about it, the best course would be to discontinue it. We feel, brethren, that if those who conduct these interviews are sensitive and wise, they can avoid such explicit questions being asked by those being interviewed. "DEAR BRETHREN," OCT. 15, 1982

Married persons should understand that if in their marital relations they are guilty of unnatural, impure, or unholy practices, they should not enter the temple unless and until they repent and discontinue any such practices. Husbands and wives who are aware of these requirements can determine by themselves their standing before the Lord. "DEAR BRETHREN," JAN. 5, 1982

[T]he laws of retribution are so devised that one cannot with impunity disregard the seventh commandment, "Thou shalt not commit adultery" (Ex. 20:14). The penalty for so doing under the Mosaic law was death. Notwithstanding the fact that in this generation's corrupt permissiveness the violation of the law of chastity is tolerated with impunity, under God's divine law it is as it has always been, a soul-destroying sin. Its self-executing penalty is spiritual death. MARION G. ROMNEY, "FIRST PRESIDENCY MESSAGE," *ENSIGN,* SEPT. 1981

We live in a culture which venerates illicit sex, streaking, trading wives, and similar crazes. How low can humans plunge! We pray with our Lord that we may be kept from being in the world. It is sad that decent people are thrown into the filthy areas of mental and spiritual pollution. We call upon all of our people to do all in their power to offset this ugly revolution. *CHURCH NEWS,* JAN. 17, 1976

Sexual immorality is made up of all kinds and degrees of offenses against the laws of God. All sexual offenses are evil, but some are more serious than others and bring a greater condemnation upon those who commit them. *PRINCIPLES,* 1976

The union of the sexes, husband and wife (and *only* husband and wife), was for the principal purpose of bringing children into the world. Sexual experiences were never intended by the Lord to be a mere plaything or merely to satisfy passions and lusts. We know of no directive from the Lord that proper sexual experience between husbands and wives need be limited totally to the procreation of children, but we find much evidence from Adam until now that no provision was ever made by the Lord for indiscriminate sex. SPENCER W. KIMBALL, "FIRST PRESIDENCY MESSAGE," *ENSIGN,* OCT. 1975

In lieu of asking specific questions about unnatural sex acts, we suggest that bishops and members of the stake presidency ask married couples who come for [temple] recommends whether in their sexual relations they engage in any unholy or impure practices. FIRST PRESIDENCY TO L---- J. C---, SEPT. 18, 1975

Let us consider some of the benefits of being morally clean. First, we might remind ourselves that there are no disadvantages, but numerous advantages, to being modest, clean, and pure. We will never have to be ashamed of our conduct. We will never bring heartache or pain to our loved ones. We will be free from the social diseases that are so prevalent and that are increasing at an alarming rate. Most important, we will have been obedient to the commandments of our Father in

Heaven that He has given for our benefit and blessing. N. ELDON TANNER, "FIRST PRESIDENCY MESSAGE," *ENSIGN,* JULY 1975

History is replete with examples of nations which have fallen in a large measure through licentiousness. *CHURCH NEWS,* OCT. 7, 1972

The Brethren wish me to tell you that there are some questions that even today should be felt to involve such delicacy and modesty as not to be the subject of common discussion. The Brethren feel that the question which you raise is such as should be answered by you and your husband and in accordance with your own convictions. The Church has never believed it necessary to issue instructions pertaining to intimate relations between husband and wife. JOSEPH ANDERSON, SECRETARY TO THE FIRST PRESIDENCY, TO L--- A------, MAR. 23, 1971; COPIES TO THE QUORUM OF THE TWELVE, MAY 19, 1971

Necking, petting, intimacies, and improprieties of every kind should not be indulged in at any time in dating or in courtship. Love and affection are precious, and virtue must never be placed in jeopardy. *STRENGTH OF YOUTH,* 1968

The doctrine of this Church is that sexual sin—the illicit sexual relations of men and women—stands, in its enormity, next to murder.

The Lord has drawn no essential distinctions between fornication, adultery, and harlotry or prostitution. Each has fallen under his solemn and awful condemnation. *IMPROVEMENT ERA,* NOV. 1942, IN *MESSAGES,* 6:170-85

Sexual purity is youth's most precious possession; it is the foundation of all righteousness. *IMPROVEMENT ERA,* MAY 1942, IN *MESSAGES,* 6:148-63

[I]t is a good for a man to realize that woman is mistress of her own body. JOSEPH ANDERSON, SECRETARY TO THE FIRST PRESIDENCY, TO MRS. W. E. C------, AUG. 7, 1935

[T]he Church of Jesus Christ of Latter-day Saints has formulated no special rules governing the associations of married people. Men and women are required to be chaste and virtuous, before and after marriage, and husband and wife make solemn covenant to be loyal to each other; but as to their mutual conduct in the marital relation, so far as sexual intercourse is concerned, they are left entirely free. The gospel of Christ is "the perfect law of liberty"; obedience to it does not come by coercion; and the exercise of unrighteous dominion is strictly forbidden among the Latter-day Saints. JOSEPH F. SMITH TO FRANK S. BELLINGS, FEB. 17, 1905

No man should exercise unrighteous power, no man should exercise power over his wife's body or mind except by her willing consent. Marital rights must be mutually enjoyed and mutually exercised. Whatsoever is more or less than this cometh of evil, and evil cometh of it. If men would delicately regard the desires of their wives—the wives would not "loathe" them. JOSEPH F. SMITH TO GEORGE L. FARRELL, APR. 22, 1897

The great, crying sin of this generation is lasciviousness in its various forms. Satan, knowing how powerful an agency this is in corrupting men and women and in driving the Spirit from them, and bringing them under condemnation before the Lord, uses it to the greatest extent possible. It requires an incessant warfare to check its spread and to prevent the people of God from becoming its victims. No people who practice or countenance these sins can be accepted of the Lord or find favor in His sight. His anger will fall upon them unless they thoroughly and heartily repent of every such evil. STATEMENT, OCT. 6, 1886, IN *MESSAGES,* 3:72-91

Smith, Joseph. ***See also*** **Church; priesthood**

We do not worship the Prophet [Joseph Smith]. We worship God our Eternal Father and the risen Lord Jesus Christ. But we acknowledge the Prophet; we proclaim him; we respect him; we reverence him as an instrument in the hands of the Almighty in restoring to the earth the ancient truths of the divine gospel, together with the priesthood through which the authority of God is exercised in the affairs of His Church and for the blessing of His people. GORDON B. HINCKLEY, "FIRST PRESIDENCY MESSAGE," *ENSIGN,* DEC. 2005

Joseph Smith has given us not only the message of the divine restoration but also the practical how-to steps to obtain personal and divine communication. JAMES E. FAUST, "FIRST PRESIDENCY MESSAGE," *ENSIGN,* OCT. 1997

The Prophet Joseph Smith was a preeminent witness of the living Christ. GORDON B. HINCKLEY, "FIRST PRESIDENCY MESSAGE," *ENSIGN,* JAN. 1997

We need not claim perfection for Joseph Smith the way we do for the Savior. Joseph's humanity was part of his strength and credibility. He never professed to be perfect; so we should not try to claim something he did not claim for himself. He knew he was only a mortal man with human feelings and imperfections, trying honestly to fulfill his divine mission. JAMES E. FAUST, "FIRST PRESIDENCY MESSAGE," *ENSIGN,* JAN. 1996

The faith of members of The Church of Jesus Christ of Latter-day Saints rests on the claim that Joseph Smith is a prophet of God, and also that he declared the coming forth of the Book of Mormon was the result of angelic visitations to him between the years 1823 and 1827. EZRA TAFT BENSON, "FIRST PRESIDENCY MESSAGE," *ENSIGN,* MAR. 1994

Anyone who has any doubt about Joseph Smith's powers of leadership need only look at the men who were attracted to him. They did not come for wealth. They did not come for political power. They were not drawn by dreams of military conquest. His offering to them was none of these; rather, it concerned only salvation through faith in the Lord Jesus Christ. It involved persecution with its pain and losses, long and lonely missions, separation from family and friends, and in many cases death itself. GORDON B. HINCKLEY, "FIRST PRESIDENCY MESSAGE," *ENSIGN,* AUG. 1983

Great was the Prophet Joseph Smith's vision. It encompassed all the peoples of mankind, wherever they live, and all generations who have walked the earth and passed on. IBID.

Through the Prophet Joseph Smith, He has restored for us, and for all mankind if they will accept it, the glorious gospel as He has brought it to earth in the meridian of time. Mormonism has its existence in that reality–it is our witness to the world. *DESERET NEWS,* DEC. 11, 1957

We solemnly bear witness that through the boy Joseph Smith, a humble instrument in the hands of Almighty God, the gospel of Jesus Christ was again made known to men, and the priesthood with its keys was restored to the earth; that the principles taught by The Church of Jesus Christ of Latter-day Saints were those that were taught by Jesus in the flesh; that as He said to Nicodemus, so it still is, that men must be born of the water and of the spirit if they are to enter the kingdom of God; that the ordinances to bestow these must, to be effective, be performed by those holding the Priesthood of God; that the rock of revelation is the rock upon which The Church of Jesus Christ of Latter-day Saints is built; and that the Lord still guides His Church by revelations of His mind and will; and that The Church of Jesus Christ of Latter-day Saints is the true Church of Christ and the only Church on the face of the earth that possesses the truths of the everlasting gospel, the right to officiate in its rites and ordinances, and that has the authority to act in the name of God, through His holy priesthood, which His Church alone possesses. *DESERET NEWS,* DEC. 20, 1947

In humility, and with full consciousness of the responsibility involved, we bear witness to the people of the world that with the appearance of the Father and the Son to the Prophet Joseph Smith in the early spring of 1820, the greatest gospel dispensation of all times was ushered in, a dispensation of light, radiating from the presence of God, illuminating the minds of men, increasing intelligence and knowledge, which is the glory of God, and by the application of which the past one hundred years have been made the miracle century of the ages. *IMPROVEMENT ERA,* MAY 1930, IN *MESSAGES,* 5:274-86

Joseph Smith was the agent through whom the Lord saw fit to begin the great latter-day work. To him the Father and Son appeared in heavenly vision, upon him the keys of the everlasting priesthood were conferred, with authority to transmit them to others, with the promise that the priesthood should never be taken from the earth again, until the purposes of the Father were accomplished. *DESERET NEWS,* DEC. 19, 1925, IN *MESSAGES,* 5:245-48

Jesus of Nazareth, the son of Mary, we regard as also the Son of God. Joseph Smith was His servant and authorized representative. We honor them both. But Jesus was the Christ, the incomparable One, the incarnation of Deity. Joseph was human, appointed and directed by the Savior, and not an object of human worship. We follow him as he followed Christ, from whom he received all the doctrines, precepts, ordinances, and authority that we recognize. *DESERET EVENING NEWS*, DEC. 17, 1910

Let no man presume for a moment that his [Joseph Smith's] place will be filled by another; for *remember he stands in his own place* and always will; and the Twelve Apostles of this dispensation stand in their own place and always will, both in time and in eternity, to minister, preside, and regulate the affairs of the whole Church. STATEMENT, AUG. 15, 1844, IN *MESSAGES*, 1:234-37

Socialism. *See also* Communism

[I]f socialism embodied all of the principles of United Order, even in that event, it would be just as distinct and from the United Order as it is at present; ... it is one thing for such principles to be administered by good and righteous men, acting by virtue of divine authority, and entirely another thing for such principles to be entrusted to men whose ambition is prompting them to ride into political power by means of a third party. Members of the Church, men holding the holy priesthood, ought to be able to discern between such things and not engage in a questionable cause of any kind, and especially after doing so to then use their Church influence as a means of putting the stamp of approval on it and recommending it to others. FIRST PRESIDENCY TO W. T. JACK, APR. 23, 1912

sons of perdition

These people, known as sons of perdition, are those who have received the Holy Spirit and then denied it, who are in open, willful rebellion against the truth. They will be cast out with Satan and his angels into a place "which is not a kingdom of glory" (D&C 88:24; see also 76:28-28). *PRINCIPLES*, 1976

Say to the brothers Hulet, and to all others, that the Lord never authorized them to say that the devil, his angels or the sons of perdition, should ever be restored; for their state of destiny was not revealed to man, is not revealed, nor ever shall be revealed, save to those who are made partakers thereof; consequently those who teach this doctrine have not received it of the Spirit of the Lord. STATEMENT, JUNE 25, 1833, IN *MESSAGES,* 1:11-12

spirit world, *see* death

spirits. *See also* premortal existence

The spirit of man is in the form of man, and the spirits of all creatures are in the likeness of their bodies. *IMPROVEMENT ERA,* NOV. 1909, IN *MESSAGES,* 4:200-06

stakes

A stake covers a specific geographical area and is composed of several wards. All members of the Church in that area belong to that stake. A stake is an administrative division organized to conduct the full program of the Church. The stake officers and organizations provide training and guidance for the wards. *PRINCIPLES,* 1976

A stake is presided over by a stake president, who is a high priest set apart by a member of the Council of the Twelve as the presiding high priest in the stake. He is assisted by two counselors, and together they are responsible for the effective operation of the Church in their area. IBID.

The stake presidency controls the affairs of the stake, and both priesthood and auxiliary organizations are under its presidency. *PRIESTHOOD STUDY GUIDE,* 1948

standard works. *See also* scriptures

[F]or many years the standard works of the Church, by which the Church should be guided, were accepted at our semi-annual conferences. The practice of proposing them each conference for acceptance and support by the people has been discontinued, but the principle stands, namely, that only those things which the Church itself accepts and adopts for its guidance can be regarded as authoritative in the sense that they are the expressed views of the Church. FIRST PRESIDENCY TO STERLING B. TALMAGE, DEC. 19, 1935

The Church of Jesus Christ of Latter-day Saints recognizes, outside the direct and heaven-inspired utterances of its prophet, seer, and revelator, four standards of doctrine, namely, the Bible, the Book of Mormon, the Doctrine and Covenants, and the Pearl of Great Price, containing the revelations of God given in times past and present for the guidance, salvation, and exaltation of His people. These books have been accepted by the Church, in general conference assembled, as its doctrinal standards, and nothing outside of them, whether true or false, has any practical bearing or significance so far as the conduct of the Church is concerned. JOSEPH F. SMITH TO LILLIE GOLSAN, JULY 16, 1902

stem cell research

[T]he Church has not taken a position on the issue of embryonic stem cell research. NEWS RELEASE, MAY 26, 2005

While the First Presidency and the Quorum of the Twelve Apostles have not taken a position at this time on the newly emerging field of stem cell research, it merits cautious scrutiny. The proclaimed potential to provide cures or treatments for many serious diseases needs careful and continuing study by conscientious, qualified investigators. As with any emerging new technology, there are concerns that must be addressed. Scientific and religious viewpoints both demand that strict moral and ethical guidelines be followed. NEWS RELEASE, "STATEMENT REGARDING STEM CELL RESEARCH," AUG. 9, 2001

sterilization. *See also* birth control

The Church strongly discourages surgical sterilization as an elective form of birth control. It should be considered only if (1) medical conditions seriously jeopardize life or health or (2) birth defects or serious trauma have rendered a person mentally incompetent and not responsible for his or her actions. Such conditions must be determined by competent medical judgment and in accordance with law. Even then, the persons responsible for this decision should consult with each other and with their bishop and should receive divine confirmation of their decision through prayer. *CHURCH HANDBOOK,* 1998

stillborn children

Temple ordinances are not performed for stillborn children. However, this does not deny the possibility that a stillborn child may be part of the family in the eternities. Parents are encouraged to trust the Lord to resolve such cases in the way He knows is best. *CHURCH HANDBOOK,* 1998

We can say without hesitation that it is safe to rely upon the mercy and wisdom of God our Father and Christ the Redeemer of the world, who is the Resurrection and the Life, as to the future status of children who are born dead. FIRST PRESIDENCY TO W. DEAN BELNAP, FEB. 12, 1970

suffering

In the pain, the agony, and the heroic endeavors of life, we pass through a refiner's fire, and the insignificant and the unimportant in our lives can melt away like dross and make our faith bright, intact, and strong. In this way the divine image can be mirrored from the soul. It is part of the purging toll exacted of some to become acquainted with God. In the agonies of life, we seem to listen better to the faint, godly whisperings of the Divine Shepherd. JAMES E. FAUST, "FIRST PRESIDENCY MESSAGE," *ENSIGN,* FEB. 2006

If there were no night, we would not appreciate the day, nor could we see the stars and the vastness of the heavens. We must partake of the bitter with the sweet. There is a divine purpose in the adversities we encounter every day. They prepare, they purge, they purify, and thus they bless. IBID.

Life is a school of experience, a time of probation. We learn as we bear our afflictions and live through our heartaches. THOMAS S. MONSON, "FIRST PRESIDENCY MESSAGE," *ENSIGN,* JUNE 2005

It may safely be assumed that no person has ever lived entirely free of suffering and tribulation, nor has there ever been a period in human history that did not have its full share of turmoil, ruin, and misery. IBID.

Whenever we are inclined to feel burdened down with the blows of life, let us remember that others have passed the same way, have endured, and then have overcome. IBID.

As part of Heavenly Father's plan of redemption, you experience adversity during mortality. Trials, disappointments, sadness, sickness, and heartache are a difficult part of life, but they can lead to spiritual growth, refinement, and progress as you turn to the Lord. *TRUE TO FAITH,* 2004

There are many things that we cannot change. We all have

difficulties and disappointments. But often these turn out to be opportunities. The Lord can measure how strong we are by how we handle these difficulties in our lives. As the Lord said to the Prophet Joseph Smith, "Know thou, my son, that all these things shall give thee experience, and shall be for thy good" (D&C 122:7).

Sometimes the Lord allows us to have trials to shape us into productive servants. In our desire to achieve, we often fail to see that the Lord is trying to prune us away from false pride and vain ambition so He can teach us discipleship. His all-seeing eye is over us and ever watching us as our Eternal Heavenly Parent. When trials come, as surely they will to all of us during mortality, let us not sink into the abyss of self-pity but remember who is at the helm, that He is there to guide us through all the storms of life. JAMES E. FAUST, "FIRST PRESIDENCY MESSAGE," *ENSIGN,* OCT. 2002

Life is full of difficulties, some minor and others of a more serious nature. There seems to be an unending supply of challenges for one and all. Our problem is that we often expect instantaneous solutions to such challenges, forgetting that frequently the heavenly virtue of patience is required. THOMAS S. MONSON, "FIRST PRESIDENCY MESSAGE," *ENSIGN,* SEPT. 2002

There is usually no quick solution to social or emotional difficulties. Those who suffer from such difficulties should exercise great care in choosing appropriate professionals to assist them. As always, members may consult with priesthood leaders for guidance in identifying sources of help that are fully consistent with gospel principles. *ENSIGN,* DEC. 1999

In the many trials of life, when we feel abandoned and when sorrow, sin, disappointment, failure, and weakness make us less than we should ever be, there can come the healing salve of the unreserved love in the grace of God. It is love that forgives and forgets, a love that lifts and blesses. It is a love that sustains a new beginning on a higher level and thereby continues "from grace to grace" (D&C 93:13). JAMES E. FAUST, "FIRST PRESIDENCY MESSAGE," *ENSIGN,* JAN. 1999

In life we all have our times of testing and growth. These trials are necessary. They are growth experiences. Though they are times of deep anguish and suffering, they are also times to draw near to God. The suffering of the Savior in Gethsemane was without question the greatest that has ever come to mankind, yet out of it came the greatest good in the promise of eternal life. JAMES E. FAUST, "FIRST PRESIDENCY MESSAGE," *ENSIGN,* FEB. 1998

Why is adversity often such a good schoolmaster? Is it because it teaches so many things? Through difficult circumstances we are often forced to learn discipline and how to work. In often unpleasant circumstances we may also be subjected to a buffeting, a honing, and a polishing that can come no other way. IBID.

More than anything else, people with problems want to be understood. This is more important to them than receiving sympathy. *CHURCH HANDBOOK 2,* 1998

We live in a complex world with daily challenges. There is a tendency to feel detached, even isolated, from the giver of every good gift. We worry that we walk alone.

From the bed of pain, from the pillow wet with the tears of loneliness, we are lifted heavenward by that divine assurance and precious promise, "I will not fail thee, nor forsake thee" (Josh. 1:5).

Such comfort is priceless as we journey along the pathway of mortality, with its many forks and turnings. Rarely is the assurance communicated by a flashing sign or a loud voice. Rather, the language of the Spirit is gentle, quiet, uplifting to the heart and soothing to the soul. THOMAS S. MONSON, "FIRST PRESIDENCY MESSAGE," *ENSIGN,* JUNE 1997

In the Lord's eternal plan, those who endure such suffering, pain, and injustice, not of their own doing, will receive compensatory blessings through the Lord's infinite mercy. NEWS RELEASE, MAY 27, 1988

Pressing on in noble endeavors, even while surrounded by a cloud of depression, will eventually bring you out on top into the sunshine. Even our master Jesus the Christ, while facing that supreme test of being temporarily left alone by our Father during the crucifixion, continued performing His labors for the children of men, and then shortly thereafter He was glorified and received a fullness of joy. While you are going through your trial, you can recall your past victories and count the blessings that you do have with a sure hope of greater ones to follow if you are faithful. And you can have that certain knowledge that in due time God will wipe away all tears and that "eye hath not seen, nor ear heard, neither have entered into the heart of man, the things which God hath prepared for them that love him" (1 Cor. 2:9). EZRA TAFT BENSON, "FIRST PRESIDENCY MESSAGE," *ENSIGN,* OCT. 1986

We join our prayers with all the others in behalf of those who mourn, that they may be comforted and the heavy burden of sadness lifted from their hearts. May they know that the Savior of mankind, who Himself is well acquainted with grief, is mindful of their tears and will ease their affliction. NEWS RELEASE, DEC. 16, 1985

No matter what else may befall us, no matter what our station in life may be, each of us is a child of God. How comforting it is to know that we can call on Him in prayer and that He is ready to hear us and will grant us those things that are for our best good. He wants our happiness and success, and most of all He wants us to return to dwell with Him forever. N. ELDON TANNER, "FIRST PRESIDENCY MESSAGE," *ENSIGN,* FEB. 1978

The future looks ominous; it is pregnant with unborn events and big with possibilities. Fear and apprehension will but unfit us for the fray. The evil of tomorrow loses much of its size as we approach it. Persistent climbing levels the hills and gives added strength to travel on. We need only faith to try, hope to inspire, and courage to endure. *CHURCH NEWS,* DEC. 21, 1968

[O]ur knowledge of the truth and our righteous living will sustain, comfort and uphold us in any emergencies through which we may be called upon to pass. *DESERET NEWS,* DEC. 12, 1956

In these times of strain and stress that shake the very foundations of our lives, all you who are weary and disconsolate, who dwell in misery and sorrow, who suffer from grievous harms and afflictions, who crave comfort and solace, who would be relieved of buffeting doubts fathered by Satan, you whose spirits are downcast and the way before you is dark, you who grieve over your trials and tribulations, all of you who need help that your mortal arm cannot give, nor your friends—you, one and all, turn to and follow and keep the commandments of our Lord and Savior, Jesus Christ, the one mediator between God and man, the propitiation for our sins and the sins of the whole world. His is the only "name under heaven given among men, whereby we must be saved.... Neither is there salvation in any other" [Acts 4:12]. He is full of grace and truth which He, not another, bestows upon us, for they came by Him. All our hope is centered in Him, and flows from Him. *DESERET NEWS,* DEC. 13, 1950

[T]he Father, who lets no sparrow fall to the ground unnoticed, guards and protects those who live righteously in Him, and ... we shall "Fear not them which kill the body, but are not able to kill the souls, but rather fear him which is able to destroy both soul and body in hell" (Matt. 10:28). *BRIEF STATEMENT,* 1943

The deplorable conditions in the world today are the direct result of failure of the children of men to keep the commandments of the Lord. As long as the world continues to ignore these commandments, so long will turmoil, strife, and misery prevail. *DESERET NEWS,* DEC. 14, 1940

The important question with us is not so much why we have these difficulties, trials, and depressions, but how nobly do we meet them. HEBER J. GRANT TO EMMA BROWN, FEB. 14, 1935

[W]e promise the people that their burdens will be lightened and surcease will come from their trials and griefs in so far as they keep the commandments of the Lord, with an eye single to His glory. *DESERET NEWS,* DEC. 15, 1934

Notwithstanding the confusion which at present prevails in this world of ours, we have much to be thankful for, and can look confidently forward to a brighter and happier day. *DESERET NEWS,* DEC. 19, 1931

The Lord has promised that all who patiently endure these tribulations to the end shall be saved. IBID.

The darkest hour precedes the dawn. The night lingers but the day is breaking with resplendent glory. *DESERET NEWS,* DEC. 22, 1917

The discord of the world is a precursor and contrast of the full and glorious harmony to follow. IBID.

While we sympathize with the suffering [in the world,] we need not ignore the blessings at hand, nor fail to enjoy the favors within our reach, extended by a bountiful Providence and gathered by industry and frugality. *DESERET NEWS,* DEC. 18, 1915, IN *MESSAGES,* 4:343-48

The knowledge that God is with us, and that His work will prevail, should buoy us up under every difficulty and every trial, having the conviction that the Lord will cause even "the wrath of man to praise Him" [Ps. 76:10]. The very efforts of the enemies of His Church to hedge up its way will be overruled by Him to accelerate its advancement. *DESERET NEWS,* DEC. 16, 1905, IN *MESSAGES,* 4:121-23

The Saints have troubles in all the world, some more, some less, but all have to exercise patience and by so doing show their devotion to God and His cause, and their works will in time shine forth out of the darkness that surrounds the world. FIRST PRESIDENCY TO "BELOVED BRETHREN AND SISTERS IN TURKEY," SEPT. 7, 1897, IN *MESSAGES,* 3:284-87

Our past experience has proved to us how willing our Father in Heaven is to hear our cries in the hours of extremity and difficulty, when we approach Him in a proper spirit and with proper faith. He is quick to hear the cries of His people and He has promised to us that if we will draw near unto Him, He will draw near unto us. *MILLENNIAL STAR,* DEC. 3, 1896, IN *MESSAGES,* 3:281-84

[H]owever much we may feel aggrieved at the acts of men towards us, we should not pray for their condemnation. Let us confess our own sins and pray that we may be forgiven for them, and leave other sinners to the Lord, who has said that judgment is His, and He will repay. FIRST PRESIDENCY TO PRESIDENTS OF STAKES AND THEIR COUNSELORS, DEC. 2, 1889, IN *MESSAGES,* 3:176-79

It appears plain that it is God's purpose to suffer His Saints to be thoroughly tried and tested, so that they may prove their integrity and know the character of the foundation upon which they build. *WOMAN'S EXPONENT,* APR. 15, 1888, IN *MESSAGES,* 3:156-63

When the Lord, for any reason, turns His face away from His people, and is slow to hear their cries, thorough repentance on their part and a complete abandonment of their evil ways are sure to bring back His favor, and to cause His countenance to shine upon them. STATEMENT, APR. 8, 1887, IN *MESSAGES,* 3:109-29

[O]ut of apparent evil, Providence will bring abundant good, and the lesson which the signs of the times should teach us is one of patience, endurance, and calm reliance on the Lord. The result will be that we shall be stronger, wiser, purer, happier for the experience gained, and the work of the Lord, delivered by His omnipotence from all the snares set for its retardation, or plans laid for its destruction, will yet triumph gloriously over all its foes, and the infinite Atonement of the Redeemer will accomplish its perfect work. The final victory of the Saints is certain; after the trial comes the reward. IBID.

They who fight against Zion shall be destroyed; and the pit which has been digged for our destruction shall be filled by those who digged it, unto their utter destruction. IBID.

The afflictions which our Father permits to come upon us will be made light unto us, and they will be made to appear as very trifling in comparison with the calamities that He has said shall come upon the ungodly inhabitants of the earth. IBID.

[W]hen the Latter-day Saints repent of their sins and devote themselves assiduously to keeping the commandments of God, their enemies cannot have much power over them. IBID.

At no time has the Lord led His people to expect that they would not have to endure trials, or not have their faith fully tested. *MILLENNIAL STAR,* MAY 17, 1886, IN *MESSAGES,* 3:46-71

[I]f you live godly in Christ Jesus, while Satan has power, you will suffer persecution. IBID.

Persecution develops character. Under its influence we all know ourselves better than we did before we felt its pressure; and we discover traits in our brethren and sisters of the existence of which, perhaps, we were in entire ignorance. IBID.

There may be storms to be endured; there may be trials to be encountered and difficulties to be overcome; and there may be seasons when clouds of darkness may envelop us and shut out the horizon from our view; yet if we humble ourselves before our God and keep the covenants we have made with Him, He will neither desert nor neglect us. IBID.

We have ever thought it better to suffer wrong than to do wrong. *MILLENNIAL STAR,* NOV. 9, 1885, IN *MESSAGES,* 3:23-41

Truths, such as God has revealed in these days, are not established without suffering and sacrifice on the part of those who espouse and advocate them. IBID.

[I]f any man or woman expects to enter into the celestial kingdom of our God without being tested to the very uttermost, they have not understood the gospel. If there is a weak spot in our nature, or if there is a fibre that can be made to quiver or to shrink, we may rest assured that it will be tested. Our own weaknesses will be brought fully to light, and in seeking for help, the strength of our God will also be made manifest to us. IBID.

[W]hile men may in their blind zeal seek to oppress us and bring us into bondage, we must not be provoked to do as they do but [rather continue] to maintain the rights, immunities, and seek for the happiness and well-being, as well as to maintain the freedom, of all men of every name, color, and creed. STATEMENT, APR. 4, 1885, IN *MESSAGES,* 3:4-12

In relation to the sickness of your wife, to which you refer, it is very distressing and painful to be so situated, both in regard to her and yourself; but such are the vicissitudes of human life, and such the weakness and infirmities pertaining to the body, that suffering from sickness and disease are not uncommon even among the good and those who are desirous to observe the law and keep the commandments of God, and while the gift of healing is a blessing imported to the Church, which we all of us ought duly to appreciate yet, at the same time, there are many people who are not healed. Some suffer and linger for a length of time, and others pass off suddenly; as it is the decree of God, and His appointment, that man must die, we cannot avert this order. JOHN TAYLOR TO S. M. LARSON, MAR. 23, 1883

He [God] has promised to fight your battles. His word has never failed. You have proved Him in times of trial and fierce persecution in the past, and He is the same God today that He was then. He has neither gone to sleep, nor is He upon a journey; and if you are faithful to Him, He will as surely deliver you in the future and fulfill all His promises to Zion as He has delivered you in the past. STATEMENT, AUG. 29, 1882, IN *MESSAGES,* 2:342-47

[I]f we, by our wickedness, bring evil on our own heads, the Lord will let us bear it till we get weary and hate iniquity. STATEMENT, JULY 2, 1833, IN *MESSAGES,* 1:16-18

suicide. ***See also*** **life, sanctity of**

It is wrong to take a life, even one's own. However, a person who commits suicide may not be responsible for his or her acts. Only God can judge such a matter. *CHURCH HANDBOOK,* 1998

It is generally assumed that no man in his right mind can commit suicide; and, therefore, the one who does so is not responsible for his acts. Under these circumstances it has been felt that it would not be fair or just to deprive such a person who is irresponsible from the blessings which come from temple endowments and sealings. JOSEPH ANDERSON, SECRETARY TO THE FIRST PRESIDENCY, TO FLOYD H. POULSEN, JAN. 19, 1948

In answer we would say that when it comes to doing temple work for that unfortunate class of people, they should be given the benefit of every doubt; that is, before we could feel justified in closing the doors of the temples against them it should be clearly shown that they were of perfectly sound mind when the act was performed and in possession of sufficient knowledge to realize that they were responsible before the Lord for the destruction of their own lives. Unless therefore it can be shown beyond doubt that your father was responsible for the suicidal act, his work should be done for him; and if it should be found in the hereafter that he is unworthy of the blessings conferred upon him, he will derive no benefit therefrom. FIRST PRESIDENCY TO W. H. SEEGMILLER, JULY 22, 1901

Suicide should be made odious among the people of God, it should be emphasized as a deadly sin, and no undue feelings of tenderness toward the unfortunate dead, or of sympathy towards the living bereaved, should prevent us denouncing it as a crime against God and humanity, against the Creator and the creation. STATEMENT, OCT. 6, 1886, IN *MESSAGES,* 3:72-91

[I]f this condition [suicide] be the result of sin, of departure from God's laws, then the unfortunate one, like the inebriate, is not altogether free from the responsibility of acts committed while in this state of mental derangement; if he is not censurable for the act itself, he is for the causes that induced it. IBID.

swearing, *see* **profanity**

T

tattooing

Latter-day prophets strongly discourage the tattooing of the body. *TRUE TO FAITH,* 2004

The Church does not look with favor upon the tattooing of the body, but this does not restrict a person from receiving a temple recommend, unless such tattooing is obscene and unbecoming in the house of the Lord. *CHURCH HANDBOOK,* 1976

Desecrating the human body by permanently marking the skin with various designs and names is discouraged. Tattooing, accomplished by inserting permanent, indelible dye through skin puncture marks, should not be permitted, except for placing a blood type or an identification number in an area of the body where it will not be noticeable. *PRINCIPLES,* 1976

taxes

Church members are obligated by the twelfth Article of Faith to obey the tax laws of the nation where they reside (see also D&C 134:5). Members who disapprove of tax laws may try to have them changed by legislation or constitutional amendment. Members who have well-founded legal objections may challenge tax laws in the courts.

Members who refuse to file a tax return, pay required income taxes, or comply with a final judgment in a tax case are in direct conflict with the law and with the teachings of the Church. *CHURCH HANDBOOK,* 1998

[A] member who deliberately refuses to pay state or federal income taxes, or to comply with any final judgment rendered in an income tax case, federal or state, is out of harmony with basic teachings of the church and may, for this reason, be considered ineligible for a temple recommend. Furthermore, we feel that such a member should not be called to a position of principal responsibility in the Church. We also feel that a member who is convicted of willfully violating either federal or state tax laws should be disciplined by a Church court to the extent warranted by the circumstances. FIRST PRESIDENCY TO ALL STAKE AND MISSION PRESIDENTS, UNITED STATES, JAN. 21, 1983

If one disapproves of the income tax law, his remedy is not to disobey or to ignore it, but rather to attempt to challenge it in the courts or to have it changed by legislation or Constitutional amendment.

It is apparent that if all persons were to refuse to obey the laws of which they disapprove, a state of anarchy would exist. FIRST PRESIDENCY TO ALL STAKE AND MISSION PRESIDENTS, UNITED STATES, SEPT. 19, 1975

tea, *see* Word of Wisdom

telestial kingdom. *See also* exaltation

Telestial glory will be reserved for individuals who "received not the gospel of Christ, neither the testimony of Jesus" (D&C 76:82). These individuals will receive their glory after being redeemed from spirit prison, which is sometimes called hell (76:84, 106). *TRUE TO FAITH,* 2004

temple garments

White undergarments [are] worn by members of the Church who have received a temple ordinance known as the endowment. The garment reminds the wearer of covenants made in the temple. *QUICK FACTS,* 2005

Once you are endowed, you have the blessing of wearing the temple garment throughout your life. You are obligated to wear it according to the instructions given in the endowment. Remember that the blessings that are related to this sacred privilege depend on your worthiness and your faithfulness in keeping temple covenants.

The garment provides a constant reminder of the covenants you have made in the temple. You should treat it with respect at all times. You should not expose it to the view of those who do not understand its significance, and you should not adjust it to accommodate different styles of clothing. When you wear it properly, it provides protection against temptation and evil. Wearing the garment is an outward expression of an inward commitment to follow the Savior. *TRUE TO FAITH,* 2004

Church members who have been clothed with the garment in a temple are obligated to wear it according to the instructions given in the endowment. *CHURCH HANDBOOK,* 1998

The garment provides a constant reminder of the covenants made in the temple. When properly worn, it provides protection against temptation and evil. IBID.

Church members who have been clothed with the garment in the temple have made a covenant to wear it throughout their lives. This has been interpreted to mean that it is worn as underclothing both day and night. This sacred covenant is between the member and the Lord. Members should seek the guidance of the Holy Spirit to answer for themselves any personal question about the wearing of the garment. Church leaders and others including temple workers should refrain from giving unauthorized instructions and opinions concerning when the garment might be removed. The promise of protection and blessings is conditioned upon worthiness and faithfulness in keeping the covenant.

The fundamental principle ought to be to wear the garment and not to find occasions to remove it. Thus, members should not remove either all or part of the garment to work in the yard or to lounge around the home in swimwear or immodest clothing. Nor should they remove it to participate in recreational activities that can reasonably be done with the garment worn properly beneath regular clothing. When the garment must be removed, such as for swimming, it should be restored as soon as possible.

The principles of modesty and keeping the body appropriately covered are implicit in the covenant and should govern the nature of all clothing worn. Endowed members of the Church wear the garment as a reminder of the sacred covenants they have made with the Lord and also as a protection against temptation and evil. How it is worn is an outward expression of an inward commitment to follow the Savior. "DEAR BRETHREN," OCT. 10, 1988

Endowed members are to wear garments in styles the Church has approved.

An endowed member who stops wearing garments, but who has not been excommunicated, may begin wearing them again without permission. A person who has been excommunicated is authorized to wear garments again only after a General Authority has restored his blessings. He should begin wearing them immediately, without waiting to go to the temple. *CHURCH HANDBOOK,* 1983

[E]ach person who wears the garment is answerable to the Lord for properly wearing and caring for it. "DEAR BRETHREN," DEC. 15, 1979

One who has received his temple endowment should wear regulation garments under his outer clothing while performing baptisms. *CHURCH HANDBOOK,* 1976

When garments are too worn for use, they may be completely burned or the marks of the priesthood should be removed from them and burned or cut into small pieces. The garment should then be cut up so the location of the marks cannot be identified. The fabrics of which garments were made have no further significance as sacred clothing. IBID.

The covenants taken in the temple incident and attached to the wearing of garments contemplate that they will be worn at all times. No exception to these covenants is found anywhere in the ceremonies. These covenants run between the one making them and the Lord. These covenants so made take on the nature of commandments of the Lord. "DEAR BRETHREN," MAR. 17, 1969; SEE ALSO "DEAR BRETHREN," AUG. 31, 1964

Every effort should be made to protect the garments from the gaze and raillery of scoffers. This may cause considerable inconvenience at times, but tact, discretion, and wisdom can do much to alleviate this inconvenience. If the scoffing [should] become unbearable and the wearer ... consider he was really "hindered" by the scoffers from wearing the garments, and if he should therefore ["decide that the Lord would" want him to] lay them aside, then the wearer should resume the wearing of the normal garment at the earliest possible moment. IBID.

The wearing of the garment is the subject of direct covenant between the Lord and the covenant maker, who must determine to what extent he will keep his covenants. To break our covenants is to lose the protection and blessings promised from obedience thereto. IBID.

It has come to our attention that in some of the temples instruction has been given to those going through to receive their endowments prior to entering into the marriage covenant that they must not remove the temple garment during the time of sexual relations.

We have authorized no such instruction or advice. We feel that this is a matter of such intimate nature that it must be left with the persons concerned. FIRST PRESIDENCY TO PRESIDENTS OF TEMPLES, MAY 16, 1968

[T]he wearing of the garment is an individual responsibility. It is associated with sacred obligations entered into by the wearer with the Lord in the temple; consequently, the conscience of the wearer must guide when circumstances seem to justify a modification of these obligations. The sacredness of the garment should be ever present and uppermost in the wearer's mind. FIRST PRESIDENCY, LETTER DATED OCT. 30, 1942, IN *MESSAGES,* 6:186

It is the duty of all persons who have been through the temple to see that the garment is not subjected to undue publicity, and to unite in an earnest effort to re-establish and to maintain the reverence it merits. *CHURCH HANDBOOK,* 1940

One of the most important obligations of the Church is to prepare its youth to receive their endowments. Boys and girls should be taught to look forward to going to the temple as one of the richest opportunities of their lives. They should understand that here are given the highest blessings which men obtain in this world. They should be early impressed with the sanctity of the marriage covenant and with its fundamental place in our concept of eternal welfare and happiness.

They should also be made to know that the garment of the holy priesthood will be given to them in the temple ceremony, and that it represents something very sacred which is not to be looked upon lightly nor sacrificed to the dictates of fashion and worldly opinion. It must be made clear to them that it is such an indispensable part of the temple ceremony that if they do not make up their minds to always wear it, and respect it, they are not entitled to the endowments of the temple. "DEAR BRETHREN," JULY 20, 1938

We permit people who are engaged in athletics to remove the garment where necessary while so engaged. There would be no objection to one whose employment required her to do so, removing the temple garment when necessary. HEBER J. GRANT TO GRANT A. KENDALL, SEPT. 20, 1935

The garment is associated with some of the most sacred covenants which members of the Church make. Neither the covenants nor the garment should be known by anyone who does not understand to a degree at least their true significance. DAVID O. MCKAY TO GEORGE F. RICHARDS, JOSEPH FIELDING SMITH, STEPHEN L. RICHARDS, AND MELVIN J. BALLARD, JUNE 29, 1935

It may be observed that no fixed pattern of the temple garment has ever been given, and that the present style of garment differs very materially from that in use in the early history of the Church, at which time a garment without collar and with buttons was frequently used. FIRST PRESIDENCY TO PRESIDENTS OF STAKES AND PRESIDENTS OF TEMPLES, JUNE 14, 1923

temple work

Only in Latter-day Saint temples are preserved in an indissoluble union for all eternity the precious associations of mortality. Among many things of a doctrinal nature that distinguish this Church from all others is the work that occurs in the house of the Lord under divine priesthood authority.

GORDON B. HINCKLEY, "FIRST PRESIDENCY MESSAGE," *ENSIGN,* MAR. 2006

Every man or woman who goes into the house of the Lord leaves there a better man or woman than he or she was when he or she entered the house of the Lord. The house of the Lord will have a refining effect upon you. It will cultivate unselfishness within your lives. It will build righteousness. It will impress upon you the importance of doing what you ought to do. Go to the house of the Lord. IBID.

In the temple we make sacred covenants and are endowed with, or are given, a gift of power and knowledge from on high. This power helps us in our daily lives and enables us to build God's kingdom. In the temple we can also be married for time and eternity, thus making it possible for families to be together forever in God's presence. *PREACH MY GOSPEL,* 2005

Temples are literally houses of the Lord. They are holy places of worship where the Lord may visit. Only the home can compare with temples in sacredness. *TRUE TO FAITH,* 2004

One ordinance we receive in the temple is the endowment. The word *endowment* means "gift," and the temple endowment truly is a gift from God. The ordinance consists of a series of instructions and includes covenants we make to live righteously and comply with the requirements of the gospel. The endowment helps us focus on the Savior, His role in our Heavenly Father's plan, and our commitment to follow Him. IBID.

Many in the spirit world embrace the gospel. However, they cannot receive priesthood ordinances for themselves because they do not have physical bodies. In holy temples, we have the privilege of receiving ordinances in their behalf. These ordinances include baptism, confirmation, Melchizedek Priesthood ordination (for men), the endowment, the marriage sealing, and the sealing of children to parents. IBID.

All the ordinances which take place in the House of the Lord become expressions of our belief in that fundamental and basic doctrine of the immortality of the human soul. As we redouble our efforts and our faithfulness in going to the temple, the Lord will bless us. *CHURCH NEWS,* MAR. 22, 2003

In the temples of the Lord, we learn obedience. We learn sacrifice. We make the vows of chastity and have our lives consecrated to holy purposes. It is possible for us to be purged and purified and to have our sins washed away so that we may come before the Lord as clean, white, and spotless as the newly fallen snow. JAMES E. FAUST, "FIRST PRESIDENCY MESSAGE," *ENSIGN,* AUG. 2001

As the Saints come into the sacrosanct washing and anointing rooms and are washed, they will be spiritually cleansed. As they are anointed, they will be renewed and regenerated in soul and spirit. IBID.

Ordinances that are performed for the dead are effective only if the deceased person chooses to accept them and becomes qualified to receive them (see D&C 138:19, 32-34). *CHURCH HANDBOOK,* 1998

In temples, worthy Church members receive ordinances that are essential for exaltation. Each ordinance includes covenants and promised blessings. In this way members receive important knowledge of "things which have been kept hid from before the foundation of the world" (D&C 124:41).

Temples are places of safety and refuge from the world. They are sources of strength for righteous living. They strengthen families as members learn sacred truths and serve those who have died without receiving the ordinances of the gospel. *CHURCH HANDBOOK 2,* 1998

The washing and anointing are the first part of the endowment. They are also called initiatory ordinances. They are administered to each person privately. They promise blessings in the present and the future (see D&C 124:39).

The endowment ordinance explains the purpose of life, the mission and Atonement of Jesus Christ, and Heavenly Father's plan for the exaltation of His children. Through this ordinance, Church members enter into covenants of sacrifice, consecration, and fidelity. They also receive a gift of power from God (D&C 38:32, 38; 95:8; 105:12, 18, 33; 109:13, 22). IBID.

People who died without a knowledge of the gospel, but who would have received it, are promised that they will be heirs to the celestial kingdom (see D&C 137:7-10). IBID.

The people in the spirit world may exercise faith in Jesus Christ and accept the gospel message, but because they do not have physical bodies, the gospel ordinances must be performed vicariously for them on earth. Church members have a responsibility to provide these ordinances for their own ancestral families. This work is performed in temples. Ordinances that have been performed for the dead are effective when the deceased persons choose to accept them and become qualified to receive them (see D&C 138:19, 32-34). IBID.

[K]eeping the covenants associated with the endowment can be the foundation for great joy in mortality. IBID.

The divine plan of happiness enables family relationships to be perpetuated beyond the grave. Sacred ordinances and covenants make it possible for individuals to return to the presence of God and for families to be united eternally. *CHURCH NEWS*, SEPT. 30, 1995

Church members should not submit for temple ordinances the names of celebrities and non-approved groups, such as Jewish Holocaust victims. *CHURCH NEWS,* JULY 8, 1995

The endowment is another ordinance performed in our temples. It consists of two parts: first, a series of instructions, and second, promises or covenants that the person receiving the endowment makes–promises to live righteously and comply with the requirements of the gospel of Jesus Christ. The endowment is an ordinance for the great blessing of the Saints–both living and dead. Thus it is also an ordinance performed by the living in behalf of deceased individuals; it is performed for those for whom baptismal work has already been performed. HOWARD W. HUNTER, "FIRST PRESIDENCY MESSAGE," *ENSIGN,* FEB. 1995

The restored gospel focuses on the ordinances of the holy temple as an essential step toward eternal life. As more members of the Church attend the temple, they and their families will enjoy needed blessings. *ENSIGN,* NOV. 1994

Temples are sacred for the closest communion between the Lord and those receiving the highest and most sacred ordinances of the holy priesthood. It is in the temple that things of the earth are joined with the things of heaven. HOWARD W. HUNTER, "FIRST PRESIDENCY MESSAGE," *ENSIGN,* OCT. 1994

Let us be a temple-attending and a temple-loving people. Let us hasten to the temple as frequently as time and means and personal circumstances allow. Let us go not only for our kindred dead, but let us also go for the personal blessing of temple worship, for the sanctity and safety which is provided within those hallowed and consecrated walls. The temple is a place of beauty, it is a place of revelation, it is a place of peace. It is the house of the Lord. It is holy unto the Lord. It should be holy unto us. IBID.

Temple worship is sacred. Those who desire to enter a temple should be worthy and should appreciate the purpose and eternal significance of temple ordinances and covenants. They also should understand the solemn and sacred responsibilities assumed by those who make temple covenants. *BULLETIN,* 1994-2

The Lord has commanded His people in all ages of the world to build temples "that the Son of Man might have a place to manifest himself to his people" (D&C 109:5). Temples play a major role in perfecting the Saints and in redeeming the dead. In temples worthy Saints receive the highest ordinances of the gospel for themselves and for those who did not receive them in mortality. *CHURCH HANDBOOK,* 1989

In considering ordinances for the deceased, we need not attempt to determine individual worthiness, whether an ordinance will be accepted, or the probable feelings of other deceased individuals affected by the proposed ordinance. In order to be binding in eternity, any ordinance in behalf of the dead must be accepted by the individuals involved, merited by individual worthiness, and sealed by the Holy Spirit of Promise. These determinations must, of necessity, be made beyond the veil. "DEAR BRETHREN," DEC. 8, 1988

Only members who have received their endowments may be buried in temple clothing. An endowed person who stopped wearing garments before his death may be clothed in temple clothing for burial if the family so requests, unless he was excommunicated. An endowed person who has committed suicide may be buried in temple clothing, unless he was excommunicated. Excommunicated persons whose blessings have not been restored may not be buried in temple clothing. *CHURCH HANDBOOK,* 1983

Brethren should wear clothing that is appropriate for sacrament meeting when they go to the temple.

While performing temple ordinances, brethren wear approved garments and either the approved one-piece white suit (white tie is optional) or white trousers with a long-sleeved white shirt and white tie. They also wear white stockings and white shoes or slippers with white, light tan, or gray soles.

Sisters should not wear slacks when they go to the temple. They should dress modestly. If they wear hats or head scarves, they should remove them at the temple entrance.

Sisters may wear plain combs, small barrettes, and white ribbons in the temple to keep their hair in place. Hairstyles, makeup, and nail polish should be conservative. Heavy makeup, loud colors, and large and ornate jewelry are out of place.

While performing temple ordinances, sisters wear approved garments and a white dress with long sleeves and a modestly high neckline. They should also wear white hose and white shoes or slippers with low or medium heels and white, light tan, or gray soles.

Brides may wear their wedding dresses in the temple. They should be white, have long sleeves and modestly high necklines, and have all sheer materials lined. Brides may wear their wedding dresses during the endowment session but must remove the trains for the session. They may not wear gowns with long dress pants in the temple.

Children must wear white clothing in the temple. IBID.

In temple work is found the very essence of selfless service. GORDON B. HINCKLEY, "FIRST PRESIDENCY MESSAGE," *ENSIGN,* AUG. 1982

The temple endowment includes certain sacred covenants which place the individual under obligation to observe these throughout life. Those who go to the temple for the first time should be both worthy and sufficiently mature to assess their capacity to keep these covenants thereafter, whether by marrying an active Church member or by righteous living, though unmarried. "DEAR BRETHREN," JULY 1, 1982

Temples of The Church of Jesus Christ of Latter-day Saints are an affirmative expression to all the world of the faith millions of Latter-day Saints have in the immortality of the soul. All of the activity carried on within these sacred edifices is based on the premise that all mortal beings who have been on Earth are in reality immortal. GORDON B. HINCKLEY, "FIRST PRESIDENCY MESSAGE," *ENSIGN,* FEB. 1982

We give our witness that the doctrines and practices of the Church encompass salvation and exaltation, not only for those who are living, but also for the dead, and that in sacred temples built for this purpose a great vicarious work is going forward in behalf of those who have died, so that all men and women of all generations may become the beneficiaries of the saving ordinances of the gospel of the Master. This great, selfless labor is one of the distinguishing features of this restored Church of Jesus Christ. *CHURCH NEWS,* APR. 12, 1980

[W]e want to stress that while members should be encouraged to go to the temple, quotas should never be used. Quotas sometimes cause people to go grudgingly and sometimes lose the spirit of the work. The decision as to when to attend the temple must be left up to every person based on his own circumstances and desires. A visit to the temple to do work for the dead should result in a happy spiritual experience. This is possible only when patrons visit voluntarily without pressure from any source. "DEAR BRETHREN," UNITED STATES AND CANADA, MAR. 28, 1979

The temples are reserved for sacred ordinances pertaining to the living and the dead. Worthy members of the Church should go to the temples as often as possible to participate in this important work. One of the ordinances performed in the temple is that of the endowment, which comprises a course of instruction relating to the eternal journey of man and woman from the preearthly existence through the earthly experience and on to the exaltation each may attain. SPENCER W. KIMBALL, "FIRST PRESIDENCY MESSAGE," *ENSIGN,* JAN. 1977

Those conducting temple recommend interviews should make clear to applicants for temple recommends what the Lord expects as to worthiness and that the representations the applicants make are being made to the Lord through the interviewing priesthood officer. "DEAR BRETHREN," JULY 6, 1976

Ordinance work for the dead, performed in the temples of God, will continue during the Millennium until every worthy soul has the opportunity of receiving all the blessings of the fullness of the gospel. "BASIC DOCTRINES," 1971

[T]he receipt by any person of the temple endowment is a most serious matter–the blessings promised and the covenants made relating to the living of their lives, indeed, the whole ceremony, is of the very last importance. We feel that for an unworthy person to go through the temple and receive his endowments merely adds to his culpability and consequent loss of the blessings promised in the temple and also increases the responsibility before the Lord for past misdeeds which may or may not be thoroughly repented of, and in addition to his responsibility for his conduct with reference to further transgression. FIRST PRESIDENCY TO PRESIDENTS OF MISSIONS, AUG. 25, 1960

Worthy Church members should be encouraged to get recommends and do temple work, but they should not be called on "missions" to the temples to perform ordinances by proxy for the dead. *HELPS AND SUGGESTIONS,* 1956

[T]he temple ceremonies themselves should never be discussed, nor information concerning them be given, to persons who have not already been through the temple, and so far as possible all discussions concerning these ceremonies between and among persons should take place only within the temple itself. FIRST PRESIDENCY TO PRESIDENTS OF EUROPEAN MISSIONS, NOV. 4, 1955

The giving of a recommend to enter into the house of the Lord and to participate in the ordinances therein performed is a most serious matter, not a mere formality to get the member past the entrance to the temple. Bishops should, of course, urge all members of their wards to fit themselves, by right thinking and living, to enter the temple to do temple work, and should urge the worthy members to get recommends; nevertheless, bishops should not indiscriminately urge all members of their wards to come and get recommends for that purpose. Bishops should always remember that only those who are really worthy members of the Church should be given recommends. "DEAR BRETHREN," JAN. 6, 1941, IN *PROGRESS,* 1941

[T]he performance of work in the temple is one of the highest privileges and prerogatives which belong to members in the Church. Only the worthy are entitled to the privilege of going to the temple. IBID.

So far as the Lord has revealed His will on the matter, it is far better not to receive the endowment than to receive it and then to violate the undertakings and obligations and covenants that pertain thereto. FIRST PRESIDENCY TO HYRUM B. CALDER, MAR. 25, 1938

The endowment is given but once, and the blessings pertaining thereto are lost only by excommunication from the Church. HEBER J. GRANT TO WILLIAM C. HUISH SR., NOV. 23, 1934

The fact is that every blessing pronounced upon those who go through the temple is given on condition of obedience to the principles and ordinances upon which that blessing is predicated. Any person who fails to comply with the requirements will deprive himself or herself of the blessing. He who arrogates to himself the thought that simply because he has received his endowments he can violate moral laws and escape paying the penalty to the "uttermost farthing" entertains a delusion. HEBER J. GRANT TO NELLIE LEE, NOV. 22, 1934

The Church is the only organization in existence that teaches the doctrine and administers the ordinances of baptism for the dead, which we associate with other vicarious administrations in behalf of our departed relatives. *DESERET NEWS,* DEC. 22, 1928, IN *MESSAGES,* 5:264-66

Each new temple forms an additional bond between the heavens and the earth, marking a new epoch in the mighty work of vicarious redemption by the living for the dead—enabling the Saints to be indeed saviors upon Mount Zion. *DESERET NEWS*, DEC. 17, 1927, IN *MESSAGES,* 5:254-57

The salvation of the dead is one of the cardinal purposes for which the everlasting gospel was restored and the Church of Christ established in this day. *DESERET NEWS,* DEC. 20, 1924, IN *MESSAGES,* 5:240-42

The temples are not open to the public. They are for the performance of sacred ordinances, having in view the salvation of the living and the dead. The principle ceremonies are baptisms, endowments, marriages, sealings, and adoptions. Much of this work, that in behalf of the dead, is of a vicarious character. With the Latter-day Saints there is hope of salvation for those who have departed this life without obeying the gospel, if they will yield obedience to its requirements in the other world, the place of departed spirits. The gospel will be preached to them by servants of the Lord who have entered into paradise, and they who manifest faith and repent ... can be baptized for here, receiving in like manner other ministrations to the end that they may be exalted and glorified. *DESERET NEWS,* NOV. 4, 1911, IN *MESSAGES,* 4:231-51

Because of their Masonic characters, the ceremonies of the temple are sacred and not for the public. IBID.

The command of God is for the Saints to labor with their might for the redemption of their dead, for, as the Prophet says: "It is the greatest responsibility that God has laid upon us, to seek after our dead." *DESERET NEWS,* DEC. 19, 1908, IN *MESSAGES,* 4:188-94

It stands to reason that while the gospel may be preached unto all, the good and the bad, or rather those who would repent and those who would not repent, in the spirit world the same as it is here, that redemption will only come to those who repent and obey. JOSEPH F. SMITH TO JOSEPH R. SMITH, SEPT. 13, 1899

[I]t is better to do the work for many who are unworthy than to neglect one who is [unworthy]. IBID.

In answer to your question regarding children born in the

covenant and those not so favored, it may be said that all the blessings belong to those born in the covenant and to none others. All will have to be brought into the covenant, hence the law of adoption, as we commonly call it. The birth of those born in the covenant is legitimate and recognized in the heavens. They are the heirs. Before others can become like unto them they must be adopted by and through the ordinances of the house of the Lord, provided in the gospel. As there is legitimate marriage recognized in the heavens by which the union of the parties becomes eternal, so also there must be legitimate birth. If originally we were born outside those united in the eternal bonds of celestial marriage then we have to be sealed to our parents after they have been thus united, or in some few exceptional cases, to others, whom we may select. And what is done for the living can be done by us for our dead. GEORGE REYNOLDS TO HENRY S. TANNER, MAR. 1, 1895

There is no labor in which the Latter-day Saints feel more deeply interested than in the building and completing of temples. *MILLENNIAL STAR,* MAY 16, 1892, IN *MESSAGES,* 3:234-36

There is no reason why young people, who are worthy, should be denied the privilege of their endowments, provided they are old enough to comprehend the principles of the gospel and the nature of a solemn covenant. JOSEPH F. SMITH TO JESSE B. MARTIN, MAR. 11, 1890

No right-feeling Latter-day Saint can think upon this subject [temple work] without being thrilled with heavenly joy for what God has done for us in our generation, furnishing us, as He has done, with every facility to prepare us, our posterity and our ancestors, for that eternal world which lies beyond the present life. STATEMENT, OCT. 10, 1887, IN *MESSAGES,* 3:133-55

terrestrial kingdom. ***See also*** **exaltation**

[I]ndividuals in the terrestrial kingdom will be honorable people "who were blinded by the craftiness of men" (D&C 76:75). This group will include members of the Church who were "not valiant in the testimony of Jesus" (76:79). It will also include those who rejected the opportunity to receive the gospel in mortality but who later received it in the postmortal spirit world (76:73-74). *TRUE TO FAITH,* 2004

testimony. ***See also*** **conversion**

Each of us has to receive our own witness concerning Jesus as the Christ. We cannot get it secondhand from someone else. JAMES E. FAUST, "FIRST PRESIDENCY MESSAGE," *ENSIGN,* MAR. 2005

A testimony is a spiritual witness and assurance given by the Holy Ghost. To bear testimony is to give a simple, direct declaration of belief—a feeling, an assurance, a conviction of gospel truth. *PREACH MY GOSPEL,* 2005

Absolutely basic to our faith is our testimony of Jesus Christ as the Son of God, who under divine plan was born in Bethlehem of Judea. GORDON B. HINCKLEY, "FIRST PRESIDENCY MESSAGE," *ENSIGN,* FEB. 2004

A testimony is a spiritual witness given by the Holy Ghost. The foundation of a testimony is the knowledge that Heavenly Father lives and loves us; that Jesus Christ lives, that He is the Son of God, and that He carried out the infinite Atonement; that Joseph Smith is the prophet of God who was called to restore the gospel; that we are led by a living prophet today; and that The Church of Jesus Christ of Latter-day Saints is the Savior's true Church on the earth. With this foundation, a testimony grows to include all principles of the gospel. *TRUE TO FAITH,* 2004

In this dispensation, when the Lord declared this to be "the only true and living church upon the face of the whole earth" (D&C 1:30), we were immediately put in a position from which we cannot shrink and which we each must face with humility and courage. Every true member of the Lord's Church who lives and breathes the spirit of the gospel of the Master knows something of that feeling as he or she associates with others. But once having gained a testimony, we are to live with it. We are to live with our conscience. We are to live with our God. GORDON B. HINCKLEY, "FIRST PRESIDENCY MESSAGE," *ENSIGN,* SEPT. 2001

A testimony is a sure knowledge, based on revelation from the Holy Ghost, that the gospel is true. *PRINCIPLES,* 1976

Every testimony should include a knowledge that Jesus is the Christ, the Son of God and the Savior of the world; that Joseph Smith is a prophet of God and was called to restore the gospel in this dispensation; and that The Church of Jesus Christ of Latter-day Saints is the only true church upon the earth. A testimony of these things leads us to all the principles of the gospel. IBID.

Because God is just, every person will have an opportunity to gain a testimony either during this life or after. However, the sooner a man builds a testimony, the greater opportunity he has to prove his faithfulness. IBID.

theology, *see* doctrine

tithing

Tithing funds are used to support the ongoing activities of the Church, such as building and maintaining temples and meetinghouses, carrying the gospel to all the world, conducting temple and family history work, and many other worldwide activities. Tithing does not pay local Church leaders, who serve without receiving payment of any kind. *PREACH MY GOSPEL,* 2005

The greatest portion of Church expenditures goes toward construction and maintenance of chapels and buildings in which to worship, meet, and learn.... The remainder is spent on other activities, including missionary and temple work, written materials in dozens of languages, and the global administration of the Church. *QUICK FACTS,* 2005

To pay a full tithe, you give one-tenth of your income to the Lord through His Church. You submit your tithing to a member of your bishopric or branch presidency. *TRUE TO FAITH,* 2004

Remember that paying tithing is not as much a matter of money as it is a matter of faith. Trust in the Lord. He gave the commandment for our benefit, and He made the accompanying promise. IBID.

Your attitude is important in paying tithing. Pay it because you love the Lord and have faith in Him. Pay it willingly with a thankful heart. Pay it first, even when you think you don't have enough money to meet your other needs. Doing so will help you overcome selfishness and be more receptive to the Spirit. *STRENGTH OF YOUTH,* 2001

These sacred contributions are used to build up God's kingdom on Earth and to assist those who are poor and needy, sick and afflicted. Blessings come to all as we bring our offerings into the Lord's storehouse (see Mal. 3:10-12). *CHURCH NEWS,* DEC. 18, 1993

The basic purpose for tithing is to provide the Church with

the means needed to carry on the Lord's work. The blessing to the giver is an ancillary return, and that blessing may not be always in the form of financial or material benefit. GORDON B. HINCKLEY, "FIRST PRESIDENCY MESSAGE," *ENSIGN,* DEC. 1989

All Church members should pay one-tenth of their annual income into the tithing fund of the Church, with the following exceptions:

1. Members without income and members entirely dependent upon Church welfare assistance.

2. Full-time missionaries. (However, missionaries should pay tithing on any personal income beyond what they receive for their support from families and others.) *CHURCH HANDBOOK,* 1985

Be liberal in your giving, that you yourselves may grow. Don't give just for the benefit of the poor, but give for your own welfare. Give enough so that you can give yourself into the kingdom of God through consecrating of your means and your time. MARION G. ROMNEY, "FIRST PRESIDENCY MESSAGE," *ENSIGN,* JULY 1982

It is our honor and privilege, our safety and promise, our great blessing to live this law of God [tithing]. To fail to meet this obligation in full is to deny ourselves the promises and is to omit a weighty matter. It is a transgression, not an inconsequential oversight. SPENCER W. KIMBALL, "FIRST PRESIDENCY MESSAGE," *ENSIGN,* MARCH 1981; SEE ALSO "DEAR BRETHREN," DEC. 2, 1980

[T]ithing is a debt which everyone owes the Lord as rent for using the things that the Lord has made and given to him to use. The Lord, to whom one owes tithing, is in a position of a preferred creditor. If there is not enough to pay all creditors, He should be paid first. You may be a little shocked by this statement, but it is true. Other creditors, however, need not worry, for the Lord always blesses the person who has faith enough to pay tithing so his or her ability to pay other creditors is not thereby reduced. MARION G. ROMNEY, "FIRST PRESIDENCY MESSAGE," *ENSIGN,* JUNE 1980

Members should be encouraged to pay tithing as they receive their income, but those who wish to pay annually may do so. *CHURCH HANDBOOK,* 1976

The law of tithing is an eternal principle, requiring each member of the Church to pay one tenth of his increase into the tithing funds of the Church. IBID.

[T]he simplest statement we know of is the statement of the Lord himself, namely, that the members of the Church should pay "one-tenth of all their interest annually" [D&C 119:4], which is understood to mean income. No one is justified in making any other statement than this.

We feel that every member of the Church is entitled to make his own decision as to what he thinks he owes the Lord and to make payment accordingly. "DEAR BRETHREN," MAR. 19, 1970

A tithe is one-tenth of a wage earner's *gross* income; a tithe is one-tenth of a professional man's income after deducting standard business expenses; a tithe is one-tenth of a farmer's income after deducting standard business operating expenses. A farmer should not include as standard business operating expense the produce which is used to sustain his family. A tithe is one-tenth of an individual's interest. *CHURCH HANDBOOK,* 1963

Tithing should be paid as the income is received. The practice of delaying the payment of tithing until the end of the year is largely responsible for the failure of many people to observe fully this law of promise. As a result they forfeit the blessings predicated upon obedience thereto. Persons wishing to pay their tithing annually may do so, but members and especially officers are encouraged to pay as the income is received. IBID.

The amount of tithing paid by an individual is strictly confidential and should not be disclosed to anyone beyond the bishopric and such other person authorized to receive tithes on behalf of the bishop. *HELPS AND SUGGESTIONS,* 1956

As we give, so will the Lord bless us. *CHURCH NEWS*, NOV. 8, 1947, IN *MESSAGES,* 6:268-69

[U]nselfish giving partakes of the spirit of Christ. *DESERET NEWS,* DEC. 15, 1945

On the question of tithing, the First Presidency have repeatedly left that matter where the revelation leaves it, namely, that you should pay one tenth of your "interest annually" [D&C 119:4], leaving it to each individual to determine how much tithing he should pay under that rule. JOSEPH ANDERSON, SECRETARY TO THE FIRST PRESIDENCY, TO J. LELAND ANDERSON, SEPT. 17, 1945

One of the most important duties of the bishop of a ward is to receive and account for the tithes of the people. By divine appointment the bishop should give this duty his personal supervision. "DEAR BRETHREN," FEB. 24, 1945, IN *MESSAGES,* 6:223-24

Aged persons without incomes; women who have no income separate from that of their husbands; children who have no individual source of revenue; and persons dependent entirely upon federal or other relief are exempt from the payment of tithes. Those receiving federal or other relief may be considered exempt because the relief rendered is supposedly only sufficient to supply their absolute needs. All Latter-day Saints should be encouraged to cultivate the spirit and practice of tithe-paying when conditions are such that they are able to earn. *CHURCH HANDBOOK,* 1940

The revelation contained in section 119 of the Doctrine and Covenants states that the Lord requires one-tenth of all their interest annually. This is understood to mean that any one having income from salary, profits, dividends, etc., or from any other source, shall pay one-tenth of the same without deducting living expenses. FIRST PRESIDENCY TO ELLEN SAWYER, AUG. 27, 1935

Children eight years of age or over who have been baptized are amenable to the law of tithing and should be encouraged to tithe their own earnings or money actually received by them. At least they should be given the opportunity to pay some tithing each year, no matter how small the amount. *CHURCH HANDBOOK,* 1934

Neither the amount of tithes paid by any of the members, nor their names should be discussed by the bishopric openly. The amount of tithes paid is strictly a confidential matter and should not be given any publicity. IBID.

The law of tithing requires—as a free-will offering—one tenth of what one earns, that is generally understood to mean what one produces, or accumulates, or gains by his labor. JOSEPH F. SMITH TO ANDREW K. SMITH, JULY 12, 1912

Where a wife has no income separate from that of her husband, she should not be classed as a non-tithepayer. But when a wife has interests apart from those of her husband and in her own name, a tenth of the income is due as tithing, which should be credited in her name on the tithing record. *CHURCH HANDBOOK,* 1909

The Lord will hold all to a strict accountability for the use made of the means [tithing] they [bishops] receive which is donated for the up-building of His kingdom. STATEMENT, APR. 1876, IN *MESSAGES,* 2:277-78

tobacco, *see* Word of Wisdom

tolerance

It does not matter our nationality. It does not matter where we were born. It does not matter whether our hair is light or dark. It does not matter the shape of our eyes. Each of us is a child of God. GORDON B. HINCKLEY, "FIRST PRESIDENCY MESSAGE," *ENSIGN*, FEB. 2007

The Church views all humankind as children of the same Heavenly Father, literally brothers and sisters. *QUICK FACTS,* 2005

Our love for those around us increases when we remember that we are all children of God—that we are spirit brothers and sisters. The love that results from this realization has the power to transcend all boundaries of nation, creed, and color. *TRUE TO FAITH,* 2004

Much that is inspiring, noble, and worthy of the highest respect is found in many other faiths. Missionaries and other Church members must be sensitive and respectful toward the beliefs of others and avoid giving offense. *CHURCH HANDBOOK,* 1998

We repudiate efforts to deny to any person his or her inalienable dignity and rights on the abhorrent and tragic theory of the superiority of one race or color over another. THOMAS S. MONSON, "FIRST PRESIDENCY MESSAGE," *ENSIGN,* MAR. 1988

[P]ublic attacks on a religious body are offensive to the Christian spirit of tolerance and the American heritage of fair play. NEWS RELEASE, MAR. 27, 1984

Love is the only force that can erase the differences between people, that can bridge chasms of bitterness. GORDON B. HINCKLEY, "FIRST PRESIDENCY MESSAGE," *ENSIGN,* MAR. 1984

We do not think it either wise or appropriate to react to all criticisms nor to challenge those responsible for them. Nor is it wise to enter into debates with them either individually or before audiences.

In the spirit of the Master, whom we love and serve, we should "turn the other cheek" [Matt. 5:39] and "pray for them which despitefully use you" [5:44]. "DEAR BRETHREN," DEC. 1, 1983

We implore all people, whoever and wherever they are, to banish hate from their lives, to fill their hearts with charity, patience, long-suffering, and forgiveness.

As a matter of doctrine and practice, leaders of The Church of Jesus Christ of Latter-day Saints have consistently counseled members of the Church to observe the constitutional law of the land in which they live and to refuse all association with organizations that would deprive citizens of their civil and religious rights.

We deplore the efforts of organizations and individuals that foster racial prejudice, feed upon religious intolerance, and resort to terrorism, crime, and violent interference with private conduct and public activity.

Peace, order, and dignity cannot long survive in society when hatred, intolerance, and suspicion motivate human behavior.

We reaffirm that all may enjoy perfect contentment and peace by following the footsteps of Jesus Christ, who said "I am the light of the world: he that followeth me shall not walk in darkness, but shall have the light of life" (John 8:12). *CHURCH NEWS,* JAN. 2, 1982

This love of which the Savior spoke, and which He emphasizes as being the most important thing in life [John 15:12], must begin in the home and then be carried into our daily lives. Tolerance and respect for others' beliefs must be taught in the home. Children must learn to love and live and play with those of differing beliefs, while being staunch and true to their own convictions and teachings. N. ELDON TANNER, "FIRST PRESIDENCY MESSAGE," *ENSIGN,* JULY 1980

Our message therefore is one of special love and concern for the eternal welfare of all men and women, regardless of religious belief, race, or nationality, knowing that we are truly brothers and sisters because we are sons and daughters of the same Eternal Father. "STATEMENT OF THE FIRST PRESIDENCY REGARDING GOD'S GUIDANCE TO ALL MANKIND," FEB. 15, 1978

We respect our Father's other children of all sects, parties, and denominations, and have no desire except to see they receive the added light and knowledge that has come to us by revelation, and to become with us inheritors of the great blessings of the restoration of the gospel. JOSEPH FIELDING SMITH, "FIRST PRESIDENCY MESSAGE," *ENSIGN,* SEPT. 1971

[W]e know something of the sufferings of those who are discriminated against in a denial of their civil rights and constitutional privileges. Our early history as a church is a tragic story of persecution and oppression. Our people repeatedly were denied the protection of the law. They were driven and plundered, robbed, and murdered by mobs, who in many instances were aided and abetted by those sworn to uphold the law. We as a people have experienced the bitter fruits of civil discrimination and mob violence. FIRST PRESIDENCY TO ALL STAKE AND MISSION PRESIDENTS, DEC. 15, 1969

In developing that love and concern for one another, while awaiting revelations yet to come, let us hope that with respect to these religious differences, we may gain reinforcement for understanding and appreciation for such differences. They challenge our common similarities, as children of one Father, to enlarge the out-reachings of our divine souls. IBID.

[T]here is in this Church no doctrine, belief, or practice that is intended to deny the enjoyment of full civil rights by any person, regardless of race, color, or creed.

We say again, as we have said many times before, that we believe that all men are the children of the same God and that it is a moral evil for any person or group of persons to deny any human being the right to gainful employment, to full educational opportunity, and to every privilege of citizenship, just as it is a moral evil to deny him the right to worship according to the dictates of his own conscience.

We have consistently and persistently upheld the Constitution of the United States, and as far as we are concerned this means upholding the Constitutional rights of every citizen of the United States.

We call upon all men everywhere, both within and outside the Church, to commit themselves to the establishment of full civil equality for all of God's children. Anything less than this defeats our high ideal of the brotherhood of man. *DESERET NEWS,* OCT. 7, 1963

We pray for all our Father's children who recognize and hold sacred the brotherhood of man, which emanates from divine parentage. We would foster that brotherhood by all righteous means. We are grateful for friends–good friends–the world over who may not be affiliated with our cause. We are thankful for the melting away of unwarranted prejudice, and for better understanding of our purposes and our procedures. We wish all might recognize that our objectives are altruistic in nature. We desire only the blessings of our fellowmen. *DESERET NEWS,* DEC. 10, 1958

Every man's place before God is holy. Each has a position of honor and trust in the divine family. To sustain that position, not wealth, nor social prestige, nor color of skin, nor domicile is essential, but "intelligence, or the light of truth" [D&C 93:29] is essential, as are also "clean hands and a pure heart" [Ps. 24:4], which are intended by the psalmist to comprehend the whole sphere of virtue, with which humanity is divinely endowed. *DESERET NEWS,* DEC. 12, 1956

We are all God's children; we are all blessed with His love and by His mindfulness. We all have a common brotherhood, for we have the common fatherhood of God. *DESERET NEWS,* DEC. 18, 1943

Woe will be the part of those who plant hate in the hearts of the youth, and of the people, for God will not hold them guiltless; they are sowing the wind, their victims will reap the whirlwinds. Hate is born of Satan; love is the offspring of God. We must drive out hate from our hearts, every one of us, and permit it not again to enter. *IMPROVEMENT ERA,* MAY 1942, IN *MESSAGES,* 6:148-63

It is the duty of these representatives [of the Church] to manifest brotherly love, first toward one another, then toward all mankind, to seek unity, harmony, and peace in organizations within the Church, and then by precept and example extend these virtues throughout the world. *DESERET NEWS*, DEC. 19, 1936

No matter in what land we may dwell, the gospel of the Lord Jesus Christ makes us brothers and sisters, interested in each other, eager to understand and know each other. *IMPROVEMENT ERA*, DEC. 1932, IN *MESSAGES*, 5:311

[W]e are all children of the Eternal One, who is the Father of spirits. *DESERET NEWS*, DEC. 20, 1930, IN *MESSAGES*, 5:286-89

We are all brethren and sisters, not some of us masters and others underlings. *LIAHONA*, FEB. 24, 1914, IN *MESSAGES*, 4:303-304

[W]e do not for a moment impugn the motives of those who originated the various systems of religion, neither do we utter a word of criticism against those who honestly believe in them. "DEAR BRETHREN," DEC. 16, 1907, IN *MESSAGES*, 4:167-71

We regard all people as the children of the Eternal Father, and therefore as our brothers and sisters. We seek their welfare, we endeavor to enlighten them, we desire their happiness, progress, and salvation. STATEMENT, DEC. 25, 1903, IN *MESSAGES*, 4:78-83

transgression

[S]erious transgression is defined as a deliberate and major offense against morality. It includes (but is not limited to) attempted murder, rape, forcible sexual abuse, spouse abuse, intentional serious physical injury of others, adultery, fornication, homosexual relations, deliberate abandonment of family responsibilities, robbery, burglary, theft, embezzlement, sale of illegal drugs, fraud, perjury, and false swearing. *CHURCH HANDBOOK*, 1998

transsexuality

Church leaders counsel against elective transsexual operations. If a member is contemplating such an operation, a presiding officer should inform him of this counsel and advise him that the operation may be cause for formal Church discipline. *CHURCH HANDBOOK,* 1998

Trinity, ***see*** **Godhead**

truth

Truth is a knowledge of things as they really are, were, and will be. It does not change with conditions or time. Truth is the same in every age and culture. God is the source of all truth. We can have faith in Him because we know He will teach us only truth. God wants all His children to know the truth. Therefore, He reveals the truths necessary for salvation through prophets and apostles. He reveals truth to us personally through the scriptures and personal revelation. *PREACH MY GOSPEL,* 2005

Spiritual truth must be bonded to faith and righteousness to be fully understood. The Apostle Paul reminded us that the misuse of the truth changes it into a lie (see Rom. 1:25). JAMES E. FAUST, "FIRST PRESIDENCY MESSAGE," *ENSIGN,* JULY 2000

If men are really humble, they will realize that they *discover* but do not *create* truth. SPENCER W. KIMBALL, "FIRST PRESIDENCY MESSAGE," *ENSIGN,* SEPT. 1978

We know that there is no greater boon to happiness and eternal joy than the knowledge of the truth. *DESERET NEWS,* DEC. 10, 1958

Youth must be taught that truth cannot be blinked [at] or

put aside; it must be accepted. FIRST PRESIDENCY TO JOSEPH FIELDING SMITH, JOHN A. WIDTSOE, HAROLD B. LEE, AND MARION G. ROMNEY, AUG. 9, 1944, IN *MESSAGES,* 6:209-15

Error cannot confound truth, and the Church is foundationed and clothed in truth, which in the end has always and must always triumph. *DESERET NEWS,* SEPT. 12, 1934

All truth, from whatever source it seems to emanate, in science, in art, in philosophy, in theology, in discovery or invention, which promotes happiness and elevates mankind, is from the Father of Light who sent His Son Jesus Christ of Nazareth into the world to uplift His sons and daughters and bring them out of darkness, ignorance, and sin into communion with Him and obedience to His laws. Glory and praise be unto Him for this great and crowning mercy! *DESERET NEWS,* DEC. 16, 1905, IN *MESSAGES,* 4:121-23

[W]e think it folly to submit the claims of our Church or the priesthood to the arbitrament of man. The Lord has said, "By their fruits, ye shall know them" [Matt. 7:20]; and to these we can confidently point, feeling satisfied that the people who are seeking for truth and looking for the evidence which the truth always furnishes can more readily obtain this knowledge by calm investigation and close observation than by controversy. *DESERET NEWS WEEKLY,* JUNE 2, 1894, IN *MESSAGES,* 3:260-61

[T]he truth should be told though the heavens fall, whenever the proper time comes to tell it. There may be times, however, when silence is wisdom, even in regard to the truth, tho' it might be gospel truth and essential to the salvation of mankind. JOSEPH F. SMITH TO ZENOS N. GURLEY, JUNE 19, 1889

Truth is "Mormonism." God is the author of it. STATEMENT, MAR. 25, 1839, IN *MESSAGES,* 1:88-104

Twelve Apostles, Quorum of. ***See also*** **priesthood**

Members of the Quorum of the Twelve Apostles are "special witnesses of the name of Christ in all the world" (D&C 107:23). They act under the direction of the First Presidency "to build up the church, and regulate all the affairs of the same in all nations" (107:33). They "open the door [to the nations] by the proclamation of the gospel of Jesus Christ" (107:35).

The Twelve direct the calling of stake patriarchs (107:39). They also "ordain and set in order all the other officers of the church" (107:58).

Along with the First Presidency, the Twelve are prophets, seers, and revelators and hold the keys of the kingdom of God on earth (27:12-13; 110:13-16; 112:30-32). *CHURCH HANDBOOK,* 1998

The primary call of a General Authority is his ecclesiastical responsibility. Except for family responsibilities, all others are secondary to this. *CHURCH NEWS,* JAN. 20, 1996

Under the First Presidency, the Council of the Twelve Apostles is organized to proclaim the gospel in all the world and to administer the affairs of the Church. *PRINCIPLES,* 1976

When the President of the Church dies, the First Presidency is dissolved, and the Council of the Twelve becomes the presiding body of the Church until a new President is chosen. IBID.

W

war. ***See also*** **conscientious objection; peace**

As members of The Church of Jesus Christ of Latter-day Saints, we are a people of peace. We follow the Savior, who is the Prince of Peace. We look forward to His millennial reign, when wars will end and peace will be restored to the earth (see Isa. 2:4). However, we recognize that in this world, government leaders sometimes send military troops to war to defend their nations and ideals. *TRUE TO FAITH,* 2004

If Latter-day Saints must go to war, they should go in a spirit of truth and righteousness, with a desire to do good. They should go with love in their hearts for all God's children, including those on the opposing side. Then, if they are required to shed another's blood, their action will not be counted as a sin. IBID.

[W]ar is the devil's own game and ... among its most serious victims is truth. GORDON B. HINCKLEY, "FIRST PRESIDENCY MESSAGE," *ENSIGN,* OCT. 1990

We live in a world of pomp and muscle, of strutting that glorifies jet thrust and far-flying warheads. It is the same kind of strutting that produced the misery of the days of Caesar, Genghis Khan, Napoleon, and Hitler. NEWS RELEASE, DEC. 15, 1983

We are a warlike people, easily distracted from our assignment of preparing for the coming of the Lord. When enemies rise up, we commit vast resources to the fabrication of gods of stone and steel—ships, planes, missiles, fortifications—and depend on them for protection and deliverance. When threatened, we become anti-enemy instead of pro-kingdom of God; we train a man in the art of war and call him a patriot, thus, in the manner of Satan's counterfeit of true patriotism, perverting the Savior's teaching:

"Love your enemies, bless them that curse you, do good to them that hate you, and pray for them which despitefully use you, and persecute you;

"That ye may be the children of your Father which is in heaven" (Matt. 5:44-45). SPENCER W. KIMBALL, "FIRST PRESIDENCY MESSAGE," *ENSIGN,* JUNE 1976

Wars should be avoided whenever possible; however, men have the right to protect themselves from those who unjustly try to take away their freedom and property. *PRINCIPLES,* 1976

Since those who battle for a righteous cause will not be held responsible for bloodshed, the responsibility rests upon those leaders who create contention and cause wars. IBID.

The futility of war as a remedial factor of social and political ills is becoming more and more apparent. It is timely, therefore, while the recent spread of barbarism and violence over Europe and the Orient is still shocking the sensibilities of humanity, for the nations to seek as never before ways and means of renouncing war forever. *DESERET NEWS,* DEC. 14, 1946

Great standing armies have always been the tools of ambitious dictators to the destruction of freedom. *IMPROVEMENT ERA,* FEB. 1946, IN *MESSAGES,* 6:239-42

It is a tragedy of war that the innocent must suffer. *DESERET NEWS,* DEC. 15, 1945

Wars spring from wickedness. As a destructive fire devastates productive fields and growing forests, wars engulf the innocent and righteous as well as the wicked. *IMPROVEMENT ERA,* JAN. 1943, IN *MESSAGES,* 6:188-91

[T]he Church is and must be against war, for war is of Satan and this Church is the Church of Christ, who taught peace and righteousness and brotherhood of man. *IMPROVEMENT ERA,* NOV. 1942, IN *MESSAGES,* 6:170-85

[I]nternational disputes can and should be settled by peaceful means. This is the way of the Lord. IBID.

God is not pleased either with war or with the wickedness which always heralds it. When He uses war, it is to wipe out sin and unrighteousness. *IMPROVEMENT ERA,* NOV. 1940, IN *MESSAGES,* 6:115-17

The divine law on the taking of human life was proclaimed at Sinai and in the Garden. This law, we declare, is equally binding upon men and upon nations. It embraces war.

We further declare that God is grieved by war and that He will hold subject to the eternal punishments of His will those who wage it unrighteously. *DESERET NEWS,* OCT. 14, 1939, IN *MESSAGES,* 6:90-93

The conflict of nations is one of the signs of His coming. *DESERET NEWS,* DEC. 18, 1915, IN *MESSAGES,* 4:343-48

We abhor tyranny, we resent oppression, but we do not believe in retaliation for real or supposed injuries. We seek to enjoy and exercise the spirit that inspired the world's Redeemer who, we believe, will eventually, be its king. STATEMENT, DEC. 25, 1903, IN *MESSAGES,* 4:78-83

wards

A ward is a Church unit organized for administering the programs of the Church. Members of the ward meet together frequently for spiritual and social purposes. *PRINCIPLES,* 1976

wealth

The Lord has blessed us as a people with a prosperity unequaled in times past. The resources that have been placed in our power are good and necessary to our work here on the earth. But I am afraid that many of us have been surfeited with flocks and herds and acres and barns and wealth and have begun to worship them as false gods, and they have power over us. Do we have more of these good things than our faith can stand? Many people spend most of their time working in the service of a self-image that includes sufficient money, stocks, bonds, investment portfolios, property, credit cards, furnishings, automobiles, and the like to *guarantee* carnal security throughout, it is hoped, a long and happy life. Forgotten is the fact that our assignment is to use these many resources in our families and quorums to build up the kingdom of God—to further the missionary effort and the genealogical and temple work; to raise our children up as fruitful servants unto the Lord; to bless others in every way, that they may also be fruitful. Instead, we expend these blessings on our own desires, and as Moroni said, "Ye adorn yourselves with that which hath no life, and yet suffer the hungry, and the needy, and the naked, and the sick and the afflicted to pass by you, and notice them not" (Morm. 8:39). SPENCER W. KIMBALL, "FIRST PRESIDENCY MESSAGE," *ENSIGN,* JUNE 1976

While millions in the world hunger, other millions eat too much and otherwise waste food. Teach your children to use food frugally. *CHURCH NEWS,* DEC. 21, 1974

With all these temporal blessings it is not pleasing to the Lord that men should selfishly forget their source, nor turn deaf ears to the calls set forth in the gospel of Christ. Neither is it pleasing to Him that we should become mercenary, overstepping the bounds of wisdom in speculations and unwise investment, with a view to further selfishly enriching ourselves. He delights in moderation and in a spirit of unselfishness and love for our fellows. *DESERET NEWS,* DEC. 14, 1907, IN *MESSAGES,* 4:171-73

Let the well-to-do remember that all are not equally prosperous, that the poor we have always with us, and that it is our duty to look after the needy, to care for the sick and sorrowing, and prevent as far as possible human suffering. Let creditors be merciful, let debtors be honest, and let all who have in plenty open their hearts and hands and give freely unto those who have not. *DESERET NEWS,* DEC. 20, 1902

The law of liberality appears to be one of the safeguards which the Lord has adopted to avert from His people the evil consequences which follow the possession of wealth. STATEMENT, OCT. 10, 1887, IN *MESSAGES,* 3:133-55

The experience of mankind has shown that the people of communities and nations among whom wealth is the most equally distributed enjoy the largest degree of liberty, are the least exposed to tyranny and oppression, and suffer the least from luxurious habits which beget vice. STATEMENT, JULY 10, 1875, IN *MESSAGES,* 2:267-72

One of the great evils with which our own nation is menaced at the present time is the wonderful growth of wealth in the hands of a comparatively few individuals. The very liberties for which our fathers contended so steadfastly and courageously, and which they bequeathed to us as a priceless legacy, are endangered by the monstrous power which this accumulation of wealth gives to a few individuals and a few powerful corporations. By its seductive influence results are accomplished which, were it more equally distributed, would be impossible under our form of government. It threatens to give shape to the legislation, both state and national, of the entire country. If this evil should not be checked, and measures not be taken to prevent the continued enormous growth of riches among the class already rich, and the painful increase of destitution and want among the poor, the nation is liable to be overtaken by disaster; for, according to history, such a tendency among nations once powerful was the sure precursor of ruin. IBID.

We are stewards only over all that we possess, for the earth is the Lord's and the fullness thereof. Therefore let us be wise stewards, and not neglecting to put to usury our means and increasing our substance, yet so order our course that we shall be able to give an account of our stewardship that shall prove creditable to ourselves and advantageous to the cause which we have espoused, that our faith may be made manifest by our works and our whole lives and existence bear to be tested at the shrine of truth and knowledge, of wisdom and righteousness towards our God. FIRST PRESIDENCY TO THE IRON COUNTY SAINTS, OCT. 1851

Gold is good in its place—it is good in the hands of a good man to do good with, but in the hands of a wicked man it often proves a curse instead of a blessing. Gold is a good servant, but a miserable, blind, and helpless god and at last will have to be purified by fire, with all its followers. *MILLENNIAL STAR,* AUG. 15, 1850, IN *MESSAGES,* 2:40-49

The true use of gold is for paving streets, covering houses, and making culinary dishes, and when the Saints shall have preached the gospel, raised grain, and built up cities enough, the Lord will open up the way for a supply of gold to the perfect satisfaction of His people; until then, let them not be over-anxious, for the treasures of the earth are in the Lord's storehouse, and He will open the doors thereof when and where He pleases. *MILLENNIAL STAR,* APR. 15, 1850, IN *MESSAGES,* 2:30-37

weapons and militarism

Churches are dedicated for the worship of God and as havens from the cares and concerns of the world. The carrying of lethal weapons, concealed or otherwise, within their walls is inappropriate except as required by officers of the law. NEWS RELEASE, JAN. 16, 2004

[W]e repeat our warnings against the terrifying arms race in which the nations of the earth are presently engaged. We deplore in particular the building of vast arsenals of nuclear weaponry. We are advised that there is already enough such weaponry to destroy in large measure our civilization, with consequent suffering and misery of incalculable extent. *HERALD,* PROVO, UTAH, MAY 6, 1981

[H]istory indicates that men have seldom created armaments that eventually were not put to use. IBID.

As we witness the increasing tensions among the peoples of the earth, with a consequent escalation of arms, including the building of huge arsenals of nuclear weaponry in our own land, we feel a deep and growing concern. We deplore the use of nuclear weapons with their terrible potential for the destruction of life, property, and even of civilization itself.

We realize that such weaponry exists in a number of nations and we understand the responsibility of our military leaders who are charged with the defense of the nation to prepare measures to repel any aggression.

But while recognizing the need for strength, we are enjoined by the word of the Lord "to renounce war and proclaim peace" [D&C 98:16]. *CHURCH NEWS,* APR. 18, 1981

Our greatest strength will come of the righteousness of the people. There is a power in the universe over and above the arms of war. That power is available to those who in a spirit of humility and brotherhood seek it. Hence the need to turn our hearts to God. IBID.

[A]s we contemplate [Christ's] birth, and reflect on the words of the angelic chorus, we are dismayed by the growing tensions among the nations and the unrestricted building of arsenals of war, including huge and threatening nuclear weaponry. Nuclear war, when unleashed on a scale for which the nations are preparing, spares no living thing within the perimeter of its initial destructive force, and sears and maims and kills wherever its pervasive cloud reaches. NEWS RELEASE, DEC. 20, 1980

The Church of Jesus Christ of Latter-day Saints is in the world to establish peace among mankind. Though brute power, greed, and lust are today, as in the past, dominant forces in civilization, yet followers of the Prince of Peace must not despair; for in the fulfillment of God's purposes, "peace, unweaponed, conquers all." *DESERET NEWS,* DEC. 14, 1946

[T]he possession of great military power always breeds thirst for domination, for empire, and for a rule by might, not right. *IMPROVEMENT ERA,* FEB. 1946, IN *MESSAGES,* 6:239-42

Responsive to the ancient wisdom, "Train up a child in the way he should go: and when he is old, he will not depart from it" [Prov. 22:6], obedient to the divine message that heralded the birth of Jesus the Christ, the Savior and Redeemer of the world, "... on earth peace, good will toward men" [Luke 2:14], and knowing that our Constitution and the government set up under it were inspired of God and should be preserved to the blessing not only of our own citizenry but, as an example, to the blessing of all the world, we have the honor respectfully to urge that you do your utmost to defeat any plan designed to bring about the compulsory military service of our citizenry. Should it be urged that our complete armament is necessary for our safety, it may be confidently replied that a proper foreign policy, implemented by an effective diplomacy, can avert the dangers that are feared. IBID.

Today civilized nations are sitting on a mountain of explosives, accumulated in defiance of Christ's teachings. Let the heat of hatred, suspicion, and greed become a little more intense and there will be such an international explosion as will greatly retard if not forcibly drive from the midst of mankind the hoped-for peace heralded by the heavenly hosts when the Son of Man was born. The GOOD WILL that was to usher in universal brotherhood will be replaced by envy, greed, and hate with resultant misery and death. *IMPROVEMENT ERA,* JAN. 1938, IN *MESSAGES,* 6:37-40

Through Him [Christ] wickedness shall be overcome, hatred, enmity, strife, poverty, and war abolished. This will not be accomplished, however, with bombs and battle-shot, with submarines or poison gas, but with a slow but never-failing process of changing men's mental and spiritual attitude. The ways and habits of the world depend upon the thoughts and soul-convictions of men and women. If, therefore, you would change the world, you must first change people's thoughts. Only to the extent that men desire peace and brotherhood can the world be made better. Only by adhering to sound principles can peace come, either to individuals or nations. *DESERET NEWS,* DEC. 19, 1936

welfare. *See also* service

The great genius of this Church is work. Everybody works. You do not grow unless you work. Faith, testimony of the truth, is just like the muscle of my arm. If you use it, it grows strong. If you put it in a sling, it grows weak and flabby. We put people to work. We expect great things of them, and the marvelous and wonderful thing is they come through. They produce. GORDON B. HINCKLEY, "FIRST PRESIDENCY MESSAGE," *ENSIGN,* MAR. 2006

The basis of Church welfare programs is individual self-reliance, not a handout that might rob the receiver of self-respect.

Members are encouraged to provide for themselves before calling on others for help. Those who need additional help turn first to their families. When members and their families have done all they can and still have welfare needs, the Church provides temporary, life-sustaining help so that the family can get back on its feet. *QUICK FACTS,* 2005

Financing for Church welfare programs comes from an unusual source. Latter-day Saints fast—that is, do without meals—one day each month. The value of the meals missed, or more, is donated for the care of the poor and needy. In addition, volunteers provide a substantial amount of the work on Church welfare farms, in canneries, and in other facilities. IBID.

The responsibility for one's spiritual and temporal well-being rests upon the individual first, then the family, and finally the Church. Church members are expected to be self-reliant and independent to the extent of their ability. IBID.

The responsibility for your social, emotional, spiritual, physical, and economic well-being rests first on yourself, second on your family, and third on the Church. Under the inspiration of the Lord and through your own labors, you should supply yourself and your family with the spiritual and temporal necessities of life. *TRUE TO FAITH,* 2004

The Lord has always commanded His people to care for the poor and the needy. IBID.

A measure of members' love for the Lord is the love they show to others by serving and blessing them in their times of need. *CHURCH HANDBOOK 2,* 1998

We urge you, particularly priesthood brethren and Relief Society sisters, to be sensitive to the needs of the poor, the sick, and the needy. We have a Christian responsibility to see that the widows and fatherless are assisted. EZRA TAFT BENSON, "FIRST PRESIDENCY MESSAGE," *ENSIGN,* OCT. 1992

Let us be a generous people and care for those in need, both spiritually and temporally, as our Lord has charged us to do. "DEAR BRETHREN," UNITED STATES AND CANADA, DEC. 13, 1991

Church assistance is designed to help people help themselves. The rehabilitation of members is the responsibility of the individual and the family, aided by the priesthood quorum and Relief Society. We are attempting to develop independence, not dependence. The bishop seeks to build integrity, self-respect, dignity, and soundness of character in each person assisted, leading to complete self-sufficiency. THOMAS S. MONSON, "FIRST PRESIDENCY MESSAGE," *ENSIGN,* SEPT. 1986

The measure of our love for our fellowman and, in a large sense, the measure of our love for the Lord is what we do for one another and for the poor and distressed. SPENCER W. KIMBALL, "FIRST PRESIDENCY MESSAGE," *ENSIGN,* AUG. 1984

Work brings happiness, self-esteem, and prosperity. It is the means of all accomplishment; it is the opposite of idleness. We are commanded to work (see Gen. 3:19). Attempts to obtain our temporal, social, emotional, or spiritual well-being by means of a dole violate the divine mandate that we should work for what we receive. Work should be the ruling principle in the lives of our Church membership (see D&C 42:42; 56:17; 68:30-32; 75:29). IBID.

No true Latter-day Saint, while physically or emotionally able, will voluntarily shift the burden of his own or his family's well-being to someone else. So long as he can, under the inspiration of the Lord and with his own labors, he will supply himself and his family with the spiritual and temporal necessities of life (see 1 Tim. 5:8). IBID.

Can we see how critical self-reliance becomes when looked upon as the prerequisite to service, when we also know service is what godhood is all about? Without self-reliance one cannot exercise these innate desires to serve. How can we give if there is nothing there? Food for the hungry cannot come from empty shelves. Money to assist the needy cannot come from an empty purse. Support and understanding cannot come from the emotionally starved. Teaching cannot come from the unlearned. And most important of all, spiritual guidance cannot come from the spiritually weak.

There is an interdependence between those who have and those who have not. The process of giving exalts the poor and humbles the rich. In the process, both are sanctified. The poor, released from the bondage and limitations of poverty, are enabled as free men to rise to their full potential, both temporally and spiritually. The rich, by imparting of their surplus, participate in the eternal principle of giving. Once a person has been made whole, or self-reliant, he reaches out to aid others, and the cycle repeats itself. MARION G. ROMNEY, "FIRST PRESIDENCY MESSAGE," *ENSIGN*, JUNE 1984

The practice of coveting and receiving unearned benefits has now become so fixed in our society that even men of wealth, possessing the means to produce more wealth, are expecting the government to guarantee them a profit. Elections often turn on what the candidates promise to do for voters from government funds. This practice, if universally accepted and implemented in any society, will make slaves of its citizens.

We cannot afford to become wards of the government, even if we have a legal right to do so. It requires too great a sacrifice of self-respect and political, temporal, and spiritual independence. SPENCER W. KIMBALL, "FIRST PRESIDENCY MESSAGE," *ENSIGN*, APR. 1984

Members of the Church are commanded by the Lord to be self-reliant to the extent of their ability.

Every Latter-day Saint would wish to be self-supporting while physically and emotionally able, rather than voluntarily shift the burden of one's own or one's family's well-being to someone else. So long as they can, under the direction of the Lord and with individual labors, members should work to the extent of their abilities to supply themselves and their families with the spiritual and temporal necessities of life.

As guided by the Spirit of the Lord and through applying these principles, each member of the Church should make individual decisions as to what assistance is accepted. In this way, independence, self-respect, dignity, and self-reliance will be fostered and free agency maintained. "DEAR BRETHREN," JUNE 10, 1983

Self-reliance implies the individual development of skills and abilities and then their application to provide for one's own needs and wants. It further implies that one will achieve those skills through self-discipline and then, through self-restraint and charity, use those skills to bless himself and others. That the Lord expects all His children of sound mind and body to thus perform in this second estate is made clear in many scriptural passages whose central thought focuses on *work*–personal, earnest, life-sustaining work. MARION G. ROMNEY, "FIRST PRESIDENCY MESSAGE," *ENSIGN,* APR. 1981

Just as each individual is accountable for his choices and actions in spiritual matters, so also is he accountable in temporal matters. If we have been frugal and saved for a rainy day, then we can more easily weather the financial storm. If we have lived beyond our means, then we pay the consequences of our own actions when the bills come. If we have kept pace in our chosen field of labor, then we can anticipate advancement or increase as opportunity knocks. Thus, it is through our *own* efforts and decisions that we *earn* our way in this life. While the Lord will magnify us in both subtle and dramatic ways, He can only guide our footsteps when we move our feet. Ultimately, our own actions determine our blessings—or lack of them. It is a direct consequence of both agency and accountability. And since we are responsible for our actions, we are also personally accountable for their consequences. And though we cannot always directly trace the impact of our actions, they are subject to the law of the harvest—"That which we sow, we also shall reap." IBID.

It is a blessing that we are required to work, and we should do it willingly and without complaint. *CHURCH NEWS,* DEC. 21 1974

This is the essence of welfare services—not merely that men

shall be fed and clothed, though that is important—but that eternal man shall be built up by self-reliance, by creative activity, by honorable labor, by service. A generation reared in idleness cannot maintain its integrity.

Thus it is seen that from the beginning, the real long-term objective of welfare services is the building of character in the members of the Church, givers and receivers, rescuing all that is finest down deep in the inside of them and bringing to flower and fruitage the latent richness of the spirit, which after all is the mission and purpose and reason for being of this Church. "WELFARE SERVICES—MESSAGE OF THE FIRST PRESIDENCY," NOV. 1972

[W]e should be strong and self-reliant individuals, not dependent upon the largess or benefactions of government. None of the doctrines of our Church gives any sanction to the concept of a socialistic state. DAVID O. MCKAY TO ERNEST L. WILKINSON, MAY 25, 1967, IN *BYU YEARS,* 4:544-45

History, of course, is replete with the downfall of nations who, instead of assuming their own responsibility for their religious and economic welfare, mistakenly attempted to shift their individual responsibility to the government. IBID.

From the beginning, the Lord has laid upon his Church the obligation to provide the necessities of life for such of its members who are unable to provide for themselves and who do not have relatives who can and will provide for them. *WELFARE PLAN,* 1952

The immediate objectives of Church Welfare are to:

1. Place in gainful employment those who are able to work.

2. Provide employment within the Welfare Program, in so far as possible, for those who cannot be placed in gainful employment.

3. Acquire the means with which to supply the needy, for whom the Church assumes responsibility, with the necessities of life.

4. Supply such needy with the means of living, each "according to his family, according to his circumstances, and his wants and needs" (D&C 51:3). This is to be done not as a dole, but rather in recognition of faithful service in the past and a present willingness to accept the program and labor in it to the extent of his ability. IBID.

The real spirit of the welfare program is to produce that which is needed. We are fast approaching a time when it may be impossible to buy what we need no matter how much money we may have.

Our economic security for the future will be found in the exercise of our faith and the doing of our works in the further development of the Church Welfare Program. To do so will be to find favor with the Lord and bring His further blessings upon the Latter-day Saints in all the world. *DESERET NEWS,* APR. 6, 1946

The Church is vitally concerned for the temporal welfare of its members. From its organization, it has endeavored to establish and maintain the economic independence of the people by fostering industries, creating employment, and encouraging thrift, and has stood ready at all times to help faithful, active Latter-day Saints who are in need. *CHURCH HANDBOOK,* 1940

The primary responsibility, legally and morally, for caring for the needy rests with the relatives. As Paul says in his Epistle to Timothy, "but if any provide not for his own, and specially for those of his own house, he hath denied the faith and is worse than an infidel" (1 Tim. 5:8).

If relatives are not able to provide for those requiring assistance, then the Church, through the welfare organizations established in each ward and branch, should render necessary aid by supplying those for whom the Church is responsible, commodities produced by the welfare program consisting of food, clothing, and fuel. The next important step should be to make dependents self-supporting by securing permanent employment for the unemployed. IBID.

[L]et us double our efforts to bring faith, happiness, and cheer into the lives of our fellow men. Let those who are blessed with comforts and luxuries share with those who are less fortunate, not with an air of superiority, but with an attitude of appreciation expressive of the feeling that it is a privilege to invite another out of the shade and cold of penury and discouragement into the sunshine of kindness and brotherly love. *IMPROVEMENT ERA,* DEC. 1936, IN *MESSAGES,* 6:23

The aim of the Church is to help the people to help themselves. STATEMENT, OCT. 2, 1936, IN *MESSAGES,* 6:19-23

[T]he ward must be one great family of equals. *DESERET NEWS,* APR. 7, 1936, IN *MESSAGES,* 6:10-13

Poverty may be caused by any one of a number of unfavorable conditions. It may be due to sickness, injury, infirmity, unemployment, lack of education, poor management, or mental or physical deficiency. It should be relieved by getting at the source of the trouble and adopting ways and means of remedying it as permanently as possible. *CHURCH HANDBOOK,* 1934

The policy of the Church is that no faithful members nor their children shall lack for the necessities of life. IBID.

The Lord will not hold us guiltless if we shall permit any of our people to go hungry, or to be cold, unclad, or unhoused during the approaching winter. Particularly He will consider us gravely blameful if those who have heretofore paid their tithes and offerings to the Church when they had employment shall now be permitted to suffer when the general adversity has robbed them of their means of livelihoods. Whatever else happens, these faithful persons must not be permitted to come to want distress now. *DESERET NEWS,* SEPT. 2, 1933

The cries of those in distress must be hushed by our bounty. The words of the Lord require this from us. A feeling of common humanity bids it from us. IBID.

Let us not forget the obligation which rests upon us to render allegiance and service to the Lord, and that acceptable service to Him cannot be rendered without service to our fellow man. *DESERET NEWS,* DEC. 16, 1922, IN *MESSAGES,* 5:222-23

As followers of the Master who drew the little children to Him and blessed them, our immediate duty is to see that no hungry child cries in vain for bread. *IMPROVEMENT ERA,* FEB. 1921, IN *MESSAGES,* 5:188-89

While members of the Church are free to donate as they desire and are able to any charitable and worthy cause, the Church as an organization is not in a financial position to respond to the demands and requests [from charities] that are made upon it, and it is not required of its stakes, wards, quorums, or associations to use their ecclesiastical activities or influence in those directions. *DESERET NEWS,* MAY 6, 1920

The care of the poor has been a particular duty devolving upon the Church from the beginning. *DESERET NEWS,* DEC. 23, 1919, IN *MESSAGES,* 5:164-67

Our motto is not simply "Live and let live" but "Live and

help to live." We should help to make the lives of others happy and progressive. The kindly word spoken should be followed by timely actions. *DESERET NEWS*, DEC. 17, 1904, IN *MESSAGES*, 4:92-98

While it has always been the policy of our people to encourage industry and to repress idleness in every form, and to expect all persons to contribute, according to their ability, to their own support; still there are many cases where the aged and the infirm, or the unfortunate, cannot, with the utmost exertion and economy, obtain through their own labors sufficient to sustain themselves. It would be a great evil among us to encourage any class in living upon the benevolence of the community. No system of begging should be permitted. Those able to work should be furnished employment. Persons who are properly disposed will be glad to obtain it in preference to being fed with the bread of charity; and all should be encouraged to labor according to their strength. STATEMENT, OCT. 10, 1887, IN *MESSAGES*, 3:133-55

The spirit of the gospel of the Lord Jesus Christ is opposed to idleness. We do not believe that a man who has that spirit can rest content if he is not busily employed. STATEMENT, APR. 8, 1887, IN *MESSAGES*, 3:109-29

Let there be no rich among us from whose tables fall only crumbs to feed a wounded Lazarus. Rather let us, each and all, do our part honorably, justly, charitably, and well. The Church of Christ has given us a worthy example, let us follow it so that God may forgive our debts as we forgive our debtors. *DESERET NEWS*, APR. 21, 1880, IN *MESSAGES*, 2:326-30

It is the duty of the rich to relieve the suffering poor, to administer to their necessities, and faithfully apply their means to the gathering of Israel, the spread of the gospel, and the building up of the kingdom. *MILLENNIAL STAR,* JULY 8, 1854, IN *MESSAGES,* 2:127-43

[I]f there are any among you who aspire after their own aggrandizement, and seek their own opulence, while their brethren are groaning in poverty and are under sore trials and temptations, they cannot be benefited by the intercession of the Holy Spirit, which makest intercession for us day and night with groanings that cannot be uttered.

We ought at all times to be very careful that such highmindedness shall never have place in our hearts; but condescend to men of low estate, and with all long-suffering bear the infirmities of the weak. STATEMENT, MAR. 25, 1839, IN *MESSAGES,* 1:88-104

wives, *see* parents

women

[I]t is a mistake for women to think that life begins only upon marriage. A woman must have an identity and be useful and feel important and needed whether she is single or married. She must also feel that she has something to offer. JAMES E. FAUST, "FIRST PRESIDENCY MESSAGE," *ENSIGN,* JUNE 1998

Although the priesthood is bestowed only on worthy male members of the Church, both men and women partake of its blessings. *CHURCH HANDBOOK 2,* 1998

The Relief Society serves under the guidance of the priesthood as the Lord's organization for sisters in the Church. The purpose of Relief Society is to assist priesthood leaders in carrying out the mission of the Church by helping sisters and families come unto Christ. The Relief Society helps sisters and their families receive all essential priesthood ordinances, keep the associated covenants, and qualify for exaltation and eternal life. IBID.

[W]e should not overlook the fact that, particularly in the absence of the father, a mother may pray with her children and call down the Lord's blessings upon them. She does not act by virtue of priesthood conferred upon her, but by virtue of her God-given responsibility to govern her household in righteousness. SPENCER W. KIMBALL, "FIRST PRESIDENCY MESSAGE," *ENSIGN,* JAN. 1984

The history of the Church clearly demonstrates the long-standing concern of its leaders that women, as daughters of God, should have without discrimination every political, economic, and educational opportunity. Where there now exist deficiencies concerning these matters, they can and should be corrected by specific legislation. Additionally, because of their unique capacities and responsibilities as wives and mothers, women should be the beneficiaries of such special laws as will safeguard their welfare and the interests of children and families. "DEAR BRETHREN," UNITED STATES, OCT. 12, 1978

From its beginnings, The Church of Jesus Christ of Latter-day Saints has championed the rights of women in our society. We recognize that there have been injustices to women before the law and in society in general. There are additional rights to which women are entitled. We would prefer to see specific injustices resolved individually under appropriate specific laws [rather than by Constitutional amendment]. NEWS RELEASE, AUG. 24, 1978

Latter-day Saint women, from the beginning of the Church and continuing today, know how deeply the Church encourages them to exercise their free agency. They also know that in the Church, or in any organization or activity for that matter, free agency must be coupled with responsibility. Individual freedom without such responsibility leads to chaos. Latter-day

Saint women are strongly encouraged to develop their individual talents, to broaden their learning, and to expand their contributions to activities such as religious, governmental, cultural, educational, and community pursuits. IBID.

One of the auxiliary organizations to the priesthood is the Relief Society, the organization for women. Its members comprise local Relief Societies in wards and branches throughout the world.

Its purpose is two-fold: the education and spiritual development of its members and compassionate service to the individual, the family, and the community. *PRINCIPLES,* 1976

Next to motherhood, the holiest thing we know on earth is radiant, innocent, obedient girlhood. "DEAR HOME BUILDERS," OCT. 1941, IN *MESSAGES,* 6:133-34

The true spirit of The Church of Jesus Christ of Latter-day Saints gives to woman the highest place of honor in human life. To maintain and to merit this high dignity, she must possess those virtues which have always, and which will ever, demand the respect and love of mankind. To know what these virtues are, let everyone think of his own mother. With her picture in mind, each will agree that "a beautiful and chaste woman is the perfect workmanship of God."

Woman possesses power to ennoble or to degrade. It is she who gives life to the babe, who wields gradually and constantly the impress of character to childhood and youth, who inspires manhood to noble ambition or entices and ensnares it to defeat and degradation, who makes home a heaven of bliss or a den of discontent, who at her best gives to life the sweetest hopes and choicest blessings.

Anything, therefore, is to be most highly commended and encouraged which has as its motive the ennoblement of womankind–beauty, modesty sincerity, sympathy, cheerfulness, reverence, and many other sublime virtues must be hers whose subtle and benign influence is such a potent factor in the progress and destiny of the human race. *IMPROVEMENT ERA,* MAY 1935, IN *MESSAGES,* 6:5-6

Women, not being heirs to the priesthood except as they enjoy and participate in its blessings through their husbands, are not identified with the priesthood quorums and consequently do not receive the religious instruction and training imparted at quorum meetings.

One of the purposes of the organization of the Relief Society was that a system might be inaugurated by which study of religious subjects, or Church doctrine and government, might be pursued by women. "DEAR BRETHREN AND SISTERS," OCT. 5, 1922, IN *MESSAGES,* 5:216-19

[T]he same God who created Adam, created Eve, "male and female created He them; and blessed them and called their name Adam" [Gen. 1:27]. Who are women? The mothers of the whole human family. They were all born of women, who were created and prepared as companions and helpmeets for man. *MILLENNIAL STAR,* MAY 17, 1886, IN *MESSAGES,* 3:46-71

Word of Wisdom. *See also* alcohol; tobacco

The Word of Wisdom is a law of health revealed by the Lord for our physical and spiritual benefit. *TRUE TO FAITH,* 2004

In the Word of Wisdom, the Lord commands us not to take the following substances into our bodies:

Alcoholic drinks (see D&C 89:5-7).

Tobacco (89:8).

Tea and coffee (89:9; latter-day prophets have taught that the term "hot drinks" refers to tea and coffee). IBID.

Anything harmful that people purposefully take into their bodies is not in harmony with the Word of Wisdom. This is especially true of illegal drugs, which can destroy those who become addicted to them. Stay entirely away from them. Do not experiment with them. The abuse of prescription drugs also leads to destructive addiction. IBID.

Eat nutritious food, exercise regularly, and get enough sleep. When you do all these things, you remain free from harmful addictions and have control over your life. You gain the blessings of a healthy body, an alert mind, and the guidance of the Holy Ghost. *STRENGTH OF YOUTH,* 2001

Never let Satan or others lead you to think that breaking the Word of Wisdom will make you happier or more attractive. IBID.

In general, the more food we eat in its natural state–without additives–and the less it is refined, the healthier it will be for us. Food can affect the mind, and deficiencies of certain elements in the body can promote mental depression. A good physical examination periodically is a safeguard and may spot problems that can be remedied. Rest and physical exercise are essential, and a walk in the fresh air can refresh the spirit. Wholesome recreation is part of our religion and is a necessary change of pace; even its anticipation can lift the spirit. EZRA TAFT BENSON, "FIRST PRESIDENCY MESSAGE," *ENSIGN,* OCT. 1986

The breaking of the Word of Wisdom is often the beginning of the breaking of many other commandments. *PRINCIPLES,* 1976

There has been no official interpretation of [the] Word of Wisdom except that which was given by the Brethren in the very early days of the Church when it was declared that "hot drinks" [D&C 89:9] meant tea and coffee.

While the use of beverages where the deleterious effects have been removed might not be considered breaking the Word of Wisdom, it is well to avoid in all cases the appearance of evil by refraining from the use of drinks which have the appearance, the smell, and the taste of that which we have been counseled not to use. FIRST PRESIDENCY, LETTER DATED APR. 17, 1975

The Church's law pertaining to proper diet and care of the body is contained in a revelation given to the Prophet Joseph Smith under date of February 27, 1833 [D&C 89]. That revelation admonishes church members to use judgment and temperance in the use of all food and drink. It prohibits the use of alcoholic beverages, hot drinks (interpreted to mean tea and coffee), and tobacco. It also prohibits the use of all other substances which may be injurious to the body or which might be said to be in violation of the spirit of the revelation. It also encourages the sparing use of meats but prohibits some outright. On the affirmative side, this health code encourages the eating of all fruits and vegetables and encourages the use of whole grain. "ATTITUDES," 1974

In the revelation [Word of Wisdom] itself it states that it was given "not by commandment or constraint, but as a word of wisdom showing forth the order and will of God, adapted to the capacity of the weak and weakest of all saints" [D&C 89:2-3], and in this spirit and understanding this revelation was received and acknowledged by the Church. To be a law to the Church it must be given to and accepted by the Church as such. But while it has never been given in a formal way to the Church as a commandment, nor accepted by the Church in a formal way as such, President Brigham Young, in speaking on the Word of Wisdom on a certain occasion at a conference in the Tabernacle, made a statement to the effect that the Lord now required of the Church a strict observance of that revelation. In this connection we may add that while the revelation known as the Word of Wisdom was not given in the beginning by way of commandment or constraint, and therefore not mandatory, it should be observed by all Saints in the light of a commandment, as the same blessings follow its observance given in the light and spirit of a word of wisdom as would follow its observance if given to the Church as a law. FIRST PRESIDENCY TO MAX H. PARKIN, AUG. 9, 1972

The drinking of cocoa and chocolate, as it is ordinarily indulged in, that is, without making a habit of it, could not be regarded as breaking the Word of Wisdom. But the drinking of cocoa and chocolate may be carried to such an extent as to result in great bodily harm, and this of course would be a violation of the spirit of the revelation called the Word of Wisdom. FIRST PRESIDENCY TO JACK V. BARTON, JUNE 15, 1970, QUOTING AN EARLIER UNDATED STATEMENT

Leaders of the Church have advised against the use of any beverage containing harmful, habit-forming drugs or ingredients under circumstances that would result in the acquiring of the habit. The use of a beverage from which the deleterious ingredients have been removed would not be considered as breaking the Word of Wisdom. FIRST PRESIDENCY TO W. DEAN BELNAP, FEB. 12, 1970

[W]hile the Word of Wisdom mentions neither tea nor coffee, nevertheless, while the Prophet [Joseph Smith] was still living, his brother Hyrum specifically stated that "hot drinks" [D&C 89:9] meant tea and coffee; and it has been also generally understood that it is the active drugs in those beverages that make them harmful and that where those drugs have been removed, the harmful effect resulting therefrom is absent. JOSEPH ANDERSON, SECRETARY TO THE FIRST PRESIDENCY, TO J. LELAND ANDERSON, SEPT. 17, 1945

[A]s to the Word of Wisdom, the drinking of a beverage made from the coffee bean from which all caffeine and other deleterious drugs have been removed is not regarded as violating the Word of Wisdom. JOSEPH ANDERSON, SECRETARY TO THE FIRST PRESIDENCY, TO J. LELAND ANDERSON, AUG. 20, 1945

Our understanding is that this revelation [Word of Wisdom] stands today in the same light as it did when it was first given, and must so remain until the Lord shall see fit to supplement it in any way deemed fit and proper by Him, and when that day comes the Church will know it and vote upon it in the same way that all the other revelations contained in the Doctrine and Covenants were received and accepted, namely, by vote at the general conference of the Church.

We wish it understood, however, that the members of the Church are under just as much obligation to receive and carry out the advice and admonitions given in this revelation as it now reads in the Doctrine and Covenants as they would be if it were given as a commandment, for the results as they affect our temporal salvation are just the same whether given by way of advice or by way of command. And besides, the revelation, it will be admitted by all Church members, is the will and the word of the Lord, and therefore it should be our good pleasure to receive and be guided not only by it but by every word that proceeds from the mouth of God as well. In this sense the revelation known as the Word of Wisdom is a commandment.

But it should be borne in mind that the revelation was not given by commandment or constraint. If it had been thus given, doubtless the great body of the Church from the beginning would have been brought under condemnation through transgression of a law of God, for in that event it would have been a law to the Church, and this means that the penalty of a broken law, namely justice and judgment, would have to be inflicted. FIRST PRESIDENCY TO J. Z. STEWART, MAR. 15, 1912

You ask if it is considered that the drinking of cocoa is contrary to the teachings of the Word of Wisdom? We would say that while cocoa is not specifically mentioned in connection with those things forbidden, we would not consider it a healthful practice for anyone to indulge in it as a daily drink; in fact, some physicians now give it as their opinion that it is a harmful and unhealthful beverage, placing it on a level with tea and coffee. FIRST PRESIDENCY TO WILLIAM ARMSTRONG, OCT. 2, 1908

It is fair to presume that if the practice in the early days, when this revelation [Word of Wisdom] was given, had been to drink tea and coffee cold instead of hot, the wording of the revelation would have been slightly different from what it is, as the essence of its meaning without doubt is the habitual drinking of tea and coffee or any other stimulating beverage. And therefore to drink tea or coffee cold instead of hot with the idea that it is not a violation of the Word of Wisdom because a cold drink is thus indulged in and not a hot drink would simply be an evasion.

But it is one thing to drink tea and coffee in the ordinary way, that is, to make a practice of doing so, and especially of taking those beverages strong, and another thing entirely to drink tea or coffee as a medicine. All such things were created in the beginning for the use of man, that is, for a wise use, and it is for the Saints to know for themselves what constitutes a wise use and to govern themselves accordingly. This is the spirit in which the revelation called the Word of Wisdom should be understood and taught. FIRST PRESIDENCY TO C. R. HAKES, AUG. 1, 1902

world, condition of

We live in complex times. We are confronted by very serious problems. Some of us are faced with sickness, with economic difficulties, with worry and concern over many matters. Our refuge, our peace, our well-being lie in the way of the Lord. GORDON B. HINCKLEY, "FIRST PRESIDENCY MESSAGE," *ENSIGN*, FEB. 2007

Today we are barraged by multitudes of voices telling us how to live, how to gratify our passions, how to have it all. At our fingertips we have software, databases, television channels, interactive computer modems, satellite receivers, and communications networks that suffocate us with information. There are fewer places of refuge and serenity. Our young people are bombarded with evil and wickedness like no other generation. JAMES E. FAUST, "FIRST PRESIDENCY MESSAGE," *ENSIGN,* JUNE 2006

One reason for the spiritual sickness of our society is that so many do not know or care about what is morally right and wrong. So many things are justified on the basis of expediency and the acquiring of money and goods. In recent times, those few individuals and institutions that have been courageous enough to stand up and speak out against adultery, dishonesty, violence, and other forms of evil are often held up to ridicule. Many things are just plain and simply wrong, whether they are illegal or not. Those who persist in following after the evil things of the world cannot know "the peace of God, which passeth all understanding" (Ps. 147:3). JAMES E. FAUST, "FIRST PRESIDENCY MESSAGE," *ENSIGN,* JULY 2005

We live in a day of shifting values, of changing standards, of will-o'-the-wisp programs that blossom in the morning and die in the evening. We see this in government, we see it in public and private morality, we see it in the homes of the people, we see it in the churches, and we even see it among some of our own members who are led away by the sophistry of men.

Men everywhere seem to be groping as in darkness, casting aside the traditions that were the strength of our society yet unable to find a new star to guide them. GORDON B. HINCKLEY, "FIRST PRESIDENCY MESSAGE," *ENSIGN,* JAN. 2005

Legal restraints against deviant moral behavior are eroding under legislative enactments and court opinions. This is done in the name of freedom of speech, freedom of the press, freedom of choice in so-called personal matters. But the bitter fruit of these so-called freedoms has been enslavement to debauching habits and behavior that leads only to destruction. GORDON B. HINCKLEY, "FIRST PRESIDENCY MESSAGE," *ENSIGN,* SEPT. 2004

Like the leprosy of yesteryear are the plagues of today. They linger; they debilitate; they destroy. They are to be found everywhere. Their pervasiveness knows no boundaries. We know them as selfishness, greed, indulgence, cruelty, and crime, to identify but a few. Surfeited with their poison, we tend to criticize, to complain, to blame, and, slowly but surely, to abandon the positives and adopt the negatives of life. THOMAS S. MONSON, "FIRST PRESIDENCY MESSAGE," *ENSIGN,* FEB. 2000

It is not always easy to live in the world and not be a part of it. We cannot live entirely with our own or unto ourselves, nor would we wish to. We must mingle with others. In so doing, we can be gracious. We can be inoffensive. We can avoid any spirit or attitude of self-righteousness. But we can maintain our standards. The natural tendency will be otherwise, and many have succumbed to it. GORDON B. HINCKLEY, "FIRST PRESIDENCY MESSAGE," *ENSIGN,* JULY 1990

Our society is afflicted by a spirit of thoughtless arrogance unbecoming those who have been so magnificently blessed. How grateful we should be for the bounties we enjoy. Absence of gratitude is the mark of the narrow, uneducated mind. It bespeaks a lack of knowledge and the ignorance of self-sufficiency. It expresses itself in ugly egotism and frequently in wanton mischief. We have seen our beaches, our parks, our forests littered with ugly refuse by those who evidently have no appreciation for their beauty. GORDON B. HINCKLEY, "FIRST PRESIDENCY MESSAGE," *ENSIGN,* AUG. 1988

In the four decades since the end of World War II, standards of morality have lowered again and again. Today there are more people in jail, in reformatories, on probation, and in trouble than ever before. From padded expense accounts to grand larceny, from petty crimes to crimes of passion, the figures are higher than ever and going higher. Crime spirals upward; decency careens downward. Many are on a giant roller coaster of disaster, seeking the thrills of the moment while sacrificing the joys of eternity. We conquer space but cannot control self. Thus we forfeit peace. THOMAS S. MONSON, "FIRST PRESIDENCY MESSAGE," *ENSIGN,* JULY 1988

[W]e live in a world where moral character ofttimes is relegated to a position secondary to facial beauty or personal charm. We read and hear of local, national, and international beauty contests. Throngs pay tribute to Miss America, Miss World, and Miss Universe. Athletic prowess, too, has its following. The games and contests, the Olympics, the tournaments of international scope bring forth the adoring applause of the enthralled crowd. Such are the ways of mankind. THOMAS S. MONSON, "FIRST PRESIDENCY MESSAGE," *ENSIGN,* AUG. 1987

We live in an age when, as the Lord foretold, men's hearts are failing them, not only physically but in spirit (see D&C 45:26). Many are giving up heart for the battle of life. Suicide ranks as a major cause of deaths of college students. As the showdown between good and evil approaches with its accompanying trials and tribulations, Satan is increasingly striving to overcome the Saints with despair, discouragement, despondency, and depression. EZRA TAFT BENSON, "FIRST PRESIDENCY MESSAGE," *ENSIGN,* OCT. 1986

On at least two counts, the very spirit of our times is conducive to inadequate knowledge of the Lord's counsel. First, ours is a day of specialization. Our science, our industry, our professions are all so complex and specialized that each of us is under heavy pressure to learn more and more about his own narrow field. Few, it seems, are expected to have a broad knowledge and a sound understanding of the whole area of which their specialties are but a part. Second, our age is traveling at an unprecedented and dizzy pace that is constantly being accelerated. The world and its ills crowd upon us through our media, our technology, and our life-style until we eat and sleep, rest and work, travel and wait with schedule in hand, always at top speed, and through it all we find little time to search out the counsel of the Lord. MARION G. ROMNEY, "FIRST PRESIDENCY MESSAGE," *ENSIGN,* AUG. 1985

If the world is to be improved, the process of love must make a change in the hearts of men. It can do so when we look beyond self to give our love to God and others, and do so with all our heart, with all our soul, and with all our mind. GORDON B. HINCKLEY, "FIRST PRESIDENCY MESSAGE," *ENSIGN,* MAR. 1984

Mankind generally has proved short in wisdom on two counts. First, mankind does not have all the facts; and second, mankind does not have the capacity to make maximum beneficial use of the facts it does have. MARION G. ROMNEY, "FIRST PRESIDENCY MESSAGE," *ENSIGN,* JULY 1983

Wisdom is in short supply in the world today because men do not know God, not even all those who preach of Him. Until mankind comes to a knowledge of God, we will continue in our distraction, regardless of how much other knowledge we acquire. IBID.

It is our prayer that members, through many small efforts, will make this world a safer and better place in which to live. NEWS RELEASE, JAN. 25, 1983

Ingratitude is one of the woeful failings of our society. The failure to acknowledge the sovereignty and the beneficence of God, the refusal to bend our will to His, are at the very root of the major problems in our society. NEWS RELEASE, NOV. 25, 1982

The world about us is surfeited with practices and attitudes which constantly tend to lower our standards of conduct, deprive us of the spirit of the gospel, and encourage us to ignore the revealed principles of truth. We can successfully resist these evils only by constantly reviewing and thinking about what the Lord has said about them. MARION G. ROMNEY, "FIRST PRESIDENCY MESSAGE," *ENSIGN,* DEC. 1978

Never since the gospel was restored have the influence and practices of evil been so widespread and aggressive as they are today. MARION G. ROMNEY, "FIRST PRESIDENCY MESSAGE," *ENSIGN,* APR. 1976

We are shocked at the depths to which many people of this

world go to assert their freedom. We fear that the trends of permissiveness toward immorality are destroying the moral fabric of our generation. *CHURCH NEWS,* JAN. 17, 1976

Lying is one of the cardinal sins of our day. MARION G. ROMNEY, "FIRST PRESIDENCY MESSAGE," *ENSIGN,* AUG. 1975

Great as our world accomplishments are, we are still capable of rising to far greater heights by also living "by every word that proceedeth out of the mouth of God" [Matt. 4:4]. Man cannot stand alone. *DESERET NEWS,* DEC. 15, 1962

There has perhaps never been a time in the history of our nation when the principles upon which it is founded were less honored than now. Belief in God, the very cornerstone of religious devotion, was never more under assault. The very principles by which men have lived and gauged their course of action have all been called in question with the result that there is a general confusion of the public mind, breaking away from old moorings. Many people do not know what is right, nor if there be such a thing as right or wrong apart from the caprice of the individual will. There has accordingly never been a time when it was more important for the Church to exert a steadying influence and steadfastly to use all the influence as its command for the maintenance of the principles of liberty, justice, and conformance to the ideals of a high Christian society. "DEAR BRETHREN," JULY 8, 1948, IN *MESSAGES,* 6:275-77

[T]oday the Church faces a world lying in moral lethargy and spiritual decline. *DESERET NEWS,* JULY 24, 1947

How glorious it would be if in men's lives there might exist conditions of contentment and peace—if there were an eradication from men's hearts of enmity and jealously, avarice and greed, strife and contention. But such is not the case. The daily press and radio brings news of war and its horrors, of strikes, of thefts, of political corruption, of family strifes, of murders. At a time when nature would proclaim the existence, handiwork, and glory of God, men in their blindness and selfishness choose to grovel in sin and misery of their own making. *DESERET NEWS,* DEC. 16, 1944, IN *MESSAGES,* 6:217-20

Self-promotion, not God's glorification, is the motivating factor in most people's lives. *IMPROVEMENT ERA,* JAN. 1943, IN *MESSAGES,* 6:188-91

The world needs more godliness and less godlessness; more self-discipline, less self-indulgence; more power to say with Christ, "Father, not my will, but thine be done" [Luke 22:42]. IBID.

Infidelity, atheism, unchastity, intemperance, civil corruption, greed, avarice, ambition–personal, political, national–are more powerful today than at any other time in the lives of us now living. They are pulling and thrusting us almost at will into new fields of action, new lines of thought. They are shaking the faith, undermining the morals, polluting the lives of the people. They have thrown many so far off balance in all of their activities, economic, social, political, and religious, that they stand in real danger of falling. *IMPROVEMENT ERA,* NOV. 1942, IN *MESSAGES,* 6:170-85

This is not a new world; it is an old and sinful world again returned, and now once more to be reconquered and rejuvenated. IBID.

The great need of the world today is spirituality and righteous living, based upon a belief in and a following of the laws and commandments of our Savior Jesus Christ. We shall advance and endure as we live righteously in accordance with

His gospel. "DEAR BRETHREN," DEC. 23, 1941, IN *MESSAGES,* 6:141-43

There never has been a time when the world had greater need of faith in the Lord Jesus Christ and love of Him than today; and there never has been a time when these emotions were more in evidence than is the case today among those who have taken upon them His name and covenanted to keep His commandments. *DESERET NEWS,* DEC. 17, 1927, IN *MESSAGES,* 5:254-57

Can there be any worse hells than those now on earth, created by professed followers of the Prince of Peace? *DESERET NEWS,* DEC. 18, 1915, IN *MESSAGES,* 4:343-48

We must remember that we live in a world of sin, wickedness, and sorrow, and that the enemy of all righteousness is ever on the alert to destroy the Saints and lead them into temptation, darkness, sin, and transgression. *MILLENNIAL STAR,* APR. 18, 1857, IN *MESSAGES,* 2:192-211

While the God of all the earth is pouring out His judgments upon a wicked world, in fulfillment of His word spoken by the mouth of His prophets in past and present generations, by pestilence, famine, tempest, and devouring flame, men and nations, drunk with their own fury, appear impatient to hasten their own consummation. In recklessness and wrath they destroy each other upon the rivers of water, and railroads, the wide spread lakes, and open sea; they rush to their own destruction. Nation arises against nation; civil discord engenders strife; and war, crimson war, with all its attendant horrors, lends its desolating aid to depopulate the earth. *MILLENNIAL STAR,* JULY 8, 1854, IN *MESSAGES,* 2:127-43

Behold this is a wicked generation, full of lyings, and deceit, and craftiness; and the children of the wicked are wiser than the children of light; that is, they are more crafty; and it seems that it has been the case in all ages of the world. STATEMENT, NOV. 1842, IN *MESSAGES,* 1:156-58

Who but those who can see the awful precipice upon which the world of mankind stands in this generation can labor in the vineyard of the Lord without feeling a sense of the world's deplorable situation? STATEMENT, JAN. 22, 1834, IN *MESSAGES,* 1:23-44

Appendix

First Presidencies of the Church

The First Presidency is usually comprised of the President of the Church and a first and second counselor but may, as during the administration of President David O. McKay, include as many as five counselors. Since the twentieth century, it has been customary to organize a new First Presidency within days after the previous President's death; however, in the nineteenth century the interregnum sometimes lasted several years, during which time the Quorum of the Twelve Apostles presided. When a counselor in the First Presidency dies, the President appoints a replacement, typically from the Quorum of the Twelve. The tenures of the various First Presidencies are briefly summarized below. The name of the President appears first, under the span of years of his presidency, followed by the names of all counselors who served during his administration. This information is taken from the *Church News Almanac,* published annually.

1995-present
Gordon B. Hinckley
Thomas S. Monson
James E. Faust

1994-1995
Howard W. Hunter
Gordon B. Hinckley
Thomas S. Monson

1985-1994
Ezra Taft Benson
Gordon B. Hinckley
Thomas S. Monson

1973-1985
Spencer W. Kimball
N. Eldon Tanner
Marion G. Romney
Gordon B. Hinckley

1972-1973

Harold B. Lee
N. Eldon Tanner
Marion G. Romney

1970-1972

Joseph Fielding Smith
Harold B. Lee
N. Eldon Tanner

1951-1970

David O. McKay
Stephen L Richards
J. Reuben Clark
Henry D. Moyle
Hugh B. Brown
N. Eldon Tanner
Joseph Fielding Smith
Thorpe B. Isaacson
Alvin R. Dyer

1945-1951

George Albert Smith
J. Reuben Clark
David O. McKay

1918-1945

Heber J. Grant
Anthon H. Lund
Charles W. Penrose
Anthony W. Ivins
J. Reuben Clark
David O. McKay
Charles W. Nibley

1901-1918

Joseph F. Smith
John R. Winder
Anthon H. Lund
Charles W. Penrose
John Henry Smith

1898-1901

Lorenzo Snow
George Q. Cannon
Joseph F. Smith
Rudger Clawson

1889-1898

Wilford Woodruff
George Q. Cannon
Joseph F. Smith

1880-1887

John Taylor
George Q. Cannon
Joseph F. Smith

1847-1877

Brigham Young
Heber C. Kimball
George A. Smith
John W. Young
Willard Richards
Jedediah M. Grant
Daniel H. Wells
Lorenzo Snow
Brigham Young Jr.

Albert Carrington
John W. Young
George Q. Cannon

1832-1844

Joseph Smith
Jesse Gause
Sidney Rigdon
Frederick G. Williams
Oliver Cowdery
Hyrum Smith
William Law
John C. Bennett
Amasa M. Lyman
John Smith
Joseph Smith Sr.